ANCIENT MACEDONIANS IN THE GREEK
AND ROMAN SOURCES

Ancient Macedonians in the Greek and Roman Sources

From History to Historiography

edited by

Timothy Howe

and

Frances Pownall

with the collaboration of
Beatrice Poletti

The Classical Press of Wales

First published in 2018 by
The Classical Press of Wales
15 Rosehill Terrace, Swansea SA1 6JN
Tel: +44 (0)1792 458397
www.classicalpressofwales.co.uk

Distributor
I. B. Tauris & Co Ltd,
6 Salem Rd,
London W2 4BU, UK
Tel.: +44 (0) 20 7243 1225
Fax: +44 (0) 20 7243 1226
www.ibtauris.com

Distributor in North America
ISD,
70 Enterprise Drive, Suite 2,
Bristol, CT 06010, USA
Tel: +1 (860) 584-6546
Fax: +1 (860) 516-4873
www.isdistribution.com

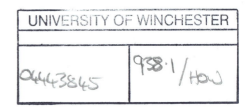

ISBN 978-1-910589-70-0

A catalogue record for this book is available from the British Library.

Typeset by Louise Jones, and printed and bound in the UK by Gomer Press, Llandysul,
Ceredigion, Wales

The Classical Press of Wales, an independent venture, was founded in 1993, initially to
support the work of classicists and ancient historians in Wales and their collaborators from
further afield. More recently it has published work initiated by scholars internationally. While
retaining a special loyalty to Wales and the Celtic countries, the Press welcomes scholarly
contributions from all parts of the world.

The symbol of the Press is the Red Kite. This bird, once widespread in Britain, was reduced by
1905 to some five individuals confined to a small area known as 'The Desert of Wales' – the
upper Tywi valley. Geneticists report that the stock was saved from terminal inbreeding by the
arrival of one stray female bird from Germany. After much careful protection, the Red Kite now
thrives – in Wales and beyond.

CONTENTS

Contents

PART IV

THE MEMORY OF ALEXANDER

INTRODUCTION

Timothy Howe and *Frances Pownall*

Since very early times, human beings have had some sense of the past, both their own and that of their community or people. This is something that has distinguished us from other species. Having said that, historiography in the narrower sense of 'intentional attempts to recover knowledge of and represent in writing true descriptions or narratives of past events' has had a rather briefer career throughout the world, though one more complex and variegated than most accounts allow (Woolf 2007, xxxv).

Woolf's observation is especially pertinent to the ancient Macedonian kingdoms, where a number of separate but related factors have rendered modern attempts to achieve an accurate and balanced assessment of past events both complicated and fraught with difficulty. First of all, the Macedonians themselves have left little trace in the textual record; there are simply no surviving historical accounts written by a Macedonian, and we are thus deprived of their own insights on themselves and their past (Rhodes 2010). Furthermore, located on the periphery of the mainland Greek world, the Macedonians remained out of the mainstream of Greek political and cultural life (despite the best efforts of a few of their Argead kings), a reality reflected in their general absence from contemporary texts (Asirvatham 2010). When the Greek sources do deign to mention the Macedonians, they tend to dismiss them as a primitive and backwards people, and even question their claim to true Hellenic ethnicity (Engels 2010). The neglect of the Macedonians by the Greek sources crystallized into outright hostility in the mid-fourth century BC, when the hegemonial aspirations of Philip II suddenly thrust Macedonia into the limelight, and it became politically expedient, particularly for certain Athenian statesmen opposed to Philip, to replace the Persians with the Macedonians as the foreign enemy *par excellence* (Harris 1994; Pownall 2004). In this process, the contemporary Greek sources began to scrutinize the unique social, political, and cultural customs of the Macedonians in order to provide further support for their classification as 'barbarians' instead of true Greeks (Asirvatham 2008).

The non-Macedonian origin of our textual evidence is not the only impediment to a full understanding of their rich and complicated past, for the large chronological gap between Macedonia's domination of the

Mediterranean world and our earliest surviving historical sources further compounds the problem. Although the period from Philip II's conquest of Greece to the kingdoms of the Successors of Alexander the Great, who divided and ruled his vast empire after his premature death, represents the heyday of Macedonian wealth and power, no contemporary narrative histories by either Greeks or Macedonians are extant (one of the great losses of the historiographical tradition), and our earliest surviving sources date from centuries later, when the Romans ruled the Mediterranean world (including the Greek city-states) and not coincidentally were experiencing their own brand of political turmoil and upheaval. By this point, the larger-than-life figure of Alexander loomed, whether as a symbol of an idealized past for Greek writers under Roman rule, or as a cautionary example of the evils of tyranny for Latin writers as allusive commentary upon their own political situations (Asirvatham 2010). In either case, it is difficult to determine to what extent contemporary biases and concerns contaminate the narrative of events by now hundreds of years in the past. And yet, unpacking the process through which history becomes historiography is what the following essays attempt to do.

Originating from a conference (*Ancient Macedonian History: A Diachronic Analysis*) organized by *The Ancient History Bulletin* and held in Athens in the summer of 2012, as part of the *10th International Conference on History: From Ancient to Modern*, these papers all reflect upon the ways in which specific Macedonian figures and events were portrayed in the later Greek and Roman sources. (We should note that not all of the original presenters offered contributions to this volume and conversely some scholars who were not able to attend the conference have contributed essays; naturally all of the essays in their present form differ significantly from their oral origins). While this crucial focus on the transformation of history into historiography offers a unifying principle for the volume as a whole, four distinct approaches emerged, which in turn reflect four complementary aspects of the main question: 1) the role of Macedonian royal women and their portrayal in the Greek and Roman sources (*Succession and the Role of Royal Women*); 2) the ways in which the later sources portrayed the political friendships and alliances of the Macedonians (Philia, *Politics, and Alliances*); 3) the Macedonian kings' own self-fashioning and how it was portrayed in the source tradition (*Royal Self-Presentation and Ideology*); and 4) the important role that Alexander the Great played as a model for later rulers in the Roman period (*The Memory of Alexander*).

The first section of the volume opens with a figure who exemplifies the divide between the historical and the historiographical: Eurydike I, mother of Philip II and grandmother of Alexander the Great. In 'A founding mother? Eurydike I, Philip II and Macedonian royal mythology', Timothy Howe examines the polarised view of Eurydike in the sources between the protective and politically savvy mother and the power-hungry and murderous harpy. As Howe observes, the divergence in the source tradition ultimately derives from the contemporary struggle for succession between the dynastic lines of Amyntas III, a situation arising from the polygamous politics of the Argead royal house. In the end, Eurydike managed to navigate the turbulent and dangerous political waters of Argead politics after the death of her husband, with offspring from Amyntas' sets of sons by different mothers vying for the kingship, and successfully positioned her own sons on the throne. The positive portrayal of Eurydike as the founding mother of the dynasty therefore stems from the influence of her sons for whom she had secured the kingship, whereas the origin of her negative portrayal as a murderess of husbands and sons lies in the propaganda circulated by their rivals for the throne. Both traditions on Eurydike, however, are appropriated by the later sources for their own narrative aims and political agendas.

Elizabeth Carney also addresses the issue of the way the sources portray the royal women who served as advocates to ensure their sons' succession to the Macedonian throne. In 'Royal women as succession advocates', she examines the cases of Eurydike, Olympias (the mother of Alexander the Great), Thessalonike (Alexander's half sister and the wife of Kassandros), and Arsinoë (daughter of Ptolemy I, and wife first of Lysimachos and then of her brother, Ptolemy II). As Carney demonstrates, in order to safeguard the succession of their sons, it was crucial for royal women to acquire military support, which they could do through the cultivation of *philia* networks, both internal and external. If this military support either did not materialize or was unsuccessful, royal women generally had no option other than dynastic violence to secure their sons' position. Although a woman's advocacy of her son's succession (at least when he was considered the rightful heir) was considered normative and appropriate, nevertheless the ancient sources demonise those royal women who resorted to dynastic violence to achieve this end (even when the violence was reciprocal), whereas they generally refrain from commenting upon male dynastic violence. While the Roman-era sources may reflect their own political *milieu* in their hostile portrayals of these royal women as murderous and vengeful, Carney (like Howe) argues that this tradition ultimately goes back to negative contemporary propaganda stemming from the complicated dynastic politics of the Argead house.

Rebecca Frank focuses particularly upon the stigmatisation of Olympias as a destructive eastern woman by one of these Roman sources, Pompeius

Trogus, whose Augustan-era history is extant only in the later summary by Justin ('A Roman Olympias: powerful women in the *Historiae Philippicae* of Pompeius Trogus'). As Frank demonstrates, in his vitriolic depiction of Olympias as a destructive political force Trogus emphasizes her role as queen and ruler and taps into the language and imagery that he also uses to describe Kleopatra VII as a powerful corrupting foreign queen, in line with Octavian's propaganda in the civil war against Antony. In this way, Trogus removes Olympias from her Macedonian context, and transforms her into a thoroughly Roman figure, through which he could offer pointed but indirect political commentary on his own era.

The second section of this collection turns from the political maneuvering of the Macedonian royal women to power politics writ large in the courts of Alexander and the Successors (Philia, *Politics, and Alliances*), with particular emphasis on the portrayal of these all-too-often ephemeral and self-serving friendships and alliances in the ancient sources. In 'Was Kallisthenes the tutor of Alexander's royal pages', Frances Pownall refutes the widespread assumption in modern scholarship that Alexander's court historian Kallisthenes held the official position of tutor of the royal pages. Pownall demonstrates that there is no evidence to support this assumption, and argues that it stems instead from two separate but complementary traditions. The first tradition, which exaggerates the closeness of Kallisthenes' connection with the pages, represents an attempt to absolve Alexander of blame for the condemnation of Kallisthenes over his alleged complicity in the Pages' Conspiracy (an accusation rooted in the machinations of his court rivals), and thus ultimately originates with the contemporary Alexander historians. The second, Roman-era, tradition transforms Kallisthenes from informal advisor of the pages into the teacher of Hermolaos, the ringleader of the conspiracy, thereby manipulating the figure of Kallisthenes into a proto-Seneca in order to offer pointed, but safely allusive, criticism of contemporary imperial politics.

Sabine Müller turns to an examination of the portrayal of Alexander's closest friend, Hephaistion, in the ancient sources ('Hephaistion – a reassessment of his career'). As she observes, evidence for the historical Hephaistion is slight, and we are therefore at the mercy of the sources in assessing both his political and military career and the nature of his private relationship with Alexander. She concludes that the most reliable source for Hephaistion is his contemporary Ptolemy, who provides a positive portrayal of him as a competent and able administrator, but appears to undercut his abilities as a military commander so as not to overshadow his own success in this sphere, through which he legitimised his subsequent kingship. Kleitarchos, who wrote at the Ptolemaic court, also depicted him favourably, and he appears to have been the first to develop the literary construct of Hephaistion as Alexander's Second Self. In the Roman-era authors, however, Kleitarchos' originally positive use of this *topos* is transformed into something negative, where the figure of Hephaistion is employed to serve as a mirror for Alexander's own moral decline and depravity. Similarly, the other tradition commonly associated with Hephaistion, his role as Alexander's lover (the Patroklos to Alexander's Achilles), has no roots in Alexander's own self-fashioning but is also a literary construct of the Roman-era sources (see also Bowden's paper), reflecting their contemporary political concerns.

Alexander Meeus ('Friendship and betrayal: the alliances among the Diadochoi') analyses the terminology employed by the literary sources to refer to the alliances between Alexander's Successors, concluding that it was not technical but was instead used loosely. It is not surprising, therefore, that the actual treaties and alliances themselves between the Successors were shifting and opportunistic, generally struck in order to achieve a particular strategic and usually military goal. None of these agreements, not even marriage alliances, implied any sort of permanent recognition of the other party's territory. These alliances, therefore, born out of short-term expediency, do not possess the constitutional significance with which modern scholarship tends to invest them, and none of them should be considered any kind of formal recognition of the definitive dismemberment of Alexander's empire (itself a modern concept which should be put to rest).

In the third section (*Royal Self-Presentation and Ideology*), we move from the representation of the friendships and alliances of the Argead kings and the Successors in the ancient literary sources to the question of their own royal self-fashioning. Victor Alonso Troncoso examines the unusually wide variety of zoological types on Argead coinage ('The animal types on the Argead coinage, wilderness and Macedonia'). As he observes, although the Argead rulers borrowed extensively from their neighbours in terms of the denominations, iconography, and style of their coinage, they nevertheless developed a unique message to be conveyed beyond the borders of Macedonia by the coins that they minted. Not only did their coins evoke the animal world, in all of its wildness, as an integral element in the Argead ideology of kingship, but they were also employed to reinforce the Hellenic identity of the Argead rulers as circulated in the constantly evolving foundation legends of the dynasty. It is only with the coinage of Philip II that the iconographical wilderness is tamed and replaced by an emphasis on panhellenic images, symbolizing his aspirations to a panhellenic empire.

Hugh Bowden ('Alexander as Achilles: Arrian's use of Homer from Troy to the Granikos') addresses one of the most common assumptions about Alexander the Great's self-fashioning, not least because it appears in all of the Alexander historians: that he consciously modelled himself upon Achilles. Although the 'Alexander as Achilles' theme originated much earlier (although almost certainly not with Alexander himself), Arrian's desire to be seen as a new Homer achieving for Alexander the sort of renown that Achilles won through his illustrious predecessor (Arr. 1.12.2–5) suggests that he deliberately constructed his narrative to highlight the parallels between Alexander and Achilles. Examining Arrian's narrative of the period from Alexander's arrival in Asia to his first major victory over the Persians at the Granikos River (1.11.6–16.7), Bowden demonstrates that this crucial stage of Alexander's campaigns is indeed tailored to reflect Achilles' pursuit of Hektor after the death of Patroklos in Books 19 to 21 of Homer's *Iliad*. Instead of attributing the differences between Arrian's narrative of the battle and those found in the other surviving accounts either to the (un)reliability of the original eyewitness sources or to the access which later writers had to these earlier sources, Bowden demonstrates that we should instead take into consideration the literary themes and requirements of his narrative and those of the other Alexander historians.

Paul Johstono ('The Grand Procession, *Galaterschlacht*, and Ptolemaic kingship') turns to the royal ideology of the Ptolemaic dynasty, focusing in particular upon Ptolemy II, who was the most successful at converting the opulent display of wealth into legitimacy and prestige. While Ptolemy II's capital-intensive strategy has generally been considered a departure from his father's more traditionally Macedonian route to the throne through success on the battlefield, Johstono demonstrates that military victory did in fact play a crucial role in the younger Ptolemy's own ideological mission. Johstono draws attention to the shields that were lavishly decorated in silver and gold and prominently displayed as trophies in the pavilion (famously described by Kallixeinos of Rhodes) constructed to host Ptolemy's guests at the Ptolemaia festival founded in honour of his parents, Ptolemy I and Berenike I. Not only did these trophies represent a conventional demonstration of martial prowess, but it is important to note that they were Galatian shields (*thyreoi*). They thus commemorated Ptolemy II's own defeat of a body of traitorous Galatian mercenaries originally hired to fight in his campaign against his rebellious half-brother Magas in 275 BC (which provides a *terminus post quem* for the disputed date of Kallixeinos' description of the festival and its attendant Grand Procession). Ptolemy's victory over the Galatians allowed him to position himself as the defender of Greek civilization against menacing barbarian invaders, which became as important a theme in the construction of his royal ideology as the extravagant display of wealth and luxury with which he is usually associated.

The fourth and final section of the volume (*The Memory of Alexander*) considers the ways in which the Successors employed the figure of Alexander the Great to legitimise their own regimes. Daniel Ogden ('Legends of Seleukos' death, from omens to revenge') examines the varied and colourful legends associated with the death of Seleukos I, founder of the Seleukid dynasty, who was murdered by Ptolemy Keraunos just after he had crossed the Hellespont en route to Macedonia and just as he was apparently (and ironically) on the verge of reconstituting Alexander's empire. As Ogden notes, many of the more obviously fabricated elements of the later tradition on Seleukos' death correspond with the Alexander tradition, especially the *Alexander Romance*.

The legacy of Alexander is also the subject of the final contribution, 'The memory of Alexander in Plutarch's Lives of Demetrios, Pyrrhos, and Eumenes', by Sulochana Asirvatham. In keeping with the emphasis on panhellenic ideology found in the biographies of other figures from the Hellenistic period (Agis, Kleomenes, Aratos, Philopoimen, and Aratos), it is no surprise that Plutarch explicitly compares the only three Successors who are the subjects of one of his Lives (Demetrios Poliorketes, Pyrrhos, and Eumenes) to the idealised Alexander that he portrays in panhellenic terms in his other works. As Asirvatham demonstrates, the use of this panhellenic Alexander as a foil against whom the Successors are measured and found wanting allows Plutarch, as a Greek intellectual, to offer tacit criticism of imperial Roman rule, as he does not apply this comparison explicitly to any of the would-be Roman imitators of Alexander.

The essays in this collection examine various aspects of the ways in which the ancient sources excerpt, format, reinterpret and even sometimes misinterpret the historical information on ancient Macedonians in order to serve their own literary and political aims and agendas. Recent scholarship has emphasized the extent to which the Roman-era sources have appropriated the figure of Alexander in particular to provide commentary upon contemporary political events and figures (e.g., Spencer 2002 and Beard 2011). While the overlay of Roman-era moralising that occludes our understanding of the 'historical' Alexander cannot be denied (e.g., Bowden 2013), it is by no means the only distorting influence in the historiographical tradition on ancient Macedonians. As we have previously demonstrated (Howe 2013; Pownall 2014), the layers of 'invented tradition' that entwined themselves around the figure of Alexander do not originate with our (mostly) Roman-era sources but much earlier, at the time of the struggles of Alexander's contemporaries to legitimise and justify their own claims to kingship. Thus, the process of historical distortion begins with the very first Alexander historians.

The authors of the essays in this collection broaden the scope of the question by considering the extent to which contemporary concerns have affected the portrayal in the later sources not only of Alexander himself, but also of his predecessors in the Argead dynasty and his Successors after his death. Although Roman-era contamination is pervasive in the historiographical tradition, it is clear that the manipulation of ancient Macedonian history generally occurs much earlier, and its origins are rooted in contemporary political rivalries arising from (depending on the period in question) the complicated dynastic politics of the Argead royal house, the efforts of Alexander himself to redefine Macedonian kingship, and the competing strategies of the Successors to lay claim to his legacy in the wars that engulfed Alexander's newly-acquired empire after his death. In other words, there are competing agendas in the source tradition dating all the way back to contemporary events, which the later sources then manipulate for their own literary and political aims. It is only by stripping away the multiple layers of distorting accretions which have been grafted on by the time of our first extant historical accounts that we can attempt to recover what Woolf has termed 'true descriptions or narratives of past events.' But by taking into account the full complexity of the source tradition, we are left with a much richer and (dare we say) more balanced reflection of both the history and the historiography of ancient Macedonia.

Bibliography

Asirvatham, S. R.

2008 'The Roots of Macedonian Ambiguity in Classical Athenian Literature', in T. Howe and J. Reames (eds), *Macedonian Legacies: Studies in Ancient Macedonian History and Culture in Honor of Eugene N. Borza*, Claremont, CA, 235–55.

2010 'Perspectives on the Macedonians from Greece, Rome, and Beyond', in J. Roisman and I. Worthington (eds) *A Companion to Ancient Macedonia*, Malden, MA, 99–124.

Beard, M.

2011 'Alexander: how great?', *The New York Review of Books* 27 October 2011, 35–37.

Bowden, H.

2013 'On Kissing and Making Up: Court Protocol and Historiography in Alexander the Great's "Experiment with *Proskynesis*"', *BICS* 56, 55–77.

Engels, J.

2010 'Macedonians and Greeks', in J. Roisman and I. Worthington (eds) *A Companion to Ancient Macedonia*, Malden, MA, 81–98.

Harris, E. M.

1994 *Aeschines and Athenian Politics*, Oxford.

Howe, T.
    2013   'The Diadochi, Invented Tradition, and Alexander's Expedition to Siwah', in V. Alonso Troncoso and E. A. Anson (eds) *After Alexander: The Time of the Diadochi* (323–281 BC), Oxford, 57–70.

Pownall, F.
    2004   *Lessons from the Past. The Moral Use of History in Fourth-Century Prose*, Ann Arbor.
    2014   'Callisthenes in Africa: The Historian's Role at Siwah and in the *Proskynesis* Controversy', in P. Bosman (ed.) *Alexander in Africa, Acta Classica* Supplementum V, Pretoria, 56–71.

Rhodes, P. J.
    2010   'The Literary and Epigraphic Evidence to the Roman Conquest', in J. Roisman and I. Worthington (eds) *A Companion to Ancient Macedonia*, Malden, MA, 23–40.

Spencer, D.
    2002   *The Roman Alexander: Reading a Cultural Myth*, Exeter.

Woolf, D.
    2007   'Historiography', in M. C. Horowitz (ed.) *New Dictionary of the History of Ideas* vol. 1, Detroit, xxxv–lxxxviii.

PART I

SUCCESSION AND THE ROLE OF WOMEN

1

A FOUNDING MOTHER? EURYDIKE I, PHILIP II AND MACEDONIAN ROYAL MYTHOLOGY

Timothy Howe

Alexander [II] succumbed to the treachery of his mother Eurydike. Although Eurydike had once been caught in adultery, Amyntas had nevertheless spared her life for the sake of the children they had in common, unaware that she would one day prove their undoing. Alexander's brother, Perdikkas [III], likewise became the victim of a treacherous plot on her part. It was indeed a cruel blow that these children should have been murdered by their mother and sacrificed to her lust when it was consideration of these same children that had once rescued her from punishment for her crimes. The murder of Perdikkas seemed all the more scandalous in that the mother's pity was not stirred even by the fact that he had an infant son (Justin 7.5.4–8; translation Yardley 1994).

Eurydike, mother of Philip II and grandmother of Alexander the Great, had a polarised reputation in Greco-Roman Antiquity. The fourth-century BC Athenian orator Aischines, and the second-century AD Roman biographer Plutarch, characterise Eurydike as a caring, nurturing, and above all politically savvy, protective mother (Aeschin. 2.26–29 and Plut. *De Educ. Puer.* 20.14).[1] In contrast, the first-century BC Pompeius Trogus, via his third-century AD epitomiser Justin, portrays Eurydike as a lust-driven, power-hungry, grasping harpy (Justin 7.4.7, 7.5.4–8, 7.6.2). For its part, modern scholarship has largely followed the paths well trodden by these ancient authorities: either attempting to cleanse Eurydike from the misogyny of the sources (Macurdy 1927; 1932; Mortensen 1992; Carney 2000, 40–6; 2012, 308–9); or highlighting Eurydike's politicking and thus perpetuating the ancient authors' conclusions, if not their vitriol and gender biases (e.g., Borza 1990, 190–5; Hammond 1994, 16–17; Worthington 2008, 15, 245, nn. 3–5). But apart from linking Eurydike's reputation to

Philip's panhellenic propaganda (Carney 2007; 2012; Mitchell 2007; Lane Fox 2011b, 262) there has been little consideration for how this mother/adulteress dichotomy originally came to exist and what its creation in mid-fourth-century Macedon, and proliferation in contemporary Athens, might mean for both Eurydike the historical actor and Eurydike the historiographical literary character.[2] In what follows, we attempt to trace the positive and negative Eurydike '*mythoi*' through their various source contexts to their origins in the closing years of Amyntas III's reign.

To begin this process, it is important to acknowledge that any original eyewitness accounts to Eurydike's actions have not survived to the present day. Even the orator Aischines, who was a personal friend of Philip II (Dem. 19.278–84) and records generally positive information about Eurydike, was a small child in distant Athens during Amyntas III's and Ptolemy Alorites' reigns and thus not personally a witness to the events he recounted. Aischines and his contemporary, Theopompos of Chios, would have access only to information that Philip, or his friends and enemies, made accessible.[3] Thus, for the reigns of Amyntas III, Ptolemy Alorites, and Eurdike's sons Alexander II and Perdikkas III, we are left with the Roman-era works of Diodoros, Plutarch, and Justin-Trogus, all of whom built their narratives by researching (i.e., 'data-mining') the fourth-century BC accounts of Ephoros, Marsyas of Pella and Theopompos of Chios, to name the authors they most regularly acknowledge.[4] As A. B. Bosworth explains in his analysis of Roman historiography, these Roman-era writers' aims and methods were as follows:

> the nature of the game was to operate with the material at one's disposal, identifying and criticizing falsehood and bias, combining details from several sources into a composite picture not paralleled in any single source, but not adding invention of one's own (Bosworth 2003, 194).

And yet, even though ancient historiographers in the Roman period may have reported information from their sources as faithfully as Bosworth suggests, they were themselves not immune to embellishment, synthesis and selective reporting in service to their own literary agendas (Woodman 1988; Howe 2015b).

Consequently, while Diodoros, Plutarch and Justin-Trogus do preserve much content and even some rhetorical tone and bias that was present in their own sources, we should not assume that their narratives are simply a facsimile of the lost originals. Diodoros, Plutarch and Trogus were literary stylists in their own right, with their own literary purposes, audiences and interests.[5] Accordingly, then, these Roman-era accounts must be seen as complicated pastiches of information and historical contexts, with some original content preserved, some extracted and synthesised from multiple sources, and some simply interpolated by the Roman author and offered to readers as 'what is likely to have been said and done'. What is clear, however, is that the Roman authors did not make up their accounts out of whole cloth. They worked with evidence and themes that already existed in their own primary and secondary sources in their efforts to excerpt and format historical content. As literary artists with their own authorial agendas they sifted through sources, chose what to put in their books, and, finally, chose how to interpret what information they included (e.g., Stadter 1978; Bosworth 1994; Howe 2015b). Most importantly for our purposes here, though, the Hellenistic- and Roman-era authors used all their rhetorical skills to sway a reader into accepting certain 'truths' so they might better understand their own world.[6] All too often the Macedonians served as a distorted mirror for such 'truths' when Romans (and Greeks like Diodoros and Plutarch living in a Roman world) sought to mine the past for that peculiar content against which they might weigh the moral implications of contemporary decisions, policies and rulers. As Justin's epitome of Trogus puts it, 'I omitted what did not make pleasurable reading or serve to provide a moral' (*praef.* 4, translation Yardley 1994).

This need for historical material to serve as a moral message to contemporary audiences is central to understanding why particular source material has survived in later accounts. Augustan-era Latin historians like Trogus and Livy, as well as Second Sophistic Greek authors like Plutarch, grounded their narratives in moral education, what Justin calls in his preface 'providing a moral'.[7] Such moralising seems particularly evident when the subject under analysis involves women. As Rebecca Frank discusses in this volume, the Roman authors deploy anecdotes about historical women (especially Macedonian women) as conniving, exploitative and socially and politically dangerous in order to contextualize and thus comment on women who are publically active in their own contemporary Rome. By retrojecting certain character traits onto historic and legendary women, the Roman historiographers are then able to 're-present' contemporary politicised women such as Fulvia, Livia and Kleopatra VII of Egypt in ways their audience can safely assess. Consequently, Olympias, Eurydike and other queens from the 'past' become proxies through which authors and their audiences can safely discuss contemporary figures outside of the politically divisive, and thus dangerous, realms of direct commentary. Indeed, in an era dominated by Antonius' fall from power and Octavian's triumph over Kleopatra, it would be difficult for authors and their audiences *not* to see powerful royal women as corrupters of morals and threats to the *Res Publica*.

Such historiographic moralizing was not unique to Augustan Rome, however; by the time of Livy and Trogus, historians and biographers of Greece and Rome had long been using examples of good and bad behaviour from the near and distant past as lenses through which to view the present and shape expectations for the future (Hau 2016). Indeed, this historical mirroring seems particularly important for the fourth-century BC accounts that Trogus, Diodoros and Plutarch combed for information about Eurydike and her sons.

We should note, though, that the fourth-century historiographers deployed markedly different methods from their first-century descendants. Theopompos of Chios, for example, passed on both true and untrue content seemingly irrespective of accuracy, simply because those particular contents fitted his rhetorical purpose and literary agendas.[8] And he was not alone: Frances Pownall in her thorough and innovative study of fourth-century historiography, argues that it was common for aristocratic Athenian intellectuals to misrepresent the past so that they could create alternative *aristocratic* versions of the past that could function in opposition to competing *democratic* versions (Pownall 2004, 1–10; cf. Flower 1994, 184–210). This discord between the aristocratic and the democratic can be seen clearly in the orations of Aischines and Demosthenes (Harris 1994; Pownall 2002).[9] For historians and orators of the fourth century, then, historical accuracy seems to have been much less a priority than rhetorical or philosophical hypothesising (or moralising). Consequently, many competing 'truths' were assembled in the fourth century BC whose accuracy was never intended to be evaluated by objective standards. And these competing anecdotes were later researched and compiled by Hellenistic and Roman authors in their historiographic narratives.

Thus, anecdotes from the fourth-century authors about famous individuals like Philip II and his mother Eurydike were unwittingly passed on by Roman writers, though not always without commentary. Because the Roman historiographers trusted their sources to a certain extent, Diodoros, Trogus and Plutarch transmitted to their audiences potentially inaccurate, or highly 'edited', commented and recontextualised content that had itself been assembled and highly edited for ideological conformity by fourth-century historians and orators. As Bosworth noted, the methods under which the Roman historiographers worked drove them to sift through these earlier accounts, identify important case studies, and format their research into composite narratives that were useful and relevant to contemporary audiences (Bosworth 2003, 167; Hau 2016). And since this type of research prized the authentic over the invented, Roman authors did not greatly alter the content they received beyond inserting dialogue and framing passages. For the Roman-era literary masters, synthesis, attribution and 'truth' were the way to literary reputation (Kraus and Woodman 1997; Bosworth 2003; cf. Hau 2016). To sum up, then, Diodoros, Plutarch and Trogus did not invent content (*pace* Mortensen 1992) but instead chose specific fourth-century anecdotes because of subject compatibility and developed their conclusions, dialogue and syntheses accordingly; thus, authentic fourth-century *exempla* served as especially powerful mirrors in which to view contemporary 'royals'. For this reason, we can reasonably conclude that traces of authentic, anti- and pro-Eurydike rhetoric were present in the fourth century. Indeed, if such fourth-century originals did not exist to point the way, it is very unlikely that Eurydike would attract much attention as a worthy exemplar of the perils (and virtues) of female power.[10] To put it another way: the Roman-era authors needed content on which to build their accounts and would not have used Eurydike's adultery, motherhood or politicking if they had not found those themes through their own research among earlier works.

While a certain amount of mixing and matching of sources inevitably occurred, the especially vituperative nature of Justin's portrayal of Eurydike seems to owe much to Theopompos' original work.[11] The negative aspects of Theopompos' *Philippic History*, and particularly his often dark assessment of Philip's character, seemed to resonate with later Roman authors and audiences, interested as they were in the vice of rulers and the moral decline it inspired.[12] A prime example can be seen in a passage preserved by Athenaios (6.260c–261a):[13]

> Theopompos records about each of the two [Dionysios and Philip] in the forty-ninth (book), writing as follows: [F 225a begins] 'Philip rejected men who were orderly in their behaviour and took care of their private property, but he honoured in praise men who were extravagant and living in dice and drink. As a result, not only did he equip them to have these things, but he also made them experts in every sort of injustice and loathsome behavior. For what was there of shameful or terrible [deeds] not attached to them, or what of good and upright [deeds] was not absent? Did not some of them, though they were adult males, continue to shave and make themselves smooth, and others dare to have sex with one another, though having beards? They also led around two or three of those prostituting themselves with them, and they supplied the same intimacies to the others. Whence one might justly suppose them to be not companions (*hetairous*) but male prostitutes (*hetairas*), call them not soldiers but streetwalkers. [F 225c begins] For though man-killers (*androphonoi*) by nature, they were man-whores (*andropornoi*) by character. [F 225a and F 225c end]. In addition, instead of sobriety they loved drunkenness, but instead of orderly living they sought thieving and murdering. And they thought telling the truth and keeping their agreements not proper for them; but they undertook swearing false oaths and cheating in the most holy places. They were careless with their

possessions, but were desirous of what they lacked, even though possessing a certain part of Europe. For I believe during that time that the companions were not more than eight hundred, having no less earth for cultivation than ten thousand of the Greeks possessing the most productive and extensive land' (translation, Morison *BNJ*).

Despite this and other famous examples, however, Theopompos' *Philippic History* should not be understood as wholly negative towards Philip and his family. Theopompos preserved both positive and negative anecdotes, so that his audience could gain a deeper understanding of his subject (Pownall 2004; 2005). If viewed holistically, the surviving fragments suggest that Theopompos combined a respect for Philip's many virtues with a condemnation of his vices. Take, for instance, Fragment 27 (Polybios 8.9.1–4):

> In this regard one would especially rebuke Theopompos, who in the beginning of his treatise on Philip [II] said that what especially encouraged him to set upon his enterprise was that Europe had never produced any man at all like Philip son of Amyntas.[14] (2) Immediately afterwards, both in the preface and throughout the entire history, he reveals that he [Philip] was completely powerless over women, with the result that even he ruined his own household by himself because of his impulsive and ostentatious [behavior] in this regard, (3) and also that he was most unjust and had the worst intentions in building friendships and alliances, and that he reduced to utter slavery and took by surprise most cities by treachery and violence, (4) and that he was by nature passionately eager for drinking unmixed wine, with the result even in broad daylight he frequently appeared drunk to his friends. (*FGrH* 115 F 27; translation, Morison *BNJ*)

Here, we see that Polybios does not approve of Theopompos' more nuanced view of Philip. The fact that Polybios takes time to criticise this approach suggests it was not uncommon in Theopompos' *Philippika*. Unfortunately, Polybios' reception of Theopompos was not unique: this highly nuanced balance between virtue and vice was rarely valued by later authors who used the *Philippika* as a source for moralising content. Positive qualities, or at the very least positive qualities as reported by Theopompos, resonated with the later authors and their audiences only in very specific contexts (see below). For the most part, Theopompos' positive comments were viewed with suspicion *because* they came from Theopompos, an author who by then had become famous for the savagery of his barbs. Plutarch's comment (*Lysander* 30.2–3, *FGrH* 115 F 333) that Theopompos was more trustworthy when he praised than when he blamed, because he preferred blaming to praising, encapsulates the perspective well.

Such a view, however, colours how modern scholars have come to understand Theopompos and his works (Connor 1967; Flower 1994, 211–3;

Pownall 2004, 143–75). As a result, Theopompos' content has been decontextualised from how he arranged it in his original work and just like their Roman predecessors, modern scholars have prioritised the negative over the positive. As Pownall (2004, 173–5; 2005) notes, Theopompos in the *Philippika* offered a subtle interpretation of Philip II of Macedon's virtues and vices so that he could explore the links between royal power and corruption, of both of which Theopompos considered Philip the culmination. In the tension Theopompos builds between public success and personal failure, Pownall sees a deep irony that runs through the *Philippic History*: Philip is a strong king who has put his kingdom on the path to regional power, even though he himself is a flawed and often vice-ridden human being. For Theopompos' purposes, then, Philip's successes make him much more worthy as a character study than the debauched, deluded and weak rulers of contemporary democratic Athens. Theopompos' Athenians (unlike Philip, with whom they share many vices) were not able to achieve lasting political or military success and thus are seen as vice-ridden failures, unable or unwilling to achieve greatness. In selecting this focus, Theopompos seems particularly ruthless, going so far as to deliberately misrepresent the past at times in order to expose and ridicule how the flattery of political rhetoric could nurture the very worst personal vices in a leader and thereby cause his (and his city's) destruction (Pownall 2004, 2–10).

Unfortunately for our study of Philip II's mother Eurydike, it was Theopompos' criticism of Eurydike's un-womanly power-seeking, faction building and flattery of usurpers such as Ptolemy Alorites that attracted Trogus. Thus, Eurydike and her political actions were arranged anew for the Roman audience and re-contextualised as character studies in amoral female behaviour (Mortensen 1992). With this in mind, I do not think it is coincidence that Trogus chose Theopompos' title, *Philippika*, for his own 'universal' history.[15] The tension between vice and virtue, public and private that so drew Theopompos and allowed him to comment on democratic Athens would be powerful to Trogus as he offered moral context to those living in Late Republican and Augustan Rome. The dichotomy between Augustus' public moralising and the vices of own household would fit well into Theopompos' analytic models of public success and private failure.

But Theopompos' original text seems to have presented a more nuanced picture of Philip's mother than we might see in Trogus. In much the same way as Trogus was drawn to Theopompos' discussion of Eurydike's womanly vices, Nepos was drawn to Theopompos' treatment of Eurydike's womanly *virtues*:

> He [Iphikrates], moreover, possessed a great spirit and body and a commanding form, so that by his own appearance he would inspire admiration for himself in anyone, but he was lacking in his work ethic and had little endurance, as Theopompos reminds us, but truly was a good citizen and very trustworthy. (2) This was both made evident in other affairs, as well as in protecting the children of the Macedonian Amyntas. For Eurydike, mother of Perdikkas and Philip, fled with these two children to Iphikrates when Amyntas died and was protected by his forces. (Nepos, *Iph.* 11.3.1–2; Theopompos *FGrH* 115 F 289; translation Morison)

Here, Iphikrates is presented by Nepos as an honourable and good Athenian citizen who is both trustworthy and hardworking – he seems to have none of the vices that Theopompos so deplores in later Athenian leaders. Eurydike, too, is shown in a very traditional and appropriate role, as a good mother intent on protecting her children. As such she can serve as an example for other women. It is likely that Theopompos' account of Eurydike's character has benefitted from Philip's propagandistic attempts to cleanse his mother's reputation (see below). Carney has observed: as he became more involved in the politics of the Greek *poleis*, Philip would be highly invested in presenting his mother in ways traditionally acceptable to his southern Greek audience (Carney 2007). Hence, Theopompos can understand Eurydike as a good mother who uses bonds of *philia* to protect her children (see Carney, this volume, for other examples of royal Macedonian women exercising *philia* in this manner). Nonetheless, the reality and the reasons behind Iphikrates' presence in Macedon might be less culturally and politically acceptable than Nepos suggests since Eurydike is deploying him in a political fashion, as a factional leader on behalf of her sons Perdikkas and Philip.

We see much the same content used by Plutarch in his essay on education. Here, Plutarch illustrates the value of a nurturing family to a young boy's intellectual development. Consequently Eurydike as a nurturing and supportive mother plays a central role and any political motives recede into the background:

> We must endeavour, therefore, to employ every proper device for the discipline of our children, emulating the example of Eurydice, who, although she was an Illyrian and an utter barbarian, yet late in life took up education in the interest of her children's studies. The inscription which she dedicated to the Muses sufficiently attests her love for her children:
>
>> Eurydice of Hierapolis
>> Made to the Muses this her offering
>> When she had gained her soul's desire to learn.
>> Mother of young and lusty sons was she,

And by her diligence attained to learn
Letters, wherein lies buried all our lore[16]
(Plut. *De Educ. Puer.* 20.14; translation Babbitt, 1927).

In these instances from Nepos and Plutarch, traditionally positive material about Eurydike in her acceptable role as mother to Philip and his brothers resonated because stories about good mothers were *useful* for their wider rhetorical purposes – education for Plutarch, and honourable (aristocratic?) leadership for Nepos. In a similar fashion, traditionally negative examples of Eurydike in her unacceptable role (to non-Macedonian audiences) as factional leader and adulteress resonated with Trogus because he could use them as examples of what women should never do. It is important to acknowledge, though, that both the mother *and* the factional leader motif are present in the Roman citations as individual authors foreground aspects of Eurydike's character and actions that best serve their literary agendas.

But if many of our negative and positive portrayals derive from Hellenistic and Roman preservation, recontextualisation and reinterpretation of fourth-century content, how might we understand the pro-Philip (and pro-Eurydike) information presented by the only fourth-century account about Eurydike to survive intact to the present, that from the Athenian orator Aischines? It seems likely that since Aischines was politically and financially indebted to Philip, he might have been susceptible to preserving stories about Philip's family as reported by Philip and Philip's allies.[17] Indeed, Aischines could himself serve as a point of dissemination for Philip's message that his mother was a good, traditionally acceptable, non-threatening mother and wife. Thus, Aischines' speeches, together with the inscriptions dedicated by Eurydike and Philip after Philip became king, are a valuable source for understanding Philip's own propaganda that his mother was a good, traditionally acceptable and non-threatening royal woman and wife as it was assembled and deployed to address and counter the propaganda generated by his factional enemies, the earliest of which seem to be his older half-brothers and their mother Gygaia. As I hope to show in the analysis that follows, these portrayals of Eurydike (positive and negative), that Roman authors and fourth-century Greek historiographers and orators found so useful to their moral messages, ultimately derived from infighting among the various Macedonian royals competing for the Argead throne during the reigns of Alexander II, Ptolemy Alorites, Perdikkas III and Philip II.

But before we jump into the familial politics of fourth-century Macedon, it is necessary to revisit the evidence relating to Argead succession and the patterns that have emerged from over a century of modern scholarship. Beginning in the late nineteenth century, it was common to perceive

9

Macedonian kingship as a formal, almost constitutional monarchy, not unlike contemporary European examples. Accordingly, strict rules governed succession: upon the death of the previous king the army (Hammond and Griffith 1979, 152–8, Hammond 1989, 58–64) or the aristocracy (Errington 1978) would choose a new king according to set protocols. The pool of candidates from which these 'assemblies' might choose could potentially be quite diverse because, as multiple historical examples demonstrated, anyone of the royal Argead blood could be a contender. Although some scholars have argued that those 'born in the purple' (porphyrogeniture) were preferred over those who were not (Hatzopoulos 1986, 1.276–80), or that the first son had priority (primogeniture) (Hatzopoulos 1986, 1.276–80; cf. Carney 1983, 260–72; 2000, 23–7 and Borza 1990, 177, 243–4; 1999, 11–15), or that the previous king's choice (heir-designation) played a key role (Greenwalt 1989), the dataset is not statistically large enough, or consistent over a long enough period of time, to provide a clear answer. Part of the problem with synthesising the surviving data is that all of these criteria and many others seem to have been relevant for various Argeads at various times. As a result, we see examples of primogeniture, porphyrogeniture, heir-designation, and military force (and combinations of these) all playing roles in the historical selection of Macedonian kings. This range of experience has led Edward Anson to conclude that 'the Macedonian kingship during the Argead dynasty did not possess a very systematic succession process. There were, however, elements that suggest the existence of certain *nomoi* related to royal succession' (2009, 278).

Unfortunately, those *nomoi* or laws governing succession seem to be broken more than they are upheld, leading other scholars to suggest that the Macedonian kingship was not institutional at all but situational (Borza 1990, 236–41; 1999, 11–15; Mitchell 2007, 65). According to this view, the Macedonian king acted as he saw fit and he either survived his decisions or perished because of them. Consequently, Argeads became kings because they could hold the throne. As a warlord, a 'first among equals' figure, the Macedonian monarch would of necessity live a precarious existence, holding together his realm by the force of his will and the extent of his alliances and friendships.

Macedonian queens had a similar experience, though their options were even more circumscribed because of restrictions imposed by traditional gender roles (Mirón Pérez 2000; Müller 2002; 2011; 2013; Carney 2010; 2012; 2015). When they act in traditionally acceptable ways, such as giving birth to males and showing by their very femininity an ability to bind clans and thereby preserve the legitimacy of male relatives, particularly sons and husbands, they are praised by the sources inevitably articulated from a male perspective (e.g., Theopompos *FGrH* 115 F 289). But when queens overshadow males in times of crisis then that same persistence and pervasiveness inherent in their dynastic power can seem threatening and draw criticism from male authors. And yet, royal women are most visible in times of crisis, especially times of succession, because of their traditional role as mothers of royal heirs and natural continuators of dynasties. Consequently, royal women in the Macedonian court serve as natural foci of factional power when a king dies, since they are well placed to keep sons and daughters together and thereby maintain the networks of friendship, *philia*, that were of pivotal significance to negotiations of status and power.

And so, when a king died, or as often happened, was killed by a rival, there was a free-for-all succession, in which women as much as men could form factions of friends and allies and thereby create a new Macedonian warlord. As Lynette Mitchell puts it:

> it was social relations that governed the Macedonian royal household and created power and, as long as he [the king] was an Argead, it was the individual's ability to control these relationships that determined whether he had and then kept a place on the royal Macedonian throne (2007, 62).

In this view, which seems to fit the evidence better than any constitutional argument in which formal rules arbitrated royal power, there is no real process for succession other than family power and its network of factionalism. All available evidence bears this out: each Macedonian king came to power for different reasons in different circumstances, but one thing was consistent – all successful contenders were Argeads, all used family connections and all had to fight rivals to gain their positions (Fernández Nieto 2005, 42–3). As a result, the Macedonian kingdom tended to be rather fragile and particularly dependent on personalities and relationships. Factional infighting, then, was the norm, rather than the exception (Mitchell 2007, 65), and families and familial bonds came to have particular resonance among the Macedonian royals (Greenwalt 1988a; 1988b; 1989; Ogden 2011; Carney 2012). As such, familial reputation could be a powerful tool as different branches of the Argead tree attempted to leverage and legitimate their claims while at the same time discounting and de-legitimating the claims of their dynastic rivals (Greenwalt 1988b; Carney 2015, 148–9).

It should not surprise us, then, that divergent, polarised family *mythoi* dominate Argead history. For the history of Eurydike, family *mythoi* seem to cluster around four main themes: 1) Eurydike's marriage to Amyntas III and admittance to the Argead court; 2) her 'kingmaking' role immediately following Amyntas' death; 3) her factional leadership during and immediately following Alexander II's murder; and finally 4) her lobbying of Iphikrates to assist in Perdikkas III's accession to the Argead throne.

First divergence: Eurydike's ethnicity

As noted earlier, all of the extant *mythoi* agree that Eurydike, the mother of Alexander II, Perdikkas III and Philip II, was closely involved in royal policy decisions and ambitious for and protective of her sons. But apart from Eurydike's female gender, this description could easily fit any of the Argead royals, who were an ambitious and rather treacherous lot. Taken as a whole, Argead history reads like a Victorian novel: rival claimants, unexpected heirs and murders disguised as hunting accidents. Add Macedonian royal polygamy to the mix and we have a perfect storm of family drama, as Greenwalt and others have noticed (Greenwalt 1989; Carney 1992; 1995; Odgen 1999, 3–29). If we probe this dynamic, status-shifting nature of the Macedonian court more deeply, though, we can see why Eurydike's entry as Amyntas' third and last wife was guaranteed to create ripples in the royal social structure.[18] As an outsider from Upper Macedonia, with mixed Macedonian and Illyrian ancestry, Eurydike's arrival at court would challenge existing status relationships and cause many positions and identities to be renegotiated.[19] Indeed, we might compare Eurydike's advent with the better-known example of Philip's seventh and last wife Kleopatra (see Figure 1 for the relevant genealogical data), for, like Kleopatra, Eurydike married Amyntas after he was established as king.

Opposition and counter-opposition seem to manifest first as an attack on, and subsequently as a defense of, Eurydike's familial identity. Two traditions come down to us from the *Suda*: 1) Eurydike is Lyncestian and noble, a member of the Upper Macedonian Royal House[20] (Strabo 7.7.8; *Suda s.v.* Leonnatos; Heckel 2006, 147); and 2) she is an outsider, an Illyrian[21] (*Suda s.v.* Karanos). Plutarch, in a section otherwise favourable to Eurydike, goes so far as to call her 'an Illyrian and an utter barbarian' (Plut. *De Educ. Puer.* 20.14). This barbarian slur seems to have had a long life, being deployed later to discredit Eurydike's children (Alexander II, Perdikkas III and Philip II), who not only were linked to barbarous Illyria but were also called supposititious, and therefore doubly unsuitable for the Argead throne.[22]

Were the *Suda* the only source to report this data, we could explain it away as an error of the (admittedly incautious) lexicographer, but as early as the mid-fourth century BC and the speeches of Demosthenes, we see Philip criticized as an illegitimate son of Amyntas (Dem. 9.31; Libanius, *Argumenta orationum Demosthenicarum Pr.*18).[23] Being anti-Philip Demosthenes

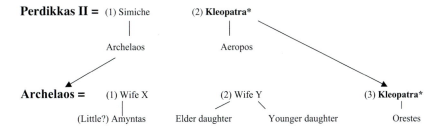

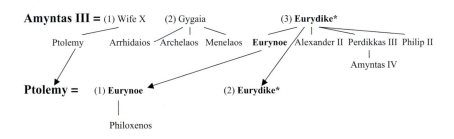

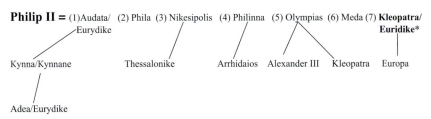

Fig. 1. Argead family trees

is not the most reliable source on the subject of Philip, though we must give his account weight, since the Athenians had also dedicated a statue to Philip at Kynosarges, the city's symbolic home for bastards (Clement of Alexandria, *Protrepticus* 4.54).[24] At least in Athens the stories about Philip's illegitimacy had teeth. It is also unlikely that the linkage between Eurydike and Illyria is simply a confusion with Philip's first wife, the Illyrian princess Audata, whom Philip renamed Eurydike after he married her (Heckel 1983; Ogden 1999, 15–16). Following Ogden, I think it likely that these familiar slurs have their origins in the conflict between Gygaia and Eurydike while Amyntas was still alive (Ogden 1999, 16). Questions about Eurydike's ethnicity fit best if located during her first few months at court, when her advent would most disrupt existing relationships. Again, a comparison with

13

Philip and Alexander and Olympias and Kleopatra might be useful, in order to identify patterns. Gygaia was Lower Macedonian just like Philip's seventh wife Kleopatra.[25] Olympias was an outsider from another royal house just like Eurydike, though Molossian and not Lyncestian in this case. Immediately before Philip's murder, Kleopatra's guardian Attalos is said to have attempted to sideline Alexander by claiming he was foreign, barbarian; he also hinted he was not a true son of Philip (Plut. *Alex* 9.5–14; Satyros, *apud* Athenaios *Deipnosophistae*, 13.557d). It is telling that Eurydike and her sons are attacked in a similar fashion a generation earlier, with the same intended result: lessening Eurydike and her sons' factional power and ability to create networks of *philia* among court stakeholders. And in Eurydike's case it seems to have worked: something certainly made Eurydike and her children unpopular (Diod. 15.71; 16.2.4). What better way to cut support than to stress Eurydike's and her family's connections to Macedon's worst enemy at the time, Illyria?

Publicising Eurydike's alleged infidelity to Amyntas and hence the non-Argead status for Alexander, Perdikkas and Philip would also be effective, as it both undermined Eurydike as a chaste and loyal wife and cut her children out of the royal succession. As not only barbarians but also illegitimate sons of Amyntas, Alexander, Perdikkas and Philip should not inherit the throne. If this reading is correct, and the stress on Illyrian ethnicity and illegitimacy had their origins in the polygamous politics of the household of Amyntas, as Ogden suggests, then Demosthenes (and his contemporary Theopompos) could have simply picked up a narrative already in place, a much more effective, powerful and safe tactic than simple invention. Diodoros, Justin-Trogus, and Plutarch (as well as Libanius and the *Suda*) then deploy these traditions as their own agendas demanded.

Of course, we would then expect Philip and his brothers to be invested in preserving an alternative view of their mother and their origins and we are well rewarded: in 346 BC Aischines reiterates that Amyntas was the father of Eurydike's little children (Aischines 2.28). But the damage control seems to predate Aischines. As early as 360 BC, Philip and Eurydike made significant dedications at royal Aigai and Dion (Saatsoglou-Paliadeli 2000, 393, n. 41) to the goddess Eukleia, 'good reputation', most likely to counter all of the bad press Eurydike had received from Gygaia and her sons.[26]

Second divergence: Who succeeds Amyntas?

Amyntas III died in 369 and, as usually happens with a vacant throne, there was factional strife, during which, it seems, Eurydike played a central role in holding together the family's *philia* networks. Unfortunately, as with

Eurydike's ethnicity, we again have a divergent tradition: Diodoros claims that Ptolemy, an older son of Amyntas II, was king (15.71.1 and 77.5);[27] Aischines (2.26) and Plutarch (*Pel.* 27.3), who closely follows him, have Alexander II, with Ptolemy serving as regent until Alexander's majority;[28] the scholiast on Aischines 2 takes a middle ground, having Ptolemy first regent and then king;[29] and Justin does not mention Ptolemy at all, choosing instead to focus closely on Eurydike and her children, so he can document Eurydike's manipulative nature and unfeminine political role. Significantly, all sources agree that Eurydike was the main power-broker at this time, using her factional network to seat the next king.

Ogden, following the scholiast on Aischines 2, explores the nature of Eurydike's network in detail and has argued that she married Ptolemy in order to keep the two strands of Amyntas' polygamous household united against the third – Gygaia and her three sons Archelaos, Arrhidaios and Menelaos. If his assessment is correct, then Ptolemy and Eurydike ally to deepen an already strong tie, for Ptolemy had been married to Amyntas' daughter with Eurydike, Eurynoe. Although it is possible that Ptolemy was concurrently and polygamously married to both mother and daughter, it seems likely that Eurynoe is no longer alive (Justin does not mention a divorce between Ptolemy Alorites and Eurynoe and he is not one to pass up such an opportunity). In any event, Eurydike marries Ptolemy to solidify the alliance between two strands of Amyntas' family against the third, as other young Argead widows have done with their dead husband's sons. Kleopatra, Perdikkas II's youngest and most recent wife, married his son Archelaos in order to ground Archelaos' accession and strengthen his *philia* networks (Arist. *Pol.* 1311b; Plato, *Gorgias* 471a–d; Ogden 1999, 9–10).[30] In the end, the fact that we do not hear from Gygaia or her sons until *after* Ptolemy's death suggests that the Eurydike-Ptolemy alliance worked and any threats from Gygaia's faction had been neutralised.

And yet, the alliance between Eurydike and Ptolemy was not wholly successful since Eurydike's eldest son Alexander II did not approve of his mother's and half-brother Ptolemy's actions. In response, Alexander took himself off to Thessaly so that he might drum up support from the Aleuadai against Ptolemy, and his Thessalian ally, Alexander of Pherai (Diod. 15.61.2–3). So bad did the tension between these two strands of Eurydike's family become that the next year, 368 BC, the Theban general Pelopidas had to march into both Thessaly and Macedonia and forcefully impose a settlement on Alexander II and Ptolemy (Plut. *Pel.* 26). Both Philip, Alexander II's youngest brother, and Philoxenos, Ptolemy's only reported son, were taken to Thebes as hostages to ensure compliance with the peace settlement (Plut. *Pel.* 27.4; Diod. 15.67.4; Justin 6.9.7, 7.5.2–3).

Given the need for Pelopidas' involvement in Macedonian politics, it seems clear that different factions of Macedonians supported Ptolemy's and Alexander's claims the throne. It also seems that Ptolemy, as the oldest son of Amyntas, and husband to both Amyntas' youngest wife and her daughter, had the position and powerbase both within and without the royal family to succeed his father. In this case, Eurydike had chosen the safe bet, Ptolemy, and may have expected Alexander to wait until he was older and more able to control the family faction. Indeed, the tradition that Ptolemy was merely regent and not king suggests that Eurydike was planning for Alexander's ultimate accession. But Alexander would not wait and chose to ignore his mother's policy and become a usurper. This tension within Eurydike's faction would not have gone unnoticed by Gygaia and her sons and must surely be the inspiration for slurs about Ptolemy and Eurydike. It is even possible that Alexander II himself contributed in no small part to such attempts to delegitimize Ptolemy.

Another potential source would be Perdikkas III (who later killed Ptolemy) and his younger brother Philip II, the successors of Alexander II. As usurpers themselves, Perdikkas and Philip would be invested in creating and preserving a narrative of Alexander as the legitimate heir and Ptolemy as the rebel usurper. Whether they initially agreed with Alexander's actions or not, once he left the family faction and set his sights on the Argead throne and then was murdered by Ptolemy (or at his behest), Philip and Perdikkas could not deny that Alexander and Ptolemy were enemies. What is interesting for our purposes is that the account preserved in Aischines does not dispute Ptolemy's royal power; it merely downgrades him to regent. A regent and a murderer. And that is where we must turn next.

Third divergence: the murder of Alexander II

In the spring of 368 BC, Diodoros reports that Ptolemy of Aloros, son of Amyntas, killed Alexander II (Diod. 15.71.1). A fragment from Marsyas of Pella is more neutral (*FGrH* 135 F 3; 135–6 F 11 = Athen. 14.629d), reporting that Alexander was killed (accidentally?) during a Macedonian war ceremony by Apollophanes of Pydna and others 'close to Ptolemy'.[31] Justin-Trogus takes the most extreme view, concluding that Eurydike and Ptolemy colluded to kill Alexander together (Justin 7.5.4–8, 7.6.2). In fact, Justin uses the murder of Alexander to showcase Eurydike's disregard for traditionally female concerns such as children and family. In his assessment, Eurydike has so far deviated from the feminine norm that she plots against her own children; even worse, Eurydike is so evil, so beyond proper family values, that after her son's murder she stayed married to his murderer,

Ptolemy. The parallels with Justin's stories of Eurydike's earlier adulterous behaviour while married to Amyntas are clear and seem to benefit the same group – Gygaia and her sons.

In order to explain Eurydike's and Ptolemy's entanglement in Alexander's murder, it might be useful to engage Macedonian amphimetric rivalry, that is, the physical and psychological rivalry between children of different mothers in a polygamous household (Ogden 1999, xix–xx, 3–40; 2011, 99–104). The illegitimacy claims against Philip and his brothers, and the charges of Illyrian ethnicity against Eurydike herself, are examples of this type of psychological warfare that Gygaia and her sons deployed against Eurydike, Alexander, Perdikkas and Philip. Linking Eurydike to Alexander's murder seems to fit within this genre, for it would not benefit Perdikkas or Philip to cultivate negative traditions about their own mother. Eurydike's sons would be invested in suppressing Eurydike's role in their brother Alexander's death entirely. Indeed, cultivating bad *kleos* against both Ptolemy and Eurydike and highlighting factional violence between those two amphimetric wings of Amyntas's house would benefit *only* Gygaia and her sons Archelaos, Arrhidaios and Menelaos.

Amphimetric rivalry also helps illuminate how Ptolemy becomes fully enmeshed in some traditions about Alexander's death but not others. By investing in stories about Alexander II as a legitimate king, who is then murdered by Ptolemy's supporters, Perdikkas creates a justification to avenge his brother and seize the throne himself.[32] Family honour dictates he kill Ptolemy. Consequently, Perdikkas is not a usurper but a righteous regicide and avenger who punishes his brother's killer and thereby frees his mother from a bad marriage. Further, by painting Alexander II as a murdered king, Perdikkas can then claim Macedon as Alexander II's heir. Clearly, this is the account of events that Philip later preferred. As we see in the pro-Philip Aischines, Eurydike was betrayed by friends, by her *philia*, by the faction she and Ptolemy had crafted (Aischines 2.26; Ogden 1999, 15–16). This 'Ptolemy and the *philia* as regicides' narrative legitimates Perdikkas while at the same time pardons Eurydike in a traditionally gendered way: Eurydike the dutiful wife was betrayed by her husband Ptolemy. With her son dead, and her husband a murderer, Eurydike can be accepted by Perdikkas (and Philip) and incorporated into their *philia*, their faction. Moreover, by stressing traditional feminine roles such as wife and mother, Eurydike's reputation can be rehabilitated by her sons (whether she might wish it or not). In a sense, a mythos of 'Eurydike the mother' can over-write that of 'Eurydike the factional leader'; it can also function as a safe and necessary alternative to other more negative *mythoi*, such as 'Eurydike the son-killer'.

Eurydike's place in all of this family conflict is perhaps the most interesting and at the same time the most elusive: just like Kleopatra, wife of both Perdikkas II and his son Archelaos, Eurydike stayed with her second husband even though the son from her first husband was murdered under suspicious circumstances (Ogden 1999, 16). This seems to suggest that Eurydike did not believe Ptolemy guilty of Alexander's murder.[33] It also suggests that she did not recognize or openly support Alexander's bid for the throne. But Eurydike's staying with Ptolemy, even after Alexander's murder, made good political sense at the time – it protected the amphimetric faction she and Ptolemy had built and protected her children from Amyntas's older heirs, Gygaia's sons. Eurydike must have recognized that a power-bid like that attempted by Alexander, and resolved by Pelopidas, would not be wise. Clearly, Alexander was not popular among the Macedonian military elites; his murder at a war-ceremony indicated that. There could be no clearer way that the Macedonian warriors could indicate a vote of no confidence. Ptolemy was the safer choice for the family, even if it meant sacrificing the rebellious Alexander to save Perdikkas and Philip.

And here again, Eurydike stepped up to rally her faction, her friends and her remaining sons. With Pelopidas at the border, there was a pressing need for Eurydike to hold the two Argead strands together and thus preserve the kingdom so Perdikkas (or Philip) could rule after Ptolemy. But Eurydike was not all-powerful. She could not force her sons to follow the policy she and Ptolemy had formulated. Thus, like Alexander, Perdikkas also decided to break with his mother and usurp the throne. To cover his tracks he declaimed Ptolemy as a regicide. It is likely that Philip invested in and further perpetuated this tradition because he as his brother's heir would also be heir to a usurped kingdom, if Ptolemy was known as a legitimate king.

Fourth Divergence: Perdikkas' Accession and Pausanias' Rebellion
Nonetheless, Perdikkas soon discovered that he could not rule alone. He needed his mother's connections and resources to battle a distantly-related Argead contender named Pausanias, who had invaded Macedonia from the east. With Ptolemy gone, Eurydike could now back her son, though she seems to have lost control of the faction she and Ptolemy had created. I think Aischines's comment that Eurydike was 'betrayed by her friends' indicates this. Gygaia's family also reappears after Ptolemy's murder, taking full advantage of the current instability between the other Argead factions. One wonders if Pausanias's favourability with the Macedonian people had anything to do with Gygaia's earlier anti-Eurydike propaganda, or Perdikkas' murder of Ptolemy. Whatever the case, Eurydike was certainly

in possession of a healthy dose of bad *kleos* that would take many years to cleanse (Carney 2007).

Yet once again, Eurydike steps up and provides leadership for her sons. Bereft of support among the Macedonians, Eurydike persuaded Iphikrates, the Athenian general in the region to take the field and drive off Pausanias (Aischines 2.28). Eurydike, not Perdikkas III, saved the family. Eurydike set her son on the throne and she did so with the help of the Athenians, not a coalition of Macedonians, whom she could not longer call on for support. And while the Athenian support certainly aided Perdikkas, it would not have made Eurydike popular in Macedon. I have no doubt that this generated even more bad *kleos*.

Conclusions

In the end, Eurydike managed to navigate the turbulent and dangerous political waters of Argead politics after the death of her husband. Like many Argead women we see her only in times of crisis, where it was acceptable and necessary for her to keep her family's factional network together. Although her reputation is polarised in the sources, both negative and positive accounts agree that Eurydike did what was best for her faction. She continually held the family *philia* networks together and was able to pass on her husbands' thrones to her children, often despite those children's own actions or wishes. Indeed, unlike other Argead women Eurydike cultivated the family networks and marshaled military support even when her sons might wish otherwise. Eurydike played a long game that above all ensured a safe and stable Macedon for *some* of her sons to inherit. Although she could not rule herself, she used all resources at her disposal to keep her faction and the kingdom of Macedon intact.

And I suppose that best explains both the historical and historiographical Eurydikes. Eurydike is remembered as beloved by Philip for keeping him alive and preserving his throne, just as she is despised by rivals, such as Gygaia and her faction, for the same reasons. Indeed, so important is Eurydike to Philip's line that he renames his first wife Eurydike in her honour (Heckel 1983; cf. Badian 1982). And so we see two Eurydikes in our sources: the grasping harpy and the founding mother. In the end, I suspect the truth is somewhere between Trogus and Aischines. Eurydike was a powerful royal woman who did what she could to ensure that at least one of her sons ruled Macedon. She was undoubtedly the founding mother for Philip and Alexander the Great's dynasty and in many ways presages the royal women of the Successor kingdoms.

Acknowledgements

I should like to thank Sheila Ager, Beth Carney, Bill Greenwalt, Waldemar Heckel, Daniel Ogden and, above all, my co-editor Frances Pownall for their insight and assistance. Of course, any errors of fact and logic are mine alone.

Notes

[1] A similar perspective can be found in Nepos *Iph.* 3.2.1–2 (Theopompos *FGrH* 115 F 289).

[2] Mortensen 1992 focuses primarily on Justin's bias and analyses this in terms of sexual stereotyping, which many have followed. Cf. Carney 2000, 44. While this approach explores why Justin and Trogus might find such negative portrayals useful, Mortensen does not engage Trogus' fourth-century sources to any significant degree and does not trace these negative portrayals much farther back in time than the Hellenistic period. From an entirely different direction, Ogden 1999, 13–16 briefly evaluates the rivalries that generated the varied traditions about Eurydike and opens the door for many fruitful connections. Nonetheless, his brief assessment does not expand the argument to contextualize the family politics he identifies within the fourth-century literary and epigraphic sources. Carney 2000, 44–6; 2007; 2012, 308–9, links these rivalries to Eurydike's bad *kleos* and analyses Philip II's efforts to rehabilitate Eurydike's reputation through public monuments. She does not, however, engage the origins of the bad *kleos* beyond noting some links between Argead royal politics and negative stories: 'Though a tradition that makes Eurydike murderous and adulterous survives (Just. 7.4.7, 5.4–8), it is now clear that this tradition is invalid, likely a consequence of propaganda by Gygaea's faction (Diod. 15.71.1; Ath. 14.629d; Mortensen 1992; Ogden 1999, 11–16), and that the historical Eurydike played a part in securing and maintaining her sons on the throne by her participation in internal and international *philia* networks' (2012, 308). Further work, such as Carney's chapter in this volume, moves on from this foundation to consider Eurydike as a 'succession advocate' for her sons Alexander II, Perdikkas III and Philip II. Like Carney, Lane Fox 2011a, 210; 2011b, 261–2, also links Eurydike's bad *kleos*, which he calls the 'black legend', to the Macedonian family politics of the fourth century. Yet he too offers little analysis of the source tradition that curated and preserved this 'black legend' for our later sources.

[3] Harris 1995, 50–62, 70–7 suggests that Aischines' relationship was more complex and nuanced than Demosthenes allows. See Mitchell 1997, 181–6 for an analysis of the political implications of Philip's relationships with various Athenian statesmen at the time of the embassies of 346, especially in terms of Demosthenes' allegations of bribery and interference.

[4] Diodoros: Goukowski 1977, ix–xxiii; 2016, vii–xix; McQueen 1995, 8–14. Trogus: Lane Fox 1986; Alonzo-Núñez 1987; Yardley 2003. Plutarch: Pelling 1980; Duff 1999.

[5] Drews 1962; Pelling 1980; Alonzo-Núñez 1987; Sacks 1990, chapters 1 and 2; Shrimpton 1991, 128–9; Ambaglio 1995; Duff 1999, chapter 1; 2011; Lefèvre 2002; Yardley 2009; Goukowski 2016, vii–xix. For Diodoros in particular it is no

longer accepted (e.g., Hammond 1937) that whenever Diodoros names no source in books 11 through 16 of the *Bibliotheke*, he is automatically reproducing Ephoros. See Pownall 2004, 118, for a recent assessment. For Trogus the issue is compounded by the fact that we do not have his original text, only Justin's epitome; see Yardley 2003.

[6] For discussions of 'Roman' historiographic methods see, e.g., Woodman 1988, 70–116; Kraus and Woodman 1997, 5–6. Such careful winnowing of evidence seems to have been in play during the fourth century as well; e.g., Pownall 2004, 1–36.

[7] For the role of *paideia*, moral education, in the writing of the Roman historians, especially those from the Second Sophistic, see, e.g., Anderson 2009, esp. 211ff., and Asirvatham, this volume. For Trogus, especially the moralising perspectives he shares with his contemporary historiographer Livy, see Yardley 2003, 20–78.

[8] As Riginos' study of Philip II's many injuries demonstrates, fourth-century authors would deliberately misrepresent events in efforts to score a rhetorical or moral point (Riginos 1994).

[9] For Pownall (2004, 1), prioritising the moral message over all else had a profound impact on the genre of historiography itself, shaping the genre for subsequent Greek and Roman historians.

[10] Lefèvre 2002 argues that Diodoros in particular put careful attention into researching the individual rulers he chose to include as character studies. See also Chamoux 1983.

[11] Lane Fox 1986, Heckel 1980, and Hammond 1991 have all convincingly argued that the most likely candidates for the stories about Eurydike and her sons are Theopompos of Chios and Marsyas of Pella. Lane Fox, in particular, argues that Trogus primarily follows Theopompos, while his near contemporary Diodoros uses primarily Marsyas. Cf. Shrimpton 1991, 128–9. I find unconvincing Talbert's view that while Diodoros made some use of Theopompos, his main source for the period under study was 'an unknown historian' (Talbert 1974, 33–7).

[12] *FGrH* 115 F 162 (transl. Morison *BNJ*): 'Theopompos in the twenty-sixth (book) of the Histories says, "Philip, recognizing that the Thessalians were dissolute and licentious in their lifestyle, prepared parties for them and endeavoured to please them in every way by dancing and partying and submitting to every sort of corruption – by nature he was a buffoon, getting drunk daily and delighting in the pursuits that lead to those things and to the so-called 'men of wit' who tell and make jokes – and he won over more of the Thessalians who associated with him by means of parties than by bribes".' The character of Philip's associates and family also comes under attack, e.g., *FGrH* 115 F 134; F 162; F 209; F. 224; F 225b; F 236.

[13] See also F 282.

[14] Here Polybios seems especially troubled by Theopompos' inconsistency. For further discussion of Polybios' critical attitude towards Theopompos, see Bearzot 2005, 55–71. Pownall 2004, 169, suggests (following Connor 1967) that Polybios missed Theopompos' irony here and instead took him at his word.

[15] Ogden 2002, xiii–xiv, comes to a similar conclusion, though from a different perspective.

[16] This epigram is part of an inscription that relates to Eurydike's late education and is from a dedication she made for the sake of citizen women to the Muses (Le Bohec-Bouhet 2006, 190–2). This seems to have been part of a group statue base, likely containing an image of Eurydike, perhaps as part of a dynastic group (Saatsoglou-Paliadeli 2000, 397–400).

[17] For the connections between Philip and Aischines see Dem. 18.51–2, 284; Mitchell 1997, 181–6.

[18] Lane Fox 2011, 231 states that Gygaia was the younger wife, and while this thesis has its attractions, Lane Fox's argument is not convincing. See Zahrnt 2006 for a discussion of Amyntas' policies and the challenges he faced during the early years of his reign.

[19] I follow Heckel 1983; 2006, 122 that Eurydike was half-Illyrian. For a full discussion of the arguments for and against see Heckel 1983; cf. Mortensen 1992. For a discussion of the ever-shifting female identities within the Argead court see Carney 1995; 2000; 2012

[20] See Ogden 1999, 13, for analysis.

[21] Oikonomides 1983; Kapetanopoulos 1994; Heckel 2009, 147. See Ogden 1999, 33, n. 55 for additional bibliography.

[22] This is also found in the *Suda* (*s.v.* Karanos), conceptually linked to Eurydike's own problematic ethnicity, suggesting a common source tradition.

[23] See Ogden 1999, 34, n. 66 for bibliography.

[24] Ogden 1996, 202.

[25] See Howe 2015a for full bibliography.

[26] So argues Carney 2007, 31–3, though she sees this as a much later development and orchestrated by Philip II as part of his policy to shore up the family's *kleos*, good fortune (cf. Palagia 2010; Schultz 2007). Oikonomides 1983; Lane Fox 2011b, 262; Le Bohec-Bouhet 2006, 190–2. For a recent discussions of the inscription and accompanying statue see Saatsoglou-Paliadeli 2007.

[27] See Ogden 1999, 14–16 for Ptolemy as Amyntas' son. Lane Fox 2011b, 232 disputes this evidence, arguing that Diodoros' text is defective. His emendation of *Basisleuontos,* while innovative and clever is, at present, not yet convincing

[28] Meeus 2009, 297–8.

[29] Tod 2. #129, ll.20–21 has Amyntas and Alexander mentioned as oath-takers in an alliance with the Athenians (Psoma 2014; cf. Pafford 2011). The third name is missing and there is certainly room here for Ptolemy Alorites. Ptolemy's role, if any here, is likely impossible to recover since a Ptolemaios is also mentioned as an envoy later in the text (Anson 2009, 282). Numismatics also is of little help: Hammond and Griffith, 1979, 192 tentatively ascribe some bronze coins to Alexander II but these are highly problematic (Greenwalt 1994).

[30] Archelaos soon killed Kleopatra's son by Perdikkas II, Airopos, so as to remove any rivals, a move not dissimilar to Ptolemy's killing of Alexander II. Harder 1985, 146; cf. Greenwalt 1985.

[31] Demosthenes (19.194–5) reports that Apollophanes was later 'treacherously murdered' by Philip and his daughters were kept as hostages, only to be released by Satyros, an Athenian *xenos* of Apollophanes (Heskel 1996, 48). While an ambassador to the Macedonian court, Satyros asked Philip to release Apollophanes'

daughters into his custody so that he could find them suitable husbands. This seems to me one more indication that while *men* were dangerous rivals to a sitting Macedonian king, women could be quite useful in creating and maintaining *philia* relationships (Herman 1987, 121; Mirón Pérez 2000; Carney, this volume).

[32] And Philip later has a reason to go after Olynthos. As Demosthenes (19.194–5), reports, Philip uses Olynthos' harbouring of Apollophanes, one of Alexander II's murderers, as a pretext for invasion.

[33] Or could Eurydike have believed she had no other option, either to stay in power or to stay alive? Kleopatra II reconciled with her brother-husband Ptolemy VIII even after he had killed one (maybe even three) of her sons: Justin 38.8.11–15; 39.2.2.

Bibliography

Alonso-Núñez, J. M.
  1987 'An Augustan World History: The "Historiae Philippicae" of Pompeius Trogus', *G&R* 34, 56–72.
Ambaglio, D.
  1995 *La Biblioteca Storica di Diodoro Siculo: problemi e metodo*, Como.
Anderson, G.
  2009 *The Second Sophistic: A Cultural Phenomenon in the Roman Empire*, London.
Anson, E.
  2009 'Philip II, Amyntas Perdicca, and Macedonian Royal Succession', *Historia* 58, 276–86.
Badian, E.
  1982 'Eurydike', in W. L. Adams and E. N. Borza (eds) *Philip II, Alexander the Great and the Macedonian Heritage*, Washington, DC, 99–110.
Bearzot, C.
  2005 'Polybio e Teopompo', in G. Schepens and J. Bollansée (eds) *The Shadow of Polybius: Intertextuality as a Research Tool in Greek Historiography*, Leuven, 55–71.
Borza, E. N.
  1990 *In the Shadow of Olympus: The Emergence of Macedon*, Princeton.
  1999 *Before Alexander: Constructing Early Macedonia*, Claremont, CA.
Bosworth, A. B.
  1994 'Arrian and Rome: the Minor Works', *ANRW* 2.34.1, 226–75.
  2003 'Plus ça change... Ancient Historians and their Sources', *ClassAnt* 22.2, 167–98.
Carney, E.
  1983 'Regicide in Macedonia', *PP* 211, 260–72. [Reprinted with Afterword in *King and Court in Ancient Macedonia: Rivalry, Treason and Conspiracy*, Swansea, 2016]
  1992 'The Politics of Polygamy: Olympias, Alexander and the Murder of Philip II', *Historia* 41, 169–89. [Reprinted with Afterword in *King and Court in Ancient Macedonia: Rivalry, Treason and Conspiracy*, Swansea, 2016]

1995 'Women and *Basileia*: Legitimacy and Female Political Action in Macedon', *CJ* 90, 367–91. [Reprinted with Afterword in *King and Court in Ancient Macedonia: Rivalry, Treason and Conspiracy*, Swansea, 2016]

2000 *Women and Monarchy in Macedonia*, Norman, OK.

2007 'The Philippeum, Women, and the Formation of Dynastic Image', in W. Heckel, L. Tritle and P. Wheatley (eds) *Alexander's Empire. Formulation to Decay*, Claremont, CA, 27–60. [Reprinted with afterward in *King and Court in Ancient Macedonia: Rivalry, Treason and Conspiracy*, Swansea, 2016]

2010 'Macedonian Women', in J. Roisman and I. Worthington (eds) *A Companion to Ancient Macedonia*, Malden, MA, 409–27.

2012 'Oikos Keeping: Women and Monarchy in the Macedonian Tradition', in S. L. James and S. Dillon (eds) *A Companion to Women in the Ancient World*, Malden, MA, 304–15.

2015 'Dynastic Loyalty and Dynastic Collapse in Macedonia', in P. Wheatley and E. J. Baynham (eds) *East and West in the World Empire of Alexander the Great*, Oxford, 147–62.

Chamoux, F.

1983 'Diodore et la Macédoine', *AM* 3, 57–66.

Connor, W. R.

1967 'History without Heroes: Theopompus' Treatment of Philip of Macedon', *GRBS* 8, 133–54.

Drews, R.

1962 'Diodorus and his Sources', *AJPh* 83, 383–92.

Duff, T.

1999 *Plutarch's Lives: Exploring Virtue and Vice*, Oxford.

2011 'The Structure of the Plutarchan Book', *ClassAnt* 30, 213–78.

Errington, R. M.

1978 'The Nature of the Macedonian State under the Monarchy', *Chiron* 8, 77–133.

1990 *A History of Macedonia*, Berkeley and Los Angeles.

Fernández Nieto, F. J.

2005 'La designación del sucesor en el antiguo reino de Macedonia', in V. Alonso Troncoso (ed.) *La figura del sucesor en la realeza helenística*, Madrid, 29–44.

Flower, M.

1994 *Theopompus of Chios. History and Rhetoric in the Fourth Century BC*, Oxford.

Goukowsky, P.

1977 *Diodore de Sicile. Bibliothèque historique, Tome X, Livre XV. Collection des universités de France*, Paris.

1991 'Les maisons princières de Macédoine de Perdikkas II à Philippe II', in P. Goukowsky and C. Brixhe (eds) *Summikta, histoire, archéologie, épigraphie*, Nancy, 43–66.

2016 'Notice' in Gaillard-Goukowsky, D. and P. Goukowsky (eds) *Diodore de Sicile. Bibliothèque historique, Tome XI, Livre XVI. Collection des universités de France*, Paris, vii–ccxl.

Greenwalt, W. S.
 1985 'The Introduction of Caranus into the Argead List', *GRBS* 26, 43–9.
 1988a 'The Marriageability Age at the Argead Court', *CW* 8, 93–7.
 1988b 'Amyntas III and the Political Stability of Argead Macedonia', *AncW* 18, 34–44.
 1989 'Polygamy and Succession in Argead Macedonia', *Arethusa* 22, 19–45.
 1993 'The Iconographical Significance of Amyntas III's Mounted Hunter Stater', *AM* 5, 509–19.
 1994 'The Production of Coinage from Archelaus to Perdiccas III and the Evolution of Argead Macedonia', in I. Worthington (ed.) *Ventures into Greek History*, Oxford, 122–3.
 2008 'Philip II and Olympias on Samothrace: A Clue to Macedonian Politics during the 360s', in T. Howe and J. Reames (eds) *Macedonian Legacies: Studies in Ancient Macedonian History and Culture in Honor of Eugene N. Borza*, Claremont, CA, 79–108.
 2010 'Macedonia, Illyria and Epirus', in J. Roisman and I. Worthington (eds) *A Companion to Ancient Macedonia*, Malden, MA, 279–305.
 2015 'Thracian and Macedonian Kingship', in J. Valeva, E. Nankov and D. Graninger (eds) *A Companion to Ancient Thrace*, Malden, MA, 337–51.
Hammond, N. G. L.
 1937–38 'The Sources of Diodorus XVI', *CQ* 31, 79–91 and 32, 37–51.
 1989 *The Macedonian State: The Origins, Institutions and History*, Oxford.
 1991 'The Sources of Justin on Macedonia to the Death of Philip', *CQ* 41, 496–508.
 1994 *Philip of Macedon*, London.
Hammond, N. G. L. and Griffith, G. T.
 1979 *A History of Macedonia, II: 550–336 BC*, Oxford.
Harder, A.
 1985 *Eurpides' Kresphontes and Archelaos*, Leiden.
Harris, E. M.
 1994 *Aeschines and Athenian Politics*, Oxford.
Hau, L. I.
 2016 *Moral History from Herodotus to Diodorus Siculus*, Edinburgh.
Hazopoulos, M. B.
 1985 'Η Ομηρεία του Φιλίππου του Αμύντα στις Θήβες', Αρχαιογνωσία 4, 37–58.
 1986 'Succession and Regency in Classical Macedonia', *AM* 4, 279–92.
 1996 *Macedonian Institutions under the Kings*, 2 vols, Athens.
Heckel, W.
 1980 'Marsyas of Pella, Historian of Macedon', *Hermes* 108, 444–62.
 1983 'Adea-Eurydike', *Glotta* 61.1, 40–2.
 2006 *Who's Who in the Age of Alexander the Great*, Malden, MA.
Herman, G.
 1987 *Ritualised Friendship and the Greek City*, Cambridge.
Heskel, J.
 1996 'Philip II and Argaios: A Pretender's Story', in R. W. Wallace and

E. M. Harris (eds) *Transitions to Empire: Essays in Greco-Roman History, 360–146 BC, in honor of E. Badian*, Norman, OK, 37–56.

Howe, T.
  2015a 'Cleopatra-Eurydike, Olympias and a "Weak" Alexander', in P. Wheatley and E. J. Baynham (eds) *East and West in the World Empire of Alexander the Great*, Oxford, 133–46.
  2015b 'Arrian and "Roman" Military Tactics. Alexander's Campaign Against the Autonomous Thracians', in T. Howe, E. Garvin and G. Wrightson (eds) *Greece, Macedon and Persia: Studies in Social, Political and Military History in Honour of Waldemar Heckel*, Oxford, 87–93.

Kapetanopoulos, E.
  1994 'Sirrhas', *AncW* 25.1, 9–14.

Kraus, C. S. and Woodman, A. J.
  1997 *Latin Historians*, Oxford.

Lane Fox, R.
  1986 'Theopompus of Chios and the Greek World 411–322 BC', in J. Boardman (ed.) *Chios*, Oxford, 105–20.
  2011a '399–369 BC', in R. Lane Fox (ed.) *Brill's Companion to Ancient Macedon. Studies in the Archaeology and History of Macedon, 650 BC–300 AD*, Leiden, 209–34.
  2011b 'The 360s', in R. Lane Fox (ed.) *Brill's Companion to Ancient Macedon. Studies in the Archaeology and History of Macedon, 650 BC–300 AD*, Leiden, 257–70.

Le Bohec-Bouhet, S.
  2006 'Réflexions sur la place de la femme dans la Macédoine antique', in A.-M. Guimier-Sorbets, M. B. Hatzopoulos and Y. Morizot (eds) *Rois, cités, nécropoles: institutions, rites et monuments en Macédoine*, Athens, 187–98.

Lefèvre, F.
  2002 'Le Livre XVI de Diodore de Sicile: Observations sur la composition et sur le traitement des grands personnages', *REG* 115, 518–37.

Macurdy, G. H.
  1927 'Queen Eurydice and the Evidence for Woman-Power in Early Macedonia,' *AJP* 48, 201–14.
  1932 *Hellenistic Queens: Study of Woman Power in Macedonia, Seleucid, Syria, and Ptolemaic Egypt*, Baltimore.

Marsh, D. A.
  1995 'The Kings of Macedon: 399–369 BC', *Historia* 44, 257–82.

Meeus, A.
  2009 'Some Institutional Problems Concerning the Succession to Alexander the Great: *Protasia* and Chiliarchy', *Historia* 58, 287–310.

Miller, M. C. J.
  1986 'The Macedonian Pretender Pausanias and his Coinage', *AncW* 13, 23–7.

Mirón Pérez, M. D.
  2000 'Transmitters and Representatives of Power: Royal Women in Ancient Macedonia', *AncSoc* 30, 35–52.

Mitchell, L.
  1997   *Greeks Bearing Gifts: The Public Use of Private Relationships in the Greek World, 435–323 BC*, Cambridge.
  2007   'Born to Rule? Succession in the Argead Royal House', in W. Heckel, L. Tritle and P. Wheatley (eds) *Alexander's Empire. Formulation to Decay*, Claremont, CA, 61–74.
Morison, W. S.
  2014   'Theopompos of Chios (115),' in I. Worthington, ed., *Brills New Jacoby*, Leiden.
Mortensen, K.
  1992   'Eurydike: demonic or devoted mother?', *AHB* 6, 156–71.
Müller, S.
  2007   'Im Interesse des oikos: Handlungsräume der antiken makedonischen Königinnen', *FemStud* 2, 258–70.
  2011   'Oikos, Prestige und wirtschaftliche Handlungsräume von Argeadinnen und hellenistischen Königinnen', in J. E. Fries and U. Rambuschek (eds) *Von wirtschaftlicher Macht und militärischer Stärke Beiträge zur archäologischen Geschlechterforschung*, Münster, 95–114.
  2013   'Das symbolische Kapital der makedonischen Herrscherfrauen', in C. Kunst (ed.) *Matronage. Soziale Netzwerke von Herrscherfrauen im Altertum in diachroner Perspektive*, Osnabrück, 31–42.
Ogden, D.
  1996   *Greek Bastardy in the Classical and Hellenistic Periods*, Oxford.
  1999   *Polygamy, Prostitutes and Death*, Swansea and London.
  2002   'Introduction: From Chaos to Cleopatra', in D. Ogden (ed.) *The Hellenistic World: New Perspectives*, Swansea, iv–xxv.
  2011   'The Royal Families of Argead Macedon and the Hellenistic World', in B. Rawson (ed.) *A Companion to Families in the Greek and Roman Worlds*, Malden, MA, 92–107.
Oikonomides, A. N.
  1983   'A New Greek Inscription from Vergina and Eurydike Mother of Philip', *AncW* 7, 62–4.
Pafford, I.
  2011   'Amyntas son of Perdiccas. King of the Macedonians, at the Sanctuary of Troponios at Lebadeia', *AncW* 42, 211–22.
Palagia, O.
  2010   'Philip's Eurydike in the Philippeum at Olympia', in E. Carney and D. Ogden (eds) *Philip II and Alexander: Lives and Afterlives*, Oxford, 33–41.
Pelling, C.
  1980   'Plutarch's Adaptation of his Source-Material', *JHS* 100, 127–40. [reprinted in *Plutarch and History*, Swansea, 2011].
Pownall, F.
  2002   'Theopompus' View of Demosthenes' , M. Joyal (ed.) *Altum: Seventy-Five Years of Classical Studies in Newfoundland*, St. John's, Newfoundland, 63–7.

2004   *Lessons from the Past. The Moral Use of History in Fourth-Century Prose*, Ann Arbor.

2005   'The Rhetoric of Theopompus', *Cahiers des Études Anciennes* 42, 255–78.

2008   'Theopompos and the Public Documentation of Fifth-Century Athens', in C. Cooper (ed.) *Epigraphy and the Greek Historian*, Toronto, 119–28.

Psoma, S.
2014   'Athens and the Macedonian Kingdom from Perdikkas II to Philip II', *REA* 116.1, 133–44.

Riginos, A. S.
1994   'The Wounding of Philip of Macedon: Fact and Fabrication', *JHS* 114, 103–19.

Saatsoglou-Paliadeli, C.
2000   'Queenly Appearances at Vergina-Aegae: Old and New Epigraphic and Literary evidence', *AA* 3, 387–404.

2002   'Βεργίνα 2000–2002. Ανασκαφή στο Ιερό της Εύκλειας', Το Αρχαιολογικό Έργο στη Μακεδονία και τη Θράκη 16, 479–90.

2007   'Arts and Politics in the Macedonian Court Before Alexander', *AM* 7, 345–55.

Sacks, K.
1990   *Diodorus Siculus and the First Century*, Princeton.

Schultz, P.
2007   'Leochares' Argead Portraits in the Philippeion', in P. Schultz and R. von den Hoff (eds) *Early Hellenistic Portraiture: Image, Style, Context*, Cambridge, 205–33.

Shrimpton, G. S.
1991   *Theopompus the Historian*, Montreal.

Stadter, P. A.
1978   'The *Ars Tactica* of Arrian: tradition and originality', *CP* 73, 117–28.

Talbert, R. J. A.
1974   *Timoleon and the Revival of Greek Sicily 344–317 BC*, Cambridge.

Woodman, A. J.
1988   *Rhetoric in Classical Historiography*, London.

Worthington, I.
2008   *Philip II of Macedonia*, New Haven, CT.

Yardley, J. C.
2003   *Justin and Pompeius Trogus. A Study of the Language of Justin's Epitome of Trogus*, Toronto.

Zahrnt, M.
2006   'Amyntas III: Fall und Aufstieg eines Makedonenkönigs', *Hermes* 134.2, 127–41.

2

ROYAL WOMEN AS SUCCESSION ADVOCATES

Elizabeth Carney

In the Argead era and that of the Successors, no consistent succession pattern was established, primarily because of the practice of royal polygamy. In this situation, royal women often served as advocates for their sons' (or grandsons') succession to the throne and also as supporters of their continued rule. Although kings' sisters and the brothers of royal mothers sometimes contributed to these efforts, mothers and sons formed the basic succession unit.[1] Though ancient authors tend to portray the women's motivation for such advocacy in emotional terms (e.g. revenge, lust), political self-interest and dynastic concerns were surely also powerful, possibly more powerful, motives.[2] Greater power and prominence tended to derive from being a royal mother, especially a widowed royal mother, than simply from being a royal wife or a royal widow, as discussion of the careers of Eurydike, Olympias, and Arsinoë will demonstrate. Sons did not always agree with their mothers on what their appropriate roles in succession efforts should be.

As I examine the succession advocacy of four royal women, I will focus on two topics: factors that led to success or failure and the normative role for royal women in succession struggles. While it is chance that sufficient material remains to discuss this topic for these four women, a pattern appears to emerge, one that the difference in their specific circumstances seems to confirm.

Let me begin with Eurydike, daughter of Sirras.[3] Amyntas III had three sons by Eurydike and three by Gygaia. In the end, all of Eurydike's sons would reign and none of Gygaia's. Mortensen[4] has shown that Justin's account (7.4.7–8, 5.4–8) of Eurydike working with murderous violence against the succession of her own sons is fiction, probably the consequence of the struggle for dominance between Amyntas' two sets of sons by different mothers, a type of struggle Ogden[5] has termed 'amphimetric'. Such struggles generated slurs about royal mothers which were intended to bring into question the royal parentage of their sons (thus their right to rule) but also to generate doubts about the status and even ethnicity of the mothers.[6] Eurydike's eldest son, Alexander II, did succeed his father, but was soon after (c. 368) murdered by another Argead named Ptolemy (Diod. 15.71.1; Ath. 629d; Plut. *Pel.* 26–7). This same man may have married the royal widow Eurydike;[7] certainly he served as regent for her remaining sons.[8] Then yet another Argead named Pausanias returned to Macedonia with an army, took a number of towns, and gained the support of many Macedonians.

According to Aischines (2.26–9),[9] at this moment of crisis, Eurydike acted. She summoned Iphikrates, an Athenian general operating against nearby Amphipolis, and sought his aid, reminding him that Amyntas had made him his son,[10] terming him, in a private context, a brother of her sons and in public, 'our' friend (*philos*), as well as citing the friendship of the Athenians to Amyntas. Iphikrates did indeed drive Pausanias out. The *Suda* (*s.v.* 'Karanos') terms Eurydike and the Athenian general allies (*symmachoi*).[11] It is possible that Ptolemy and Eurydike acted jointly,[12] but that his role disappeared from the literary tradition because of his murder of the eldest of Eurydike's sons. In any event, whether acting on her own or with Ptolemy, Eurydike took diplomatic action in the context of her role as mother; she couched her argument in terms of kinship and friendship ties with Iphikrates as an individual, as well as friendship[13] with the Athenians in general. Eurydike was clearly versed in the reciprocal nature of Hellenic understanding of *philia*. Moreover, Aischines (2.26) asserted that Eurydike and her sons had initially been betrayed by those who had claimed to be their *philoi*, implying that both domestically and internationally he understood Eurydike to be included in *philia* relationships.

While Aischines (2.28–9) certainly sentimentalizes Eurydike's advocacy of her sons' continued claim to the throne with ahistorical detail (he has her put the boys into Iphikrates' arms, though they were teenagers, and Philip may not even have been in Macedonia at the time),[14] his speech takes for granted Eurydike's involvement in private and public *philia* networks in order to safeguard what Aischines describes as Philip's and her own interest (2.29). This pattern of involvement in internal and external *philia*, often in the context of succession advocacy, recurs in the careers of other royal women. Granted the importance of reciprocity in *philia*, women's benefactions often played a role in these relationships (see below).[15] Their participation in such networks was part of the larger pattern of male and female faction-building related to succession struggles at the Macedonian court.[16]

Subsequent to the Iphikrates episode, Perdikkas, Eurydike's second son, managed to kill off Ptolemy and rule in his own right (Diod. 15.77.5). When Perdikkas died in battle, Eurydike's youngest son, Philip II, took the throne and held it against various Argead claimants including Gygaia's sons.

Eurydike continued to play a public role that probably was intended to increase her prestige and thus the status of her sons. At Vergina, Eurydike made several dedications, including a statue, and possibly the entire sanctuary to the goddess Eukleia, whose priestess she could possibly have been. The sanctuary may have been related to the general plan, now commonly attributed to Philip II, of the palace-theater complex. Eurydike also made a dedication to the Muses that portrayed her, apparently in reference to the period after her husband's death, as a loving mother to her sons (Plut. *Mor.* 14c). A statue of her stood as part of some group – possibly a dynastic one – in the neighborhood of Vergina and another formed part of the dynastic group in the Philippeum at Olympia (Paus. 5.17.4, 20.9–10).[17] It is likely that all these dedications and monuments were created during the reigns of her sons, most likely during the reign of Philip II.[18] An elaborate and eerie tomb of the Macedonian type has also been attributed to her, although no specific evidence connects her to it.[19] The collection of monuments, Aischines' speech, and inscriptions establish that for Philip himself, the Athenians, and the Macedonians, Eurydike acted appropriately.

Olympias worked for the succession of her son Alexander III and for the possibility that her grandson Alexander IV would live long enough to rule in fact as well as name. According to Plutarch, Olympias made relations between Philip II and his son Alexander, already tense because of the complexity of royal polygamy, worse (*Alex.* 9.3). Plutarch even recounts a story that she poisoned Philip Arrhidaios, Philip's other son (Plut. *Alex.* 77.5). When Attalos, guardian of Philip's last bride, proposed a toast that questioned Alexander's legitimacy as an heir, Alexander chose to leave Macedonia, taking with him his mother.[20] Justin (9.7.5) claims that Olympias, back in her Molossian homeland where her brother was king, tried to persuade him to go to war with Philip; in any event, the war did not happen. Philip reconciled with his son and Olympias too (Plut. *Mor.* 179c) and Philip honored Olympias' brother by arranging his marriage to Philip's and Olympias' daughter. Olympias' connection to her brother may have been a significant factor in both these events. According to Plutarch (*Alex.* 10.1–3), Olympias and Alexander's friends precipitated Alexander's intervention in an attempted marriage alliance between Philip Arrhidaios and the daughter of Pixodaros, satrap of Karia, because they argued that the projected marriage signified that Philip intended to settle the kingdom on his half-brother rather than Alexander (Plut. *Alex.* 10.1). Plutarch (*Alex.* 10.4) and Justin (9.8.1–14) suggested that Olympias, with or without her son's knowledge, arranged or facilitated the murder of her husband and thus the succession of her son.

After her son's succession, Olympias continued to look out for her son's interests, as she understood them. Soon after Philip's death, when Alexander's hold on the Macedonian throne was not yet firm, she eliminated one rival branch of the dynasty by her murder of Philip's last wife and child.[21] After Alexander's departure, she kept her son informed about those she deemed a threat to his secure rule. She believed that Antipatros was acting too much like a king, a view which her daughter apparently shared (Plut. *Alex.* 68.3) and which Alexander himself may have come to embrace. The grain diplomacy/benefaction in which she and her daughter engaged during the reign of Alexander was probably also done in the interest, at least in part, of the stability of her son's empire.[22]

Immediately after Alexander's death, Olympias could do little for her grandson Alexander IV. However, in 319, Polyperchon, the new regent, offered Olympias a position of authority over her grandson (Diod. 18.49.4, 57.2). Alexander IV, though a king, was only a child and had a co-king, Alexander's half brother. Philip Arrhidaios was apparently not mentally competent to rule himself, but generals and his wife, Adea Eurydike, ruled for him. Olympias accompanied an army back to Macedonia led by her nephew, the current king of Molossia, and Polyperchon. Its apparent purpose was to eliminate the co-king and thus make Alexander IV's position more secure.[23] Kassandros, son of Antipatros, had allied himself with Philip Arrhidaios and Adea Eurydike, but he was not in Macedonia when the invading army arrived to confront that of the royal pair. Their army went over to Olympias and she killed both of them as well as a number of Kassandros' supporters. Kassandros, however, returned, attacked, and defeated the forces, now depleted, that supported Olympias and Alexander IV and had Olympias killed. Though he did not kill Alexander IV for several years, he immediately deprived him of the symbols of kingship. The chance that Alexander IV would ever actually rule died with Olympias.[24]

A number of factors contributed to Alexander's succession and the ultimate failure of his son's. Alexander's initial military success and his son's lack of it were critical. Like Eurydike, Olympias employed a *philia* network to aid in her efforts as well as public patronage of various kinds. Unlike Eurydike, Olympias actually made use of violence in her efforts to safeguard the succession. It probably did help, though it may also have entrenched her enemies. Her efforts for her grandson failed because the *philoi* supporting her grandson by military means were defeated, not because of her continued use of violence.

Nonetheless, the extant sources roundly condemn her actions, suggesting that they were peculiarly unacceptable for a woman yet somehow deeply feminine. Justin (14.6.1) understands Olympias' dynastic violence as vengeful and womanish, in keeping with the view that women are vengeful but men take vengeance. Diodoros (19.11.9) portrays her violent acts as fulfillment of Antipatros' supposed death-bed advice that Macedonia should never be led by a woman. Their views ignore similar and often greater violent acts by the Successors. While both Diodoros (19.5.11–6) and Justin (14.6.7–12) admire Olympias' brave death, they never mention, let alone praise, the fairly obvious fact that she had risked her life for her grandson's future.

In contrast to Olympias, Thessalonike, Alexander's half-sister, spent most of her life as a dynastic pawn. Kassandros married her in 316, hoping to bring some legitimacy to his control of Macedonia by marrying the daughter of Philip (Just. 14.6.13; Diod. 19.52.1–5). She had three sons by Kassandros, but played no public role in the kingdom. His death in 297 was followed, within months, by that of their oldest son. The surviving sons apparently shared rule, a situation more likely the decision of Kassandros or a council of advisors than of Thessalonike, who was not regent.[25] Nonetheless, Antipatros, probably her older son,[26] murdered his mother, an act that precipitated the end of the dynasty. Justin (16.1.3–4) and Pausanias (9.7.3) say that Antipatros killed her because, at the time of the partition of the kingdom, she seemed more inclined to his brother. Diodoros (21.7.1) attributes the murder to Antipatros' *phthonos* (jealousy).[27]

Thessalonike failed because she had no military protection against Antipatros' violence and little experience in power politics. Justin comments that everyone considered Antipatros' crime even more terrible because there was no evidence of *fraus* (wrongdoing) in her actions. This suggests that Thessalonike was murdered not because she favoured one son over the other, but rather because she refused to favour one son to the exclusion of the other. On the other hand, her murder also demonstrates that her son Antipatros expected her whole-hearted advocacy of his succession and considered it worth the risk to kill her when he did not get it.

Arsinoë, daughter of Ptolemy I, was much more aggressively involved in at least two and possibly three succession struggles.[28] Arsinoë married Lysimachos and had three sons by him, but his considerable age and the existence of older sons meant that initially Arsinoë's sons were not likely candidates to succeed their father. Lysimachos' longevity gradually made their succession conceivable, but his adult son, Agathokles, was expected to succeed his father and had, by the mid 280s, built up a network of *philoi* committed to his succession. Nonetheless, in 283 Lysimachos had Agathokles executed and Arsinoë's oldest son became his apparent heir.

The sources all picture Arsinoë as a participant in the elimination of

Agathokles, though they vary considerably about the degree of her involvement. Memnon (*FGrH* 434 F. 1.5.6) says Lysimachos executed him through her influence.[29] Pausanias (1.10.2–4) claims that Arsinoë herself, without her husband's knowledge, killed Agathokles, at least partly because he had spurned her sexual advances. Justin (17.1.4–5), on the other hand, asserts that Lysimachos hated Agathokles and used Arsinoë to poison him. In addition, Arsinoë publicized herself and her son.[30]

In this first struggle, Arsinoë was victorious primarily because her husband sided with her and her son, apparently because he believed Agathokles had betrayed him. Strabo (13.4.1) says that Lysimachos, encompassed by troubles in his household, was compelled to kill Agathokles. Doubtless Arsinoë's influence contributed to Lysimachos' belief, but so may Agathokles' actions and his relationship with his father. The prestige of her family, now that her brother ruled Egypt,[31] her husband's affection, and her powers of patronage may also have contributed to her success. Apart from Justin,[32] the sources picture Arsinoë as a scheming woman, lecherous and treacherous, who destroyed the rightful heir.

Her victory was ephemeral. The demise of Agathokles gave Seleukos an excuse to make war and in 281 Lysimachos died in battle against him. Arsinoë and her sons tried to rebuild a base in Macedonia, but her son Ptolemy, now adult, was not acclaimed king. Seleukos invaded the European portion of Lysimachos' former realm, but was murdered by Arsinoë's half-brother, Ptolemy Keraunos, who then managed to get Seleukos' troops to recognize him as king (Memnon *FGrH* 434 F 1.8.3). Arsinoë and her sons retained control of Kassandreia.[33] At this point, Keraunos, despite a lifetime of enmity between the two families of Ptolemy I, offered to marry his half-sister.[34] According to our only source, Justin (17.2.6–8; 24.2.1–3.10), Arsinoë extracted a series of promises from Keraunos: he would adopt her sons, he would co-rule with them, proclaim her queen, would not take another wife, and would not recognize any children other than hers as his sons. Keraunos swore to all of this, but as soon as he married Arsinoë and got control of Kassandreia, he murdered her two younger sons. Doubting Keraunos' sincerity (Just. 24.2.10), her eldest son apparently departed and so escaped slaughter.

Granted that Arsinoë could easily have fled to Alexandria after Lysimachos' death, her determination to stay in Macedonia must relate primarily to her effort to secure their father's throne for her sons. Her methods were partly military, but primarily political. The disastrous marriage alliance was not enough to thwart superior military strength. Justin's florid narrative (24.3.7–9) describes Arsinoë as more concerned about her sons than herself, offering herself up in place of her sons, and devastated by their murders.

Arsinoë again fled dynastic disaster. She returned to Egypt and subsequently married her brother, Ptolemy II, having supplanted his first wife.[35] Some scholars believe the mysterious co-regent of Ptolemy II from 267–59, known as 'Ptolemy the Son', was Arsinoë's son by Lysimachos. This could mean that Arsinoë had yet again functioned as a succession advocate, convincing her husband to favor his nephew over his own sons. Granted the complexities of the evidence about the post-Macedonian career of Arsinoë's son,[36] continuing debate about the identity of Ptolemy the Son, and the possibility that, even if Ptolemy II did make his sister's son co-regent, he did so for reasons not having much to do with her actions,[37] it is difficult to say more in this context.

What have we learned? First let us think about the factors that led to successful succession advocacy. Military support was critical and women had only indirect or symbolic connection to armies. Women could, however, acquire military backing (or the threat of it) by effective use of *philia* networks (brothers seem especially important). If these methods failed, then so did they. Participation, direct or indirect, in dynastic violence, sometimes worked. Public patronage and the generation of an attractive and yet conventional public image helped, just as hostile propaganda harmed a woman and weakened her son's position, before or after her son's succession.

What was the attitude in antiquity to women known to have played a role in the succession of sons? Ancient authors condemn women associated with violent methods, even if the violence was reciprocal, whereas they rarely comment on male dynastic violence. Of course, our extant sources reflect only fragments of contemporary opinion and many of them were composed centuries after the events described, in the Roman era. As we have seen, both Diodoros and Justin condemn Olympias' use of violence; the same can be said of Memnon's and Justin's treatment of Arsinoë's supposed role in the elimination of Agathokles. Thus this topic does not seem to be one where the Roman origin of some of our sources and Greek origin of others (or their difference in period) signifies.

On the other hand, ancient sources presume that royal women would and should support their sons' path to the throne (assuming they considered the son was the rightful heir) and should work to protect them against physical danger. Significantly, the tradition that demonizes Eurydike assumes the same norm as that seen in the 'good Eurydike' tradition: a royal mother should act for her sons, not against them. Notably, both Aischines' sentimentalized description of Eurydike's intervention with Iphikrates and

Justin's florid picture of Arsinoë's attempt to save her sons from Ptolemy Keraunos imagine the safety of the succession in terms of the royal mother's embrace: Eurydike removes her sons from her own arms and lap to that of Iphikrates (Aeschin. 2. 28) and Arsinoë's sons attempt to save themselves by racing to her lap and embrace (Just. 24.3.7–9). Still, even when a woman's advocacy was deemed legitimate, it was simply expected. Such behavior was normative, natural, but not worthy of praise in itself.

Notes

[1] See discussions of royal polygamy and its consequences in Carney 1987, 1992, and 2000 and Ogden 1999; on royal mothers as succession advocates see Carney 1987, 37–8; 2000, 23–7; Müller 2013. For an overview of succession in the Argead era, see Mitchell 2007.

[2] See Carney 2000, 120 for a discussion of Olympias' possible worldly motivation, and Carney 2006, 74, for her dynastic motivation. She had either never met her grandson or just met him at the time she chose to go back to Macedonia, so affection was not likely a strong motivator in her advocacy. See below on the motivation of other royal mothers.

[3] Macurdy 1932, Mortensen 1992, Carney 2000, 40–6; Saatsoglou-Paliadeli 2000.

[4] Mortensen 1992.

[5] Ogden 1999: x. Amphimetric struggles are those between claimants who have the same father but different mothers. See his discussion of the struggles of the sons of Amyntas III: Ogden 1999, 11–16.

[6] The *Suda s.v.* 'Karanos' comments, in terms of Eurydike's sons, 'some claim they were spurious children that Eurydike introduced'. Ogden 1999 uses the term 'bastardize' to describe such attempts, but the term should not be taken literally. The point in amphimetric disputes is not whether the sons were born of a legitimate marriage but rather whether they were born of a royal father. In addition, as in the case of Attalos' famous toast hoping for legitimate heirs (Plut. *Alex.* 9.4), the references to Eurydike's Illyrian identity (*Suda s.v.* 'Karanos'; Lib. *Vit. Dem.* 9) and the notion that Philinna, mother of Philip Arrhidaios was little more than a prostitute (Plut. *Alex.* 77.5; Just. 9.8.2, 13.2.11; Ath. 13.578a), amphimetric and dynastic struggles often slighted the birth of a royal mother – her social class, her ethnicity – rather than claiming that her children were literally illegitimate.

[7] Our sole source for the marriage, however, is the scholiast on Aischines 2.29. Ogden 1999, 8–10, 23–4 and *passim*, believed marriages of kings to the widows of their predecessors (he termed them 'levirate') were more common than I do.

[8] Ptolemy's identity is much disputed. He seems to be an Argead and may be a son of Amyntas III by another wife. Ptolemy may have briefly ruled as king, but no coins with his name have been found. See recent discussions in Roisman 2010, 161–2 and Lane Fox 2011, 231–3

[9] This speech was delivered in fall 343 at Aischines' trial for malfeasance during

an embassy to Philip II in 346. Aischines, referring to his remarks to Philip in 346, reports that he referred to this incident involving Eurydike and Iphikrates c. 368.

[10] Herman 1987, 23, discussing the role of foster parentage in *xenia* (guest- or ritualized friendship), observes that though foster parentage was often romanticized, it must have been understood that it was primarily a way to create or confirm an alliance, citing Eurydike and Iphikrates as an example.

[11] Like the other ancient authors, Nepos (*Iph.* 3.2) also omits mention of Ptolemy, but has Eurydike and her sons actually taking refuge with Iphikrates, not simply having him defend them. Hammond 1979, 184 omits any reference to Eurydike and says simply that 'Ptolemy obtained help', ignoring the sources, perhaps because Aischines fictionalized some details (see below).

[12] Borza 1992, 193 makes the point that if the Ptolemy in question was the Ptolemy who had earlier represented Amyntas in a treaty with Athens (when the Macedonians supported Athenian recovery of Amphipolis), Iphikrates, trying to do just that, might well help Ptolemy and Eurydike, reflecting on the earlier link and hoping to gain their support again. At most, this would mean that both were involved. Though Ptolemy may well, despite Aischines' failure to mention him, have had a role in this affair, as Roisman 2010, 163 suggests, Roisman is unconvincing in trivializing Eurydike's role. See Howe, this volume, for further discussion of this and other issues in the career of Eurydice.

[13] Aischines (2.28) has Eurydike assert that, thanks to Iphikrates' relationship with Amyntas, it follows that in private he was the brother of her sons and in public a *philos* 'to us'. She also says that Amyntas treated the Athenians in an *oikeios* (familial, friendly) way. Jones 1999, 14 discusses the meaning of this term which derives from *oikos*.

[14] Mortensen 1992, 158, n.12.

[15] See Carney 2006, 50–2, 90–1 on royal women and *philia*. See also Müller 2013 for a broader analysis of the factors that tended to empower royal women's political efforts, particularly in terms of the succession.

[16] Mitchell 2007.

[17] Palagia 2010 argued that Eurydike in the Philippeum was Philip II's last wife; I do not find this view persuasive.

[18] See Saatsoglou-Paliadeli 2000 and Carney 2006, 90–1 and 2007 for discussion and references to the inscriptions and their possible date.

[19] See Kottaridi 2006 for references.

[20] Plutarch (*Alex.* 9.5) and Justin (9.7.5) say that Alexander took his mother, not that Philip sent them. Satyrus *ap.* Ath. 13.557e simply notes where they went, leaving open the possibility that they went separately.

[21] None of the major accounts of Alexander's reign refer to the event directly (Plut. *Alex.* 10.4, may be a euphemistic reference to the murder of Kleopatra and Alexander's attempt to distance himself from it but, if so, it does not mention the baby). The two extant accounts (Just. 9.7.12; Paus. 8.7.5) give contradictory versions, suggesting that the murders were done in private and not publicly acknowledged. Nonetheless, it seems likely that Olympias did indeed bring about their deaths. See Carney 2006, 43–8. Howe 2015 argues that Olympias murdered them entirely without her son's knowledge, in order to prevent Alexander from a

'levirate' marriage (see above) to Kleopatra. While I am not persuaded by his argument, it would suggest that mother and son both wanted to control Kleopatra and her baby/babies, but approached the problem in different ways.

[22] See Carney 2006, 50–1.

[23] Diodoros (19.11.3) says that the army restored Olympias and Alexander's son to *basileia*. Since Alexander IV was, in effect, king before he was born, Diodoros refer to political reality, not the title of *basileus*.

[24] On these events, see Carney 2006, 68–7.

[25] For a discussion of these conclusions, see Carney 1999 and Carney 2000, 157–8.

[26] Plutarch (*Pyrrh.* 6.2) says that he was Kassandros' second son and thus the elder of the surviving sons, but Porphyry (*FGrH* 260, F.3.5) says he was the younger. They must have been close in age – possibly even twins – but Antipatros' actions (see below) suggest a sense of entitlement that very likely came from being the elder, if only slightly elder, brother.

[27] Plutarch (*Demetr.* 36.1) simply reports that the brothers had each formed a faction and that Antipatros killed Thessalonike. See Landucci-Gattinoni 2009, 263–71 for a discussion of the contradictory sources for events after the death of Kassandros.

[28] See Carney 2013.

[29] He says that Lysimachos first tried to poison Agathokles (in order to conceal his murder) and then, when poison did not work, Lysimachos threw him into prison and ordered him executed, on the charge that he was plotting against his father. Memnon reveals that the actual perpetrator of Lysimachos' orders was Ptolemy Keraunos (this last probably a mistake for Arsinoë's son Ptolemy). See further Carney 2013, 41–5.

[30] She dedicated the Arsinoeum on Samothrace, almost certainly during the reign of Lysimachos (*OGIS15=IG* XII 227). It is likely that Arsinoë was promoting her son as heir and an inscription from Thebes for a statue of Arsinoë that Ptolemy, son of Lysimachos, dedicated, not for himself but for his father, may suggest that. Another statue of Arsinoë once on Delos may have formed part of the same campaign for recognition. In neither case, however, is it clear whether the statue's erection preceded or followed the death of Agathokles. (See Carney 2013, 43, ns. 59 and 60, for references.)

[31] Ptolemy II was named co-regent with his father in December 285 or January 284; Ptolemy I died in winter 283–2.

[32] Justin 17.1–8 makes Lysimachos an unnatural father and the villain of the piece and Arsinoë merely his agent.

[33] They may have controlled some other Macedonian cities as well: Trogus Prol. 24.

[34] Keraunos moved quickly to patch things up with Seleukos' son Antiochos, with Ptolemy II, and with Pyrrhus (to whom he gave military aid). Having dealt with the obvious immediate external threats, Keraunos then turned (winter 281/0) to the internal situation and the problem of Arsinoë and her sons.

[35] The scholiast on Theocritus 17.129 says that Ptolemy II found that Arsinoë I was conspiring against him with Amyntas and Chrysippus, the Rhodian physician,

and that he therefore sent her to Coptos in the Thebaid. It is often assumed that Arsinoë II engineered her predecessor's fall from grace, but no ancient source says this. Moreover, granted chronological difficulties, we cannot even be sure that Arsinoë I's fall happened before or after the return of Arsinoë II to Egypt. See further Carney 2013, 65–70. Whether Arsinoë I's disgrace jeopardized the succession of her children, at least for a time, is debatable. See below.

[36] The Prologue to book 24 reports a war between Keraunos and the combined forces of the son of Lysimachos and an Illyrian named Monimos. That effort was apparently unsuccessful. What happened to him next is unclear.

[37] The debate over the identity of Ptolemy the Son was revived by Huss 1998; see also Tunny 2000; Gygax 2000; Carney 2013, 124–6.

Bibliography

Borza, E. N.
  1992   *In the Shadow of Olympus: The Emergence of Macedon*, Princeton.
Carney, E. D.
  1999   'The Curious Death of the Antipatrid Dynasty', *AM* 6, 1, 209–16.
  2000   *Women and Monarchy in Macedonia*, Norman, OK.
  2006   *Olympias, Mother of Alexander the Great*, London and New York.
  2007   'The Philippeum, Women, and the Formation of a Dynastic Image', in W. Heckel, L. Tritle and P. Wheatley (eds) *Alexander's Empire: Formulation to Decay*, Claremont, CA, 27–70.
  2013   *Arsinoë of Egypt and Macedon: A Royal Life*, New York and Oxford.
Gygax, M. D.
  2002   'Zum Mitregenten des Ptolemaios II. Philadelphos', *Historia* 51, 49–56.
Hammond, N. G. L.
  1979   'Part One' and 'Chapter 20', in Hammond and Griffith, 1–202, 647–75.
Hammond, N.G. L. and Griffith, G. T.
  1979   *A History of Macedonia*, 2 vols. Oxford.
Hazzard, R. A.
  2000   *Imagination of a Monarchy: Studies in Ptolemaic Propaganda*, Toronto.
Herman, G.
  1987   *Ritualised Friendship and the Greek City*, Cambridge.
Höbl, G.
  2001   *A History of the Ptolemaic Empire*, London.
Howe, T.
  2015   'Cleopatra-Eurydice, Olympias, and a "Weak" Alexander', in P. Wheatley and E. Baynham (eds) *East and West in the World Empire of Alexander: Essays in Honour of Brian Bosworth*, Oxford, 133–46.
Huss, W.
  1998   'Ptolemaios der Sohn', *ZPE* 121, 229–50.
Jones, C. P.
  1999   *Kinship Diplomacy in the Ancient World*, Cambridge, MA.
Kottaridi, A.
  2006   'Couleur et signification: l'usage de la couleur dans la tombe de la reine

Eurydice', in A.-M. Guimier-Sorbets, M. B. Hatzopoulos and Y. Morizot (eds) *Rois, cités, nécropoles: institutions, rites et monuments en Macedoine*, Meletemata 45, Athens, 155–68.

Landucci Gattinoni, F.
2009 'Cassander's Wife and Heirs', in P. Wheatley and R. Hannah (eds) *Alexander and His Successors: Essays from the Antipodes*, Claremont, CA, 261–75.

Lane Fox, R.
2011 '399–69 BC', in R. Lane Fox (ed.) *Brill's Companion to Ancient Macedon: Studies in the Archaeology and History of Macedon, 650 BC–300 AD*, Leiden, 209–34.

Macurdy, G. H.
1932 *Hellenistic Queens*, Baltimore.

Mitchell, L.
2007 'Born to Rule? Succession in the Argead Royal House', in W. Heckel, L. Tritle and P. Wheatley (eds) *Alexander's Empire: Formulation to Decay*, Claremont, CA, 27–60.

Mortensen, K.
1992 'Eurydice: Demonic or Devoted Mother?', *AHB* 6, 156–71.

Müller, S.
2013 'Das symbolische Kapital von Argeadinnen und Fraue der Diadochen', in C. Kunst (ed.) *Matronage Handlungsstrategien und soziale Netzwerke antiker Herrscherfrauen*, Osnabrück, 31–42.

Ogden, D.
1999 *Polygamy, Prostitutes and Death: The Hellenistic Dynasties*, Swansea and London.

Palagia, O.
2010 'Philip's Eurydice in the Philippeum at Olympia', in E. D. Carney and D. Ogden (eds) *Philip II and Alexander the Great: Father and Son, Lives and Afterlives*, New York, 33–42.

Pomeroy, S. B.
1984 *Women in Hellenistic Egypt from Alexander to Cleopatra*, New York.

Roisman, J.
2010 'Classical Macedonia to Perdiccas III', in J. Roisman and I. Worthington (eds) *A Companion to Ancient Macedonia*, Malden, MA, 145–65.

Saatsoglou-Paliadeli, C.
2000 'Queenly Appearances at Vergina-Aegae: Old and New Epigraphic and Literary Evidence', *AA* 3, 387–403.

Tunny, J. A.
2000 'Ptolemy "the Son" Reconsidered: Are there too many Ptolemies?' *ZPE* 131, 83–92.

3

A ROMAN OLYMPIAS:
POWERFUL WOMEN IN THE *HISTORIAE PHILIPPICAE* OF POMPEIUS TROGUS

Rebecca Frank

Who was Olympias? Our sources identify her as the wife of Philip II of Macedonia and the mother of Alexander the Great. But her reputation far exceeds this narrow scope and the traditional limitations for women in the Greco-Roman world. In the extant ancient literature her character is universally maligned and she is condemned as ruthless, vengeful, and desperate for power. For authors such as Diodoros, Pompeius Trogus/ Justin, and Plutarch, Olympias serves as a symbol of madness and chaos, demonstrating the destructive influence of women in the political sphere.[1] This stigmatisation of her character colors our understanding of her role in Macedonian politics throughout her life, presenting a view that marginalises her political power and obscures her standing in the Macedonian court during her lifetime.[2] In order to understand who Olympias was and her position within the Macedonian political sphere, we first need to address the context of her treatment within the ancient literature.[3] The prominence of the figure of Alexander in the decades and centuries after his death in both popular imagination and political propaganda problematises making sweeping assessments of how and why ancient historiographers formulated their depictions of Alexander and those associated with him.[4] The time, place, and context of each individual work must be addressed with regard to the portrayal of the events and figures contained therein. The *Historiae Philippicae* of Pompeius Trogus has posed a particular challenge to historians making such assessments due to the nature of its preservation, and as a result the context of its composition and the resulting presentation of Olympias have been frequently overlooked.

The Augustan historian Pompeius Trogus produced a world history during the period following the triumviral civil wars and in the early decades of the principate in Rome. As may be suggested by the title of his work, *Historiae Philippicae*, Trogus highlighted Macedonia in particular both before and after Alexander. Although the meaning of this title continues to be the subject of much scholarly debate, Justin's epitome as well as the extant summaries of Trogus' books indicates that Macedonia, Alexander, and the Diadoch period were given extra weight in the history.[5] This interest in Alexander is not a phenomenon seen in Trogus alone, but coincides with the rhetoric surrounding Alexander and the use of his name and reputation for political motives in the late Republic and early Augustan periods. Alexander's image could be used to demonstrate political might, as utilised by Augustus, but also contained the dangerous veneer of Eastern despotism, as seen when applied to Mark Antony.[6] The rhetoric surrounding the image of Alexander in late Republican and early Augustan politics connects the portrayal of Alexander in the histories of the period with the political situation of the historiographers. Although Trogus has long been accused of being 'anti-Roman', both for the general absence of Rome from his largely Hellenistic history and for his seemingly brusque treatment when he does incorporate the Romans into his narrative, his 'Philippic' history engaged directly with some of the principal problems of his day, those concerning the nature of empire and ruler.[7]

Unfortunately, Trogus' *Historiae Philippicae* has been lost. The study of his historiographical method and agenda is made inherently problematic by the failure of his text to survive. What remains is preserved in the history produced by Justin during the late second or early third century AD.[8] While Justin's account is derivative of Trogus', earning it the title of 'epitome' by modern scholars,[9] because Trogus' text failed to survive it is difficult to attribute specific words or phrases of Justin's history to him with any degree of certainty.[10] However, this does not imply that we are unable to read Trogus through the work of Justin. In the preface to his history, Justin declares (*praef.* 4): 'I have selected what is most worthy and have omitted what was necessary neither for pleasure nor for moral instruction'.[11] As Justin informs his reader, what he has excerpted from Trogus may not be representative of the original forty-four book work.[12] But what he has transmitted most likely preserves sentiments that were, in some fashion, expressed by Trogus.[13] In this way Justin's text (henceforth Justin/Trogus) provides a glimpse into the original account of Trogus. Although it is not possible to ascertain beyond mere speculation what was in Trogus that has not been preserved, the text as it stands allows us to analyze what has been transmitted.

This analysis is not without substantial historiographical difficulties. Justin's later 'epitome' introduces the voice of another author whose authorial intent and focus may have been different from that of his predecessor.[14] But preserved along with the manuscripts of Justin is a means to check the text of Justin against that of Trogus: the so-called

Prologi. As with the *Periochae* of Livy, the *Prologi* are succinct, grammatically and stylistically simple summaries of the books of Trogus' *Historiae Philippicae*. Fundamental differences between the *Prologi* and Justin suggest that while they were eventually transmitted together, they stem from different authors and the *Prologi* could not have been based on the text of Justin.[15] In addition, the anonymous author of the *Prologi* was summarising Trogus based on his assessment of the key elements of the narrative. In spite of the arguably voiceless and dry tone of the writing, the events listed in the summaries represent a subjective choice by the author of the *Prologi*, a choice which may – or may not – reflect the true nature of the *Historiae Philippicae* of Trogus. While the *Prologi* may offer a glimpse at what was contained within the books of Trogus, usually corroborating Justin's history, their concise nature poses limitations to their utility. The presence of material in the *Prologi* not included by Justin suggests that it was most likely present in Trogus but passed over by Justin. On the other hand, material included by Justin but not found in the *Prologi* does not condemn it as invention by the later author due to the difference in scope of the 'epitome' versus the *Prologi*. This chapter aims to scrutinise the *Historiae Philippicae* of Trogus, focusing on the Augustan-era author's portrayal of a powerful Eastern woman within his account of Alexander: Olympias.

I

Justin/Trogus' depiction of Olympias is hardly flattering. Ruled by jealousy and a desire for vengeance, she serves as an *exemplum* of the troubles wrought by a woman given access to power. She is a source of destruction and an obstacle blocking the political aspirations of others. From the moment she is introduced in the narrative she thwarts the political ambitions of her uncle Arybbas by substantiating the treaty between Molossia and Macedonia via her marriage to Philip II. According to Justin/Trogus (7.6.11–12), 'this was the cause of his downfall and of all his misfortunes'. Although Olympias is not given an active role in this affair, she is still associated closely here with the political downfall of Arybbas. Justin/Trogus has chosen to include this warning of Arybbas' future loss in the narrative with the introduction of Olympias even though the political events referenced are not recorded until the end of the following book (8.6.3–5).[16] The anticipatory nature of the linking makes it appear unlikely that this was an innovation of Justin's.[17] By linking Olympias with political intrigue and ruin from her very introduction to both the Macedonian political sphere and his history, Justin/Trogus sets the tone for her subsequent treatment in the work.[18]

43

Justin/Trogus accentuates this destructive political aspect through Olympias' involvement in the estrangement of Philip and Alexander, leading ultimately to the murder of the Macedonian king. Claiming that Olympias was put aside by Philip on a charge of adultery (9.5.9), Justin/Trogus cites her resentment and jealousy over this as the spur motivating the murder of Philip (9.7.1–2): 'It was also believed that [Pausanias] had been spurred on by Olympias, the mother of Alexander...for Olympias did not feel any less indignation at her repudiation and the preference of Kleopatra [Eurydike] over herself than Pausanias at his sexual abuse [by Philip]'.[19] Again it is Olympias, after she and Alexander left Macedonia, who attempts to persuade her brother to wage war against Philip (9.7.7). Justin/Trogus refrains from accusing Olympias outright of driving Pausanias to murder the king, instead making use of passive generalities (9.7.1: *creditum est* and 9.7.8: *creduntur*) when describing her presumed role in the murder.[20] While Justin/Trogus does not accuse Olympias directly of instigating and orchestrating Philip's assassination, he emphasises her culpability in the matter through a string of slanderous charges demonstrating her approval of Pausanias' actions. She had horses prepared for Pausanias' escape (9.7.9), placed a golden wreath on the head of the crucified Pausanias (9.7.10), had his body cremated and entombed over Philip's remains (9.7.11), and consecrated to Apollo the sword used to slay the king (9.7.13). In addition to this, Justin/Trogus reports that she slew the young child of Kleopatra Eurydike and forced the mother to hang herself (9.7.12).[21] This level of detail is a striking contrast to the typically brief style of Justin. While we cannot presume that this contrast would have been present in Trogus' *Historiae Philippicae*, it is reasonable to assume that these details were also present in that work.[22] In recounting Olympias' active participation in Macedonian political affairs during the life of Philip, Justin/Trogus not only sheds light on how she navigated her political situation, but also condemns her for this very engagement.

Justin/Trogus' criticism of Olympias is most vitriolic in his presentation of Olympias' attempts to exploit the leverage her relationship to Alexander afforded her during the political turmoil arising from the death of her son. Her continued influence in Macedonia after the death of Alexander is acknowledged in Justin/Trogus through the citation of her tacit approval of the proposed match between Perdikkas and her daughter Kleopatra (13.6.4) and in the acknowledgment of her political clout by Perdikkas' advisors (13.6.12). Regardless of Olympias' historical ability or inclination to prevent, or support, such a marriage, by inserting this clause Justin/Trogus implies that she held some authority in this matter. It is her subsequent abuse of this power that sets her up as an example of the destructive nature of female power and a symbol of the disordered nature of Macedonian society as it descended into civil war.[23]

Turning from the defeat of Eumenes in the East (14.1–4), Justin/Trogus frames the conflict in Macedonia as the result of female meddling. Adea Eurydike, the wife of Philip III Arrhidaios, is characterised as being 'overpowered by womanly jealousy [and] taking advantage of her husband's illness whose duties she was appropriating for herself' (14.5.2).[24] But Justin/Trogus make not only her husband, but also Kassandros her pawn in her bid for true royal power, scornfully noting (14.5.4): 'Kassandros, obliged by her assistance, managed nothing without the authority of her womanly audacity'. Into this context Olympias is said to enter the fray, personally leading an army against Adea Eurydike and Arrhidaios and ordering on her own authority the deaths of her rivals (14.5.9–10).[25] Although Justin/Trogus notes that Olympias was invited to return to Macedonia from Epirus where she had been residing since 331 BC, the reasons for this summons and Polyperchon's ongoing struggles with Kassandros are so contracted that they are rendered unintelligible in the account.[26] The conflict between Kassandros and Polyperchon under the pen of Justin/Trogus became purely a war between women, manipulating both kings and generals to further their personal ends.[27]

But it is after Olympias has wrested power from her female rival that the scathing tone of Justin/Trogus reaches its climax (14.6.1):

> But Olympias did not rule for long. For when she brought about the indiscriminate slaughter of the nobility more in the custom of a woman than a ruler, goodwill towards her turned into hatred.

Justin/Trogus' use of *regnavit* and *regio* are demonstrative of the treatment of Olympias in this passage. She is not merely the grandmother of the young Alexander IV, nor regent (a position which was occupied officially by Polyperchon), but is said to rule and is criticised for acting in a manner unbefitting that rank. Thus Justin/Trogus guides the reader to view Olympias not only as usurping power through violence but as subsequently abusing that very authority.

Justin's possible modifications of Trogus' narrative may be identifiable here through cross-comparison with the *Prologi. Prol.* 14 states:

> how in Macedonia Kassandros, having defeated Polyperchon and having received Munichia from the defector Nikanor, killed the mother of Alexander, Olympias, who had been besieged at Pydna.

Polyperchon's defeat is nowhere to be found in Justin's text, and he disappears from the narrative entirely after summoning Olympias to Macedonia in 14.5.1. If the tone of *Prol.* 14 may be applied to Trogus, this would indicate that Trogus' account was centered around the movements of Kassandros (as 14.1–4 follows Eumenes), rather than on Eurydike and Olympias. Yet there are reasons for dismissing the critique of Eurydike and Olympias as merely a fabrication of Justin. Unless Justin should be given credit for a greater historical understanding of the period under consideration and access to sources other than the *Historiae Philippicae*, the material which he relates concerning Olympias and Eurydike must have been gleaned from the pages of Trogus. The details of Justin/Trogus' account of Olympias here mirror closely those found in Diodoros[28] and attempts by Adea Eurydike to seize power are also well documented in other sources.[29] The numerous parallels within the source tradition for Justin/Trogus' material concerning Olympias and Adea Eurydike indicate that it is most likely not an addition to Trogus' history by Justin.[30] Furthermore, the soundness of the language, not merely the contents, is suggested by the numerous parallels with Livy in the passages in question.[31]

Although in the *Prologi*, as compared to the text of Justin, the role of Olympias is marginalised and that of Adea Eurydike passed over entirely, this does not restrict this material to being an invention of Justin. Nor does it exclude the possibility that Justin has elaborated upon the subject, expanding upon the moral undercurrent running throughout his presentation of the two royal women. Justin's choice to transmit such material found in Trogus is not surprising given his statement of authorial intent in the preface. But even if here Justin has elaborated on a theme, it is an elaboration and does not change the likelihood, or the impact, of its presence in the work of Trogus.

Finally, Justin/Trogus lingers over the death of Olympias, pausing in the narrative to draw out the manner of her assassination at the hands of Kassandros. This scene is notable not only in its length but also in its vivid description of her final actions (14.6.9–12):

> But Olympias, when she saw resolute soldiers coming towards her, approached them in her regal vestments, supported by two handmaids. The assassins, upon seeing her, struck by the fate of her previous majesty and by the great many names of kings she recalled to memory, halted, until men were sent by Kassandros who would pierce her through. She did not flee the sword nor the wounds, nor cry like a woman, but she submitted to death in the manner of brave men for the glory of her ancestral family, so that you were able to recognise Alexander even in his dying mother. It is said moreover that while dying she arranged her hair and covered her legs with her dress, lest anything should seem to be unseemly in her appearance.

Justin/Trogus' Olympias dies a noble death.[32] In spite of the repeated criticism leveled at both her and Adea Euryice as being *muliebris* previously

(14.5.2, 5.5, 6.1), in her manner of death Olympias is described as acting *not* in the manner of a woman (*muliebriter*), but of an exemplary man (*virorum fortium more*). While Diodoros (19.51.5) also adds that Olympias died 'letting slip no base or womanly plea',[33] Justin/Trogus is alone among the ancient sources in his description of her modesty in death.[34] This emphasis on her dignity and virtue is an abrupt switch from Justin/Trogus' previous treatment of her as the unremorseful murderer of her husband, Kleopatra Eurydike and her young daughter, Adea Eurydike and Arrhidaios, and the unnamed nobility who succumbed to her *womanly* wrath.

The figure of Olympias seen in Justin/Trogus is a multifaceted one. She is a powerful woman who inserts herself into the political sphere and is not above ruthless murder to satisfy her ambitions. When she is able to wield her power unchecked, her destructive (womanly) instincts are made fully manifest and betray the trust conferred upon her by the Macedonian people. And yet in death, her former dignity is once more allowed to shine through as she becomes the embodiment of the Argead dynasty, all hopes of which are lost with her assassination at the hands of Kassandros.

Such a change in characterisation from a grasping and ruthless woman to one exhibiting male *virtus* as she approaches her death is not unprecedented in Augustan-era literature, as is seen most notably in Horace's Kleopatra Ode (*Odes*, 1.37, see below). This connection between Justin/Trogus' Olympias and the Ptolemaic Kleopatra is best understood in light of the tenor set by Octavian explaining and justifying his political and military struggle with fellow *triumvir*, Mark Antony.

II

At the height of the Roman civil wars and in their aftermath, Octavian demonstrated himself to be adept at manipulating the nature of his struggle with Antony. Making use of a deformed portrayal of Kleopatra, he effectively shaped the Battle of Actium into a foreign war against the savage, autocratic East rather a civil war between himself and the (Roman) Antony.[35] While he could not remove Antony from the conflict, he could cast aside the blame from his opponent and hold up the corrupting, seductive influence of Kleopatra as the root cause of the political upheaval.[36] Portraying himself as the perfect Roman, preserver of traditional Republican values,[37] Octavian strove to present the Roman people with a contrast: the noble Roman fighting against the power-hungry barbarians.[38] In order to accomplish this, Octavian endeavored to cloak himself in legitimacy, distancing himself from the royal aspirations of his predecessor and emphasising his adherence to the strict limitations of legality in spite of his opponent's flouting of those same principles.[39] By thus couching his language in terms of tradition and precedent, Octavian was able to wield autocratic power while waging a war against that very ideal.

The link between Augustus and the Augustan-era writers has been, and continues to be, the subject of much scholarly debate. Syme suggested the imperial-era authors were effectively puppets controlled by the emperor and directed to sing his praises.[40] Ahl likewise argued for a direct, coercive propaganda model while acknowledging that the Augustan authors may not have believed the message they were nonetheless propagating.[41] More recently however, scholarship has turned to consider a more nuanced role for Augustus in the literary culture of Rome. White (1993) suggests that Augustus operated within the traditional sphere of literary patrons and argues that there is no evidence to suggest an overt literary propaganda campaign, though the scale of Augustus' *auctoritas* and *dignitas* meant his influence was felt in all aspects of Roman life.[42] More radically, Galinsky questions whether the poetry may be said to contain such 'propaganda' at all, noting the many other poetic and cultural influences on the Augustan era writers and emphasising the subtle nature of Augustan influence on the poets.[43] Regardless of the source of the portrayal of Kleopatra and Actium in Augustan-era literature, whether the authors were limited to this view or adopted it willingly, its consistency in the Augustan authors – both in poetry and in prose – is notable.[44]

Horace's Kleopatra Ode (*Odes* 1.37) presents a vivid depiction of the Battle of Actium. Describing Kleopatra as a *fatale monstrum*,[45] a horrible Eastern queen plotting the utter ruin of Rome,[46] Horace's rancorous words wholeheartedly embrace Octavian's propaganda surrounding the downfall of Antony.[47] This is especially apparent in the absence of one of the primary players in the war from the poem: Antony, against whom the battle of Actium was actually being waged, goes unmentioned.[48] It is Kleopatra, the bestial, drunken foreigner, who threatens Rome and whose barbarity is overcome by the triumph of Octavian, not her lover Antony, the celebrated Roman general. Furthermore, while Horace glosses over Antony's role in the civil war, he celebrates Octavian as the skilled hunter, exacting justice from a depraved yet ultimately powerless queen.[49] And yet, as with the death of Olympias in Justin/Trogus, Kleopatra does not die a shameful or 'womanly' death (*Odes* 1.37.21–29):

> Who, seeking to die more nobly, did not display womanly fear of the sword (*nec muliebriter expavit ensem*)[50] nor did she flee to hidden shores with her fleet, but she endured to gaze at her fallen city with a serene face, and courageously handled savage serpents (*fortis*[51] *et asperas tractare serpentes*) so that she might drink the black venom, more fiercely intent upon death.

48

The implications of this portrayal of Kleopatra's death are unclear. Does Horace mean to exonerate the Egyptian queen, granting her the dignity of a noble death, or does this sudden turn of countenance suggest ridicule of Octavian's characterisation of her? It may well be, as Galinsky concludes, 'it is left for the reader to define and delimit the exact emphases and connotations'.[52] But whatever Horace's intentions were behind the shift, it is the same character reversal that Justin/Trogus' Olympias undergoes immediately before her death.

There are other notable parallels. Both Kleopatra and Olympias are foreign – Eastern – queens who dared to take power for themselves. Justin/Trogus' Olympias is a symbol and agent of destruction, at times apparently descending to senseless violence for no other purported reason than female jealousy. Likewise the Augustan Kleopatra was a blend of savage brutality and female seduction who corrupted Antony and dared to challenge Rome. Additionally, as demonstrated aptly in the case of Kleopatra, both her and Olympias' abilities to defend their reputations died with them.

The civil war between Antony and Octavian appears in no part of Justin's 'epitome'. It would appear, therefore, that Trogus had astutely avoided any mention of the conflict. But the *Prologi* reveal an odd truth: parts of the Roman civil wars, including the Battle of Actium, must have appeared in the work of Trogus, but were deliberately passed over by Justin.[53] Book 40 of Justin continues a discussion of the collapse of the Ptolemaic kingdom begun in the previous book, but fails to finish it. Reaching the defeat of Tigranes and the reorganisation of the East by Pompey, Justin ends the book and continues in book 41 with the Parthians, failing to see the Ptolemaic kingdom through to its conclusion. Not so in the *Prologi*. Justin's narrative follows the framework of the *Prologi* through to the seizure of Syria by the Romans, but where his book ends, *Prol.* 40 continues:

> How at Alexandria after the death of Ptolemy Lathyros he was replaced by his sons: one of these was given Cyprus, which the Romans took away with the proposal of P. Clodius; the other (Ptolemy XIV), having been accused of sedition in Alexandria, escaped to Rome, and regained his rule with the aid of the war waged by Gabinius. How when he died his sister Kleopatra (VII) succeeded to the throne, who after Marcus Antonius became ensnared by love for her destroyed the reign of the Ptolemies with the conclusion of the battle of Actium.[54]

The narrative structure given in *Prol.* 40 fits the pattern seen throughout the rest of the *Historiae Philippicae*, that is, tracing the rise *and fall* of empires. But more importantly here, it provides evidence of Trogus' treatment of Kleopatra. In the words of the author of the *Prologi*, Kleopatra lured Antony with her charms and made herself the last Ptolemaic pharaoh by ending her dynasty with her defeat in the Battle of Actium. As in Horace,

Kleopatra is the dominant actor in this account and Antony's only role that of passive victim rather than active participant in the conflict. In fact, no other reference to the civil war of the 30s is given in either the *Prologi* or Justin. Antony himself in both the *Prologi* (*Prol.* 40 aside) and Justin/ Trogus is limited to the context of the Parthians: twice in reference to Antony's campaigns (Just. 41.2.6 and 42.5.3, *Prol.* 42), and once to the Parthians giving aid to Brutus and Cassius in their fight against Augustus and Antony (Just. 42.4.7). In this context the civil war between Caesar and Pompey is acknowledged to explain the actions of the Persians,[55] but nowhere is there any mention of the conflict between Antony and Octavian. If this snippet from the *Prologi* accurately represents Trogus' *Historiae Philippicae*, it would appear that Trogus fashioned his Kleopatra in line with the Augustan image: a powerful, corrupting woman against whom the 'civil' war was truly being waged.

By tapping into this language used for Kleopatra to describe Olympias – her noble (manly) death as seen in Horace, her rule as queen in her own right, and her womanly cruelty – Trogus connected the ancient kingdom of Macedonia with his own present circumstances, the wars of the Successors with the civil war between Octavian and Antony. His discussion of the rise and fall of empires reveals a remarkable circularity: just as Kleopatra brought an end to the reign of the Ptolemies in Egypt, so too did Olympias for the Argeads in Macedonia.[56] While there were Argeads still living, including her grandchildren Alexander IV and Herakles, they did not survive for long and were never in any position to wield power.[57] The two women became symbolic figures who are both portrayed as bringing about their own deaths through their actions and are condemned for taking their kingdom down with them.

Not only would Trogus' Roman audience have identified Olympias with Kleopatra, the historian's language itself urges his readers towards that conclusion. Additionally, in emphasising Olympias' role as a queen and ruler, he places her on par with Kleopatra, squarely in the political context of the Roman author rather than in her own Macedonian setting.[58] Constructing an image of barbarity and manipulation, Trogus fashions an Olympias with whom his contemporaries could identify and through whom they could read their own political turbulence. By invoking terminology and imagery reminiscent of Kleopatra, Trogus can construct a vision of Macedonia that mirrors his own sociopolitical context thereby enabling him to fashion a political narrative through the use of comparison and analogy. As a result, through the manipulation of language and the retrospective nature of historiography, Trogus' Olympias becomes Kleopatra, and his Kleopatra, Olympias.

Notes

I am most grateful to Timothy Howe for his unfailing advice and support.

[1] e.g. Just. 9.7, 14.6.1; Diod. 19.11.2–9; Plut. *Alex.* 9.3.

[2] For a general overview of the problems inherent in the study of powerful women in antiquity, see Carney 2006, 1–4 (and on Olympias in particular) 125–37.

[3] For an overview of modern scholarship on Olympias, see Macurdy 1932, 22–4; Greenwalt 1989, 19–45; Carney 2009, 189–202.

[4] For the significance of Alexander as a political and cultural symbol, see Spencer 2002.

[5] For the significance of the title and the prominence of Macedonia and Alexander within the work, see Seel 1955, 27–36; Urban 1982, 82–96; Develin 1985, 110–15; Alonso-Núñez 1987, 58–9; J.C. Yardley and W. Heckel 1997, 24–5.

[6] Spencer 2002, 24–6, 41–53, 175 and Pollini 2012, 162–203.

[7] See Levene 2007, 287–89 and Atkinson 2000, 308–10, 317–18. For a discussion (and refutation) of Trogus' theorised anti-Roman bias, see Adler 2006, 383–407 and Pendergast 1961.

[8] For the debate concerning the dating of Justin and Trogus, see Yardley and Heckel 1997, 10–13 and Barnes 1998, 589–93.

[9] For a discussion of the use of 'epitome' for Justin's history, see Yardley and Heckel 1997, 15–19. Justin himself makes no claim to be producing an 'epitome' of Trogus, but he makes clear that his history stems directly – and only – from Trogus' *Historiae Philippicae*. Here I will use the label of 'epitome' in referring to the text of Justin for convenience, rather than from a belief that this is an accurate description of Justin's history. See also Jal 1987, 196–200.

[10] Yardley's (2003) thorough analysis of the language of the *Epitome* is of much value for dating Justin as well as understanding the nature of his writing. However, while it possible to demonstrate with relative certainty what language cannot have been used by Trogus, it is much more difficult to prove what was his.

[11] All texts of Justin/Trogus and the *Prologi* are those of O. Seel's 1985 Teubner. All translations are my own.

[12] On the discrepancies between Trogus and Justin, see Jal 1987, 197–8 and Yardley and Heckel 1997, 22–4.

[13] As Develin 1994, 6 notes: 'Justin must have found Trogus amenable, so that he could readily draw upon the original for moral examples'.

[14] Develin 1994, 110–115 argues that the title is a nod to the moralistic nature of Theopompus' work, indicating that the attention to virtue and vice in Justin/Trogus may be a reflection of a focus of the original author as well as the later. See also n. 4 above.

[15] For an overview of the *Prologi* and an assessment of the date of their composition, see Lucidi 1975, 173–80.

[16] The marriage between Olympias and Philip took place in 357 as part of an anti-Illyrian alliance between Macedonia and Molossia, while Arybbas was not supplanted by Alexander (brother of Olympias) until 342. See Borza 1990, 211. Although the nature of the epitome may distort the narrative distance between these incidents in Trogus' history, it does not change the anticipatory nature of the passage in question. The *Prologi* agree with Justin in recording the deposition of

Arrybas at the end of book 8. While the *Prologi* do not record the marriage of Olympias in book 7, the highly abridged nature of the *Prologi* does not allow conclusions to be made from this on whether the anticipation was an innovation of Justin or residual from Trogus.

[17] Further support of this comes from the Livian appearance of the phrase. Yardley (2003, 21–3, 36) argues that the Livian influence on Trogus was 'deep and pervasive'. However, he admits that while 'the number of striking similarities of expression between the two, some of which appear to be deliberate echoes' points overwhelmingly to a relationship between the works, it is difficult to ascribe any particular word or phrase to both Trogus and Livy. Further complicating this attempt is Tacitus' use of Livian expressions, including the one in question here. For a possible link between Tacitus and Trogus, see Goodyear 1982, 23–4.

[18] As this is historically speaking Olympias' first political relevance, it is highly unlikely that Trogus discussed Olympias before this event.

[19] Justin/Trogus' claim that Philip divorced Olympias, either for adultery (9.5.9 and 11.11.3–5) or out of desire for Kleopatra Eurydike (9.7.2 and 9.7.12), displays several deep flaws: a failure to understand the polygamous nature of Macedonian royal marriages, the application of Roman divorce practices to the Macedonians, and the tainting of the historical narrative by the highly-fictionalised Alexander Romances in which the charge of adultery is applied to Olympias as a result of Alexander's supposed divine parentage. The effect of the Roman monogamous lens is especially clear in Justin/Trogus' omission of any of Philip's other marriages, making Olympias the first wife of the king and passing over Philip's marriage to Meda of Odessa between those to Olympias and Kleopatra Eurydike. Even Philip III Arrhidaios' mother is denied the status of a wife, being merely an unnamed Larissan dancer (9.8.2). For Philip II's marriages, see Tronson 1984, 116–26. The sexual jealousy attributed to Olympias in 9.7.2 and 9.7.12, appears to have no basis in historical reality, a position strengthened by Philip's marriage to Meda between those with Olympias and Kleopatra Eurydike. If Olympias' actions were merely stemming from jealousy at being replaced in the king's affections, her temper should have been roused by the earlier intruder into the royal house. See also Fredricksmeyer 1990, 301; Carney 2000, 18–27, 52–81; and Müller 2010, 170–1.

[20] For the death of Philip II, see, e.g., Müller 2010, 182–3; Borza 1990, 227; and Bosworth 1971, 93–105.

[21] For Olympias' role, and possible motivations, see Howe 2015, 145–6.

[22] As with the *Prologi* discussed above, the absence of Olympias, and Alexander, from the murder of Philip in *Prol.* 9 does not demonstrate that these accusations were not present in Trogus. The highly abbreviated nature of the *Prologi* is not conducive to such conclusions.

[23] For Justin/Trogus' vivid description of the civil war, see 13.6.7.

[24] Yardley 2003, 147 identifies the close resemblance of the phrase *muliebri aemulatione* to Tacitus *Ann.* 2.43.4: *aemulatione muliebri* (see also *Ann.* 4.40.3: *aemulatione feminarum*). However, he also notes that the following phrase (Just. 14.5.5: *muliebris audaciae*) has a parallel in Livy 1.46.6: *muliebri...audacia*. Taking into account Justin's declared interest in moralising (see *praef.* 4 and above), it is

eminently possible that Justin has elaborated on the theme of female ambition here. However, this does not prohibit Trogus from having ventured similar comments on this theme as seen in the appropriation of a Livian construction in 14.5.5. Yardley, Wheatley & Heckel (2011, 3–8, 197) suggest that these remarks may have derived from Hieronymos of Kardia transmitted through the unfavorable lens of Duris of Samos.

[25] Here as well the language indicates a preference for Eurydike over the supposed king of Macedonia, Philip III Arrhidaios: *cuius issu et Eurydice et rex occiditur* ('by the order of whom both Eurydike and the king were killed').

[26] Justin/Trogus elides both time and political circumstance in describing this period. According to Diodoros, Polyperchon asked Olympias to join him in Macedonia multiple times before she finally agreed (18.49.4, 18.57.2, 19.11.1–2). For the historical and literary chronology, see Wheatley and Heckel's excellent commentary in Yardley, Wheatley & Heckel 2011, 193–203. It is unclear to what extent the defects of the narrative are due to Justin's 'excerpting' approach and what is the result of Trogus' historiographical practice (or that of his sources).

[27] On the persistence of this notion in both ancient and modern scholarship, see Carney 2000, 115–16.

[28] Diod. 18.49.4 = Just. 14.5.1, Diod. 19.11.2–5 = Just. 14.5.9–10, Diod. 19.11.8–9 = Just. 14.6.1, Diod. 19.35.1 = Just. 14.5.8, and Diod. 19.35.5 = Just. 14.6.2–3. This similarity may be explained easily by the heavy reliance on Hieronymos of Kardia by both Trogus and Diodoros; Yardley, Wheatley, & Heckel 2011, 5.

[29] For example, Arrian *FGrH* 156, F 9.30–33 and Diod. 18.39.1–4. See also Carney 2000, 132–7. Carney (2000, 140) rightly contrasts the vividness of Diodoros' account of the death of Adea Eurydike and Arrhidaios with that of Justin/Trogus, but her assessment of Justin/Trogus as a 'matter-of-fact' treatment needs further scrutiny. Given the highly abbreviated nature of Justin/Trogus, and the quantity of prominent events in the wars of the Successors he omits (such as the death of Antipatros), Justin/Trogus' mention of not only the deaths, but also his placing total power in the hands of Olympias cannot be passed over as an inconsequential element of his account.

[30] This assessment is not to say that the transmitted accounts represent accurately historical reality. The atmosphere of the wars between the Successors increased the polemic between contenders for power and historiography quickly became a means to promote personal legitimacy and castigate the claims of rivals. Additionally, the presence of such defamatory material in the sources used by Trogus does not remove the import of his historiographical choice to include such material in his history. On Kassandros in particular, see Landucci Gattinoni 2010, 113–21.

[31] Yardley (2003, 20–23, 47–8) notes a number of Livian phrases scattered throughout Just. 14.5.1–6.13 that suggests he may have preserved some of Trogus' language in these passages: 14.5.4 *muliebris audaciae* (see above), 5.8 *turbatus Macedoniae status*, 5.10 *potitus regno*, 6.5 *cum fame ferroque urgeretur*, 6.5 *obsidionis taedio*, 6.7 *sine respectu pristinae maiestatis*, 6.10 *memoriae occurrentibus*. See also Just. 14.1.8: 'so great was the veneration of Alexander's greatness that even through the tracks

of women the favor of his sacred name was sought after' (*tanta veneratio magnitudinis Alexandri erat, ut etiam per vestigia mulierum favor sacrati eius nominis quaereretur*) in comparison to Livy 4.21.3: *favore nominis moturum se aliquid ratus*. For the Tacitean parallel (*Hist.* 2.72.1: *nominis favor manebat*) see above; cf. Yardley 2003, 46. For the courtship of Kleopatra described here, see Meeus 2009, 63–92.

[32] The account given by Trogus was presumably comparatively substantial, earning it mention in the *Prologi* where the other deaths of the period (Antipatros, Polyperchon, Adea Eurydike and Philip III Arrhidaios) did not. Similarly, the tone and content in Justin may be assumed to have been copied from Trogus due to the close parallels with Diodoros (see above).

[33] The choice of wording between the two authors is pronounced. Where Justin/Trogus describes Olympias' *maiestas* (14.6.7, 10), Diodoros uses the comparable term ἀξίωμα (19.51.3, 5, 6). The parallel uses of *maiestas* and ἀξίωμα in Justin/Trogus and Diodoros indicates Justin/Trogus' *maiestas* may represent a Latin translation of the Greek from a shared source (see above).

[34] Note also the parallels with descriptions of the death of Caesar, particularly that of Suetonius, *Iulius* 82.2. Also containing mention of Caesar covering himself during his murder are Plutarch, *Julius Caesar* 66.12, Valerius Maximus 4.5.6, and Appian *Bellum Civile* 2.117. The closeness of the accounts given in these widely varying source media from the reign of Tiberius onwards indicates that this story was widely circulated during the early Principate. The detail of Olympias covering herself as she lay dying may be a Roman addition to the story of her death by Trogus, as Yardley, Wheatley, & Heckel (2011, 211) suggest, deliberately recalling the assassination of Caesar.

[35] Eder 1990, 83–104; Galinsky 1996, 75, 81–2. See also Wyke 1992, 113.

[36] E.g., Ahl 1984, 44–6.

[37] E.g., *Res Gestae Divi Augusti* 6, 34.

[38] For Octavian's manipulation of his image, see Armstrong 2008, 340–356 and Zanker 1990, 33–77.

[39] Ramage 1985, 229.

[40] Syme 1959, 57–76.

[41] Ahl 1984, 55–9. As Feeney (2002, 173) notes aptly, however, the interplay between poet and emperor was not one-directional, and present in Horace's poetry is evidence for how 'Augustus and Horace depend on each other for the immortality they both covet so much'.

[42] White 1993, 95–155. Bowditch (2010, 57–8, 61–4, 72–3) also identifies the difficulties involved in assessing the beliefs of the poet from his poetry.

[43] Galinsky 1996, 3–24, 225–31.

[44] E.g. Horace *Epod.* 9, Propertius 3.11.29–72 and 4.6, Virgil, *Aeneid* 8.678–88 and 696–719, Cassius Dio 50.24.3–7, Velleius Paterculus 85 and 87, and prolific throughout Plutarch's *Antonius*. See also Wyke 1992, 98–116.

[45] Hor. *Odes* 1.37.21. For a discussion of the phrase, see Luce 1963, 251–7 and Galinsky 2003, 19–23.

[46] Hor. *Odes* 1.37.6–10: 'The queen was plotting mad ruins for the Capitol and death for the empire along with her flock of disreputable men' (*Capitolio / regina dementis ruinas / funus et imperio parabat / contaminato cum grege turpium / morbo virorum*).

On the use of *regina* for Kleopatra, see Nisbet and Hubbard 1970, 413.

[47] Lowrie 2007, 77 and Galinsky 1996, 81–2. Horace's toadying to Augustus is also magnified in his 'Letter to Augustus' (*Epistles* 2.1), especially 2.1.1–4: 'When you alone bear so many and such great troubles, when you protect Italy with arms, when you adorn her with morals, when you improve her with laws, I should sin against the public good if I should waste your time with long speech, Caesar' (*Cum tot sustineas et tanta negotia solus, / res Italas armis tuteris, moribus ornes, / legibus emendes, in publica commoda peccem, / si longo sermone morer tua tempora, Caesar*). On the sincerity of this letter, see Ahl 1984, 55–8; Feeney, 2002, 172–87; Galinsky 1996, 126–8.

[48] Nisbet and Hubbard 1970, 407–10.

[49] Hor. *Odes* 1.37.17–21: 'just as a swift hawk hunts gentle doves or a hare, to put that dangerous monster in chains' (...*accipiter velut / mollis columbas aut leporem citus / venator in campis nivalis / Haemoniae, daret ut catenis / fatale monstrum*). See Wyke 1992, 112–13.

[50] Cf. Just. 14.6.11: *non refugientem gladium sed nec vulnera aut muliebriter vociferantem* (see above).

[51] Cf. Just. 14.6.11: *sed virorum fortium more* (see above).

[52] Galinsky 2003, 19.

[53] Jal 1987, 198. It is difficult to discern why Justin has omitted this passage. The language of the author of the *Prologi* indicates that the section was ripe for similar explication on the seductive dangers of women, a topic he does not skimp on at other points in the work. Book 39, for example, lays out the machinations of Kleopatra II (39.1.2, 4), Kleopatra III (39.3.1–3, 4.1–6), and Kleopatra IV (39.3.2–11), as well as of Tryphaena (39.3.5–12). See also his treatment of Eurydike, mother of Philip II of Macedonia (7.4.7).

[54] The Battle of Actium unfolds in a similar fashion in the *Periochae* (132–3) of Livy. The connection here between Antony and Octavian is made much more explicit, though Kleopatra remains the pervasive and corrupting force and one against whom Octavian can celebrate a triumph.

[55] Just. 42.4.6: 'Soon after these affairs were completed civil war was born among Romans between Caesar and Pompey' (*his ita gestis non magno post tempore Romanis inter Caesarem Pompeiumque civile bellum oritur*).

[56] Carney (1994, 357–80) provides a thorough overview of the complications and problems leading to the end of the Argead dynasty.

[57] For their deaths (also perpetrated by Kassandros) see 15.2.3–5. The only remaining Argead of dynastic import was Thessalonike, daughter of Philip II (though Justin/Trogus wrongly grants Arrhidaios patrimony), whom Kassandros married after the death of Olympias (14.6.13).

[58] For the Romanisation of Macedonian relationships in Justin/Trogus, see Tronson 1984, 123, though he does not extend his analysis to the issue of queenship.

Bibliography

Adler, E.
  2006   'Who's Anti-Roman? Sallust and Pompeius Trogus on Mithridates', *CJ* 101, 383–407.

Ahl, F.
  1984   'The Rider and the Horse: Politics and Power in Roman Poetry from Horace to Statius', *ANRW* II.32.1, 40–110.

Alonso-Núñez, J. M.
  1987   'An Augustan World History: The "Historiae Philippicae" of Pompeius Trogus', *G& R* 34, 56–72.

Armstrong, G. E.
  2008   'Sacrificial Iconography: Creating History, Making Myth, and Negotiation Ideology on the Ara Pacis Augustae,' *Religion & Theology* 15, 340–56.

Atkinson, J.
  2000   'Alexander Sources of the Early Empire', in A.B. Bosworth and E. J. Baynham (eds) *Alexander the Great in Fact and Fiction*, Oxford, 307–25.

Barnes, T. D.
  1998   'Two Passages of Justin,' *CQ* 48, 589–93.

Borza, E. N.
  1990   *In the Shadow of Olympus: The Emergence of Macedon*, Princeton.

Bosworth, A. B.
  1971   'Philip II and Upper Macedonia,' *CQ* 21, 93–105.

Bowditch, P. L.
  2010   'Horace and Imperial Patronage,' in G. Davis, (ed.) *A Companion to Horace*, Malden, MA, 53–74.

Carney, E. D.
  1994   'Olympias, Adea Eurydice, and the end of the Argead dynasty', in I. Worthington (ed.) *Ventures into Greek History*, Oxford, 357–80.
  2000   *Women and Monarchy in Macedonia*, Norman, OK.
  2006   *Olympias: Mother of Alexander the Great*, New York.
  2009   'Alexander and his Terrible Mother', in W. Heckel and L. A. Tritle (eds) *Alexander the Great: A New History*, Malden, MA, 189–202.

Develin, R.
  1985   'Pompeius Trogus and Philippic History', *Storia della Storiografia* 8, 110–15.
  1994   'Introduction', in *Justin: Epitome of the Philippic History of Pompeius Trogus*, tr. J. C. Yardley, Atlanta, 1–11.

Eder, W.
  1990   'Augustus and the Power of Tradition: The Augustan Principate as Binding Link between Republic and Empire', in K. A. Raaflaub and M. Toher (eds) *Between Republic and Empire: Interpretations of Augustus and His Principate*, 71–122, Berkeley.

Feeney, D.
  2002   '*Una cum scriptore meo*: Poetry, Principate, and the traditions of literary history in the Epistle to Augustus', in D. Feeney and A. J. Woodman (eds) *Traditions and Contexts in the Poetry of Horace,* Cambridge, 172–87.

Fredricksmeyer, E. A.
    1990   'Alexander and Philip: Emulation and Resentment', *CJ* 85, 300–15.
Galinsky, K.
    1996   *Augustan Culture: An Interpretive Introduction*, Princeton.
    2003   'Horace's Cleopatra and Virgil's Dido', in A. F. Basson and W. J. Dominik (eds) *Literature, Art, History: Studies on Classical Antiquity and Tradition in Honour of W. J. Henderson*, Frankfurt, 17–23.
Goodyear, F. D. R.
    1982   'On the Character and Text of Justin's Compilation of Trogus,' *Proceedings of the African Classical Associations* 16, 1–24.
Greenwalt, W.
    1989   'Polygamy and Succession in Argead Macedonia', *Arethusa* 22, 19–45.
Howe, T.
    2015   'Cleopatra-Eurydice, Olympias, and a "Weak" Alexander', in P. Wheatley and E. J. Baynham (eds) *East and West in the World Empire of Alexander the Great*, Oxford, 133–46.
Jal, P.
    1987   'À propos des *Histoires Philippiques*: quelques remarques', *RÉL* 65, 196–200.
Landucci Gattinoni, F.
    2010   'Cassander and the Legacy of Philip II and Alexander III in Diodorus' *Library*', in E. Carney and D. Ogden (eds) *Philip II and Alexander the Great: Father and Son, Lives and Afterlives,* Oxford, 113–22.
Levene, D. S.
    2007   'Roman Historiography in the Late Republic', in J. Marincola (ed.) *A Companion to Greek and Roman Historiography*, Malden, MA, 275–89.
Lowrie, M.
    2007   'Horace and Augustus', in S. Harrison (ed.) *The Cambridge Companion to Horace*, Cambridge, 77–89.
Luce, J. V.
    1963   'Cleopatra as Fatale Monstrum (Horace, *Carm.* 1.37.21),' *CQ* 13, 251–57.
Lucidi, F.
    1975   'Nota ai "Prologi" delle *Historiae Philippicae* di Pompeo Trogo,' *Rivista di Cultura Classica e Medioevale* 17, 173–80.
Macurdy, G. H.
    1932   *Hellenistic Queens: A Study of Woman-Power in Macedonia, Seleucid Syria, and Ptolemaic Egypt*, Chicago.
Meeus, A.
    2009   'Kleopatra and the Diadochoi,' in P. Van Nuffelen (ed.) *Faces of Hellenism: Studies in the History of the Eastern Mediterranean (4th Century BC– 5th Century AD). Studia Hellenistica 48*, Leuven, 63–92.
Müller, S.
    2010   'Philip II', in J. Roisman and I. Worthington (eds) *A Companion to Ancient Macedonia*, Malden, MA, 166–71.
Nisbet, R. G. M and Hubbard, M. A.
    1970   *Commentary on Horace: Odes Book I*, Oxford.

Pendergast, J.
   1961   'The Philosophy of the History of Pompeius Trogus,' PhD diss., University of Illinois.
Pollini, J.
   2012   *From Republic to Empire: Rhetoric, Religion, and Power in the Visual Culture of Ancient Rome*, Norman, OK.
Ramage, E. S.
   1985   'Augustus' Treatment of Julius Caesar', *Historia* 34, 223–45.
Seel, O.
   1955   *Die Praefatio des Pompeius Trogus*, Erlangen.
Spencer, D.
   2002   *The Roman Alexander: Reading a Cultural Myth*, Exeter.
Syme, R.
   1959   'Livy and Augustus', *HSCP* 64, 27–87.
Tronson, A.
   1984   'Satyrus the Peripatetic and the Marriages of Philip II', *JHS* 104, 116–26.
Urban, R.
   1982   '"Historiae Philippicae" bei Pompeius Trogus: Versuch einer Deutung', *Historia* 31.1, 82–96.
White, P.
   1993   *Promised Verse: Poets in the Society of Augustan Rome*, Cambridge.
Wyke, M.
   1992   'Augustan Cleopatras: Female Power and Poetic Authority', in A. Powell (ed.) *Roman Poetry and Propaganda in the Age of Augustus*, London, 98–140.
Yardley, J. C.
   2003   *Justin and Pompeius Trogus: A Study of the Language of Justin's Epitome of Trogus*, Toronto.
Yardley, J. C. and Heckel, W.
   1997   *Justin: Epitome of the Philippic History of Pompeius Trogus Books 11–12: Alexander the Great*, Oxford.
Yardley, J. C., Wheatley, P. and Heckel, W.
   2011   *Justin: Epitome of the Philippic History of Pompeius Trogus, Vol. II Books 13–15: The Successors to Alexander the Great*, Oxford.
Zanker, P.
   1990   *The Power of Images in the Age of Augustus*, Ann Arbor.

PART II

PHILIA, POLITICS AND ALLIANCES

4

WAS KALLISTHENES THE TUTOR OF ALEXANDER'S ROYAL PAGES?

Frances Pownall

It is a commonplace in modern scholarship that Alexander's court historian Kallisthenes served as the tutor of the Royal Pages during Alexander's expedition;[1] R. D. Milns (2006/07, 234) has gone so far as to suggest that 'the Pages rather than historical composition were his prime responsibility and duty'. A review of the source material, however, reveals no firm evidence to support this widespread assumption that Kallisthenes ever held an official position as the Pages' Tutor. In fact, all of the evidence associating Kallisthenes with the Pages in any way at all is connected with the so-called Pages' Conspiracy against Alexander, which renders it suspect because his alleged complicity in the plot led directly to his trial and condemnation (*FGrH* 124 T 6–8). As I shall argue, the pervasive myth that Kallisthenes was the Pages' tutor stems from two separate but complementary traditions: (1) the contemporary apologetic Alexander historians, who justified Kallisthenes' condemnation by emphasising the closeness of his connection with the Pages, and (2) contamination from the imperial *milieu* of the Roman-era sources, particularly Curtius, who subtly reworked the episode to provide a more explicit parallel for Nero's elimination of his own erstwhile tutor, Seneca the Younger, an important stage in the emperor's increasing tyranny.

Let us begin with a review of the evidence for Kallisthenes' association with the Pages, young members of the Macedonian elite who formed part of the king's immediate entourage as teenagers in a somewhat servile capacity as a rite of passage and later joined the ranks of the Companions.[2] Curtius, our earliest source,[3] claims (8.6.24) only that Kallisthenes served as the Pages' confidant, particularly when they were criticising Alexander:

> Callisthenes was certainly not named as one involved in the plot, but it did come out that he was in the habit of giving a ready ear to the talk of the pages when they were criticizing and finding fault with the king. (trans. J. Yardley)[4]

Similarly, in his *Life of Alexander*, Plutarch makes two references to Kallisthenes' alleged influence over the Pages which serve to bookend his discussion of the growing rift between Alexander and Kallisthenes. The first reference is vague (Plut. *Alex*. 53.1): 'Kallisthenes, who was eagerly sought after by the young men because of his facility with words, aroused the hostility of the other sophists and flatterers.'[5] Here, Plutarch simply states that Kallisthenes' oratorical ability was the reason for his popularity with the younger generation, but does not suggest that he exercised any official role in the Pages' rhetorical education. Similarly, he concludes this section by saying (*Alex*. 55.1–2):

> At that point, courtiers such as Lysimachos and Hagnon repeatedly claimed that the sophist used to go around priding himself as if he were planning to bring down a tyranny (ὡς ἐπὶ καταλύσει τυραννίδος μέγα φρονοῦντα), and that the youth were gathering around him and paying particular attention to him as if he alone were a free man among these tens of thousands (ὡς μόνον ἐλεύθερον ἐν τοσαύταις μυριάσι). It is for this reason that when the plot against Alexander, of Hermolaos and his fellow conspirators, was brought to light, the slanders of his accusers appeared plausible.[6]

In Plutarch, as in Curtius, any association with the Pages as a group only comes out in the context of the Pages' Conspiracy, where both remark that the allegation that Kallisthenes was complicit gained credence precisely because he exercised considerable influence over the younger generation.

The Pages' Conspiracy was a plot against the life of Alexander by a cabal of the younger Macedonian elite, whose leader, Hermolaos, had a personal score to settle with the king, having been flogged and humiliated after he anticipated Alexander in striking a wild boar during a hunt (Arr. 4.13.2 and Curt. 8.6.8–10).[7] The conspirators planned to kill Alexander while he was asleep (guarding the king was one of the duties of the Royal Pages), but the attempt on the king's life was foiled when he stayed up all night drinking on the appointed day, and the delay led to the revelation of the plot (Arr. 4.13.4–6; Curt. 8.6.12–20). Coming on the heels of Alexander's failed attempt to introduce *proskynēsis* to his own court ritual,[8] which was thwarted by Kallisthenes himself,[9] the plot is generally interpreted as a backlash by the more conservative element in the Macedonian elite to the changes that Alexander was making to the traditional conception of kingship.[10]

All the extant sources emphasise how Kallisthenes' tactless outspokenness, culminating in his vocal opposition to Alexander's innovations at court, earned him the ill-will of the king (Curt. 8.5.13 and 8.6.1; Arr. 4.12.1–7; cf. Plut. *Alex.* 53.1–55.1). It is also explicit in Plutarch's account, and implicit in those of both Curtius and Arrian, that the machinations behind the scenes of Kallisthenes' rivals at court, who were competing with him for influence over Alexander and the rewards and benefits that would ensue from the king's favour, also played a significant role in the accusation that he was complicit in the Pages' Conspiracy.[11] The hostility between Kallisthenes and the philosopher Anaxarchos is well attested,[12] and other members of the intellectual entourage of Alexander who are mentioned in contexts of rivalry with Kallisthenes include Lysimachos and Hagnon (Plut. *Alex.* 55.1, cited above), the epic poet Agis of Argos,[13] and Demetrios the son of Pythonax, who was one of Alexander's Companions.[14] It seems likely that the allegations against Kallisthenes were not due simply to his own tactless outspokenness, but in no small part also to the efforts of his rivals at court to eliminate a competitor.

In any case, Kallisthenes' opposition to Alexander in the *proskynēsis* affair and his association with the Pages (however informal or tenuous, and almost certainly exaggerated by his court rivals) made the allegation that he was involved easy to believe and it became the official version, even though both Plutarch (*Alex.* 55.5) and Curtius (8.6.24) claim that the Pages themselves denied that Kallisthenes had any role in the conspiracy and refused to incriminate him. Arrian (4.14.1), however, provides an alternative version:

> Aristoboulos (*FGrH* 139 F 31) says that the Pages claimed that Kallisthenes had incited them to the conspiracy, and Ptolemy says the same thing (*FGrH* 138 F 16). Most of the sources, however, do not concur with this account, but say that because of the previously-existing enmity between Kallisthenes and Alexander and the fact that Hermolaos was on especially friendly terms with Kallisthenes (ὅτι ὁ Ἑρμόλαος ἐς τὰ μάλιστα ἐπιτήδειος ἦν τῷ Καλλισθένει), Alexander readily believed the worst about Kallisthenes.

Ptolemy and Aristoboulos, Arrian's principal sources (Arr. *pro.* 1–2),[15] both wrote apologetic accounts of Alexander, and their motive appears to have been to absolve the king of responsibility for the subsequent trial and death of Kallisthenes by alleging that the historian had incited the Pages (Bosworth 1995, 90), doubtless adhering to the official version of the incident that Alexander wished to be promulgated. In contrast to the apologetic treatment of Alexander by the early sources (Ptolemy and Aristoboulos were both contemporaries who participated in the expedition to Asia), the majority of the sources (who are not named by Arrian, but we find traces of this tradition in both Plutarch and Curtius) suggest that after the rift occurred between Alexander and Kallisthenes, thanks to the latter's 'inopportune outspokenness and overweening foolishness' (Arr. 4.12.7: ἐπὶ τῇ ἀκαίρῳ τε παρρησίᾳ καὶ ὑπερόγκῳ ἀβελτερίᾳ), Alexander took advantage of Kallisthenes' complicity in the plot, or according to the more sinister version retailed by Justin (15.3.3; cf. 12.7.2), engineered it himself,[16] as an opportunity to eliminate one of his more vocal critics.

What is more interesting for our purposes than the question of Kallisthenes' guilt or innocence (which seems to be driven less by any actual evidence than by the efforts of the sources, depending on their agenda, to absolve either Kallisthenes or Alexander), is the other reason given by Arrian (that is, besides Kallisthenes' reckless tendency to speak his mind) as to why his implication in the plot was so readily believed, namely his friendship with the leader of the conspiracy, Hermolaos. Arrian also refers to the association between the two men in a slightly earlier passage, when he introduces Hermolaos at the beginning of his narrative of the conspiracy (4.13.2) as someone who 'appeared to be interested in philosophy and for that reason was a follower (θεραπεύειν) of Kallisthenes'. While the precise meaning of this phrase remains (perhaps intentionally) ambiguous, the verb θεραπεύειν has the connotation of attending upon someone or ingratiating oneself with someone, and, it should be noted, is not normally used in the context of a teacher-student relationship.

Plutarch says nothing specific about an association between Kallisthenes and Hermolaos, and it is likely that any such link was exaggerated by the contemporary apologetic Alexander historians in order to implicate Kallisthenes in the Pages' Conspiracy (cf. Heckel 2006, 138). Instead, Plutarch states (*Alex.* 55.2) that those who denounced Kallisthenes recounted as 'proof' a conversation which allegedly took place between the two men. According to Kallisthenes' 'slanderers', when Hermolaos asked him how he might become the most famous man of all, he replied, 'By killing the most famous man', and then proceeded to encourage him to do just that. This anecdote, with its pithy incitement to regicide, does not inspire confidence in its veracity, especially when it appears to be derived from a stock type circulating in the anecdotal tradition, for the very same anecdote is attached also to Pausanias, Philip's assassin, who is alleged to have consulted the sophist Hermokrates (who is otherwise unattested), under whom he had studied, as to how he might become famous, and to have received the same answer.[17]

Arrian (4.10.3–4) recounts a similar anecdote, although he does not personally endorse it, according to which Kallisthenes was once asked by Philotas whom the Athenians held in the greatest honour, to which he responded with the names of the 'tyrant-slayers' Harmodios and Aristogeiton (cf. Thuc. 6.54–5), because they killed one of the tyrants and brought an end to the tyranny,[18] and then named Athens as a possible site of asylum for a tyrannicide, for the Athenians gave refuge to the Herakleidai and then defeated Eurystheus on their behalf (cf. Hdt. 9.27.2).[19]

It is generally thought that these anecdotes, which in which Kallisthenes is represented as encouraging Hermolaos to assassinate Alexander, were originally circulated (very likely in the first instance by Aristoboulos and Ptolemy) as another piece of 'evidence' employed by Kallisthenes' accusers to prove his guilt (e.g., Hamilton 1969, 154 and Bosworth 1995, 76), and Arrian's anecdote was particularly useful in this regard because it linked Kallisthenes to Philotas, whose trial and execution for allegedly plotting against Alexander's life had taken place some three years previously.[20] Because Plutarch and Arrian do not believe that Kallisthenes actually was complicit in the Pages' Conspiracy (as seen above), neither of them endorses these anecdotes personally. But if that is the case, why then do they choose to recount these anecdotes at all?

It is important to note the context for this anecdote in Arrian, for it comes between his narrative of Alexander's murder of Kleitos and the *proskynēsis* episode. This is in a section of the *Anabasis* which Brian Bosworth has called 'The Great Digression' (Bosworth 1995, 45), where Arrian breaks away from strict chronological sequence in his generally encomiastic narrative to provide (relatively muted) criticism of Alexander on moral grounds for succumbing to oriental luxury and the barbarian mode of kingship and to emphasise the gulf between the monarch and his subjects after the mutilation of Bessos (Arr. 4.7.4), by narrating as a unified whole the murder of Kleitos, the *proskynēsis* episode, the Pages' Conspiracy, and Kallisthenes' condemnation.[21] Thus, Arrian's purpose in recounting this episode in this section of his narrative is not to absolve Alexander by implicating Kallisthenes in the conspiracy led by Hermolaos, but quite the opposite, that is, to portray Alexander as a tyrant. By equating Hermolaos and the Pages with the Athenian tyrannicides, Arrian is simultaneously equating Alexander with the Peisistratid tyrants of Athens. The reference to the mythological *exemplum* of Athens' provision of refuge to the suppliant Herakleidai reinforces this portrayal of Alexander, for it equates Alexander with Eurystheus, a stock tyrannical figure in Athenian patriotic oratory (cf. Bosworth 1995, 77).

Similarly, the context for Plutarch's version of the anecdote according to which Kallisthenes incites Hermolaos to regicide occurs in a section of his *Life* which emphasises the deterioration in Alexander's character. According to Plutarch, this deterioration occurred after the capture of Bessos (whose death legitimised Alexander's position as the true successor to the Achaemenid monarchy), and he, like Arrian, telescopes the chronology (cf. Plut. *Alex.* 56.1) of events from the murder of Kleitos to Kallisthenes' condemnation in order to illustrate more effectively Alexander's descent into orientalism and autocracy.[22] Futhermore, although Plutarch does distance himself by putting these comments into the mouth of Kallisthenes' slanderers, he suggests explicitly in the narrative leading up to this anecdote (cited earlier) that the rift between Kallisthenes and Alexander was one involving freedom versus tyranny. The question of how to maintain freedom (of speech at least, for true political freedom had been out of the question now for centuries) while living under autocratic rule was particularly acute for imperial Greek writers,[23] and thanks to Plutarch's education at the Academy, he adopted Plato's views that the tyrant's rule was by definition illegitimate and its very lack of restraint encouraged excessive behaviour generally associated with barbarians.[24] The figure of Kallisthenes, then, offers Plutarch a useful lens through which to address the issues of Hellenism and virtue,[25] even if he only does so at the subtexual level in his generally apologetic portrayal of Alexander.

Curtius recounts a similar anecdote (8.6.25), immediately after his narrative of the revelation of the Pages' Conspiracy and observation (cited above) that although Kallisthenes was not named as a participant in the plot, he did wield extensive influence over the Pages:

> Some people also assert that, when Hermolaus complained before Callisthenes of having been flogged by Alexander, Callisthenes commented that they ought to remember that they were men (*meminisse debere eos iam viros esse*); but they did add that it is unclear whether this remark was made to comfort Hermolaus after his beating or to provoke resentment in the young men. (trans. J. Yardley)

Although Curtius qualifies this ambiguous anecdote by claiming that it is unclear whether his remarks were intended to comfort Hermolaos or to incite resentment against the king, and like both Arrian and Plutarch he does not personally endorse it, in a later context he does refer to it again, and this time his speaker (Alexander himself) explicitly links it to the attempted regicide (Curt. 8.8.19):

> As for your Kallisthenes, the only person to think you a man (*cui uni vir videris*) (because you are an assassin), I know why you want him brought forward. It is so that the insults which you sometimes uttered against me and sometimes heard from him can be repeated by his lips before this gathering. Were he a Macedonian I would have introduced him here along with you – a teacher truly worthy of his pupil (*dignissimum te discipulo magistrum*). (trans. J. Yardley)

The verbal echoes between Alexander's sarcastic reference to Kallisthenes as Harmolaos' evil regicide-inciting teacher and the vaguely threatening (but not specific) advice that Kallisthenes was alleged to have given Hermolaos after his flogging explicitly draw the parallel between these two episodes. Furthermore, it is here that we find the first reference to Kallisthenes as Hermolaos' teacher.

It is important, however, to observe that this reference occurs in a highly rhetorical set of paired speeches. Immediately before his own defense speech (Curt. 8.7.3–15), Hermolaos explains to Alexander why he spearheaded the conspiracy against him (8.7.1): 'We plotted to kill you because you have begun to act not as a king with his free-born subjects but as a master with his slaves' (*occidendi te consilium iniimus, quia non ut ingenuis imperare coepisti, sed quasi in mancipia dominari*; trans. J. Yardley). Alexander then offers a sarcastic point-by-point *apologia* against the charges of Hermolaos (8.8.1–19), of which his glancing reference to the 'tyrannicide' anecdote and his implication that Kallisthenes was his teacher constitutes the peroration. In addition to this jeering statement in the peroration, the Curtian Alexander responds (in indirect discourse) to Hermolaos' father, who had leapt up to his son's defense immediately prior to Hermolaos' accusatory speech (8.7.3):

> Alexander restrained the father and told Hermolaus to state what he had learned from his teacher, Callisthenes (*rex inhibito patre dicere Hermolaum iubet, quae ex magistro didicisset Callisthene*; trans. J. Yardley).

Alexander then opens his own speech with another reference to Kallisthenes as Hermolaos' teacher (Curt. 8.8.1):

> The king replied: "The falseness of these charges (which that fellow has picked up from his teacher) is obvious from my patience (*at rex: 'quam falsa sint', inquit, 'quae iste tradita a magistro suo dixit, patientia mea ostendit*; trans. J. Yardley).

Curtius is thus the only ancient source who refers explicitly to Kallisthenes as Hermolaos' teacher, and he does so three times in this rhetorically charged context, always putting it into the mouth of Alexander. Taken out of context, these explicit references may appear to provide confirmation that Kallisthenes was Hermolaos' teacher, but in fact they are not at all straightforward but very ambiguous, occurring as they do in this mocking and sarcastic speech of the Curtian Alexander, and they raise a number of related questions. Does Curtius himself endorse the statement that Kallisthenes was Hermolaos' teacher or does he mean it as pure sarcasm on the part of Alexander? If the Curtian Alexander is actually imputing that Kallisthenes was Hermolaos' teacher, does he mean that he served as his teacher in some sort of official capacity, or does he just mean that he encouraged him to commit regicide, as the anecdotes that circulated as 'evidence' of Kallisthenes' guilt or of Alexander' tyranny (depending on the source) imply?

On a purely rhetorical level, it is important to note that these references to Kallisthenes as Hermolaos' teacher do not occur in any kind of authorial statement by Curtius himself, but are attributed to Alexander in his *apologia* in which it is necessary for the king to justify his condemnation of Kallisthenes by presenting Hermolaos, and by extension, the Pages as mere dupes of their unscrupulous teacher (Baynham 1998, 198). The rhetorical necessity in this context for Alexander to portray Kallisthenes as the tutor of the Pages raises serious doubts about the veracity of this tradition, attested only by Curtius. Another red flag is the attribution of the teacher-student relationship, which is attested nowhere else, to Kallisthenes and Hermolaos, for it was a common tendency of the biographical tradition in antiquity to impute this relationship to any association between a younger contemporary and an older intellectual.[26]

Given these red flags, we must ask to what extent Curtius' Roman imperial context colours his portrayal of Alexander's condemnation of Kallisthenenes in general, and the relationship between Kallisthenes and Hermolaos in particular. As both Elizabeth Baynham and Diana Spencer have demonstrated, Alexander's sarcasm in his speech replying to Hermolaos' accusations against him is best read as a minatory intervention by Curtius himself on the abuse of absolute power by Alexander, in direct response to contemporary intellectual debates on the autocracy exercised by the Julio-Claudian emperors.[27] Hence it comes as no surprise that the same theme of freedom versus tyranny that is implicit in this context in both Plutarch and Arrian, who, after all, also reflect in varying ways their (slightly later) Roman imperial intellectual *milieu*, is both explicit and emphasised in Curtius.[28] Nor is it a coincidence, as Brian Bosworth has argued (2004), that substantial echoes of Alexander's court as portrayed by Curtius underlie Tacitus' portrait of imperial Rome, providing a highly elaborated and carefully constructed subtextual commentary on the nature of autocratic power.

Writing, as Curtius almost certainly was,[29] in this intellectual *milieu* which implicitly contrasted the contemporary Roman emperors with the tyrannical behaviour of Alexander,[30] I suggest that we look for contemporary Roman concerns, particularly Nero's relationship with the philosopher Seneca, in Curtius' portrayal of the association between Kallisthenes and Hermolaos on the one hand, and Kallisthenes and Alexander on the other.[31] It is tempting to see Neronian echoes lurking behind the references in the sources to Kallisthenes as a 'sophist' and a philosopher on the one hand, and teacher on the other.[32] There is no evidence at all, despite his kinship with Aristotle, that Kallisthenes actually practiced philosophy of any kind (Bosworth 1995, 73), and it was his reputation as a professional historian, coupled with his willingess to narrate events from a pro-Macedonian perspective, that elicited the invitation from Alexander to accompany the expedition in the capacity of official court historian.[33] Nor is there any evidence that Kallisthenes ever taught; interestingly the elder Seneca puts into the mouth of the Augustan rhetorician L. Cestius Pius the statement that he was the tutor (*praeceptor*) of Alexander himself (*Suas.* 1.5), although tellingly the context is one of the freedom (or, rather, the lack thereof) of speech of public intellectuals when offering (even facetious) criticism of kings.[34] To paraphrase Ernst Badian, who in a seminal article inaugurated the methods of modern source criticism of the Alexander historians: if we know that a historical account is not true, how and why did it come into existence (Badian 1958, 147)?

I believe that a number of factors come into play in this particular (and ultimately erroneous) characterisation of Kallisthenes. First of all, the label of philosopher was an easy one to attach to Kallisthenes, because he was related to Aristotle. Second, the term 'sophist,' which in an Athenian context in the late fifth century originally meant itinerant intellectual and teacher, later (thanks to the influence of Plato) took on a negative connotation as a purveyor of false and immoral wisdom (as opposed to true philosophy). It therefore may have begun to be applied to Kallisthenes very early on for, as we have seen, Alexander's official version of his former court historian's trial and condemnation implicated him in the Pages' Conspiracy, and his name and reputation became tarnished almost immediately. Third, presenting Kallisthenes, the corrupter of the youth in his alleged incitement of the Pages to conspiracy, as a philosopher, presented an obvious parallel to the figure of Sokrates, the foundational figure for Hellenistic philosophy (Long 1988), who was sentenced to death in 399 for his own alleged corruption of the Athenian youth, and usefully could be employed either as a positive or a negative *exemplum* (Haake 2004, 476), depending on the agenda of the source. Finally, the application of the labels of philosopher and sophist to Kallisthenes can be viewed as literary constructs, designed to explain his eloquence (the key element of the sophist in the Second Sophistic),[35] particularly in his effective (if ultimately self-destructive) opposition to Alexander's attempt to introduce *proskynēsis* to the Macedonian court.[36]

For Roman authors of the early Empire, the representation of Kallisthenes as a teacher and philosopher would, of course, serve to reinforce the parallel between him and contemporary victims of their own *parrhēsia*.[37] I would argue, however, that there is a more precise political point in Curtius' emphatic representation of Kallisthenes as a philosopher and teacher. By presenting Kallisthenes in this way, Curtius echoes the relationship between Nero and the younger Seneca, particularly in light of the similar fates of the court intellectuals at the hands of an autocratic ruler, who was rapidly growing more megalomaniacal and tyrannical.[38] As narrated vividly by Tacitus (*Ann.* 15.60.2–64.4), Nero took advantage of Seneca's implication in a conspiracy (the famous Pisonian conspiracy against Nero of AD 65) and forced him to commit suicide in order to eliminate an outspoken intellectual whose opposition had become intolerable. Ironically, Seneca's own words may have inspired this parallel, for in a digression in his *Natural Questions* (6.23.2–3) he praises Kallisthenes' resistance to a 'frenzied king' (*furibundi regis*) and claims that his death was Alexander's greatest crime. Curtius' carefully elaborated development of this parallel between Kallisthenes and Seneca allows him to offer nuanced commentary on Nero's autocracy through the portrayal of Alexander as a raging despot whose savagery extended even to his resident philosopher, court tutor, and erstwhile adviser. This negative characterisation of Alexander as tyrant, influenced by contemporary intellectual responses to autocracy, stands in stark contrast to the idealising narrative of the Greek writers of the imperial period (although glimpses of this hostile tradition do shine through the later, generally apologetic, narratives of Plutarch and Arrian, as we have seen).[39]

Returning to our original question, I have demonstrated that there is no evidence to support the common modern assumption that Kallisthenes held an official position as the Pages' tutor, or even that he taught Hermolaos, the only individual with whom he is explicitly associated in the sources. On the contrary, his only official position in Alexander's entourage was as his court historian, as Justin attests (12.6.17), whose role was to produce a history of the expedition which was to be authorised and endorsed by the young conqueror himself. Confirmation that this indeed was Kallisthenes' role has come from a somewhat surprising source, a fragment of a Hellenistic library catalogue on the wall of a gymnasium in Tauromenion, which lists Kallisthenes as Alexander's *epistolographos*, who wrote a history of Alexander.[40] The title of *epistolographos* is specific to Hellenistic administration, and pertains to the head of the royal chancellery (Battistoni 2006, 171 n. 13), but in this context, in reference to Kallisthenes' historical work, appears to be equivalent to 'secretary'.[41] Thus, this inscription simultaneously provides evidence that Alexander did indeed compose his history of Alexander's expedition in an official capacity, and confirms (at least *ex silentio*) that he did not hold the official position of the tutor of the Pages, as there is no mention (where one would expect it in the inscription) of the position of *didaskalos*, as for example in similar documents when the librarians at Alexandria are described as serving as the tutors of the children of the Ptolemies.[42]

In conclusion, there is no evidence at all that Kallisthenes ever served as tutor of the Royal Pages in any official capacity, and in fact it is very likely that his influence over the Pages in general was enhanced by contemporary apologetic sources such as Aristoboulos and Ptolemy in order to justify his implication in the Pages' Conspiracy and ultimate condemnation. Similarly, the close relationship between Kallisthenes and Hermolaos, the ringleader of the conspiracy, was almost certainly exaggerated, again by the contemporary apologetic sources, to mitigate Alexander's guilt in the condemnation and death of his court historian and former member of his inner circle. By the time that Curtius was composing his history in the early imperial period, however, the larger-than-life figure of Alexander had become an object lesson in autocratic rule. Influenced by the negative portrayal of Alexander as despot inspired by political developments in his own intellectual *milieu*, Curtius transformed Kallisthenes into a proto-Seneca in order to offer more pointed commentary on the tyranny of Nero. This tendency to read the condemnation of Kallisthenes in contemporary terms is present even in the generally idealising narratives of both Plutarch and Arrian, although Alexander's 'tyranny' in the Greek writers is confined to his descent into orientalism after the murder of Bessos. The pervasive but demonstrably false tradition that Kallisthenes was the official tutor of the Pages offers a salutary lesson that we must exercise extreme caution in separating the historical reality of the achievements of Alexander from the biases and agendas of the Roman-era sources who offer the only extant continuous narratives of his expedition.[43]

Acknowledgements

This paper was written with the support of the Social Sciences and Humanities Research Council of Canada. It has benefited greatly from the comments of audience members who heard preliminary versions of these arguments in Athens in 2012, Edmonton in 2013, and Marburg in 2015. I am especially grateful for the incisive feedback of my fellow editor, Tim Howe.

Notes

[1] See, e.g., Hamilton 1969, 154; Golan 1988, 116; Rubinsohn 1993, 1316; Müller 2003, 155; Heckel 2003, 206 n. 43 ('Aristotle and Callisthenes were both tutors of Pages') and 2006, 77 and 138 (more cautiously); Carney 2008, 150 and 152 (also more cautiously); Worthington 2014, 234.

[2] On the institution of the so-called *Basilikoi Paides*, see Heckel 1986, 279–85 and 2003, 205–6; Hammond 1990; Koulakiotis 2005; Carney 2008.

[3] Firm evidence for the date of Curtius' history of Alexander remains elusive, although there is a consensus that it was written during the early Empire. Previously, the favoured date for its composition was during the reign of Claudius; Hamilton 1988 and Atkinson 2009 (a re-statement of his earlier position), 2–14. More recently, however, the pendulum has swung to Vespasian; Baynham 1998, 201–19; Bosworth 2004, esp. 566 (in a reversal of his previous dating of Curtius to the time of Trajan's adoption in late 97); Power 2013. If I am correct in my argument below that Curtius manipulates the figure of Kallisthenes to offer more pointed criticism of Nero's tyranny, it offers further support for a Vespasianic date.

[4] *Callisthenen non ut participem facinoris nominatum esse constabat, sed solitum puerorum sermonibus vituperantium criminantiumque regem faciles aures praebere.*

[5] τοὺς δὲ ἄλλους σοφιστὰς καὶ κόλακας ὁ Καλλισθένης ἐλύπει σπουδαζόμενος μὲν ὑπὸ τῶν νέων διὰ τὸν λόγον.

[6] Lysimachos (not the future Diadoch) and Hagnon were courtiers of Alexander; Hamilton 1969, 57 and 153–4; Heckel 2006, 128 and 153.

[7] On the paramount importance of success in the royal hunt as a vehicle for the king to legitimise his position, especially *vis-à-vis* the Macedonian elite who served as his hunting entourage, see Greenwalt 1993, esp. 518; Carney 2002; Roisman 2003, 313–16. But cf. Palagia 2000, who argues that the political symbolism of the royal hunt derives from Asian iconographical conventions and therefore is not originally a Macedonian practice but can be attributed to Alexander himself. On the dual functions of the hunt in ancient Macedonia as both a symbol of royal power and a masculine rite of passage, see Cohen 2010, esp. 71–118.

[8] The modern bibliography on Alexander's attempt to introduce the Achaemenid practice of *proskynēsis* to his court ritual is enormous. The matter is complicated because the Persian court ceremonial of *proskynēsis* was conflated in the ancient sources with Alexander's alleged claims to divinity; see, e.g., Spawforth 2007, 102–12; Matarese 2013; Bowden 2013 (all with earlier bibliography). Bowden is convincing that the episode reveals less about Alexander's supposed desire to be worshipped as a god, and more about contemporary debates on the imperial ruler-cult in our Roman-era sources. If, on the other hand, there was deliberate ambiguity in the Achaemenid concept of kingship between a ruler who is himself divine and an earthly representative of the gods, as has recently been argued (Root 2013; cf. Root 2010), then the question of Alexander's aims in attempting to introduce *proskynēsis* becomes even more complex.

[9] On Kallisthenes' role in the *proskynēsis* fiasco, see Pownall 2014.

[10] Carney 1980–81 and 2008; Bosworth 1996, 112–13; Heckel 2009, 46–7; Müller 2010.

[11] On the poisonous atmosphere of personal rivalry among the intellectual elite at Alexander's court, see Borza 1981 and Roisman 1993, 302–6.

[12] Rivalry is attested between Kallisthenes and Anaxarchos in their competing attempts to comfort Alexander after Kleitos' death, which resulted in the undermining of Kallisthenes' influence with the king (Plut. *Alex.* 53.3–7; cf. Arr. 4.9.7–8), Kallisthenes' embarrassment of his rival by besting him in an argument and subtly drawing attention to his love of luxury (Plut. *Alex.* 52.8–9), and most famously when the two engaged in a debate on the *proskynēsis* question (Arr. 4.10.5–11.0; on Kallisthenes' role in this debate, see Pownall 2014, 61–5). Oddly, Curtius (8.5.10–20) replaces Anaxarchos with the otherwise unknown 'flatterer' Kleon as Kallisthenes' interlocutor in the *proskynēsis* debate. On Anaxarchos, see Borza 1981 and Bosworth 1995, 66–7.

[13] Agis of Argos: Curt. 8.5.8 and Arr. 4.9.9; cf. Bosworth 1995, 72 and Heckel 2009, 8.

[14] Demetrios, the son of Pythonax: Plut. *Alex.* 54.6 and Arr. 4.12.5; cf. Hamilton 1969, 153 and Heckel 2009, 109.

[15] Bosworth 1980, 16–34 and Stadter 1980, 69–72.

[16] Cf. Badian 2000, 88: 'Alexander, a master plotter from the plot that led to his accession, skilfully uses charges of conspiracy to strengthen his position and rid himself of possible centres of rivalry.'

[17] Hermokrates: D.S.16.94.1; Val. Max.8.14 *ext.*4 (Hermocles instead of Hermocrates).

[18] On the persistent myth in the Athenian oratorical tradition that Harmodios and Aristogeiton liberated Athens from tyranny, see e.g., Pownall 2013, esp. 339–44 (with earlier bibliography).

[19] The Athenian protection of suppliants against tyranny is a recurring theme in Attic oratory, particularly the funeral oration (e.g., Lysias 2.11–15); cf. Bosworth 1995, 77 and Steinbock 2013, esp. 54 and 187.

[20] On the trial and execution of Philotas, see Heckel 1977; Badian 2000, 62–9; Adams 2003; Reames 2008.

[21] On Arrian's (still defensive) criticism of Alexander in this digression, see Stadter 1980; 83 and 103–14; Bosworth 1988, 140–56; Bosworth 1995, 45–7.

[22] Cf. *Alex.* 52.7, where Plutarch comments that Anaxarchos 'made his (i.e., Alexander's) character especially more haughty and lawless (i.e., autocratic)' (τὸ δὲ ἦθος εἰς πολλὰ χαυνότερον καὶ παρανομώτερον ἐποίησεν). On the deterioration of Alexander's character in Plutarch's generally apologetic life, see Hamilton 1969, lxii–lxvi.

[23] On the complex question of Plutarch's Hellenism in his treatment of Alexander, see Hamilton 1969, xvii–xxi, Humbert 1991, and more recently the nuanced arguments of Whitmarsh 2002 and Asirvatham 2005.

[24] On Plutarch's view of tyranny, see Mossé 2006, with particular reference to his portrayal of the Sicilian tyrants, a topic which naturally had special relevance to Plato.

[25] Cf. Asirvatham 2001, 120: 'Callisthenes is important to Plutarch because he speaks on behalf of the Greeks at a moment when, in Plutarch's eyes, Alexander has become most barbaric: the moment when the Greeks are required to perform

proskynesis is the moment at which the Hellenisation of Orientals turns into the Orientalisation of Hellenes'.

[26] See, e.g., Lefkowitz 2012 and Chitwood 2004. Flower (1994, 49) adduces the analogous contemporary myth that Gilbert Murray studied under Wilamowitz.

[27] Spencer (2002, 135–8) comments upon Alexander's sarcasm in this speech (8.8.1–19) replying to Hermolaos' accusations against him, and reads it (136) as a 'tacit intervention into developments in Roman autocracy'; cf. Baynham 1998, 52 and 195–9 on the echoes of the Roman imperial court in this speech.

[28] Cf. Asirvatham 2010, 115: 'Curtius' overarching theme was how *fortuna* gave Alexander glory but eventually turned him from *rex* to *tyrannus*'.

[29] On his date, see n. 3 above.

[30] On Latin writers' treatment of Alexander, see Spencer 2002 and Asirvatham 2010, 114–16.

[31] See Too 1994 on Seneca's literary manipulation of his role as Nero's tutor. I thank Adrian Tronson and Tim Howe for drawing my attention to the reflections of Seneca and Nero in Kallisthenes' relationship with Alexander.

[32] Sophist: Ath.10.434d; Plut. *Alex.* 55.1 and 4; cf. 53.1. Philosopher: Plut. *Alex.* 52.2 and Arr. 4.13.2; cf. Arr. 4.10.1, where Kallisthenes is attested to have received instruction from Aristotle.

[33] Bosworth 1970; cf. Brown 1949, 226; Golan 1988, 101; Rubinsohn 1993, 1312–13; Pownall 1998, 49; *contra* Prandi (1985, 19–22), who attributes Alexander's invitation to Aristotle's influence. On the intended propagandistic function of Kallisthenes' official history of the expedition, see Zahrnt 2006.

[34] On this passage, see Spencer 2009, 271–2.

[35] Schmitz 2014, 32–41. Cf. Schmitz 2014, 40: Plutarch 'used the Second Sophistic as an ideological construct: sophists and their attitudes are often depicted as a foil to behavior that Plutarch wants to present as appropriate and reasonable'. Conversely, Plutarch in this instance appears to have portrayed Kallisthenes as a philosopher to make him a foil to Alexander's orientalising and morally dubious stance in the *proskynēsis* episode; cf. Asirvatham 2001, 120–1.

[36] Cf. S. Müller 2014, 57, who identifies three factors that obstruct our understanding of Kallisthenes' fall from grace: the hushing-up of events that occurred throughout Alexander's reign, the literary stylising of Kallisthenes' fall as a symptom of Alexander's descent into tyranny and oppression of philosophical *parrhēsia*, and Kallisthenes' idealisation as a philosophical cliché.

[37] Cf. Spencer 2009, 268: 'The figure of Callisthenes opens up, for Roman authors, strategically interesting ways of focusing on and exploring relationships between historiography, autocracy, and individual responsibility.'

[38] Cf. Spencer 2009, 270 (in reference to the *proskynēsis* episode): 'Callisthenes functions as a focus for narratological expressions of dissent'.

[39] For a useful summary of the general tendencies of the Greek imperial writers versus the Latin writers in their portrayals of Alexander, see Asirvatham 2010, 111–16.

[40] *SEG* 26.1123: first published by Mangarano 1974, with new readings by Battistoni 2006.

[41] Prandi 1985, 21–2; cf. Stadter 1980, 214 n. 38.

[42] See, e.g., the list of the librarians of Alexandria (*P. Oxy.* 10.1241 = *FGrH* 241 T 7), where it is stated explicitly that both Apollonius of Rhodes and Aristarchus served as tutors to the royal children, in addition to their duties as head of the library at Alexandria.

[43] For a similar deconstruction of the *proskynēsis* episode, see Bowden 2013.

Bibliography

Adams, W. L.
2003 'The Episode of Philotas: An Insight', in W. Heckel and L. A. Tritle (eds) *Crossroads of History: The Age of Alexander*, Claremont, CA, 113–26.

Asirvatham, S. R.
2001 'Olympias' Snake and Callisthenes' Stand: Religion and Politics in Plutarch's *Life of Alexander*', in S. Asirvatham, C. O. Pache, and J. Watrous (eds) *Between Magic and Religion: Interdisciplinary Studies in Ancient Mediterranean Religion and Society*, Lanham, MD, 93–125.
2005 'Classicism and *Romanitas* in Plutarch's *De Alexandri fortuna aut virtute*', *AJP* 126, 107–25.
2010 'Perspectives on the Macedonians from Greece, Rome, and Beyond', in J. Roisman and I. Worthington (eds) *A Companion to Ancient Macedonia*, Malden, MA, 99–124.

Atkinson, J. E.
2009 Introduction and Historical Commentary (with J. Yardley, trans.) to *Curtius Rufus: Histories of Alexander the Great, Book 10*, Oxford.

Badian, E.
1958 'The Eunuch Bagoas', *CQ* 9, 144–52.
2000 'Conspiracies', in A. B. Bosworth and E. J. Baynham (eds) *Alexander the Great in Fact and Fiction*, Oxford, 50–95.

Battistoni, F.
2006 'The Ancient *Pinakes* from Tauromenion. Some New Readings', *ZPE* 157, 169–80.

Baynham, E.
1998 *Alexander the Great: The Unique History of Quintus Curtius*, Ann Arbor.

Borza, E. N.
1981 'Anaxarchus and Callisthenes: Academic Intrigue at Alexander's Court', in H. J. Dell (ed.) *Ancient Macedonian Studies in Honor of Charles. F. Edson*, Thessalonica, 73–97.

Bosworth, A. B.
1970 'Alexander and Callisthenes', *Historia* 19, 407–13.
1980 *A Historical Commentary on Arrian's History of Alexander*, vol. 1, Oxford.
1988 *From Arrian to Alexander: Studies in Historical Interpretation*, Oxford.
1995 *A Historical Commentary on Arrian's History of Alexander*, vol. 2, Oxford.
1996 *Alexander and the East: The Tragedy of Triumph*, Oxford and New York.
2004 'Mountain and Molehill? Cornelius Tacitus and Quintus Curtius', *CQ* 54, 551–67.

Bowden, H.
    2013 'On Kissing and Making Up: Court Protocol and Historiography in Alexander the Great's "Experiment with *Proskynesis*"', *BICS* 56, 55–77.
Brown, T. S.
    1949 'Callisthenes and Alexander', *AJP* 70, 225–48.
Carney, E. D.
    1980–81 'The Conspiracy of Hermolaus', *CJ* 76, 223–31.
    2002 'Hunting and the Macedonian Elite: Sharing the Rivalry of the Chase', in D. Ogden (ed.) *The Hellenistic World: New Perspectives*, Swansea, 59–80.
    2008 'The Role of the *Basilikoi Paides* at the Argead Court', in T. Howe and J. Reames (eds) *Macedonian Legacies*, Claremont, CA, 145–64.
Chitwood, A.
    2004 *Death by Philosophy: The Biographical Tradition in the Life and Death of the Archaic Philosophers Empedocles, Heraclitus, and Democritus*, Ann Arbor.
Cohen, A.
    2010 *Art in the Era of Alexander the Great: Paradigms of Manhood and their Cultural Traditions*, Cambridge.
Flower, M. A.
    1994 *Theopompus of Chios: History and Rhetoric in the Fourth Century BC*, Oxford.
Golan, D.
    1988 'The Fate of a Court Historian, Callisthenes', *Athenaeum* 66, 99–120.
Greenwalt, W. S.
    1993 'The Iconographic Significance of Amyntas III's Mounted Hunter Stater,' *AM* 5, 509–19.
Haake, M.
    2004 'Documentary Evidence, Literary Forgery, or Manipulation of Historical Documents? Diogenes Laertius and an Athenian Honorary Decree for Zeno of Citium,' *CQ* 54, 470–83.
Hamilton, J. R.
    1969 *Plutarch: Alexander: A Commentary*, Oxford.
    1988 'The Date of Quintus Curtius Rufus', *Historia* 37, 445–56.
Hammond, N. G. L.
    1990 'Royal Pages, Personal Pages, and Boys Trained in the Macedonian Manner during the Period of the Temenid Monarchy', *Historia* 39, 261–90.
Heckel, W.
    1977 'The Conspiracy *against* Philotas', *Phoenix* 31, 9–21.
    1986 '*Somatophylakia*: A Macedonian *Cursus Honorum*', *Phoenix* 40, 279–94.
    2003 'Kings and "Companions": Observations on the Nature of Power in the Reign of Alexander', in J. Roisman (ed.) *Brill's Companion to Alexander the Great*, Leiden, 197–225.
    2006 *Who's Who in the Age of Alexander the Great*, Malden, MA.
    2009 'Alexander's Conquest of Asia', in W. Heckel and L. A. Tritle (eds) *Alexander the Great: A New History*, Malden, MA, 26–52.
Humbert, S.
    1991 'Plutarque, Alexandre, et l'Hellénisme', in S. Saïd, *HELLENISMOS*, Leiden, 169–82.

Koulakiotis, E.
   2005   'Domination et résistance à la cour d'Alexandre: Le cas des *basilikoi paides*', in V. I. Anastasiadis and P. N. Doukellis (eds) *Esclavage antique et discrimations socio-culturelles*, Berne, 167–82.

Lefkowitz, M. R.
   2012   *The Lives of the Greek Poets*, 2nd ed., Baltimore.

Long, A. A.
   1988   'Socrates in Hellenistic Philosophy', *CQ* 38, 150–71.

Mangarano, G.
   1974   'Una biblioteca storica nel ginnasio di Tauromenion e il P.Oxy. 1241,' *PP* 29, 389–409.

Matarese, C.
   2013   '*Proskynēsis* and the Gesture of the Kiss at Alexander's Court: The Creation of a New Élite', *Palamedes*, 75–85.

Milns, R. D.
   2006/07 'Callisthenes on Alexander', *Mediterranean Archaeology* 19/20, 233–7.

Mossé, C.
   2006   'Plutarch and the Sicilian Tyrants', in S. Lewis (ed.) *Ancient Tyranny*, Edinburgh, 188–96.

Müller, S.
   2003   *Maßnahmen der Herrschaftssicherung gegenüber der makedonischen Opposition bei Alexander dem Großen*, Frankfurt.

   2010   'In the Shadow of his Father: Alexander, Hermolaus, and the Legend of Philip', in E. Carney and D. Ogden (eds) *Philip II and Alexander the Great: Father and Son, Lives and Afterlives*, Oxford, 25–32.

   2014   *Alexander, Makedonien und Persien*, Berlin.

Palagia, O.
   2000   'Hephaistion's Pyre and the Royal Hunt of Alexander', in A. B. Bosworth and E. J. Baynham (eds) *Alexander the Great in Fact and Fiction*, Oxford, 167–206.

Power, T.
   2013   'Suetonius and the Date of Curtius Rufus', *Hermes* 141, 117–20.

Pownall, F. S.
   1998   'What Makes a War a Sacred War?', *Echos du Monde Classique/Classical Views* 17, 35–55.

   2013   'A Case Study in Isocrates: The Expulsion of the Peisistratids', in D. Côté and P. Fleury (eds) *Discours politique et Histoire dans l'Antiquité, Dialogues d'histoire ancienne*, Supplément 8, Besançon, 339–54.

   2014   'Callisthenes in Africa: The Historian's Role at Siwah and in the *Proskynesis* Controversy', in P. Bosman (ed.) *Alexander in Africa*, *Acta Classica* Supplementum V, Pretoria, 56–71.

Prandi, L.
   1985   *Callistene: Uno storico tra Aristotele e i re macedoni*, Milan.

Reames, J.
   2008   'Crisis and Opportunity: The Philotas Affair...Again', in T. Howe and J. Reames (eds) *Macedonian Legacies*, Claremont, CA, 165–81.

Roisman, J.
  2003   'Honor in Alexander's Campaign', in J. Roisman (ed.) *Brill's Companion to Alexander the Great*, Leiden, 279–321.
Root, M. C.
  2010   'Palace to Temple – King to Cosmos: Achaemenid Foundation Texts in Iran', in M.J. Boda and J. Novotny (eds) *From the Foundations to the Crenellation: Essays on Temple Building and the Ancient Near East and Hebrew Bible*, Münster, 165–210.
  2013   'Defining the Divine in Achaemenid Persian Kingship: The View from Bisitun', in L. Mitchell and C. Melville (eds) *Every Inch a King: Comparative Studies of Kings and Kingship in the Ancient and Medieval Worlds*, Leiden, 23–65.
Rubinsohn, W. Z.
  1993   'The Philosopher at Court-Intellectuals and Politics in the Time of Alexander the Great', *AM* 5, 1301–27.
Schmitz, T. A.
  2014   'Plutarch and the Second Sophistic', in M. Beck (ed.) *A Companion to Plutarch*, Malden, MA, 32–42.
Spawforth, A. J. S.
  2007   'The court of Alexander the Great between Europe and Asia', in A. J. S. Spawforth (ed.) *The Court and Court Society in Ancient Monarchies*, Cambridge, 82–120.
Spencer, D.
  2002   *The Roman Alexander: Reading a Cultural Myth*, Exeter.
  2009   'Roman Alexanders: Epistemology and Identity', in W. Heckel and L. A. Tritle (eds) *Alexander the Great: A New History*, Malden, MA, 251–74.
Stadter, P. A.
  1980   *Arrian of Nicomedia*, Chapel Hill.
Steinbock
  2013   *Social Memory in Athenian Public Discourse: Uses and Meaning of the Past*, Ann Arbor.
Too, Y. L.
  1994   'Educating Nero: a reading of Seneca's *Moral Epistles*', in J. Elsner and J. Masters (eds) *Reflections of Nero: Culture, History, & Representation*, Chapel Hill, 211–24.
Whitmarsh, T.
  2002   'Alexander's Hellenism and Plutarch's Textualism', *CQ* 52, 174–92.
Worthington, I.
  2014   *By the Spear: Philip II, Alexander the Great, and the Rise and Fall of the Macedonian Empire*, Oxford.
Zahrnt, M.
  2006   'Von Siwa bis Persepolis: Überlegungen zur Arbeitsweise des Kallisthenes.' *AncSoc* 36: 143–74.

5

HEPHAISTION – A RE-ASSESSMENT OF HIS CAREER

Sabine Müller

Thanks to his relationship to one of the most famous ancient conquerors, the Macedonian officer Hephaistion, son of a certain Amyntor, is an ancient celebrity. Apart from, or perhaps due to, the scanty evidence on him, one of the main issues on Hephaistion is the dynamics of reception in ancient and modern times.[1] In popular collective memory, Hephaistion is known as Alexander's best friend in the sense of having been his Aristotelian fellow pupil, boyhood friend, intimate adviser and perhaps more. So it is usually assumed that Hephaistion was Alexander's boyfriend and life partner.[2] Often, he is also labelled as Alexander's own personal Patroklos.[3] In consequence, concerning Hephaistion's afterlife, it is eye-catching that he seems to be primarily known for his personal relationship with Alexander instead of his political and military function. The fact that he had been one of Alexander's most important officers, his *hipparch*, commander of units of the important Companion Cavalry, and often his ambassador,[4] is neglected sometimes even to the point of being forgotten. On the other hand, as Hephaistion certainly played an important political role in Alexander's newly conquered empire, it is often suggested that he owed his impressive career mainly to his private connection with Alexander, hence a clear case of nepotism.[5] Therefore, scholars characterised him as 'sinister',[6] 'gehässiger Intrigant' (bitchy schemer),[7] 'im Grunde ein Nichts'(for the most part a nobody),[8] 'a particularly quarrelsome nature...an unpleasant, jealous individual',[9] 'generally unliked and unlikeable',[10] 'attractive to no one else, and therefore to Alexander alone',[11] 'handsome, spoilt, spiteful, overbearing, and fundamentally stupid'.[12] These harsh judgements are based on bringing the scanty scattered pieces of information on Hephaistion together and welding them into a final picture. However, this method is rather problematic. The result is a kind of Frankenstein's monster because there are different images of Hephaistion in the sources that are not always compatible. His portrait depends on each author's attitude towards Hephaistion and Alexander, as Arrian has already stated:

> At this point indeed historians have given varied accounts of Alexander's grief. That it was great, all have related; as to the actions it occasioned, they

differ according to the good-will or malice each felt towards Hephaistion or even towards Alexander himself.[13]

Furthermore, the value of the sources differs. The aim of this chapter is to scrutinise the evidence on Hephaistion in order to re-assess his career and check whether all the assumptions on his personal relationship with Alexander can in fact be traced back to the contemporary, eyewitness, sources, or if they should instead be rejected as later literary interpolations. In addition, it will try to create a profile of the historical Hephaistion behind all the layers of literary embroidery. By doing this, I hope to show that we do not know anything certain about Alexander's and Hephaistion's private relationship. The ideas of Hephaistion being Alexander's lover, his own personal Patroklos, or his Second Self did not stem from Alexander's political self-fashioning but were instead literary models transferred posthumously by later writers, particularly Romans. In fact, an Argead ruler did not promote his love life publicly unless for dynastic reasons (e.g. polygamous marriage, see Carney, this volume). Moreover, Alexander did not even call much public attention to his three marriages in his self-representation. Whatever he may have felt or not felt for Hephaistion, concerning his non-marital private life, he (and his contemporaries) obviously did not comment on it.

Chasing a shadow: the historical Hephaistion

The fragments of Ptolemy's *History of Alexander* (with its in fact unknown title) seem to provide helpful evidence on Hephaistion. Ptolemy knew him personally and built his career in the Macedonian empire at the same time as Hephaistion. Because both were Alexander's trusted men belonging to his inner circle, they worked closely together. Ptolemy informs us that Hephaistion came from Pella and that his father was called Amyntor.[14] Waldemar Heckel has suggested that this Amyntor might have been identical with a man who, along with his offspring, was granted Athenian citizenship in an inscription dated to 334 BC.[15] And yet, we know very little about Hephaistion's early life; even Hephaistion's role in Alexander's invasion of Asia is nearly invisible in the sources. All we know is that Hephaistion seems to have served as a lesser commander of the *agēma* of the hypaspists. Heckel suggests that he was promoted to this post in 332 BC, when the former holder of the office was killed at Tyre.[16] Indeed, Hephaistion's remarkable career began only *after* Alexander eliminated the influential clan of Parmenion and Philotas and thus got his hands free to promote men of his own choosing.

Early on, Ptolemy outlines Hephaistion's career and emphasises his own importance in the political structure of Alexander's empire.[17] He also makes clear that Hephaistion and Alexander were very good friends. However, in the fragments, there is no trace that Ptolemy may have hinted that they were more than this. At least, the characterisation of Hephaistion as φίλτατος that probably comes from Ptolemy does not necessarily imply that there was a sexual aspect to their friendship.[18] In addition, there are no other hints that Ptolemy might have characterised Hephaistion as Alexander's boyfriend. It is especially significant that the episodes linking Hephaistion to Patroklos or showing him as his Alter Ego are not reported by Ptolemy, as Arrian admits.[19] The deepest insight into any relationship that Ptolemy provides is when he reports that Alexander honoured Hephaistion in 324 by giving him Drypetis, the sister of his own Achaemenid wife Stateira in marriage.[20] Even if the bridegroom regarded this marital bond as an 'honour (or obligation)',[21] it tied him dynastically to Alexander.[22] But this was a political, not a personal, step.

Throughout the extant fragments there is also no sign that Ptolemy depicted Hephaistion as Alexander's boyhood friend. This is interesting since Ptolemy probably was brought up at the court in Pella and thus will have known well the boys with whom Alexander had developed close associations.[23] Likewise, Onesikritos, one of Hephaistion's fellow officers during the Indian Campaign,[24] who wrote on Alexander's early years and probably served as Plutarch's source for his chapters on Alexander's youth,[25] does not mention Hephaistion as Alexander's fellow pupil in Mieza or as his boyhood friend living with him at the court. Nor is there any trace in the fragments of Kallisthenes that Hephaistion rose to any prominence before 331 BC.[26] All of this evidence seems to confirm Ptolemy's outline of Hephaistion's career. Thus, although Hephaistion did come from Pella, it is uncertain whether he grew up at the palace or was even an age-mate or boyhood friend of Alexander. In fact, Hephaistion may not even have entered Alexander's life before 334 when the campaign began. Hephaistion first becomes visible in fragments of the contemporary sources that are most likely to preserve the official version (Kallisthenes, Ptolemy, Aristoboulos) in about 331/330 BC.[27] In the end, at least as concerns the contemporary, eyewitness evidence, Hephaistion's early life is a complete mystery.

What is clear, however, is the fact that Ptolemy certainly did not intend to blacken Hephaistion by denying his early relationship to Alexander, for Hephaistion and Ptolemy seem to have been very close friends. Throughout his *History* Ptolemy went out of his way to commemorate Hephaistion in a very favourable way.[28] In fact, Hephaistion, alone of Alexander's 'inner circle', receives special treatment: while Ptolemy tends to depict Perdikkas,[29] and probably also Krateros, as incompetent commanders, Lysimachos,

Antigonos, and Seleukos as nearly not present, and thus not very important,[30] and Eumenes comes across as insignificant, Hephaistion was portrayed as competent, loyal, and capable, always living up to Alexander's expectations.[31] Furthermore, Ptolemy protects him against all potential reproaches: every time something went wrong or could be regarded as a potential problem or a bad decision by Alexander, according to Ptolemy, he (Ptolemy) and Hephaistion were suspiciously absent.[32] This is the case when Kleitos was murdered, when Alexander married Roxane and when Alexander nearly died during the unfortunate siege of the town of the Malloi.[33] In each case, Ptolemy and Hephaistion's absence seems to be strange and demands an explanation, which Ptolemy often gives.[34] Moreover, Aristoboulos confirms that Ptolemy witnessed the murder of Kleitos, and Kleitarchos, and other sources mention that he was present during the disaster at the town of the Malloi.[35] Looking at the reports on this event, it is odd that Hephaistion and Ptolemy who were Alexander's most trusted and important commanders at this point of time,[36] led a great number of troops just before and after the siege, but were allegedly sent away when the siege began.[37] Ptolemy claims in vague terms that he was on another mission with certain troops in order to chase other 'barbarians'.[38] In contrast to Ptolemy's usual style, it is rather strange that for once he did not precisely name his units and field of operation.[39] This unusual obscurity on his part raises the suspicion that it was a mere pretext to cover up that indeed he had been there with a high command, and thus was in part responsible for the inglorious outcome.[40] It is also striking that Ptolemy depicts his enemy Perdikkas as the one to blame for the disaster.[41] Furthermore, although Hephaistion and presumably also Ptolemy were prominent commanders during the badly organised and horrorific journey through the Gedrosian desert, Ptolemy quickly passes over the episode, being silent on any of the commanders' shortcomings.[42]

Consequently, one may deduce that it was not politically sound for Ptolemy to explain to his audience why he and Hephaistion as Alexander's close friends did not advise him better. Ptolemy's self-defensive reasons to protect himself against such potential reproaches are clear. But he was in no need to extend this protection to Hephaistion, who had died too early to be of special value as a political symbol in the times of the Successors. Thus, it can be suggested that Ptolemy wanted to honour a friend who in his lifetime had been very dear to him. Another hint may be that the rather unusual name Hephaistion[43] continued to exist in the Ptolemaic empire.[44] It would be enlightening to know whether Hephaistion's posthumous heroic honours that were also ordered to be installed in Egypt by Alexander[45] were preserved by Ptolemy and whether this was also the inspiration for the survival of the Hephaistion name in the Egyptian realm. Unfortunately, there is next to no traceable evidence for this cult in Egypt.[46] Furthermore, the Alexandrian court poetry that reflects Ptolemaic ideology is focused on Alexander and Ptolemy and does not name any of Alexander's other generals.

It is probably not by chance that Arrian is also silent on Hephaistion's role in the downfall of Philotas and Kallisthenes that is attributed to him by Curtius and Plutarch.[47] This negative image of Hephaistion as an unscrupulous schemer is presumably not contemporary nor does it stem either from Ptolemy or from Kleitarchos,[48] who tried to please the Ptolemaic house and seems to have known that Hephaistion's memory was dear to Ptolemy I (and thus also to his successors). Hence, Kleitarchos will have created a favourable portrait of Hephaistion that in the Roman context was later transformed into something negative when Hephaistion was used as a mirror-image of Alexander reflecting his moral downfall (see below).

However, as Ptolemy's literary aim was to glorify himself as Alexander's ideal successor,[49] he could not allow anyone to rank higher, not even the best friend. Therefore, he created the impression that Alexander had *two* best officers with different fields of special interest. As warrior skills ranked highest in the Macedonian war-centered culture,[50] Ptolemy depicted himself as the great commander and Hephaistion as the expert concerning organisation, diplomacy, and logistics. Clearly, this image has its flaws and demands a cautious treatment since, first and foremost, Hephaistion is visible as a military commander. Unfortunately, Ptolemy does not say much on Hephaistion's duties as a hipparch or chiliarch, or on the date of his appointment to the chiliarchy or as one of the seven *sōmatophylakes*.[51] The nature of the newly introduced chiliarchy, which despite its Persian name was an office linked with the Macedonian Companions' Cavalry,[52] is unclear.[53] Arrian states briefly:

> At any rate Alexander never appointed anyone in place of Hephaistion as chiliarch over the Companions' Cavalry, so that the name of Hephaistion might never be lost to the unit; the chiliarchy was still called Hephaistion's, and the standard went before it which had been made by his order.[54]

Diodoros mentions the chiliarchy only in a posthumous context in the time of the Successors and seems to have no exact idea about its character.[55] Probably the chiliarchy was meant to inscribe Hephaistion's position into the political structures of Alexander's empire. When he died, this gap could not be bridged and so the office lost its intended meaning.

Until the publication of *POxy* LXXI. 4808 in 2007, there was general agreement that Kleitarchos wrote under Ptolemy in Alexandria and was 'a willing promoter of Ptolemy's course'[56] who depicted him rather favourably.[57] The new evidence led to the – however debated – suggestion of a new dating of Kleitarchos as the tutor of Ptolemy IV.[58] In either case, Kleitarchos seems to have emphasised Hephaistion's role in his *History*, presumably under the impression that Ptolemy would appreciate the cultivation of Hephaistion's memory either by his contemporaries or or later on at the Ptolemaic court, as Ptolemy's heirs conserved and continued his cultural legacy and ideology.[59]

To sum up, it seems that Hephaistion was at least not tied closely into the network of the influential old Macedonian clans that controlled Macedonian politics and the campaign in the beginning.[60] His career started after Alexander had removed Parmenion and Philotas, thus freeing him to promote his own choice of men. But even concerning Hephaistion's career we know little. The historical Hephaistion, known to the contemporary sources, remains a mystery.

And yet, in much the same way as Alexander was quickly turned into an artificial figure,[61] Hephaistion too was transformed. For literary dramaturgic reasons (see below), Curtius deviated from tradition and styled Hephaistion as Alexander's friend and fellow pupil. Diodoros, Plutarch, and Trogus-Justin, who also used Kleitarchos,[62] do not confirm this, though modern scholars usually support Curtius' statement with an alleged letter written by Aristotle to Hephaistion mentioned by Diogenes Laertios.[63] Thus, thanks to Curtius, the literary *topos* of the Second Self has dominated the study of Alexander and Hephaistion.[64]

Kleitarchos, Ephippos, Curtius and the *Topos* of Hephaistion as Alexander's Second Self

Hephaistion's depiction as Alexander's Second Self was decisively influenced by a *Wandermotiv* common to different cultures in different times: the theme of the Doppelgänger,[65] first categorised by Otto Rank, a pupil of Sigmund Freud. In 1925 he pointed out that the double is a kind of reminder concerning mortality. The double often appears when the death of his Self is close at hand. Neither can live without the other. If the Second Self dies, the First Self is also doomed to die.[66] Alternatively, Carl Francis Keppler interpreted the phenomenon of the *topos* of the Alter Ego as a chance for an encounter of the Ego and a visual manifestation of his inner counter image.[67]

Two episodes stand out in depicting Hephaistion as Alexander's Second Self:[68] first of all, the famous scene when they both went into the tent of Darius' captured family after Issos.[69] Diodoros' version reads:

> So at the daybreak, the king took with him the most valued of his friends, Hephaistion, and came to the women. They were dressed alike, but Hephaistion was taller and more handsome. Sisyngambris took him for the king and did him obeisance. As the others present made signs to her and pointed to Alexander with their hands she was embarrassed by her mistake, but made a new start and did obeisance to Alexander. He, however, cut in and said, 'Never mind, Mother, for actually he too is Alexander'.[70]

The story that became a symbol of Alexander's magnanimity[71] reflects the Aristotelian image of friendship as one soul in two bodies: friendship implying equality between the two, hence duality as a measure of their love for each other.[72] However, the anecdote is most probably invented in order to illustrate Alexander's self-restraint towards the Persian royal women, thus depicting him as a merciful victor.[73] According to the official version, probably originally coming from Kallisthenes, Alexander did not visit the royal ladies himself:

> On hearing this, Alexander sent Leonnatus, one of the Companions, to them with instructions to tell them that Darius was alive (...) This is the account of Ptolemy and Aristobulus.[74]

According to this storyline, Alexander exercised so much self-control that he did not even lay eyes on Darius' wife, who was said to be the most beautiful woman in Asia. This is a clear imitation of a scene in Xenophon's *Cyropaedia* telling the same story about Cyrus II and Pantheia, one of his captives.[75] Therefore, reality and literary allusions seem to be blended: Alexander probably did not visit the royal women's tent. However, the explanation why he exercised restraint was constructed so that it might serve as a literary imitation of Xenophon.

The tale of Hephaistion being mistaken by Sisygambis probably goes back to Kleitarchos.[76] Thus, he might have been the first to present Hephaistion as Alexander's acknowledged Second Self. However, there is no hint that he also depicted him as his Patroklos. Kleitarchos' positive portrayal of Hephaistion is assumed to be most clearly reflected in Diodoros' praise of him.[77] Most probably Kleitarchos is also the source for the story that Hephaistion was sent out by Alexander to choose a new king of Sidon (in Curtius' version) and thereby proves to be a wise, calm and reliable diplomat.[78]

The theme of the significant other was probably employed even earlier but in a negative way by Ephippos, who wrote *On the Death/Funeral of Alexander and Hephaistion* shortly after 323 BC.[79] This work is usually characterised as a hostile pamphlet of a disgruntled Olynthian written for disgruntled Greeks – such as, for example, the Thebans.[80] Ephippos commented on the un-Hellenic habits at Alexander's court, criticising the Macedonian drinking customs and attributing Alexander's death to the wrath of Dionysus because of Alexander's destruction of Thebes.[81] As Hephaistion might have died during the Dionysia,[82] the parallel was close at hand. Therefore, Ephippos may have echoed contemporary rumours. According to Aristoboulos, who had a special taste for prophecies and miracle stories, a seer promoted his business by boasting that he had foretold their deaths:

> Peithagoras then sacrificed first in regard to Hephaistion, and, as the lobe could not be seen on the liver of the victim, he reported this, and sealing his letter sent it to Apollodorus from Babylon to Ecbatana, showing that he had nothing to fear from Hephaistion, as in a short time he would be out of their way. Apollodorus received this letter, Aristobulos says, on the day before Hephaistion died. Then Peithagoras sacrificed again in regard to Alexander and again the liver of the victim had no lobe. Peithagoras wrote to Apollodorus in the same terms about Alexander.[83]

Thus, Alexander's death only about half a year after Hephaistion had passed away is the second major key element of the Doppelgänger theme: Alexander could not live without his Alter Ego and followed him: Hephaistion 'was the proverbial second self (...) in putting on the funeral (...) Alexander cannot avoid acting out a scene which presages his own death'.[84] Because of this underlying motif, the ancient reports on their deaths are to be treated with great caution: Hephaistion dies nearly the same way as Alexander does – reportedly, he drank about 3 litres of wine at breakfast time while being ill – and Alexander honours him like a dead king.[85] This suits the literary pattern so well that it raises suspicion. It is just too good to be true. The tradition that the ceremonies planned for Hephaistion were carried out for the late Alexander shows the extent to which their deaths were seen and styled as connected with each other.[86] The fragments of Ephippos' work, however, already reveal a certain negative twist. But the further development of this feature and manifest transformation into the story of a mutual moral decline and fall probably stem from Roman authors, namely Trogus and Curtius. Curtius in particular, possessing the literary skills to write a psychologically convincing story, may have been responsible for emphasising this negative twist, thereby creating the impression that Alexander's moral downfall was mirrored by the parallel decline of his Alter Ego.

It is most implausible that Kleitarchos was the original source for this unfavourable depiction of the two of them. Living in the Ptolemaic Egyptian realm – either under Ptolemy I or under Ptolemy IV – marked as the ideological core of the Hellenistic world by Ptolemy's entombment of Alexander's corpse there, Kleitarchos could not simply ignore the official guidelines of glorifying Alexander as Ptolemy's major source of legitimis-ation. Depicting Ptolemy's 'predecessor' as a victim of *hybris* turning into an un-Macedonian tyrant would have been in contrast to the image promoted by Ptolemy.[87] Kleitarchos could not have been that uninformed. Furthermore, as far as we can tell he obviously wanted to please and not to upset Ptolemy or one of his successors who conserved his cultural legacy and regarded Alexander as a token of their legitimisation.

Thus, it seems that Trogus and Curtius adopted the theme of Hephaistion as Alexander's Second Self from Kleitarchos but turned the originally positive narrative meant to emphasise Hephaistion's important role into something different and negative. It is difficult to guess how far Trogus went, since Justin's epitome is so abbreviated, but in any case, Curtius' work shows that he doubled Alexander's depravity by using Hephaistion as a mirror of his moral decline. First Alexander and Hephaistion were moderate students of philosophy; then they became infected by *hybris* and were transformed into nasty schemers with low morals. Consequently, Curtius' unique claim that they had been brought up and educated together falls into the context of the tent scene that established Hephaistion as Alexander's Second Self. According to the logic of the literary theme, their sharing a childhood and youth, as well as the same education, is dramaturgically necessary:

> He was by far the dearest to the king of all his friends; brought up with him, and the confidant of all his secrets, he also had more freedom than anyone else in admonishing him, a privilege which he nevertheless used in such a manner that it seemed rather to be allowed by the king than claimed by himself; and though Hephaistion was of the same age as the king, he nevertheless excelled him in bodily stature.[88]

Hephaistion is Alexander's mirror image, hence he had to share the same education. Next, Curtius shows the wise and moderate Hephaistion as Alexander's ambassador:

> Hephaistion was allowed to choose as king from among the Sidonians the one whom he thought most worthy of that high station. Hephaistion was the guest of two young men distinguished among their countrymen; when they were offered the privilege of ruling, they said that according to the custom of their country no one was admitted to that eminence unless born of royal stock. Hephaistion, admiring the lofty spirit that declined what others sought by fire and sword, said: 'Accept my congratulations, since you have been the first to appreciate how much greater it is to disdain royal power than to receive it.'[89]

There is a little ironic twist at the end when Hephaistion praises the intelligence of the men. Of course, Curtius' audience knew that this was not the way Alexander acted.

Curtius also shows Hephaistion the brave warrior mirroring Alexander's skills on the battlefield of Gaugamela:

> Hephaistion was struck in the arm by a spear (...) And if we wish justly to estimate the Macedonians of that day, we shall admit that their king was fully worthy of such subordinates, and they of so great a king.[90]

In Roman eyes, war injuries were a token of courage. However, true to the rhetorically influenced depravity story of Alexander, after Gaugamela, things changed. Curtius shows a Macedonian ruler overwhelmed by his successes becoming a tyrant. Mirroring his moral decline, Hephaistion appears to play a nasty role in the downfall of Philotas depicted by Curtius as a conspiracy against Philotas. Even worse, he transforms from the former ideal friend into Alexander's sexual plaything:

> Therefore he received the envoys of the Sacae courteously and gave them Euxenippus to accompany them; he was still very young and beloved to Alexander because of the flower of his youth. Although he equalled Hephaistion in the beauty of his body, he was certainly not equal to him in manly charm.[91]

By comparing him to this Euxenippos/Excipinus[92] whom Curtius is the only author to mention, he hints at an erotic relationship by employing pederastic phraseology.[93] Interestingly, this episode does not only offer insight into the cultural differences between Greeks and Romans but also into the way Curtius worked with his sources. It is the first time that he mentions Hephaistion's beauty. In contrast, Diodoros described him as beautiful – at least beautiful enough for the Great King's mother to mistake him as royal (according to the Greek ideal of the *kalokagathia*) – earlier in the context of the tent scene at Issos. Curtius only mentioned that Sisygambis mistook Hephaistion for the ruler because he was taller than Alexander. According to his narrative, at this point in time, Alexander and Hephaistion were still moderate decent persons unaffected by 'Eastern vices'. Hence, Curtius does not mention Hephaistion's physical beauty for a reason: in the Roman perspective this was not an attribute of the good commander. He had to be brave, wise, courageous and loyal but not beautiful. The Greek Diodoros, aware of the concept of *kalokagathia*, had no problem describing Hephaistion's good looks, probably regarding it as another token of his virtue. Curtius, however, postpones the information on Hephaistion's beauty and manly charms until his moral decline is in full bloom. Now, he could to turn Hephaistion's physical beauty against Hephaistion and Alexander by using it as another proof of their negative character development. He implies that it was first and foremost Hephaistion's beauty that attracted Alexander to him hinting at a sexual relationship. In Roman eyes, being the ruler's favourite was not appropriate behaviour for an army commander. Unfortunately Hephaistion's death scene is lost but Curtius might have taken the chance to emphasise the Second Self theme again by hinting at matters of alcohol. In summary, then, Curtius uses Hephaistion as a literary tool to emphasise Alexander's depravity. The boyhood friendship, Aristotelian education, and sexual relationship are elements of this literary pattern and do not deserve much credence.

Justin went one step further: 'Hephaistion, one of his friends, died who had been extremely dear to the king first because of his gifts of beauty and youth, then because of his willing servitude.'[94] This is the only reference to Hephaistion, who is not presented as a commander but reduced by the phrase *dotibus primo formae pueritiaeque, mox obsequiis regi percarus* to the image of Alexander's youthful sex-object. Either Justin deliberately omitted any comment by Trogus on Hephaistion's military exploits, or Trogus had already established this one-dimensional image. The use of the term *puer* for Hephaistion shows that Trogus-Justin alluded to the classical Greek pederastic concept translating it into Latin terms. There are also traces of this literary treatment of Hephaistion as Alexander's *erōmenos*, traditionally the younger part of a male couple, a teenager, in Aelian's comment:

> Note that Alexander laid a wreath on Achilles' tomb and Hephaistion on Patroclus', hinting that he was the object of Alexander's love, as Patroclus was of Achilles (...) A story circulates that these ceremonies while planned for Hephaistion, were carried out for Alexander on his death, because mourning for the young man *(meirakion)* was not yet completed when the death overtook Alexander.[95]

The claim that Hephaistion was very young is also expressed by the word *meirakion*.

To sum up, obviously, there is a traceable development: Hephaistion transforms from Alexander's best friend and capable general (Ptolemy; Kallisthenes?) into his Second Self (Kleitarchos?) who also drinks himself to death (Ephippos?), is his boyhood friend, fellow pupil and lover (Curtius) and finally his much younger boyfriend (Trogus-Justin; Aelian). It seems to be significant that the Greek authors depicting Hephaistion as Alexander's Second Self did so without the negative twist applied by the Roman authors.[96]

Diodoros: Closer to Kleitarchos' Version?

Diodoros depicts Hephaistion as Alexander's Second Self without the negative twist and thus may have been closer to Kleitarchos' narrative than Roman authors like Trogus and Curtius. In Diodoros, Hephaistion is portrayed as an important and loyal officer, especially during the Indian campaign. For example, Diodoros is silent on the fact that the friction between Krateros and Hephaistion made the separation of the troops on their way back from the Hydaspes necessary. However, he quotes a (probably spurious) letter by Hephaistion to Olympias in which he tells her quite arrogantly:

> Stop quarreling with us and do not be angry or menacing. If you persist, we shall not be much disturbed. You know that Alexander means more to us than anything.[97]

But, as Elizabeth Carney pointed out, this mainly serves to illustrate the alleged quarrelsome nature of Olympias without being directed against Hephaistion.[98] It is implied, though, that jealous Olympias even interferes with Alexander's best friend. Apart from these and other similar examples, Hephaistion seems most important to Diodoros when he dies and the theme of the Second Self reaches its climax. At this point, Diodoros feels the need to remind his audience of Hephaistion's special nature by retelling the tent story:

> At their first meeting with Darius' mother, when she from ignorance had bowed to Hephaistion supposing him to be the king and was distressed when this was called to her attention, Alexander had said: 'Never mind, mother. For actually he too is Alexander'.[99]

According to the Doppelgänger motif, Alexander is doomed to die. Conspicuously, he also fell ill with fever after heavy drinking. In addition, it is implied that it was a self-fulfilling prophecy as he seems to have provoked his early end by ordering the Persian sacred fire to be extinguished. Diodoros emphasises that this was the custom of the Persians only when their king died.[100] Perhaps the parallelism of their deaths led to Diodoros' mistake that Alexander gave the order to worship Hephaistion as a god while in fact he received cultic honours as a hero.[101]

Plutarch: Virtues and Vices
Due to Plutarch's aim to use Alexander as a moral example by creating a kind of (pseudo-) psychological profile, Hephaistion appears as a marker of either Alexander's virtues or his vices in his *Life of Alexander*. In the scattered information preserved by the *Moralia*, Hephaistion is a marker only of Alexander's virtues. Thus an example of Hephaistion serving as proof of Alexander's magnanimity and philosophical generosity can be found in the famous episode:

> Once, when he was reading a confidential letter from his mother, and Hephaistion, who, as it happened, was sitting beside him, was quite openly reading it too, Alexander did not stop him, but merely placed his own

signet-ring on Hephaistion's lips, sealing them to silence with a friend's confidence. 'Like a philosopher!'[102]

Plutarch seems to have regarded this exchange as a major proof of Alexander's virtue as he quotes it no fewer than four times in his work (once in the *Life of Alexander*, three times in the *Moralia*).[103] Another probably spurious letter written by Alexander to Hephaistion serves to prove that Alexander was an ideal friend according to the demands of Greek philosophy:

> And yet in the most trifling attentions which he paid his familiar friends there were marks of great good-will and esteem (...) To Hephaistion, who was absent on some business, he wrote that while they were diverting themselves with hunting an ichneumon, Craterus encountered the lance of Perdiccas and was wounded in the thighs (...) And it is astonishing that he had time to write so many letters for his friends.[104]

Presumably, the comment on the lance encountering Krateros' thighs while hunting this peculiar animal indicates that this in fact was an indecent joke.[105] The letter might have been made up by an anonymous later author, who regarded it as funny to imagine that Alexander spent his leisure time writing naughty letters to Hephaistion while the latter was on a mission.

In the *Life of Alexander*, Hephaistion appears as a marker also of Alexander's depravity in the context of the 'orientalisation' of his court. Plutarch attributes these tendencies partly to the bad influence of his flatterers.[106] In this context, Hephaistion is mentioned as one of the schemers responsible for Philotas' downfall. Thus he forms part of the vicious circle controlling Philotas' torture.[107] Furthermore, he is said to have organised the introduction of *proskynēsis* and to have denounced Kallisthenes.[108] In addition, Plutarch mentions that Hephaistion quarrelled with Eumenes and Krateros and finally fell ill after an excessive un-Greek drinking session.[109] At least, he is the only source providing the alternative tradition that Hephaistion died from food poisoning from a rotten chicken.[110] Alexander's grief is also characterised as excessive and un-Greek, culminating in the execution of Hephaistion's doctor and the slaying of the Cossaeans.[111] Hence, in Plutarch, the portrait of Hephaistion is completely dependent on the portrait of Alexander: Hephaistion mirrors Alexander's moral development.

A time for romance? Arrian and the Patroklos theme

Arrian knew about the tradition presenting Hephaistion as Alexander's lover. His teacher Epiktetos, whose lessons Arrian had collected and published, applied the term *erōmenos* to Hephaistion.[112] Arrian also knew the reports by Ptolemy, Kleitarchos, and Aristoboulos. He claimed to aim at reconstructing a neutral and sober image of Alexander, doing justice to his deeds as a conqueror. However, Arrian's portrait of Alexander was also coloured by his own socio-cultural concepts of the ideal emperor or king.[113] Arrian also seems to have been been heavily influenced by his own experience serving under Hadrian and by the latter's patronage of Greek culture.[114] In regard to the depiction of Hephaistion and his relationship to Alexander, Arrian seems to have gone his own way. Thus, it is possible that Arrian himself inserted the romantic Patroklos *topos* into Alexander's relationship with Hephaistion. It is important to notice that he was aware of the erotic implications attributed to Achilles and Patroklos in the Greek literary tradition.[115]

Arrian stated that he wanted to rely mainly on Ptolemy and Aristoboulos, but made exceptions to this rule, especially in the case of Hephaistion, where in three distinct sections Arrian chose to mention a version that was not confirmed by his main sources: first when Alexander allegedly placed a wreath on Patroklos' tomb at Ilion;[116] second during the famous tent scene at Issos;[117] and third when describing Alexander's expressions of grief when Hephaistion died:

> I regard it as not unlikely that Alexander cut off his hair over the corpse, especially considering his emulation of Achilles, with whom he had a rivalry from boyhood.[118]

It is unlikely that Arrian invented this comparison – he was not the first to mention it – but he seems to have elaborated it in a very influential way.[119] Philip Stadter has cleverly suggested that Arrian was thinking of Hadrian and his lover Antinous while describing Alexander and Hephaistion.[120] In this case Arrian's Macedonian couple would in fact have been the romanticised idea of a Roman couple disguised as a 'modernised' version of a Homeric couple, thus very far away indeed from the historical Hephaistion and Alexander.

Three to tango: Lucian's ironic contribution

Arrian's contemporary, the Syrian satirist Lucian, may have known him personally from Athens. In any case he obviously knew his work and mocked his far-fetched literary ambitions as well as prominent aspects of his image of Alexander.[121] In a famous *ekphrasis*,[122] intended to win the hearts of all the Macedonians at once, Lucian describes a painting by the Greek artist Aëtion showing Alexander's wedding night with Roxane.[123] It is important to keep in mind that the *ekphrasis* is embedded in a context of satire and irony:[124]

The scene is a very beautiful chamber, and in it there is a bridal couch with Roxane, a very lovely maiden, sitting upon it, her eyes cast down in modesty, for Alexander is standing there. There are smiling Cupids: one is standing behind her removing the veil from her head and showing Roxane to her husband; another like a true servant is taking the sandal off her foot, already preparing her for bed; a third Cupid has hold of Alexander's *chlamys* and is pulling him with all his might towards Roxane. The king himself is holding out a garland to the maiden and their best man and helper, Hephaistion, is there with a blazing torch in his hand, leaning on a very handsome youth – I think he is Hymenaeus (his name is not inscribed). On the other side of the picture are more Cupids playing among Alexander's armour (...) All this is not needless triviality and a waste of labour. Aëtion is calling attention to Alexander's other love – war – implying that in his love for Roxane he did not forget his armour.[125]

Of course, in Lucian's day, when Macedonian glory had long since faded, it was a good idea to speak about the most successful warrior king who had developed into an iconic figure. Probably the Macedonians (and Romans) would have appreciated a description of Alexander victorious in battle. But Lucian chooses an event that was highly unpopular with the Macedonians: Alexander's marriage to a nameless barbarian whose father and allies he failed to defeat in battle.[126] Furthermore, Lucian makes clear that the reluctant bridegroom has to be dragged with force towards his bride by one of the *erōtes*, away from his beautiful male companions,[127] Hephaistion holding a torch and the pretty youth who according to Lucian might be Hymenaeus, the god of marriage. However, usually Hymenaeus is depicted with a torch. Thus, perhaps the lovely youngster (*meirakion*) whom the person with the torch leans on is in fact meant to be Hephaistion. Hence, the question is raised as to why Hymenaeus seems to link Hephaistion and Alexander rather than Alexander and Roxane.

Such an *ekphrasis* would surely not have pleased any Macedonian audience. I have suggested that Lucian satirises Aëtion's actual painting showing the wedding of Ninos and Semiramis mentioned by Pliny.[128] Probably an old woman carrying the torch also formed part of this painting. Thus, it is possible that Lucian mocks the romanticised perception of Alexander and Hephaistion in his days as presented by Arrian.[129]

Conclusions

There is no proof that Alexander and Hephaistion were boyhood friends or fellow pupils. We do not even know whether Hephaistion grew up at the court in Pella. Perhaps he joined the campaign just at its beginning in 334. Certainly, the historical Hephaistion would have been militarily and politically very important for Alexander during the Asian campaign, but since Alexander and the contemporary sources did not tell the public about the nature of their private relationship, any speculation about a possible love affair probably brought up by the Romans is useless.[130] None of these features can be traced back to Alexander's own political self-fashioning. Indeed, much of what we have now accepted about Hephaistion was mainly influenced by Hellenistic and Roman receptions, such as the Doppelgänger theme, the Patroklos theme, and the assumption that he had been Alexander's *erōmenos*. In any case, as I have attempted to show here, Hephaistion's image should be separated from Alexander's. Unlike our sources, we must try to treat him as an autonomous person and move beyond literary concepts like that of the 'Second Self'.

Acknowledgements

I am grateful to Liz Baynham, Reinhold Bichler, Malcolm Davies, Waldemar Heckel, Johannes Heinrichs, Tim Howe, Frances Pownall, Anneli Purchase, Kai Ruffing and Gerhard Wirth for their kind support and helpful advice.

Notes

[1] On Hephaistion see Müller 2014, 218–23; Heckel 2013; Müller 2013a, 2011b; 2011c; Heckel 2009, 133–7; 1992, 65–90; Wirth 1967.

[2] Cf. Ogden 2012, 157–67; 2009, 210–12; Reames-Zimmerman 1999, 92; Heckel 1993, 65–6; Hamilton 1969, 130; Wirth 1967, 1022; Berve 1926, 173.

[3] Cf. Reames-Zimmerman 1999; Hamilton 1969, 130.

[4] Arr. *An.* 3.27.4; 5.20.6; 5.21.2–6; 6.28.3–4; Plut. *Alex.* 47.5; Diod. 17.91.1–2; Curt. 8.12.6.

[5] Heckel 2006, 133–4. See also Bosworth 1980a, 364–5.

[6] Badian 1958, 150.

[7] Badian 1998, 350. Cf. Hamilton 1969, 131.

[8] Schachermeyr 1973, 512.

[9] Heckel 1992, 72–3, 83.

[10] Heckel 2006, 133.

[11] Carney 1975, 221.

[12] Green 1970, 253.

[13] Arr. *An.* 7.14.2. Translation: P.A. Brunt.

[14] Arr. *An.* 6.28.4.

[15] IG II² 405. Cf. Heckel 1991. The probable links of Hephaistion's family to Athens might perhaps help to explain why Demosthenes sent his intimate Aristion to Hephaistion in 332/1 BC for the sake of securing reconciliation with Alexander (Marsyas, *FGrHist* 135/6 F2; cf. Aeschin. 3.162). Cf. Heckel 2006, 133. Athenian connections might also be the reason for the unusual name of Amyntor's son as there are some contemporary individuals called Hephaistion attested at Athens, cf. Fraser/Matthews 1994, 208. Probably, the name had something to do with the sanctuary of Hephaistos at the Agora of Athens (Paus. 1.14.6; Harpokration

κ 27) and his special veneration. On the myth connecting Hephaistos and Athena, see Apollodor. *Bibl.* 3.14.6.

[16] Cf. Heckel 2006, 133 (based on Diod. 17.61.3). For Admetus' death see Arr. *An.* 2.23.5; Diod. 17.45.6.

[17] See Howe 2015 for Ptolemy's early emphasis on his importance to Alexander's military successes.

[18] Arr. *An.* 3.27.4.

[19] Arr. *An.* 1.12.1; 2.12.6; probably also 7.14.4.

[20] Curt. 9.10.6; Arr. *An.* 7.4.5; 5.6; Diod. 17.107.6.

[21] Atkinson 2009, 154.

[22] Cf. Wirth 1967, 1023. See also Olbrycht 2004, 47. Cf. Arr. *An.* 7.4.5.

[23] Arr. *An.* 3.6.5; Plut. *Alex.* 10.4. Cf. Heckel 2006, 235.

[24] On Onesikritos see Müller 2012; Heckel 2006, 183–4; Winiarczyk 2007; Pédech 1984, 71–157; Pearson 1960, 83–111.

[25] Cf. Hammond 1993, 58; Pédech 1984, 77, 98–9; Hamilton 1969, liii.

[26] Cf. Müller 2011c, 433–4, 438–40; Heckel 1992, 67.

[27] Polyaen. 4,3,27. Marsyas of Pella, a half-brother of Antigonos, who is regarded as an insider mentions that in 331 Demosthenes sent his young favourite Aristeion to Hephaistion in order to negotiate a reconciliation with Alexander (*FGrH* 135 F2). Cf. Müller 2011c, 437–8; Heckel 2006, 46, 110; Berve 1926, 170.

[28] Cf. Müller 2013a; 2011c, 443–4.

[29] Arr. *An.* 1.8.1; 21.1–3. Cf. Errington 1969; Berve 1926, 335. *Contra*: Roisman 1984, 375–85; Ellis 2002, 21.

[30] Cf. Bosworth 1995, 281; Errington 1969, 234–42.

[31] For example, he is responsible for the important task of crossing of rivers, namely the Indus (Arr. *An.* 4.22.7; 4.28.5; 5.3.5; Curt. 8.10.2.; 8.12.4). Cf. Rollinger 2013, 9. See also his mission in Arr. *An.* 6.20.1.

[32] Cf. Müller 2014, 84–8; Müller 2011b, 444.

[33] Marriage with Roxane: Curt. 8.4.24–30; Arr. *An.* 4.19.5–6; Kleitos: Arr. *An.* 4.8.9 (cf. Rabe 1964, 109–11); *contra*: Curt. 7.1.45–46. Cf. Berve 1926, 331.

[34] Howe 2008; 2015.

[35] Arr. *An.* 4.8.4–9; 6.11.8; Curt. 8.1.43–47; 9.5.21.

[36] Cf. Wirth 1993a, 346, n. 300: Hephaistion had a leading command. See also Pearson 1960, 208: Ptolemy's report on the siege of the town of the Malloi was of an unusually unspecific nature.

[37] Arr. *An.* 6.5.5. 6.2–3; 13.1.

[38] Arr. *An.* 6.11.8; Curt. 9.5.21.

[39] Cf. Pearson 1960, 191.

[40] Cf. Müller 2003, 191–2.

[41] Arr. *An.* 6.6.4–6; 9.1–2.

[42] Arr. *An.* 6.23–26.

[43] Cf. Fraser/Matthews, 2005, 160; Pape/Benseler 1959, 476.

[44] Sel. Pap. I 97 (a soldier in the army of the Ptolemies in 168 BC); the *epistratēgos* of Thebes Hephaistion under Ptolemy XI (cf. Huß 2001, 700); the Alexandrian metrician Hephaistion of the second century AD; Hephaistion of Thebes, the author of an astrological work in the fourth century AD; Ptolemaios Chennos or

Ptolemaios Hephaistion from Alexandria living in the first century AD, whose father is said to have borne the name Hephaistion too. However, according to Lucian (*Pro Im.* 27), in his day many people were called Hephaistion. But this is difficult to confirm. Lucian mentions this in the context of criticising the ambitions of human beings to bear the names of the gods: 'But how many there are who have copied the very names of the gods, calling themselves Dionysius, Hephaistion, Zeno, Poseidonius, Hermes!' (translation: A. M. Harmon).

[45] Arr. *An.* 7.23.6–8 mentions this in the mysterious letter to Kleomenes whose authenticity is debated. According to this letter, Alexander wanted a hero's shrine to be built in Alexandria and on the isle of Pharos and that his name should be written into the contracts of traders. Pearson 1954/55, 449–50 even thinks that the letter was forged by Ptolemy.

[46] There are traces of Hephaistion's cult only at Athens and Pella. Cf. Palagia 2000, 168; Bosworth 1996, 129; Treves 1939. Interestingly, the name Hephaistion continues to exist in Athens for centuries, cf. Fraser/Matthews 1994, 208. Hypereides also seems to attest the existence of Hephaistion's cult at Athens. Polemically, he gets exasperated with the Macedonians' impertinence in forcing the Athenians to venerate their 'household slaves' (οἰκέται) (Hyp. 6.21). Of course, the plural is an exaggeration.

[47] Curt. 6.8.17; 6.11.10; Plut *Alex.* 49.6–7; 55.1. Cf. Arr. *An.* 3.26.1–2; 27.4; 4.14.3–4. Cf. Badian 2000, 64–75. On Curtius' version see also Rollinger 2009, 266–71.

[48] *Contra*: Atkinson 1994, 212–46.

[49] Cf. Howe 2008.

[50] Cf. Müller 2011c, 159–62.

[51] Arr. *An.* 3.27.4 (hipparch); 6.28.4; Diod. 17.61.3 (*sōmatophylax*); Arr. *An.* 7.14.9–10 (chiliarch).

[52] Cf. Müller 2011c, 440–1; Briant 2010, 74; Bosworth 1980b, 5, A. 34, 14. *Contra* Meeus 2009, 303, 308, 310.

[53] Cf. Meeus 2009, 302–3. See also Heckel 2006, 136; Bosworth 1988b, 276; Errington 1969, 240; Wirth 1967, 1023.

[54] Arr. *An.* 7.14.9–10. Translation: P.A. Brunt. It was certainly not the type of chiliarchy Curt. (5.2.3) mentions while obviously thinking of models provided by Xenophon. Cf. Lenfant 2011, 358. See also Arr. *An.* 5.23.7.

[55] Diod. 18.48.4. Cf. Arr. *Succ.* 1ª.3.

[56] Atkinson 2009, 20.

[57] Cf. Atkinson 2009, 21; Zambrini 2006, 216; Baynham 2003, 10; Wirth 1993, 202; Stoneman 1997, 4.

[58] Cf. Beresford/Parsons/Pobjoy 2007, 27–36. See also Parker 2009, 28–55. The new dating is rejected by Prandi 2012.

[59] Cf. Müller 2013a.

[60] Cf. Müller 2003, 31–2; Reames-Zimmerman 1998, 67; Heckel 1985, 289.

[61] See Wirth 1993b.

[62] Cf. Zambrini 2006, 216; Prandi 1996, 84–148; Bosworth 1976, 1.

[63] Diog. Laert. 5.27. The reliability of Diogenes Laertios here is a significant problem, since the letter to Hephaistion is listed among other letters by Aristotle

to members of Alexander's family and entourage, such as Olympias and Philip, who were certainly not his pupils. The genre and context have been hopelessly confused.

[64] Cf. Müller 2011b, 120–4; 2011c, 445–51.

[65] Cf. Müller 2011b, 117–24.

[66] Cf. Rank 1993, 115–17.

[67] Cf. Keppler 1972, 200–1.

[68] I would like to thank Malcolm Davies for pointing out to me that Hephaistion as the companion of a descendant of Heracles might have also been styled by ancient authors as the second Heracles applied proverbially to Theseus, who is sometimes represented as ally or collaborator in Heracles' adventures. Cf. Erbse 1950, 102, 158.

[69] Curt. 3.12.15–26; Diod. 17.37.5–38.2; 114.2; Arr. *An.* 2.12.5–8. Cf. Val. Max. 4.7ext. 2a; Suda s.v. Hephaistion (660 Adler). Cf. Bosworth 1980a, 222.

[70] Diod. 17.37.5–38.2. Translation: C. B. Welles. Diodoros calls her Sisyngambris, Curtius Sisygambis.

[71] Cf. Bosworth 1980, 222.

[72] Arist. *Eth. Nic.* 1156 B, 1157 B, 1159 B; Diog. Laert. 5.20; Plut. *Mor.* 93 E. Cf. Konstan 1997, 42, 75.

[73] Cf. Atkinson 1980, 250.

[74] Arr. *An.* 2.12.5–6. Translation: P.A. Brunt.

[75] Xen. *Cyr.* 5.1.7. Cf. Müller 2014, 49. On the impact of the *Cyropaedia* see Rollinger 2014, 169–70. On Cyrus II as Alexander's Persian role model see Olbrycht 2014, 52–7; Müller 2011a, 113–17; Briant 2010, 110–11; Wiesehöfer 2005, 150; Wiesehöfer 1994, 36.

[76] Cf. Baynham 1998, 80; McKechnie 2005, 431.

[77] Diod. 17.37.5–6; 17.114.2.

[78] Curt. 4.1.16–18. Cf. Plut. *Mor.* 340 C–D (Paphos); Diod. 17.47.1–4 (Tyros). Justin (11.10.9) locates it in Sidon, too, but does not mention Hephaistion. According to him, Alexander himself enthroned the king. Cf. Müller 2011c, 437; Atkinson 1980, 278–83.

[79] Ath. 4.146 C–D; 10.434 A–B; 12.537 D.

[80] Cf. Pearson 1960, 64–7.

[81] Ath. 3.120 C–E. Cf. Müller 2011c, 449; Heckel 1992, 88; Mossman 1988, 91; Bosworth 1988a, 173–84; Mederer 1936, 97–8, 137–8, 162.

[82] Cf. Wirth 1967, 1023.

[83] Arr. *An.* 7.18.2–3. Translation: P. A. Brunt. Cf. Plut. *Alex.* 73.2 (Pythagoras); App. *BC* 2,152. See Heckel 2006, 40–41, 194; Yardley and Heckel 1997, 279; Mederer 1936, 124–6.

[84] McKechnie 1995, 418–19.

[85] Diod. 17.110.7–8; Arr. *An.* 7.14.1; 7.14.4; Polyaen. 4.3.31; Plut. *Alex.* 72.1–2. Cf. Bosworth 1988a, 171–2, 176–7.

[86] Ael. *VH* 7.8. Cf. McKechnie 1995, 418–19.

[87] His successors adopted and continued to promote this image: in Alexandrian court poetry, Alexander is still a glorious hero: Poseidipp. *Ep.* 31 AB; 65 AB. Cf. Müller 2014, 247–53; Lianou 2010.

[88] Curt. 3.12.15–16. Translation: J.C. Rolfe.

[89] Curt. 4.1.16–18. Translation: J.C. Rolfe. Cf. Müller 2011c, 446.

[90] Curt. 4.16.32–33. Translation: J.C. Rolfe.

[91] Curt. 7.9.19. Translation: D. Ogden. The *aetatis flore* (flower of youth) mentioned by Curtius (or *pueritiae flore*) is often connected with implications of pederastic sexual attraction. Cf. Yardley 2003, 111.

[92] There are variants of his name in the manuscripts: *euxenippon; excipinon*. H. E. Foss (1851) suggests *escipinon*. K. Müller and H. Schönfeld (1954) read *elpinicon*. E. Hedicke (1867) suggested Euxenippos and is followed by Rolfe (1946), LCL, vol. II, 210, n. 3. Cf. Ogden 2009, 211, n. 58; Reames-Zimmerman 1999, 91. On Euxenippos, see Heckel 1992, 291–2; Berve 1926, 158.

[93] Cf. Müller 2014, 142, n. 742; Müller 2011c, 447–8; Ogden 2009, 210–11, n. 59. Curtius seems to imply that this Euxenippos/Excinipus formed part of a certain kind of 'escort service'. In any case, in Roman eyes, he was not an honourable companion for a group of ambassadors.

[94] Just. 12.12.11–12. Translation: J. C. Yardley.

[95] Ael. *VH*. 12.7; 7.8. Translation: G. P. Goold.

[96] On Greek versus Roman attitudes to Alexander, see Asirvatham 2010, 99–124.

[97] Diod. 17.114.3. Translation: C. B. Welles.

[98] Cf. Carney 2006, 57, 167, n. 108; 2003, 240.

[99] Diod. 17.114.2. Translation: C. B. Welles. Cf. McKechnie 1995, 418–19.

[100] Diod. 17.114.4–5. Cf. Brosius 2003, 181; Palagia 2000, 168.

[101] Diod. 17.115.6; cf. Luc. *Cal.* 17; Just. 12.12.12. Correct: Arr. *An.* 7.23.6; Plut. *Alex.* 75.2–3; *Pelop.* 34.2. Cf. *Bull. Ép.* 1992, no. 309 (around 325–300 BC): Διογένης Ηφαιστίωνι ἥρως. Cf. Palagia 2000, 168, n. 6; Bosworth 1996, 129; Hammond 1989, 234; Treves 1939, 56–7.

[102] Plut. *Mor.* 332 F–333 A. Translation: F. C. Babbitt.

[103] Plut. *Mor.* 180 D; 332 F– 333 A; 339 F– 340 A; *Alex.* 39.5. Cf. Carney 2006, 57, 126, 133.

[104] Plut. *Alex.* 41.2–3; 42.1. Translation: B. Perrin.

[105] An *ichneumōn*, also known as an Egyptian mongoose, is a little slender long-tailed animal able to rise up quickly by stiffening his back: Aristot. *HA* 612 A; Ael. *NA* 6.38.

[106] Plut. *Mor.* 60 B–C; 65 C–F.

[107] Plut. *Alex.* 49.6–7.

[108] Plut. *Alex.* 55.1.

[109] Plut. *Eum.* 2.1–2; 2.4–5; 3.1–2; *Alex.* 47,5–7; *Mor.* 337 A. Cf. Arr. *An.* 7.13.1; 7.14.9.

[110] Plut. *Alex.* 72.1–2.

[111] Plut. *Alex.* 72.1–3.

[112] Epict. 2.22.17. Cf. Arr. *An.* 7.14.5–6.

[113] *Contra*: Pearson 1960, 188.

[114] On Arrian and Hadrian see Syme 1982, 190, 203, 208–9.

[115] Arr. *Per.* 23.4. Cf. Stadter 1980, 38–9. Aeschin. 1.133; 1.142–144; Plat. *Symp.* 179 E–180 B. Cf. Konstan 1997, 37.

[116] Arr. *An.* 1.12.1. Cf. Ael. *VH* 12.7. Interestingly, in his *Periplus of the Euxine*

Sea, Arrian mentions that on the 'island of Achilles' (*Per.* 21.1–23.4), Achilles and Patroklos are honoured with equal respect by offerings and inscriptions. On the *Periplus* see Bosworth 1993, 242–4.

[117] Arr. *An.* 2.12.5–8.

[118] Arr. *An.* 7.11.14.

[119] Cf. Müller 2011c, 452–3.

[120] Cf. Stadter 1980, 39, 169.

[121] Luc. *Alex.* 2. Cf. Müller 2013b.

[122] Cf. Müller 2011b, 125–6; Noll 2005, 33–5.

[123] Luc. *Hdt.* 7–8.

[124] Ironically, Lucian compares himself to Herodotus who allegedly tried the same in Greece by reading his *Histories* to the masses in Olympia as 'the quickest and least troublesome path to fame and a reputation for both himself and his works (...): This was the shortcut to glory'. (Luc. *Hdt.* 1.3. Translation: K. Kilburn). Lucian's satire is manifest: According to him, Herodotus chose the *opisthodon*, the backside of the temple for his ambitious plan–where in fact nobody could see him. Consequently, this anecdote is regarded as fictitious. Cf. Erbse 1955, 102–3.

[125] Luc. *Hdt.* 5–6. Translation: K. Kilburn.

[126] Curt. 8.4.30; 10.6.13–14.

[127] Cf. Stewart 2003, 41.

[128] Plin. *NH* 35.78. Cf. Bröker and Müller 2004, 5. In the Greco-Roman literary tradition, Semiramis appears as a 'femme en habit d'homme', producing a decadent son, Ninyas, with her husband. Cf. Azoulay/Sébillote Cuchet 2011, 116.

[129] Cf. Müller 2011c, 439–40. It would not have been the first time that he makes fun of Arrian and his literary ambitions and pretensions, cf. Luc. *Alex.* 2. See Müller 2013b; Whitmarsh 2005, 68, n. 43; Wirth 1964, 233; *PIR²* T 210.

[130] In addition, Hephaistion was not styled as his Patroklos in Alexander's propaganda, because, as Waldemar Heckel has shown, Alexander himself never imitated Achilles systematically (Heckel 2015). Accepted by Müller 2011a, 433; 2011b, 121. *Contra* Ameling 1988.

Bibliography

Ameling, W.
    1988   'Alexander und Achilleus', in W. Will and J. Heinrichs (eds) *Zu Alexander d. Gr. FS G. Wirth, II*, Amsterdam, 657–92.

Atkinson, J. E.
    1980, 1994, 2009 *A Commentary on Q. Curtius Rufus' Historiae Alexandri Magni, Books 3 and 4; 5 to 7,2; 10*, Amsterdam; Oxford.

Asirvatham, S.
    2010   'Perspectives on the Macedonians from Greece, Rome and Beyond', in J. Roisman and I. Worthington (eds) *Blackwell's Companion to Ancient Macedonia*, London, 99–124.

Azoulay, V. and Sébillote, V.
    2011   'Parures, genre et politique: les vêtements comme opérateur dans les

Persika de Ctésias', in L. Bodiou et al. (eds) *Parures et artifice: Le corps exposé dans l'Antiquité*, Paris, 113–28.

Badian, E.
   1958   'The Eunuch Bagoas', *CQ* 8, 144–57.
   1998   'Hephaistion', *DNP* 5, 350.
   2000   'Conspiracies', in A. B. Bosworth and E. Baynham (eds) *Alexander the Great in Fact and Fiction*, Oxford, 50–95.
Baynham, E.
   1998   *Alexander the Great. The Unique History of Quintus Curtius*, Ann Arbor.
Beresford, A. G., Parsons, P. J. and Pobjoy, M. P.
   2007   '4808. On Hellenistic Historians', *POxy LXXI*, London, 27–36.
Berve, H.
   1926   *Das Alexanderreich auf prosopographischer Grundlage, II*, Munich.
Bosworth, A. B.
   1976   'Arrian and the Alexander Vulgate', in A. B. Bosworth and D. van Berchem (eds) *Alexandre le Grand. Image et réalité*, Geneva, 1–46.
   1980a, 1995 *A Historical Commentary on Arrian's History of Alexander*, 2 vols., Oxford.
   1980b 'Alexander and the Iranians', *JHS* 100, 1–21.
   1988a *From Arrian to Alexander*, Oxford.
   1988b *Conquest and Empire*, Cambridge.
   1993   'Arrian and Rome: The Minor Scripts', *ANRW* II 34.1, 226–75.
   1996   *Alexander and the East. The Tragedy of Triumph*, Oxford.
Briant, P.
   2010   *Alexander the Great and his Empire*, Princeton.
Bröker, G. and Müller, W.
   2004   'Aëtion', *AKL*, 5–6.
Brosius, M.
   2003   'Alexander and the Persians', in J. Roisman (ed.) *Brill's Companion to Alexander the Great*, Leiden, 169–93.
Carney, E. D.
   1975   *Alexander the Great and the Macedonian Aristocracy*, Ph.D. Dissertation, Duke University.
   2003   'Women in Alexander's Court', in J. Roisman (ed.) *Brill's Companion to Alexander the Great*, Leiden, 227–52.
   2006   *Olympias, Mother of Alexander the Great*, London and New York.
Ellis, W. M.
   2002   *Ptolemy of Egypt*, London and New York.
Erbse, H.
   1950   *Untersuchungen zu den attizistischen Lexica*, Berlin.
   1955   'Vier Bemerkungen zu Herodot', *RhM* 98, 99–120.
Errington, R. M.
   1969   'Bias in Ptolemy's *History of Alexander*', *CQ* 19, 233–42.
Fraser, P. M. and Matthews, E.
   1994; 2005 *A Lexicon of Greek Personal Names, II: Attica; IV: Macedonia, Thrace, Northern Regions of the Black Sea*, Oxford.

Green, P.
1970   *Alexander the Great*, London.
Hamilton, J.R.
1969   *Plutarch, Alexander. A Commentary*, Oxford.
Hammond, N. G. L.
1993   *Sources for Alexander the Great*, Cambridge.
1989   *The Macedonian State*, Oxford.
Heckel, W.
1978   'The *somatophylakes* of Alexander the Great', *Historia* 27, 224–8.
1985   'The Boyhood Friends of Alexander the Great', *Emerita* 53, 285–9.
1991   'Hephaistion "the Athenian"', *ZPE* 87, 39–41.
1992   *The Marshals of Alexander's Empire*, London and New York.
2003   'King and "Companions"', in J. Roisman (ed.) *Brill's Companion to Alexander the Great*, Leiden, 197–225.
2006   *Who's Who in the Age of Alexander the Great*, Oxford.
2013   'Hephaistion, Macedonian', *EAH*, 3132–3.
2015   'Alexander, Achilleus, and Heracles: Between Myth and History', in Baynham, E. and Wheatley, P. (eds), *East and West in the World Empire of Alexander: Essays in honour of Brian Bosworth*, Oxford, 21–33.
Howe, T.
2008   'Alexander in India: Ptolemy as Near Eastern Historiographer', in T. Howe and J. Reames (eds) *Macedonian Legacies*, Claremont, CA, 215–33.
2015   'Introducing Ptolemy: Alexander at the Persian Gates', in W. Heckel, S. Müller, G. Wrightson (eds) *The Many Faces of War in the Ancient World*, Newcastle upon Tyne, 168–97.
Huß, W.
2001   *Ägypten in hellenistischer Zeit 332–30 v. Chr.*, Munich.
Keppler, C. F.
1972   *The Literature of the Second Self*, Tucson.
Konstan, D.
1997   *Friendship in the Classical World*, Cambridge.
Lenfant, D.
2011   *Les Perses vus par les Grecs*, Paris.
McKechnie, P.
1995   'Diodorus Siculus and Hephaistion's Pyre', *CQ* 45, 418–32.
Mederer, E.
1936   *Die Alexanderlegenden bei den ältesten Alexanderhistorikern*, Stuttgart.
Meeus, A.
2009   'Some Institutional Problems concerning the Succession to Alexander the Great', *Historia* 58, 287–310.
Mossman, J. M.
1988   'Tragedy and Epic in Plutarch's *Alexander*', *JHS* 108, 83–93.
Müller, S.
2003   *Maßnahmen der Herrschaftssicherung gegenüber der makedonischen Opposition bei Alexander dem Großen*, Frankfurt.

2011a 'Die frühen Perserkönige im kulturellen Gedächtnis der Makedonen und in der Propaganda Alexanders d. Gr.', *Gymnasium* 118, 105–33.

2011b 'Der doppelte Alexander der Große', *Amaltea* 3, 115–38 (http://www.ucm.es/info/amaltea/revista/num3/muller.pdf).

2011c 'In Abhängigkeit von Alexander? Hephaistion bei den Alexanderhistoriographen', *Gymnasium* 118, 429–56.

2012 'Onesikritos und das Achaimenidenreich', *Anabasis* 2, 45–66.

2013a 'Ptolemaios und die Erinnerung an Hephaistion', *Anabasis* 3, 75–92.

2013b 'Trügerische Bilder? Lukians Umgang mit Tyrannen- und Orienttopoi in seinen Hadesszenen', *Gymnasium* 120, 169–92.

2014 *Alexander, Makedonien und Persien*, Berlin.

Noll, T.

2005 *Alexander der Große in der nachantiken bildenden Kunst*, Mainz.

Ogden, D.

2009 'Alexander's Sex Life', in W. Heckel and L. A. Tritle (eds) *Alexander the Great. A New History*, Oxford, 203–17.

2012 *Alexander the Great. Myth, Genesis and Sexuality*, Exeter.

Olbrycht, M. J.

2004 *Alexander Wielki i swiat iranski*, Rzeszów.

2014 '"An Admirer of Persian Ways": Alexander the Great's Reforms in Parthia-Hyrcania and the Iranian Heritage', in T. Daryaee et al. (eds) *Excavating an Empire. Achaemenid Persia in Longue Durée*, Costa Mesa, 37–62.

Palagia, O.

2000 'Hephaestion's Pyre and the Royal Hunt of Alexander', in A. B. Bosworth and E. Baynham (eds) *Alexander the Great in Fact and Fiction*, Oxford, 167–206.

Pape, W. and Benseler, G. E.

1959 *Wörterbuch der griechischen Eigennamen*, Graz.

Parker, V.

2009 'Source-Critical Reflections on Cleitarchus' Work', in P. Wheatley and R. Hannah (eds) *Alexander and His Successors. Essays from the Antipodes*, Claremont, 28–55.

Pearson, L.

1954/55 'The Diary and Letters of Alexander the Great', *Historia* 3, 429–54.

1960 *The Lost Histories of Alexander the Great*, New York and Oxford.

Pédech, P.

1984 *Historiens compagnons d'Alexandre*, Paris.

Prandi, L.

1996 *Fortuna e realtà dell'opera di Clitarco*, Stuttgart.

2012 'New Evidence for the Dating of Cleitarchus (*POxy* LXXI.4808)?' *Histos* 6, 15–26.

Rabe, I.

1964 *Quellenkritische Untersuchungen zu Plutarchs Alexanderbiographie.* Ph.D. Dissertation, Hamburg University.

Rank, O.

1993 *Der Doppelgänger. Eine psychoanalytische Studie*, Vienna.

Reames-Zimmerman, J.
   1998   *Hephaistion Amyntoros: Eminence Grise at the Court of Alexander the Great*, Ph.D. Dissertation, Pennsylvania State University.
   1999   'An Atypical Affair? Alexander the Great, Hephaistion Amyntoros and the Nature of their Relationship', *AHB* 13, 81–96.
   2010   'The Cult of Hephaistion', in P. Cartledge and F. Greenland (eds) *Responses to Oliver Stone's Alexander*, Madison, 183–217.
Roisman, J.
   1984   'Ptolemy and his Rivals in his History of Alexander', *CQ* 34, 373–85.
Rollinger, R.
   2013   *Alexander und die großen Ströme. Die Flussüberquerungen im Lichte altorientalischer Piorniertechniken*, Wiesbaden.
   2014   'Das teispidisch-achaimenidische Imperium', in M. Gehler and R. Rollinger (eds) *Imperien und Reiche in der Weltgeschichte*, I, Wiesbaden, 149–92.
Schachermeyr, F.
   1973   *Alexander der Große*, Vienna.
Stadter, P. A.
   1980   *Arrian of Nicomedia*, Chapel Hill.
Stewart, A.
   1993   *Faces of Power*, Berkeley.
   2003   'Alexander the Great in Greek and Roman Art', in J. Roisman (ed.) *Brill's Companion to Alexander the Great*, Leiden, 31–66.
Stoneman, R.
   1997   *Alexander the Great*, New York and London.
Syme, R.
   1982   'The Career of Arrian', *HSCPh* 86, 181–211.
Tarn, W. W.
   1948   *Alexander the Great*, 2 vols., Cambridge.
Treves, P.
   1939   'Hyperides and the Cult of Hephaestion', *CR* 53, 56–7.
Welles, C. B.
   1970   *Alexander and the Hellenistic World*, Toronto.
Whitmarsh, T.
   2005   *The Second Sophistic*, Oxford.
Wiesehöfer, J.
   1994   *Die dunklen Jahrhunderte der Persis*, Munich.
   2005   *Das antike Persien von 550 v. Chr. bis 650 n. Chr.*, Düsseldorf/Zürich.
Winiarczyk, M.
   2007   'Das Werk *Die Erziehung Alexanders* des Onesikritos von Astypalaia (FGrHist 134 F 1–39)', *Eos* 94, 197–250.
Wirth, G.
   1964   'Anmerkungen zur Arrian-Biographie', *Historia* 13, 209–45.
   1967   'Hephaistion', *DKP* 2, 1022–3.
   1993a   *Der Brand von Persepolis. Folgerungen zur Geschichte Alexanders des Großen*, Amsterdam.
   1993b   *Der Weg in die Vergessenheit. Zum Schicksal des antiken Alexanderbildes*, Vienna.

Yardley, J. C.
  2003   *Justin and Pompeius Trogus: A Study of the Language of Justin's Epitome of Trogus*, Toronto.
Yardley, J. C. and Heckel, W.
  1997   *Justin. Epitome of the Philippic History of Pompeius Trogus Books 11–12*, Oxford.
Zambrini, A.
  1996   'The Historians of Alexander,' in J. Marincola (ed.) *A Companion to Greek and Roman Historiography*, *I*, Oxford, 210–20.

6

FRIENDSHIP AND BETRAYAL: THE ALLIANCES AMONG THE DIADOCHOI

Alexander Meeus

'War puts an end to treaties, whatever be their name.'[1]

In describing the stasis in Kerkyra, Thucydides provides a long catalogue of the ways in which the civil war completely destroyed the moral order, including an observation on peace agreements:

> And if in any case oaths of reconciliation were exchanged, for the moment only they were binding, since each side had given them merely to meet the emergency, having at the time no other resource (Thucydides 3.82.7).

Such a policy of expediency was even put forward as a general rule in Thucydides' speech of the Athenian archon Euphemos at Kamarina:

> 'To an autocrat or an imperial city nothing is inconsistent which is to its interest, nor is anyone a kinsman who cannot be trusted; in every case one must be enemy or friend according to circumstances' (6.85.1).[2]

This policy was also practised in Macedonia at the time, as is illustrated for instance by the unstable relationship between Perdikkas II and Athens (Roisman 2010, esp. 148), and students of the age of the Successors may well be particularly tempted to agree with Thucydides that his account of events in Kerkyra showed the kind of 'grievous calamities' in civil wars 'such as happen and always will happen while human nature is the same' (3.82.2). Plutarch seems to have taken this approach, as is clear from his assessment of the Successors' behaviour in his *Life of Pyrrhos* (12.3 and 12.7):

> Nay, they are perpetually at war, because plots and jealousies are parts of their natures, and they treat the two words, war and peace, like current coins, using whichever happens to be for their advantage, regardless of justice; for surely they are better men when they wage war openly than when they give the names of justice and friendship to the times of inactivity and leisure which interrupt their work of injustice. (...) Whence we see that kings have no reason to find fault with popular bodies for changing sides as suits their interests; for in doing this they are but imitating the kings themselves, who are their teachers in unfaithfulness and treachery, and think him most advantaged who least observes justice.

The strongly moral tone does not alter the astuteness of the observation. Other sources utter similar judgements about particular treaties, thus for instance the *Suda* (*s.v.* Δημήτριος [Δ 431 Adler]) about the treaty between Ptolemy and Demetrios in 309/8:

> Demetrios the son of Antigonos and Ptolemy agreed that there was a treaty of alliance between them for the liberation for all Greece and for the mutual defense of each other's territory. And there was a competition between them as to which would be more of a hindrance in deed to what had been decided. (...) But the agreement between Ptolemy and Demetrios concerning the accord did not last long (trans. Hutton, SOL).

When discussing the alliance at Ipsos, Diodoros (21.1.2) notes that this too was merely a matter of expediency:

> Ptolemy, Seleukos, and Lysimachos united against King Antigonos; not so much prompted by goodwill towards one another as compelled by the fears each had for himself, they moved readily to make common cause in the supreme struggle.

Lysimachos' peace with Demetrios in 294 was likewise inspired by the former's need to have his hands free for the war with Dromichaites, as Justin (16.1.19) informs us:

> Under pressure from a war with Dromichaetes, a king of the Thracians, and fearing that he might be obliged to fight Demetrius at the same time, Lysimachus also ceded to Demetrius the other part of Macedonia which had fallen to his son-in-law Antipater, and concluded a peace with him.

Polybios' assessment – or, if you will, the assessment the Polybian narrator attributes to Aratos of Sikyon – about Hellenistic kings in general was the same:

> he knew that kings do not regard anyone as their natural foe or friend, but measure friendship and enmity by the sole standard of expediency (2.47.5).

All of this – though admittedly only the interpretation of outsiders who were prone to moralising – would suggest that we should probably not attach too much weight too such treaties and alliances in the Diadoch Wars. Indeed, scholars universally agree with the general interpretation of the sources when it comes to the lack of faithfulness of the Successors to their agreements: they were constantly making and breaking treaties, creating 'an ever-shifting pattern of alliances, treaties and betrayals' (Wheatley 1998, 20; also e.g. Austin 1986, 461 with n. 88 and Lefèvre 1998, 139 n. 98). And yet at the same time much is often made of these agreements either by investing them with far-reaching constitutional implications or with rather too strong an influence on the subsequent behaviour of the contracting parties. Thus, the alliances or treaties of 315,

311, the years after Ipsos, or 279 have all been interpreted as marking the definitive break-up of Alexander's empire. Furthermore, in interpreting the many obscure episodes in the history of the Successors it is often argued that two parties will not have attacked each other because there was a treaty between them or conversely that there cannot have been an earlier agreement when the sources report hostilities. I hope to show that because of the utterly opportunistic behaviour of the Successors none of these conclusions is valid: I shall first discuss a misconception about the relevant terminology in the sources and then analyse the lack of impact of most treaties on the behaviour of the contracting parties.[3]

1. A problem of terminology: κοινοπραγία and συμμαχία

A widespread view holds that the words κοινοπραγία and συμμαχία in the literary sources for the Successors, particularly in Diodoros, reflect a fundamental difference in the legal status of an alliance. According to this view, both terms can be used in a general sense, simply having their literal meaning of military or political collaboration, but συμμαχία can also have the specific technical meaning of a formal coalition of sovereign partners. The latter is the case, Rosen (1968, 184) claims, when the conclusion of the agreement is mentioned, i.e. when an expression like συμμαχίαν συντίθεσθαι or συμμαχίαν ποιεῖσθαι is used, or when συνθῆκαι or ὁμολογίαι are connected to the συμμαχία; yet often, he significantly adds, only interpretation will reveal whether we are facing a formal treaty and what its legal status would have been. Consequently, while anyone can set up a κοινοπραγία with someone, a συμμαχία in its technical sense is said to have been available only to those who officially have sovereign status.[4] To some extent it may be a technicality that the modern concept of sovereignty did not exist in Antiquity (Davies 1994), as the point remains that a distinction between subordinate officials and independent rulers can be made (cf. Davies 2002, 12). A more severe problem, however, seems to me that this argument assumes rather more technical precision than we can expect from an author like Diodoros.[5] Furthermore, like much of twentieth-century scholarship on Hellenistic politics, it requires a far more developed *Staatsrecht* than the sources seem to justify,[6] and one may even doubt whether it conforms to the ancient Greek understanding of what a συμμαχία was.[7]

The argument is based in large part on the rarity of the word κοινοπραγία. This noun is used only 41 times in the extant literature of Antiquity (before AD 500, as per the *TLG*); the related verb κοινοπραγεῖν only 28 times. Both are particularly common in books 18 to 20 of Diodoros, and Rosen (1968, 184–90) has argued that this reflects the usage of Hieronymos, who is the solution to so many problems in the history of the Successors. Hieronymos, it is argued, consistently distinguished sharply between κοινοπραγίαι of non-sovereign partners and συμμαχίαι of sovereign allies, and Diodoros would have scrupulously maintained the technical vocabulary of his source despite his failure to understand the distinction (cf. infra). Even regardless of my doubts whether Hieronymos actually was Diodoros' direct source for the history of the Successors,[8] I am not so convinced that the statistics actually reflect Diodoros' close reliance on any particular lost source. They rather conform to the normal pattern of incidence of typically Hellenistic prose words in occurring first in Polybios and more frequently in Diodoros while numbers go down again in Philo of Alexandria and Plutarch to then largely disappear again until Late Antiquity: the κοινοπραγ- root is not attested before Polybios, who uses it 19 times, then there are 32 instances in Diodoros, 12 in Philo and 3 in Plutarch. Between Plutarch and the fourth century CE, a single instance in Polyainos is attested. Given the tendency of occurrences of particular words in Diodoros' *Bibliotheke* to cluster (Palm 1955, 69; Hornblower 1981, 273; Meeus 2009c, 32–3), even the distribution of κοινοπραγία and κοινοπραγεῖν throughout the work need not necessarily result from the influence of Diodoros' source on the Successors.[9] Furthermore, and this seems crucial, the occurrences of κοινοπραγεῖν in the narrative on Agathokles (19.4.1. and 19.6.5) cannot go back to Hieronymos,[10] and it is not correct that the word disappears from the *Bibliotheke* after Ipsos (see 30.9.1, 31.15a.4, 32.9c.1, 37.22a.1; *pace* Rosen 1968, 185). Even when this may partially be due to their being irrelevant in the non-historical books 1–6, it is still notable that the frequency of κοινοπραγία/κοινοπραγεῖν is higher in books 21–40 (0.0076%) than in books 1–20 (0.0060%). It may be a typical Hellenistic usage that was normal for Diodoros and occurs more frequently in the books on Hellenistic history because of the cumulative effect of his sources having used it too. Thus, there may surely have been some influence from his source, as does seem to be suggested by the antonyms ἰδιοπραγία/ἰδιοπραγεῖν occurring only in book 18 and the lone instance of κοινοπραγεῖν in Polyaenus (4.6.6) also belonging to the history of the Successors (Rosen 1968, 187 and 189–90), but this can only be a partial explanation. Furthermore, I would rather doubt that in books 11–15 one can attribute to Ephoros the allegedly accurate usage of the distinction Diodoros did not understand: Ephoros wrote almost 200 years before the earliest preserved literary attestation of the word in Polybios, and more than a hundred years before the single epigraphical occurrence I have been able to find (*SEG* XXIII 547 of 201/200 BC).[11] This does not completely exclude that he used the word, but asserting that he did does seem quite hazardous.[12]

Furthermore, when it comes to the interpretation of the individual occurrences of συμμαχία and κοινοπραγία, the analysis is not always equally convincing to me.[13] The most striking instance is the discussion of the Greek alliance in the Lamian War that is supposed to show how carefully Hieronymus observed the distinction between κοινοπραγία and the συμμαχία of international law (Rosen 1968, 187–8). At 18.9.5 Diodoros says that Leosthenes was sent by the Athenian *dēmos* to Aitolia 'to arrange for common action', συνθησόμενος κοινοπραγίαν; two chapters later, at 18.11.1, when listing all the members of the Greek alliance Diodoros says that the Aitolians joined first, 'as has been said'. Here, however, he does not use the word κοινοπραγία, but he says πρῶτοι συνέθεντο τὴν συμμαχίαν, καθάπερ προείρηται. It is argued that Leosthenes simply went to Aitolia twice, first to levy a private army, and then to establish an official alliance in the name of the Athenian state. The καθάπερ προείρηται would then have been mistakenly added by Diodoros who did not know that these were two different moments.[14] The structure of these chapters is rather confusing indeed, but it seems that Diodoros himself understood what he was doing: Leosthenes had started preparing for war before the Athenians officially decided to start hostilities and Diodoros first gave a full account of Leosthenes' preparations both before (privately enlisting soldiers, 18.9.2–3) and after the war decree (receiving money and arms from Athens; sending an embassy to Aitolia, 18.9.4–5), then explained how the decree came about (18.10.1–3), and after that returned to the consequences of the decision, repeating the information about Aitolia and thus rightly inserting a cross-reference at 18.11.1. The passage about the debates in the assembly in chapter 10 constitutes a sort of digression about the demagogues in the assembly, the men of whom Philip had said that to them 'war was peace and peace was war'; it does not describe new debates after Leosthenes had already been sent and which would have led to a second mission establishing an official συμμαχία.[15] In my view, the καθάπερ προείρηται is not a mistake and simply confirms that Diodoros is using συμμαχία and κοινοπραγία synonymously (cf. Schmitt 1964, 264 n. 1).

Another example concerns the alliance of Antipatros, Krateros and Ptolemy which Diodoros describes first as a κοινοπραγία (18.25.4) and then as a συμμαχία (18.29.6). Rosen (1968, 188–9 and 196) claims that here συμμαχία only has its general meaning, which may be correct, but again it shows how both terms can be used synonymously by Diodoros, and that he was not particularly concerned to maintain a strict distinction.

Kassandros' alliance with Polyperchon in 309 is rightly called κοινοπραγία, so Rosen (1968, 207) argues, because the latter was not a sovereign partner. That Kassandros did not want to grant sovereignty to the general of the

Peloponnese is quite understandable indeed. His alliance with Polemaios, however, is called a συμμαχία, which Rosen (1968, 207) explains by stating that Polemaios independently held sway in Hellespontine Phrygia, the Kyklades and Euboia. Whatever the ambitions of Kassandros were, it is most unlikely that he would have wanted to acknowledge Polemaios as the sovereign lord of Euboia given the extreme strategic importance of Chalkis (cf. Diod. 19.78.2; Plb. 18.11.5–7). Again the obvious explanation is that κοινοπραγία and συμμαχία are simply used as synonyms in Diodoros' narrative.

At 21.1.2 Diodoros describes the coalition concluded before the battle of Ipsos in 302 as a κοινοπραγία. As all the Diadochoi were sovereign rulers since 304 at the latest, Diodoros should have written συμμαχία according to Rosen's system.[16] He argues, however, that in 315, when they concluded the very first συμμαχία, the Successors wanted to delegitimise Antigonos' claim to the entire empire and in order to do this they expressed their territorial sovereignty by concluding a συμμαχία.[17] By 302, however, they had become kings and as sovereign kings they felt no real need to stress their independence by a treaty under international law, and a less formal alliance would suffice, which had the added advantage that they would be more free to do as they wished after the battle.[18] At the same time, however, it is claimed that the aim was nothing less than a third and final re-organisation of the empire after Ipsos and Triparadeisos (Rosen 1968, 208–9). If that were the case, then surely now would have been the time when clear legal arrangements were needed, all the more so since Rosen (1968, 209–10) argues that after Ipsos they could never have concluded another κοινοπραγία because this constituted the end of the united empire: Ipsos is, after all, a curious conclusion for someone so concerned with *Staatsrecht*. With Ipsos nothing changed in the constitutional positions of the Successors: Antigonos died and especially Lysimachos and Seleukos expanded their territories, but all remained the kings they were. If they had felt the need to mark the disbanding of the empire in a formal sense in 315 when the process was incomplete, why then not mark the definitive end of the process in an equally formal way? Furthermore, how or why would they in 315 have expressed sovereignty by means of the name of their alliance while at the same time still recognising their subordinate status in dating formulas containing the name of Alexander IV? A far more obvious conclusion seems to me that συμμαχία and κοινοπραγία are simply used synonymously, and that both can refer either to a formal or to an informal alliance. Indeed at 32.9c.1, Diodoros describes a formal alliance between Ptolemy VI and Demetrios II, which contained an agreement on borders and was sanctioned by the latter's marriage to the former's daughter, as a κοινοπραγία, which again confirms its nature as a synonym of συμμαχία (Schmitt 1964, 264 n. 1).

While the practice of every author must be analysed on its own merits (Bertrand and Gruenais 1981, 68–70), the existence of such a clear technical distinction between the terms συμμαχία and κοινοπραγία in Diodoros must surely be even less likely when one observes that no such distinction exists in Polybios, who definitely was much more concerned with precision in his institutional vocabulary than Diodoros (cf. Bertrand and Gruenais 1981, 68). Rosen (1968, 185) himself notes that κοινοπραγία was used as a synonym of συμμαχία by Polybios,[19] who does indeed report κοινοπραγίαι between independent kings: at 5.107.4, for instance, it is said that Antiochos III and Attalos I conclude an alliance which is described with the words συνθέμενος πρὸς Ἄτταλον τὸν βασιλέα κοινοπραγίαν, a phrase which according to Rosen's principles reveals a legal agreement.[20] He attempts to solve the problem by styling Polybios a later historian (Rosen 1968, 185: 'Bei dem späteren Historiker Polybios...'), but this will not do, unless one can prove definitively that Diodoros' usage was completely determined by Ephoros, the source of book 17 (which Rosen does not identify) and Hieronymos in each and every instance. And indeed at 30.9.1, 31.15a.4, 32.9c.1, 37.22a.1 Diodoros must have used such later historians as Polybios.

2. The significance of the treaties and alliances of the successors

Not only has the alliance of Ptolemy, Seleukos, Kassandros and Lysimachos against Antigonos in 315 been considered a crucial step in the dismemberment of the empire, the peace treaty of 311 is often taken to be an even more important – for many already the final – stage in the process of disintegration. Thus, Welles (1934, 6) for instance contends that with this treaty 'formal recognition was accorded the dismemberment of Alexander's empire'.[21] To Rosen (1968, 205) this *völkerrechtliche* conclusion of the Third Diadoch War was the logical consequence of its start as an alliance between sovereign rulers. Cohen (1974), in turn, argues that the definitive break-up of the empire followed only after the battle of Ipsos, when the Successors started intermarrying on a rather large scale (cf. Braunert 1964, 90–1; Billows 1990, 160 n. 46). These marriages would have signalled that each of the parties recognised the others' possession of parts of the empire. Yet other scholars, such as Habicht (2006, 43), argue that the idea of the unity of the empire may have lived on until 281, and that

> the decisive turning point came with the treaty concluded in 279 or 278 by two members of the new generation, Antiochos I and Antigonos Gonatas, in which each recognised the other and renounced all claim to his territory.[22]

Thus, including the assumption of the royal title by the Successors which has also been taken as marking the end of the empire's unity, Alexander's empire definitively fell apart at least four times (311, 306–4, 301, and 279).[23]

It is striking that there are so many different suggestions for what really can only have been one moment – at least on the assumption that there was such a moment. Some do try to combine them, for instance by having one step reinforce the other (Rosen 1968 for 315, 311 and 302/1) or picturing the successive abandonment, death and burial of the idea of the empire's unity (Bengtson 1977, 371), but the variety of allegedly decisive treaties or alliances must cast doubt on the suitability of the criterion. There also seems to be a contradiction between the widespread assumption that for the Successors a treaty was merely a matter of expedience, and the other widespread assumption that these treaties have some *völkerrechtliche* significance. All of this seems strongly inspired by hindsight; if their alliances and treaties only lasted as long as was expedient and thus did not mean much to the Successors, might they then perhaps not just mean very little?

For the same reason, I am unconvinced by the argument one regularly encounters that if there were hostilities between two of the Successors there cannot have been a treaty between them, or that, conversely, if there was a treaty, there cannot have been hostilities.[24] The latter assumption, for instance, informs Horat Zuffa's (1971/2) attempt to demonstrate that Ptolemy' campaign in Greece in 308 cannot in any way have been directed against Kassandros because they were allies, which is all the more puzzling since she herself points out that the peace of 311 in no way put a stop to the mutual hostilities between Ptolemy and Antigonos (Horat Zuffa 1971/2, 100). She thus has to reject out of hand several events reported by the sources, simply to maintain the assumption that the treaty must have preserved peace between Ptolemy and Kassandros. Yet if the campaign was not directed against Kassandros, why did Ptolemy have to make peace with him when he hastily aborted the campaign (Diod. 20.37.2)?[25]

Enmity has been used as evidence against the existence of a treaty for instance in the case of the alliance between Ptolemy and Demetrios mentioned in the *Suda* (*s.v.* Δημήτριος [Δ 431 Adler]).[26] Admittedly it seems unlikely that a treaty would have existed under the exact terms stated by the *Suda*: there is indeed no reason for Ptolemy and Demetrios to free the Greeks together or to protect each other's territory. But this can easily have been the lexicographer's misrepresentation of the actual terms of the treaty. Antigonid treaties always contained the clause that the Greeks should be free: this is attested in 313 with Antigonos and Asandros (Diod. 19.75.1), in the peace of 311 (Diod. 19.105.1; *OGIS* 5, l. 53–65), and in the treaty of 302 between Kassandros and Demetrios that the latter already knew his father would never ratify (Diod. 20.111.2); one wonders if such was also true of the present treaty. Most importantly, as we have seen above, the author of the *Suda* himself notes that both parties remained as hostile after the treaty as they had been before.

3. The expediency of the successors

It remains for us to explore in more detail the expediency of the Successors which the sources emphasise so strongly (see the introduction).[27] As a matter of fact the trend of alliances that were merely expedient and did not contain any real intention of future commitment was set immediately after Alexander's death, both with respect to so-called territorial recognition and to marriage alliances.[28]

3.1 Making and breaking agreements

The top priority for many of the generals in the first debates over the succession after Alexander's death seems to have been to obtain as much power as possible for themselves (Meeus 2008, 46–51; Waterfield 2011, 20–2). Forced by the resistance of the infantry, however, they managed to agree on a compromise (Meeus 2008, 51–2; Roisman 2012, 70), but as soon as the resistance of the infantry was broken, a new round of power brokering began and the outcome was substantially different, especially for the absent Krateros, who went from being regent of the entire empire to having to share power with Antipatros in Greece and Macedonia – Meleagros had already been killed, right after his reconciliation to Perdikkas (Meeus 2008, 53–76). Relations between Perdikkas and Ptolemy seem to have been tense from the very beginning (Anson 2004, 61–2; Meeus 2008, 48–50 and 70–6), but Perdikkas agreed on the latter obtaining the rich and strategically well-situated satrapy of Egypt. Rather than this being an indication of friendly relations (Schäfer 2002, 57), Perdikkas seems to have decided at the outset that he would remove Ptolemy as soon as a suitable pretext presented itself, as is revealed by Diodoros (18.14.2) and Arrian (*Succ.* 24.1).[29] For Perdikkas, then, the agreement over the distribution of the satrapies officially sanctioned by the king surely did not bring about his acceptance of the territorial power of all involved.

Perdikkas was not the only one, of course. Leonnatos crossed to Europe under the pretext of helping Antipatros, but was really out to establish his own power in Macedon (Diod. 18.14.4; Plut. *Eum.* 3.3–5). Antigonos used his allies Seleukos and Peithon (Diod. 19.17.2) only as long as he really needed them, then lured the latter into believing that he would receive an important command in order to have him killed (Diod. 19.46.1) and was relieved that the former had fled before he would have had to kill a friend and collaborator (Diod. 19.55.6). Admittedly, Peithon himself seems to have been plotting against Antigonos (Diod. 19.46.1), but as far as we know Seleukos had not wronged him in any way and is said even to have honoured him with royal gifts and feasted the whole army (Diod. 19.55.1).[30] The coalition opposing Antigonos, Peithon and Seleukos, had been anything but free from plotting either. Plutarch (*Eum.* 13.4) describes Peukestas and Eumenes as friends, but that is surely not the impression one would get from the way their struggle for the leadership of the coalition is subsequently depicted (Plut. *Eum.* 13–16; Diod. 19.15–43; Nepos *Eum.* 7–10).

It is very much in this light that such major coalitions as the one uniting Ptolemy, Seleukos, Kassandros and Lysimachos against Antigonos in 315 should be seen. It has been observed that the larger pattern of the alliances among the Successors is that whenever one of them becomes too powerful or too aggressive, the others united against him.[31] In my view they did not act in this way because they were necessarily less ambitious, but rather because all saw their own ambitions threatened by the same enemy and considered it in their own interests to have that threat removed as soon as possible (cf. Lund 1992, 61). They could then deal with each other afterwards, and indeed most did just that when they were in a position to do so: none of the parties in the coalition of 315 was afterwards always at peace with any of the other partners, apart from Kassandros and Lysimachos who continually seem to have entertained a good relationship.[32] Furthermore, the idea that Ptolemy, Kassandros, Lysimachos and Seleukos would have wanted to break up the empire is to my mind only based on hindsight. Their ambitions were not more limited than those of Antigonos, their strategies were simply more careful, among other reasons surely because each of them wished to avoid the possibility that the others would unite in a coalition against himself (cf. Meeus 2013, 2014; Strootman 2014a).

The first to act against the interests of one of the allies was Ptolemy: in response to Antigonos' proclamation that all Greek cities should be free, he hastened to profess that he too was the champion of Greek freedom. This is explained easily enough by the motive Diodoros attributes to him, namely that he perceived 'that it was a matter of no little moment to gain the goodwill of the Greeks' (Diod. 19.62.2). The proclamation could seriously damage the interests of Kassandros, with whom he had only just concluded an alliance, as the latter had garrisons in many Greek cities. Such behaviour does not only prove that Ptolemy looked farther than the immediate future (Will 1979, 56), but it also reveals once more that a treaty had by no means an absolute significance for the Successors (cf. Adams

1974, 115). Nonetheless, for the time being Ptolemy seems to have refrained from direct actions against Kassandros (Heuß 1938, 150; Simpson 1959, 390), and he even sent out Polykleitos to support him in the Peloponnese (Diod. 19.62.5 and 64.5; *contra* Gullath 1982, 150 n. 3). This should not mean, though, that Ptolemy only proclaimed the freedom of the Greeks in his own territories, as Manni (1951, 104–5) argued in an attempt to save both the effectiveness of Ptolemy's declaration and the correct legal relationship between the satrap of Egypt and Kassandros. Such legalistic approaches can only lead us away from understanding the actual – mostly opportunistic and anarchic – actions and alliances of the Successors. Ptolemy can hardly be said to have been cooperating with Kassandros on anything but those matters which were in his own personal interest (cf. Simpson 1954, 27). Furthermore, in the winter of 315 Ptolemy already seemed prepared to give up on his allies, as he was conducting peace talks with Antigonos (Diod. 19.64.8; Meeus 2012a, 84). Eventually, however, Lysimachos and Kassandros were the first to give up the alliance in concluding a separate peace with Antigonos which initially did not include Ptolemy.[33]

Antigonos did not conclude peace because he was now also prepared to recognise the others (*pace* Billows 1990, 4); he even admits himself that one of his aims was to isolate Polyperchon (*OGIS* 5, l. 37–41), while isolating Seleukos and being fully able to concentrate on the war against him without having to fight on any other fronts was no doubt his main, but unstated, reason for wanting peace in the first place. The others had probably realised that they were not getting very far against Antigonos' superiority of means and resources (Simpson 1954). The treaty of 311 thus seems to have had much the same kind of rationale as the coalition of 315.

The treaty provided that

> Kassandros be general of Europe until Alexander, the son of Rhoxane, should come of age; that Lysimachos rule Thrace, and that Ptolemy rule Egypt and the cities adjacent thereto in Libya and Arabia; that Antigonos have first place in all Asia (Diod. 19.105.1).

In spite of what Diodoros' wording may suggest, the treaty did not limit the power of Alexander IV to the European part of the empire: documents throughout the empire continued to be dated according to the regnal years of Alexander IV (Boiy 2007, 73–104). There thus seems no reason to assume that this treaty meant the *de facto* break-up of the empire or even constitutionally fixed the dissolution of the empire. It is striking that some of the same scholars who interpreted the treaty in this sense at the same time note that it was merely a truce or a breathing-space for some or all of the parties.[34] Indeed, the Successors clearly did not recognise the borders agreed on in the treaty, and very soon most of them were at war with each other again: within a few years Ptolemy and Antigonos both tried to conquer Greece, Ptolemy tried to gain parts of Asia Minor, and Antigonos invaded Egypt.[35] That the empire did eventually fall apart does not necessarily mean that any of the parties took the territorial division this treaty contained more seriously than the aspect of peace. The sole purpose had been to create a breathing space. It is also telling how easily the others all abandoned Seleukos (*pace* e.g. Cloché 1957, 137–8).

Even more striking is Polyperchon's series of alliances in these years. That he, together with his son Alexandros, joined Antigonos at the beginning of the Third Diadoch War is only natural, as he was an enemy of Kassandros (Diod. 19.60.1, 61.1). Kassandros unsuccessfully attempted to induce him to defect soon after he had joined Antigonos (Diod. 19.63.3), and not much later his son Alexandros did so, obtaining the office of general of the Peloponnese which his father had held under Antigonos (Diod. 19.64.3–4). We are not told if Polyperchon himself also changed sides on this occasion, but he might well have done so: Ptolemy's admiral Polykleitos did not find any hostile forces in the Peloponnese after Alexandros' defection (Diod. 19.64.5) and Polyperchon seems to have had good relations with Alexandros' widow Kratesipolis.[36] Antigonos' letter to Skepsis also suggests that in 311 Polyperchon was no longer on his side, but seems to have been allied with the anti-Antigonid coalition of the other major Successors, who, however, abandoned him as part of the peace arrangements.[37] Polemaios is attested as Antigonid general in the Peloponnese at this time (Diod. 20.19.2), and it is difficult to see how Polyperchon would fit in this situation if he were still in Antigonid service.[38] Yet in 310 Polyperchon appears to be on Antigonos' side again, when he tried to bring Herakles to the throne, who had been living in Pergamon – in Antigonid territory and therefore most likely under Antigonid control (Wheatley 1998, 14–15 and 20; cf. Kleopatra in Sardes or Rhoxane and Alexander IV in Amphipolis under Kassandros). Perhaps Antigonos had invited him to re-join his cause after the revolt of Polemaios (see below) left him without a general of the Peloponnese in 310. Kassandros, however, convinced Polyperchon to join his side and do away with the young prince in 309 (Diod. 20.20.1–2 and 20.28). It would thus seem that Polyperchon joined Antigonos in the spring of 315, defected to Kassandros between late 315 and early 313, was abandoned by him in 311, and had reconciled to Antigonos by the end of 310 only to defect to Kassandros again the next year.[39]

The consecutive alliances of Polemaios, with Kassandros and Ptolemy respectively, constitute another case in point. From 315 to 310 Polemaios acted as the right-hand man of his uncle Antigonos in Asia Minor, Greece and the Aegean. Because he thought that 'he was not being honoured according to his deserts' he defected to Kassandros (Diod. 20.19.2). The next year he changed sides again, this time concluding an alliance with Ptolemy, who, however, soon decided that his new ally was too ambitious and executed him (Diod. 20.27.3).[40] His quick abandoning of Kassandros may well be due to the latter's new rapprochment with Polyperchon who was now promised the generalship of the Peloponnese (Will 1979, 72). At any rate, this quick succession of defections not only shows Polemaios' search for the most expedient alliance so typical of the period, but also reveals the determination of Ptolemy to act against Kassandros in Greece and against Antigonos in Asia so soon after the peace of 311 (Hammond 1988, 169).

These examples should suffice as illustration of the flexibility and opportunism with which the Successors approached common treaties and alliances; many more are to be found in the overview table in the appendix. It is necessary, however, briefly to consider the treaty between Antigonos Gonatas and Antiochos I (Just. 25.1.1) because of the consequences that have been attached to it, namely the alleged mutual recognition of the kings, which is said to have constituted the definitive end of the unity of Alexander's empire (see above, n. 22). Again, though the moment hardly seems so significant, and it does not seem that these rulers necessarily gave up all of their overseas ambitions, as is now revealed by an inscription from Kaunos that shows Gonatas being in control of the city in 269/8 (*IvKaunos* 4).[41] Kaunos, of course, was Ptolemaic rather than Seleukid territory, but at any rate it is clear that Gonatas operated in a wider area than has often been presumed.[42] To be sure, none of the Epigonoi seems to have been willing to risk losing everything in an attempt to gain it all, as Perdikkas, Antigonos Monophthalmos and Demetrios seem to have done, but such risk assessment need not be a sign of limited ambitions (cf. Bosworth 2002, 2–3; Meeus 2013, 118–19), as indeed throughout the Hellenistic period kings all too gladly seized opportunities to grasp for more when these offered themselves.[43] Of course, they could only do so when an enemy seemed sufficiently vulnerable and they themselves had no pressing threats to deal with, two situations which may not have occurred at the very same time all that often. The idea of a deliberately-sought balance of power belongs to the nineteenth century, not to the Hellenistic period.[44] It seems more plausible that Antigonos and Antiochos simply wanted to avoid having to fight wars on different fronts at the same time (cf. Grainger 2010, 78).

3.2 The significance of marriage alliances

I now turn to the specific case of marriage alliances, which *prima facie* would seem more solid. Yet I think it can easily be shown that even such unions do not imply permanent recognition of the other party's territory. In this respect too the trend seems to be set by Perdikkas soon after Alexander's death: while negotiations in Babylon were on-going and his position was still uncertain, he had sought an alliance with Antipatros, the strong man in Europe, who accepted the proposal and with some delay sent his daughter Nikaia to Asia to marry Perdikkas. The Babylon settlement had turned out rather well for Perdikkas, however, and after a while he seemed to deem his position quite solid, which made him lose interest in the alliance and seek the hand of Alexander's sister Kleopatra. As it happened, both women arrived in Asia around the same time, and Perdikkas hesitated about the best course of action, eventually deciding that in the short run a marriage with Nikaia would be more useful: the sources stress, though, that he simply thought he could not afford to alienate Antipatros at this point.[45] How accurately Diodoros and Justin report Perdikkas' thoughts is another question, but at the very least they represent Hellenistic thinking about marriage alliances, and their judgement in this instance seems very plausible to me. The sources' noting that the plan was temporary (see n. 45) and Perdikkas' subsequent relations with Kleopatra (Meeus 2009a, 78–9), suggest that the regent saw the marriage to Nikaia purely in terms of immediate gain and had no intention of establishing a long-term alliance with Antipatros (Seibert 1967, 13–14; Heckel 1986a, 294).

The same is true, I would argue, for the marriage alliances concluded after Ipsos, connecting Lysimachos and Ptolemy, Seleukos and Demetrios, and later also Ptolemy and Demetrios.[46] These alliances were not so much concluded with an eye to peace, but rather in the expectation of further wars (cf. Gehrke 2008, 160). Ptolemy, fearing a conflict with his neighbour Seleukos, sought a marriage with the daughter of Seleukos' other neighbour Lysimachos, in a way surrounding him. In order not to become completely isolated, Seleukos responded by establishing a marriage alliance with Demetrios who possessed a navy that could match that of Ptolemy (Bosworth 2002, 261 and 267). Ptolemy seems to have realised the potential threat from the powerful new alliance, and he himself also sought a marriage alliance with Demetrios, betrothing his daughter Ptolemais to him (Bosworth 2002, 263). Rather remarkably, the marriage agreement itself does not seem to have sufficed to establish trust between Ptolemy and Demetrios, as Ptolemy demanded hostages (Plut. *Pyrrh.* 4.3; Seibert 1967, 31). Relations between Seleukos and Demetrios were not all that warm either, as Plutarch (*Demetr.* 32.4–33.1) reports:

So far all was courtesy on the part of Seleukos. But presently he asked Demetrios to cede Kilikia to him for a sum of money, and when Demetrios would not consent, angrily demanded Tyre and Sidon from him. It seemed a violent and outrageous proceeding that one who had possessed himself of the whole domain from India to the Syrian sea should be so needy still and so beggarly in spirit as for the sake of two cities to harass a man who was his relative by marriage and had suffered a reverse of fortune. Moreover, he bore splendid testimony to the wisdom of Plato in urging the man who would be truly rich, not to make his possessions greater, but his inordinate desires fewer; since he who puts no end to his greed, this man is never rid of poverty and want. Demetrios, however, was not cowed, but declared that not even if he should lose ten thousand battles like that at Ipsus would he consent to pay for the privilege of having Seleukos as a son-in-law.

Whatever the historicity of the words Plutarch attributes to the protagonists, his presentation of the dynamics is appropriate enough. Indeed, the new family ties did not even prevent the Successors from going to war with each other, and later Seleukos did seize Kilikia (Plut. *Demetr.* 47.1; Bosworth 2002, 267 with n. 77). In 287 Ptolemy and Seleukos both joined a coalition against Demetrios in spite of the earlier marriage alliances (Plut. *Demetr.* 44.1), initiating what is sometimes called the Fifth Diadoch War. Plutarch (*Demetr.* 48.3) tells us that Seleukos did not want the help of Lysimachos, although the latter was also a member of the coalition, because he did not trust him. In spite of his marriage alliance with Lysimachos, Ptolemy seems to have allowed Demetrios to attack Lysimachos' positions soon after the establishment of the coalition (Buraselis 1982, 98; Heckel 1986b, 459–60). Even if it were correct that the Fifth Diadoch War ended with a general peace agreement amongst all the warring parties (but see Meeus 2015, 159–60), one can only conclude that its terms 'were chiefly honored in the breach' (Shear 1978, 77).

It seems clear, then, that these marriage alliances did not in any way entail permanent recognition of the ally's territory, and it seems that the women involved in these unions, far from guaranteeing peace, could often do no more than negotiate in times of tension (cf. Heckel 1986a, 295). After Demetrios' capture of Kilikia, for instance, he is said to have sent Phila to Kassandros, 'who was her brother, that she might bring to naught the denunciations of Pleistarchos' (Plut. *Demetr.* 32.3). For Demetrios, then, the marriage alliance did not mean that he had to maintain peace but rather that he had an additional means of attempting to soothe tempers after a hostile act.[47] In such a context, there seems to be no point whatsoever in talking about enemies or even allies recognizing each other in the possession of their territories.[48]

4. Conclusion

I have argued that the aim of alliances and treaties among the Successors was usually simply strategic: isolating an opponent, avoiding a war on several fronts at the same time, obtaining support against an enemy who was too strong. As we have seen, Antigonos himself even admitted as much in his letter to Skepsis, explaining that isolating Polyperchon was one of his reasons to admit Ptolemy to the peace of 311. As strategic needs changed often, so did alliances. Even when the alliance was sanctioned by a wedding, this does not necessarily seem to have implied a long term commitment from both parties. In such a context alliances and treaties surely cannot have any constitutional significance, so that none of them should be taken to signal the definitive break-up of the empire. One may well wonder whether such constitutional consequences would even have come to the minds of the Successors rather than being a mere problem of modern *Staatsrecht*. It seems that there was no such thing as permanent territorial recognition in the Hellenistic world.[49]

Acknowledgements

I would like to thank Tim Howe, Anton Powell, Frances Pownall and an anonymous reader for their helpful criticism on an earlier draft, and Stephanie Cousin for help with checking the table in the appendix. I am also indebted to the Research Foundation – Flanders (FWO) which funded a fellowship during which this study was written. Translations of Justin are from Yardley 1994; all others are from the Loeb Classical Library, unless stated otherwise.

Notes

[1] Letter of the Belgian king Leopold I to Queen Victoria (1856), quoted by Stengers 1990, 78 (I owe this reference to De Schaepdrijver 2013, 46).

[2] Cf. Scharff 2009, 321: 'So lässt sich etwa die griechische Geschichte der klassischen Zeit bei Thukydides oder in den *Hellenika* Xenophons als eine lose Kette von Eid- und damit Vertragsbruchen lesen'. See also Eckstein 2006, 38–9 and passim, and the brief but very apt comments of Christ 2010 on expediency trumping justice in Athenian foreign policy in the fourth century.

[3] To be sure, as Gehrke (2008, 161) rightly notes, 'muss man sich hier hüten, zu sehr vom späteren Ergebnis her zu denken und die Diadochen – was angesichts deren "machiavellistischen" Charakters verführerisch ist ist – ausschließlich von realpolitischen und zweckrationalen Überlegungen her zu verstehen'. Yet it does not seem to me that this the main problem of scholarship on the Successors and their alliances, and it is thus the perspective of *Realpolitik* that I shall be stressing here, while realizing full well that aiming at brevity and clarity in doing so may at times result in a somewhat too schematic image that does not pay much attention to such aspects of the problem as the consistently good relationship between

Kassandros and Lysimachos. Even so, that relationship may also have been mainly inspired by self-interest: Lund 1992, 67.

[4] Argued in detail by Rosen 1968 and accepted e.g. by Briant 1973, 184 n. 2; Müller 1973, 33 n. 117 and 62; Bizière 1975, *ad* 19.17.2; Goukowsky 1978, *ad* 18.9.5; Hornblower 1981, 169; Mendels 1984, 151 n. 132; Mehl 1986, 49 n. 61; Seibert 1991, 92 n. 19; Huß 2001, 108 n. 81 and 145 n. 391; Schäfer 2002, 138 n. 33; Landucci Gattinoni 2005, 168 n. 64; Malitz 2007, 29 with n. 72.

[5] See the important essay of Bertrand and Guernais (1981) who approach the problem of technical language in ancient texts in a very careful and insightful way. My own approach to the problem in Meeus 2009b was perhaps somewhat simplistic, but not – it seems to me – to such an extent as to invalidate the conclusions drawn there, and I would still adduce them in support of the claim that Diodoros' vocabulary cannot be studied in the way Rosen (1968) does. To the references collected earlier (Meeus 2009b, 289 n. 9) can also be added Mooren 1989.

[6] Gehrke 2008, 160. Cf. also Gehrke 1982, 247–8 on *Staatsrecht* and *Staatstheorie* in scholarship on Hellenistic politics: 'Von diesen Themen ist die einschlägige Forschung weitgehend beherrscht, mir scheint fast: daran krankt sie'. For Macedonia, see Errington 1978 and 1983, esp. 89 and 101: 'the manner of systematic legalised thinking about the Macedonian state is not an ancient but a modern phenomenon'.

[7] Scharff (2009, 326–7) argues 'dass griechische Verträge bis ins frühe 4. Jh. eben nicht als Verträge mit dem Ziel einer langfristigen Aussöhnung, sondern als Bündnisverträge zum nächsten Krieg (συμμαχία) konzipiert wurden'. I do not see why it would have been different after the early fourth century.

[8] See Landucci Gattinoni 2008, esp. xvi–xviii; Meeus 2009c, 44–56; Rathmann 2014, esp. 80–94.

[9] The whole pattern of a word not occurring in some books, rarely in others and very frequently in yet others is very normal in Diodoros and can be shown to occur also with words that clearly are typically Diodorean. I limit myself to a few examples. A somewhat similar pattern of distribution is to be observed for the word πολυχειρία which is typical of Diodoros. Of the ninety preserved attestations in ancient literature twenty are to be found in Diodoros' work. Just over 30% of these are found in a single book, book 17 (cf. 30% of all instances of the κοινοπραγ-root in the *Bibliotheke* occurring in book 18), and thus also in a single source unit (for the latter concept, see Hau 2009, 173–6). The adjective ἐλαφρός occurs at 1.87.2, 3.14.2, 4.20.1, 5.39.7, 18.46.5, 19.29.1, 19.30.3, 19.30.4, 19.30.10 and 19.84.7, while the noun ἐλαφρότης is used at 19.30.1, 19.30.2 and 31.38.1. Thus, the large majority of the occurrences belongs to the narrative on the Successors. However, as the words are found from book 1 to book 31, we may rather be facing Diodoros' typical penchant for verbal repetition (especially within 19.29–30). Similarly, almost half of the instances of the word ἐφεδρεύειν belong to the history of the Diadochoi (3.39.9, 10.22.1, 13.107.3, 14.37.3, 15.3.1, 15.34.3, 16.47.5, 16.48.3, 17.11.1, 17.12.2, 17.33.2, 18.17.5, 18.25.6, 18.72.2, 19.35.1, 19.43.4, 19.57.4, 19.71.4, 19.77.5, 19.80.1, 19.100.6, 20.47.5, 20.60.4, 20.61.3, 20.105.1, 31.4.8). Again the explanation rather seems to be Diodoros' apparent lack of interest in *variatio*.

[10] One might of course argue, as Bottin (1928) has done, that Diodoros has based his narratives on the Successors and on Agathokles on one and the same source, but that would still exclude Hieronymus who did not write Sicilian history.

[11] That the word is so rare in inscriptions surely proves Schmitt's claim (1964, 264 n. 1) that it was not part of the usual ancient Greek *Vertragssprache*, but that in itself does not say anything about its meaning in Hellenistic literary texts or indeed about the alleged quality of the word συμμαχία to reveal sovereignty.

[12] Yet Rosen (1968, 185) claims it as certain that the occurrence at 11.1.4 goes back to Ephorus while the other cases are deemed probable.

[13] Cf. Mehl 1980/1, 192 n. 54: 'im Einzelnen belastet der Autor seine Argumentation freilich mit mancher *petitio principii*'.

[14] Rosen 1968, 188: 'Diodor achtete nicht auf den Unterschied, dachte vielmehr, der Autor habe sich lediglich wiederholt, und fügte die für ihn typische, sachlich aber falsche Bemerkung καθάπερ προείρηται hinzu'.

[15] Schmitt 1992, 80 with n. 186 seems to work with the same chronology, or at least thinks there was only one mission of Leosthenes to Aitolia, as does Landucci Gattinoni 2008, 69. For different views, see e.g.: Worthington 1984, 142; Habicht 1995, 45–6.

[16] He himself is obviouly aware of this: 'Um so erstaunlicher ist es, daß συμμαχία-*societas* hier wie in der gesamten sonstigen Überlieferung nicht vorkommt' (Rosen 1968, 208).

[17] Rosen 1968, 201–3, stating 'daß die Diadochen zum ersten mal als Souveräne im völkerrechtlichen Sinn eine zwischenstaatliche Symmachie eingegangen sind. Acht Jahre nach Alexanders Tod vollzogen sie einen entscheidenden Schritt zur Auflösung der Reichseinheit'.

[18] Rosen 1968, 209: 'Die κοινοπραγία gab jedem einzelnen bei den zukünftigen Verhandlungen die größtmögliche Freiheit und zwang zu keinerlei gegenseitigen Rücksichten, wie das 311 infolge der Symmachie der Fall gewesen war'. Yet in 311 the parties of the coalition had not actually considered each other either: Kassandros and Lysimachos had already agreed on peace with Antigonos when Ptolemy found out about the negotiations and requested to join the treaty: see below.

[19] Cf. Mauersberger 1966, s.v. κοινοπραγία: 'gemeinsame Unternehmung (...), Bündnis'.

[20] Schmitt (1964, 264 n. 1) on the same basis claims that 'an unserer Stelle ist der Vertragscharakter durch συνθέμενος eindeutig bezeichnet'. Admittedly, it has been claimed that Attalos and Antiochos did not actually conclude a formal treaty on this occasion: thus e.g. Allen (1983, 59) who in support of this view strangely enough only refers to Schmitt's statement of the opposite conclusion, and simultaneously claims that the agreement implied the recognition of the Attalid kingdom as a sovereign state.

[21] Many others likewise see the treaty of 311 as the *de facto* or even *de iure* dismemberment of Alexander's empire: e.g. Braunert 1964, 83–5; Rosen 1968, 205–7; Wehrli 1968, 55, 62 and 73; Müller 1973, 107; Will 1979, 63; Mehl 1980/1, 189 n. 47; Walbank 1981, 54; Billows 1990, 135; Sherwin-White and Kuhrt 1993, 120; Huß 2001, 168; Mileta 2012, 319.

[22] See also Will 1979, 56; Grainger 1990, 210; Waterfield 2011, 210; cf. Gabbert 1997, 25.

[23] For the assumption of the royal title by the Diadochoi as the event marking the definitive break-up of the empire, see e.g. Seibert 1967, 20; Wehrli 1968, 62 and 73; Müller 1973, 107; Bengtson 1977, 371; Will 1979, 75; Walbank 1981, 56; Billows 1990, 159–60; Hammond 1999, 486; Huß 2001, 185.

[24] It is crucial here also to bear in mind the demonstration of Rhodes (2008) that a given hostile action did not necessarily constitute a breach of the treaty; whether it did seems to have depended on the *ad hoc* interpretation of the various parties involved. I am fully aware that this does in principle make my own working hypothesis that every act of hostility among the Successors constituted a breach of treaty (esp. in the table in the appendix) invalid, but we simply do not have the information to actually study this question for the age of the Successors, and the pattern as whole suggests that – obviously with some exceptions – treaties did not tend to stand long. Seleukos' attitude towards conflicts with allies in the disagreement over Koile Syria after Ipsos is telling: 'for friendship's sake he would not for the present interfere, but would consider later how best to deal with friends who chose to encroach' (Diod. 21.1.5). The matter subsequently remained a bone of contention between Ptolemies and Seleucids for many generations to come. See also Waterfield 2011, 174: 'Seleukos made out that he refrained from attacking Ptolemy out of friendship, but everyone knew that the real reason was that he was in no position to challenge Ptolemy at sea'.

[25] Cf. Hauben 2014, 260 n. 131, who concludes that Horat Zuffa's view, 'despite a careful argument, is too much in contradiction with the sources'. Simpson (1954), 27 suggests that Ptolemy's initial exclusion from the treaty of 311 (see below) also explains the open hostility between him and Kassandros in 309. This may be correct, but the assumption is surely not necessary to explain the hostility.

[26] E.g. Seibert 1969, 180–3; Horat Zuffa 1971/2, 101–4. *Contra*: Will 1979, 71; Hauben 2014, 250.

[27] I shall not concern myself in what follows with the question whether there existed formally different types of treaties and alliances among the Successors, for I have not found any indications about this in the sources.

[28] For this reason, I would also disagree with Bosworth's claim (2002, 33) that settlement is a misnomer for the arrangement the Successors made at Babylon. It may not have settled much even in the relatively short run, but by that logic the words alliance and, especially, treaty could also be considered misnomers when describing the age of the Successors. However, I would rather contend that none of these terms contains the element of stability in their definition and that abandoning them might obscure the expediency and unpredictability of Successor politics rather than illuminating them.

[29] See Meeus 2015, 163–4 for further discussion.

[30] Then again, the power struggle between Eumenes and Peukestas shows that feasting the entire army is not necessarily an innocent gesture: Diod. 19.22 and 19.24.5. As to the gifts, it is not clear if the adjective 'royal' concerns the recipient or rather the giver. At most, then, Seleukos was guilty of ambition – or perhaps that is just how far the sources take us.

[31] Perdikkas in 321–320, Antigonos in 315–311, Antigonos in 302–301 and Demetrios in 287: see e.g. Rosen 1968, 182; Habicht 1995, 54; Bosworth 2002, 267.

[32] Whether there were hostilities between Ptolemy and Lysimachos is debated: see Buraselis 1982, 97–9; Meeus 2014, 303 with n. 150.

[33] *OGIS* 5, l. 26–31; Simpson 1954, 26–7. Kassandros had already negotiated with Antigonos before, at the Hellespont in the summer of 313, but these talks came to nothing: Diod. 19.75.6; *OGIS* 5, l. 5–8. In light of these negotiations and those of Ptolemy and Antigonos in 315, I would not say that Ptolemy's initial absence from the peace talks of 311 is particularly puzzling or that we need to explain it in terms of his being otherwise engaged (*pace* Burstein 2015, 125): his struggle over Syria with the Antigonids and his closer connection with Seleukos might be sufficient explanation.

[34] E.g. Wehrli 1968, 56; Will 1979, 67; Walbank 1981, 54; Huß 2001, 168. See above, n. 21, for the interpretation of the treaty as the end of the empire's unity.

[35] Cf. Wheatley 1998, 20: 'Even after the peace of 311/10, which theoretically signalled a lull in hostilities, the dynasts continued to struggle with each other, particularly for control of Greece'; Waterfield 2011, 125: 'Of course, no one believed that this was the peace to end all wars. (...) Never has Ambrose Bierce's definition of peace as "a period of cheating between periods of fighting" been more appropriate'.

[36] At 19.74.2 Diodoros writes that Polyperchon held Sikyon and Korinthos, but before (19.67.2) and after (20.37.1) that time he describes Kratesipolis as being in control of the city: this suggests that she collaborated with Polyperchon.

[37] *OGIS* 5, l. 37–41. Antigonos seems to imply that Polyperchon was allied with Kassandros and Ptolemy before the peace was concluded as the treaty would isolate him from his allies (μηθενὸς αὐτῶι συνορκοῦντος): the most plausible reading seems to me that Polyperchon had joined the alliance and that Antigonos could deal with him more easily once the allies (first Kassandros and Lysimachos, then also Ptolemy) would give up on him. Other interpretations exist, however: Bosworth (2002, 243) reads it as Antigonos giving up his official support for Polyperchon as a concession to Kassandros and thus follows Heckel (1992, 202–3) in taking l. 40–1 as a reference to potential allies.

[38] If Polyperchon was no longer on Antigonos' side in the final years of the Third Diadoch War, that would also explain the Peloponnesian interventions of Telesphoros much better (*pace* Bosworth 2002, 243 n. 121).

[39] Wheatley (1998) argues for a different chronology for Polyperchon's movements after 311 and places the reconciliation with Antigonos in 309 and the new defection to Kassandros in 308, assuming confusion in Diodoros (ibid., 16). However, I see no problem in accepting that Diodoros is at this point consistently and correctly applying his equation of the campaigning season with the year of the archon who took office during that campaign year (see Smith 1961; Meeus 2012a). I would thus place the alliance of Polemaios and Kassandros in the spring of 310, Polyperchon's championing of Herakles and preparation for war late in 310, Polyperchon's invasion of Macedon and his reconciliation with Kassandros in the (early?) spring of 309 and Polemaios' defection to Ptolemy later that spring or in the early summer of 309. That Polemaios' defection to Ptolemy is mentioned before

Polyperchon's invasion of Macedon, need not be a problem: Diodoros states that Polyperchon's invasion happened at the same time as Ptolemy' operations of the spring of 309, which include the alliance with Polemaios. At 20.28.1 he thus moves back in time when he reports European affairs of that spring after having dealt with Asia (a similar narrative structure can also be observed in some parts of book 19: Meeus 2012a, 87). The Marmor Parium (*FGrHist* 239 F B18) dates both the deaths of Alexander IV and Herakles under the archonship of Hieromnemon, which is consistent with the chronology proposed here, if Alexander IV was murdered after the Athenian new year in 310. Wheatley (1998, 15 and 18) argues that the Marmor Parium is wrong here. At any rate, the point of Polyperchon's frequent changing of side is not affected by this chronological uncertainty.

[40] Some hold that the alliance of Polemaios and Kassandros was simply a mistake by Diodoros who wrote 'Kassandros' while he should have written 'Ptolemy': e.g. Horat Zuffa 1971/2, 100–1 with further references in n. 7. Yet the fickleness of Polemaios that is implied when one accepts both the alliance with Ptolemy and that with Kassandros as historical, would not at all be surprising in this period of shifting alliances; that Diodoros speaks of defection from Antigonos on both occasions is an equally likely case of confusion as the mistaken substitution of names.

[41] See the commentary of Marek (2006, 134–6) in the *editio princeps*. There is some debate over the date of the inscription, and e.g. Meadows (2006, 463 n. 20) claims that 'identification of this Antigonus with Antigonus Gonatas is out of the question', but Marek's arguments seem conclusive: attributing the decree to the reign of Monophthalmos creates even greater problems; thus also Hermann *ad SEG* XLVII 1568 and Kuzmin 2015.

[42] Cf. already Buraselis 1982, 118–119; Austin 1986, 461 n. 88.

[43] Austin 1986, 456–7; Meeus 2012b, 73; Strootman 2014a, 320–1 and 2014b.

[44] Cf. Ager 2003, and 49–50; Heinen 2003, 36; Strootman 2014b, 44. One regularly reads claims about the Epigonoi accepting the new reality, but it obviously was a new reality only in hindsight: in 279 no one even had the faintest clue of what the map of Alexander's empire would look like ten years later, let alone in the farther future. See recently e.g. Waterfield 2011, 210–11 and Stewart 2014, 59: 'Their successors – lesser but wiser men – accepted the new reality. The unified empire was a bygone dream; the kingdoms had come to stay'.

[45] Diod. 18.23.3: οὔπω δὲ βουλόμενος ἀποκαλύψασθαι πρὸς τὴν ἐπιβολὴν κατὰ μὲν τὸ παρὸν ἦγε τὴν Νίκαιαν, ὅπως μὴ τὸν Ἀντίπατρον ἀλλότριον ἔχῃ ταῖς ἰδίαις ἐπιβολαῖς ('But not wishing as yet to reveal his design, he married Nicaea for the time, so that he might not render Antipater hostile to his own undertakings'); Just. 13.6.5–6: *sed prius Antipatrum sub adfinitatis obtentu capere cupiebat. Itaque fingit se in matrimonium filiam eius petere, quo facilius ab eo supplementum tironum ex Macedonia obtineret* ('First, however, he wished to use the pretext of family alliance to ensnare Antipater. He therefore pretended that he wished to marry the latter's daughter, his object being to facilitate the acquisition of fresh levies of recruits from Macedonia'); Meeus 2009a, 75–8; Yardley, Wheatley and Heckel 2011, 140–1.

[46] *Pace* Cohen 1974. Cf. also Heckel's (1986a, 294) particularly apt comments on marriage alliances: 'The importance of "political" marriage is almost certainly overestimated by modern scholars. Far from predicting the political inclinations

of an individual, evidence of connection by marriage serves rather to confirm the existence of political cooperation at a time in the past (...) and an intention to continue such cooperation, at least for the period immediately following the wedding. But expediency outweighs commitment to the marriage vow, and, in a number of known cases, the political impact of the union scarcely outlasts the "honeymoon"'. For an overview of the marriages of the Successors after Ipsos, see Seibert 1967, 130–1 and his discussions ibid., *passim*; Cohen 1974, 178–9; Ogden 1999, 59, 74, 120–4 and 175–6.

[47] Cf. Seibert 1967, 18–19 with the nuances added by Bosworth 2002, 262–3 with n. 64. See also Heckel (1986a, 294), who observes that 'political marriages appear to have served the interests of the bridegrooms more often than those of the fathers-in-law'. Of course, drastic solutions were always available, as when Antiochos III ordered his sister Antiochis to kill her husband Xerxes (Johannes Antiochenus F 53 [*FHG* IV, p. 557]) or when Ptolemy VI took his daughter away from his old ally to marry her to a new ally (Diod. 32.9c.1).

[48] Cf. Bevan 1968, 36: 'the tension between one party and another, the friendships and antagonisms, varied continually according to the circumstances of the moment'; Bosworth 2002, 266: 'The constant factor was the mutual suspicion of the leading dynasts. Ipsus had created even more tensions than it resolved'; Waterfield 2011, 174: 'What emerged after Ipsos was not so much a balance of power as a balance of fear'. The argument of recognition has also been applied to the mutual use of the royal title in diplomatic interchanges between the Successors, but seems equally irrelevant there (Meeus 2013, 139 n. 49).

[49] As Austin (1986, 461) rightly observed about Hellenistic kings in general, 'the notion of fixed, stable frontiers is one that is alien to the world of the kings, and it is perhaps no accident that so little is known of treaties made at the conclusion of wars between kings, which may therefore have been conceived as temporary truces without any long-term commitments'. Strootman (2014a, 322) likewise notes the kings' 'refusal to acknowledge borders'.

Bibliography

Adams, W. L.
  1974   Cassander, Macedonia, and the Policy of Coalition, 323–301 BC, diss. University of Virginia.
Ager, S. L.
  2003   'An Uneasy Balance. From the Death of Seleukos to the Battle of Raphia', in A. Erskine (ed.) *A Companion to the Hellenistic World*, Oxford, 35–50.
Allen, R. E.
  1983   *The Attalid Kingdom. A Constitutional History*, Oxford.
Anson, E. M.
  2004   *Eumenes of Cardia. A Greek among Macedonians* (Ancient Mediterranean and Medieval Texts and Contexts. Studies in Philo of Alexandria and Mediterranean Antiquity 3), Boston.
Austin, M. M.
  1986   'Hellenistic Kings, War, and the Economy', *CQ* n.s. 36, 450–66.

Bengtson, H.
   1977[5]   *Griechische Geschichte. Von den Anfängen bis in die römische Kaiserzeit*, Munich.
Bertrand, J.-M. and Gruenais, M.-P.
   1981   'Sur les termes réputés techniques dans les sources anciennes: l'exemple de "topos"', *Langage et société* 16, 67–82.
Bevan, E. R.
   1968[2]   *The House of Ptolemy. A History of Egypt under the Ptolemaic Dynasty*, London.
Billows, R. A.
   1990   *Antigonos the One-Eyed and the Creation of the Hellenistic State* (Hellenistic Culture and Society 4), Berkeley.
Bizière, F.
   1975   (ed., trad.), *Diodore de Sicile*. Bibliothèque historique, *Livre XIX* (Collection des Universités de France), Paris.
Boiy, T.
   2007   *Between High and Low. A Chronology of the Early Hellenistic Period* (Oikoumene. Studien zur antiken Weltgeschichte 5), Frankfurt am Main.
Bosworth, A. B.
   2002   *The Legacy of Alexander. Politics, Warfare, and Propaganda under the Successors*, Oxford.
Bottin, C.
   1928   'Les sources de Diodore de Sicile pour l'histoire de Pyrrhus, des successeurs d'Alexandre-le-Grand et d'Agathocle', *RBPh* 7, 1307–27.
Braunert, H.
   1964   'Hegemoniale Bestrebungen der hellenistischen Großmächte in Politik und Wirtschaft', *Historia* 13, 80–104.
Briant, P.
   1973   *Antigone le Borgne. Les débuts de sa carrière et les problèmes de l'assemblée macédonienne* (Annales littéraires de l'Université de Besançon 152 – Centre de recherches d'histoire ancienne 10), Paris.
Buraselis, K.
   1982   *Das hellenistische Makedonien und die Ägäis. Forschungen zur Politik des Kassandros und der drei ersten Antigoniden im Ägäischen Meer und in Westkleinasien* (Münchener Beiträge zur Papyrusforschung und antiken Rechtsgeschichte 73), Munich.
Burstein, S. M.
   2015   'Alexander's Unintended Legacy: Borders', in T. Howe, E. E. Garvin and G. Wrightson (eds) *Greece, Macedon and Persia: Studies in Social, Political and Military History in honour of Waldemar Heckel*, Oxford, 118–26.
Christ, M. R.
   2010   Review of P. Hunt, 2010 *War, Peace, and Alliance in Demosthenes' Athens*, Cambridge 2010, *BMCR* 2010.10.57 (http://bmcr.brynmawr.edu/2010/2010-10-57.html).
Cloché, P.
   1957   'La coalition de 315–311 av. J.-C. contre Antigone le Borgne', *CRAI* 101, 130–9.

Cohen, G. M.
  1974   'The Diadochoi and the New Monarchies', *Athenaeum* 52, 177–9.
Davies, J. K.
  1994   'On the non-usability of the concept of 'sovereignty' in an ancient Greek
         context', in L. Aigner Foresti *et al.* (eds) *Federazioni e federalismo nell'Europa
         antica* (Alle radici della casa comune europea 1), Milan, 51–65.
  2002   'The Interpenetration of Hellenistic Sovereignties', in D. Ogden (ed.)
         The Hellenistic World. New Perspectives, Swansea, 1–21.
De Schaepdrijver, S.
  2013   *De Groote Oorlog. Het Koninkrijk België tijdens de Eerste Wereldoorlog*, Antwerp.
Eckstein, A. M.
  2006   *Mediterranean Anarchy, Interstate War, and the Rise of Rome* (Hellenistic
         Culture and Society 48), Berkeley.
Errington, R. M.
  1978   'The Nature of the Macedonian State under the Monarchy', *Chiron* 8,
         77–133.
  1983   'The Historiographical Origins of Macedonian *Staatsrecht*', *AM* 3, 89–101.
Gabbert, J. J.
  1997   *Antigonus II Gonatas. A Poltical Biography*, London.
Gehrke, H. J.
  1982   'Der siegreiche König. Überlegungen zur hellenistischen Monarchie',
         AKG 64, 247–77.
  2008⁴ *Geschichte des Hellenismus* (Oldenbourg Grundriß der Geschichte 1B),
         Munich.
Goukowsky, P.
  1978   (ed. trad.), *Diodore de Sicile*. Bibliothèque historique, *livre XVIII*
         (Collection des Unversités de France), Paris.
Grainger, J. D.
  1990   *Seleukos Nikator. Constructing a Hellenistic Kingdom*, London.
  2010   *The Syrian Wars* (Mnemosyne Suppl. 320), Leiden.
Gullath, B.
  1982   *Untersuchungen zur Geschichte Boiotiens in der Zeit Alexanders und der Diadochen*
         (Europäische Hochschulschriften III, 169), Frankfurt am Main.
Habicht, C.
  1995   *Athen. Die Geschichte der Stadt in hellenistischer Zeit*, Munich.
  2006   *The Hellenistic Monarchies. Selected Papers*, Ann Arbor.
Hammond, N. G. L.
  1988   with F. W. Walbank, *A History of Macedonia* III, *336–167 BC*, Oxford.
  1999   'The Nature of the Hellenistic States', *AM* 6, 483–8.
Hau, L. I.
  2009   'The Burden of Good Fortune in Diodoros of Sicily: a Case for
         Originality?', *Historia* 58, 171–97.
Hauben, H.
  2014   'Ptolemy's Grand Tour', in H. Hauben and A. Meeus (eds) *The Age of
         the Successors and the Creation of the Hellenistic Dynasties (323–276 BC)* (Studia
         Hellenistica 53), Leuven, 235–61.

Heckel, W.
  1986a   'Factions and Macedonian Politics in the Reign of Alexander the Great', *AM 6*, 293–305.
  1986b   'Review of Buraselis 1982', *Phoenix* 40, 458–61.
  1992   *The Marshals of Alexander's Empire*, London.
Heinen, H.
  2003   *Geschichte des Hellenismus. Von Alexander bis Kleopatra* (Wissen in der Beck'schen Reihe), Munich.
Heuß, A.
  1938   'Antigonos Monophthalmos und die griechischen Städte', *Hermes* 73, 133–94.
Horat Zuffa, G.
  1971/2 'Tolemeo I in Grecia', *AttiVen* 130, 99–112.
Hornblower, J.
  1981   *Hieronymus of Cardia*, Oxford.
Huß, W.
  2001   *Ägypten in hellenistischer Zeit. 332–30 v. Chr.*, Munich.
Kuzmin Y.
  2015   'The Antigonids, Caunus and the so-called "Era of Monophthalmus": Some Observations Prompted by a New Inscription', in V. Goušchin and P. J. Rhodes (eds) *Deformations and Crises of Ancient Civil Communities*, Stuttgart, 73–85.
Landucci Gattinoni, F.
  2005   'La tradizione su Seleuco in Diodoro XVIII–XX', in C. Bearzot and F. Landucci (eds) *Diodoro e l'altra Grecia. Macedonia, Occidente, Ellenismo nella Biblioteca storica*, Milan, 155–81.
  2008   *Diodoro Siculo,* Biblioteca Storica, *Libro XVIII. Commento Storico*, Milan.
Lefèvre, F.
  1998   'Traité de paix entre Démétrios Poliorcète et la confédération étolienne (fin 289?)', *BCH* 122, 109–41.
Lund, H. S.
  1992   *Lysimachos. A Study in Early Hellenistic Kingship*, London.
Malitz, J.
  2007   'Von Alexander bis Kleopatra. Die Politische Geschichte', in G. Weber (ed.) *Kulturgeschichte des Hellenismus. Von Alexander dem Großen bis Kleopatra*, Stuttgart, 13–55.
Manni, E.
  1951   *Demetrio Poliorcete*, Rome.
Marek, C.
  2006   *Die Inschriften von Kaunos* (Vestigia 55), Munich.
Mauersberger, A.
  1966 *Polybios-Lexikon* I.3 (η-κ), Berlin.
Meadows, A.
  2006   'The Ptolemaic Annexation of Lycia: *SEG* 27.929', in K. Dörtlük *et al.* (eds) *The IIIrd Symposium on Lycia, 07–10 November 2005, Antalya. Symposium Proceedings*, Antalya, 459–70.

Meeus, A.

2008   'The Power Struggle of the Diadochoi in Babylon, 323 BC', *AncSoc* 38, 39–82.

2009a   'Kleopatra and the Diadochoi', in P. Van Nuffelen (ed.) *Faces of Hellenism. Studies in the History of the Eastern Mediterranean (4th century BC– 5th century AD)* (Studia Hellenistica 48), Leuven, 63–92.

2009b   'Some Institutional Problems concerning the Succession to Alexander the Great: *Prostasia* and Chiliarchy', *Historia* 58, 287–310.

2009c   *The History of the Diadochoi in Book XIX of Diodorus Siculus'* Bibliotheca Historica. *A Historical and Historiographical Commentary*, diss. Leuven.

2012a   'Diodorus and the Chronology of the Third Diadoch War', *Phoenix* 66, 74–96.

2012b   'Review of Waterfield 2011', *AHB Online Reviews* 2, 70–4.

2013   'Confusing Aim and Result? Hindsight and the Disintegration of Alexander the Great's Empire', in A. Powell (ed.) *Hindsight in Greek and Roman History*, Swansea, 113–47.

2014   'The Territorial Ambitions of Ptolemy I', in H. Hauben and A. Meeus (eds) *The Age of the Successors and the Creation of the Hellenistic Dynasties (323–276 BC)* (Studia Hellenistica 53), Leuven, 263–306.

2015   'The Career of Sostratos of Knidos: Politics, Diplomacy and the Alexandrian Building Programme in the Early Hellenistic Period', in T. Howe, E. E. Garvin and G. Wrightson (eds) *Greece, Macedon and Persia: Studies in Social, Political and Military History in Honour of Waldemar Heckel*, Oxford, 143–71.

Mehl, A.

1980/1 'Ἀδορίκτητος χώρα. Kritische Bemerkungen zum «Speererwerb» in Politik und Völkerrecht der hellenistische Epoche', *AncSoc* 11/12, 173–212.

1986   *Seleukos Nikator und sein Reich* I. Teil, *Seleukos' Leben und die Entwicklung seiner Machtposition* (Studia Hellenistica 28), Leuven.

Mendels, D.

1984   'Aetolia 331–301: Frustration, Political Power, and Survival', *Historia* 33, 129–80.

Mileta, C.

2012   'Ein Agon um Macht und Ehre. Beobachtungen zu den agonalen Aspekten der Königserhebungen im ›Jahr der Könige‹', in A. Lichtenberger *et al.* (eds) *Das Diadem der hellenistischen Herrscher. Übernahme, Transformation oder Neuschöpfung eines Herrschaftszeichens?* (Euros 1), Bonn, 315–34.

Mooren, L.

1989   'Ptolemaic and Hellenistic Institutions in Literary Sources', in L. Criscuolo and G. Geraci (eds) *Egitto e Storia antica dall'Ellenismo all'età araba. Bilancio di un confronto*, Bologna, 573–81.

Müller, O.

1973   *Antigonos Monophthalamos und 'Das Jahr der Könige.' Untersuchungen zur Begründung der hellenistischen Monarchien, 306–304 v.Chr.* (Saarbrücker Beiträge zur Altertumskunde 11), Bonn.

Ogden, D.
   1999   *Polygamy, Prostitutes and Death. The Hellenistic Dynasties*, Swansea and London.

Palm, J.
   1955   *Über Sprache und Stil des Diodoros von Sizilien*, Lund.

Rathmann, M.
   2014   'Diodor und seine Quellen. Zur Kompilationstechnik des Historiographen', in H. Hauben and A. Meeus (eds) *The Age of the Successors and the Creation of the Hellenistic Dynasties (323–276 BC)* (Studia Hellenistica 53), Leuven, 49–113.

Rhodes, P. J.
   2008   'Making and Breaking Treaties in the Greek World', in P. de Souza and J. France (eds) *War and Peace in Ancient and Medieval History*, Cambridge, 6–27.

Roisman, J.
   2010   'Classical Macedonia to Perdiccas III', in J. Roisman and I. Worthington (eds) *A Companion to Ancient Macedonia*, Malden, MA, 145–65.
   2012   *Alexander's Veterans and the Early Wars of the Successors*, Austin.

Rosen, K.
   1968   'Die Bündnisformen der Diadochen und der Zerfall des Alexanderreiches', *AClass* 11, 182–210.

Schäfer, C.
   2002   *Eumenes von Kardia und der Kampf um die Macht im Alexanderreich* (Frankfurter Althistorische Beiträge 9), Frankfurt am Main.

Scharff, S.
   2009   '„Da sie als erste, gegen die Eide, Schaden verübten,..." – Zur Bedeutung von Vertragseiden im zwischenstaatlichen Bereich bei den Griechen', *Zeitschrift für Altorientalische und Biblische Rechtsgeschichte* 15, 316–32.

Schmitt, H. H.
   1964   *Untersuchungen zur Geschichte Antiochos' des Großen und seiner Zeit* (Historia Einzelschriften 6), Wiesbaden.

Schmitt, O.
   1992   *Der Lamische Krieg*, Bonn.

Seibert, J.
   1967   *Historische Beiträge zu den dynastischen Verbindungen in hellenistischer Zeit* (Historia Einzelschriften 10), Wiesbaden.
   1969   *Untersuchungen zur Geschichte Ptolemaios' I.* (Münchener Beiträge zur Papyrusforschung und antiken Rechtsgeschichte 56), Munich.
   1991   'Zur Begründung von Herrschaftsanspruch und Herrschaftslegitimierung in der frühen Diadochenzeit', in id. (ed.) *Hellenistische Studien. Gedenkschrift für Hermann Bengtson* (Münchener Arbeiten zur Alten Geschichte 5), Munich, 87–100.

Shear, T. L., Jr.
   1978   *Kallias of Sphettos and the Revolt of Athens in 286 BC.* (Hesperia. Supplement 17), Princeton.

Sherwin-White, S. and Kuhrt, A.
   1993   *From Samarkhand to Sardis. A New Approach to the Seleucid Empire*, London.
Simpson, R. H.
   1954   'The Historical Circumstances of the Peace of 311', *JHS* 74, 25–31.
   1959   'Antigonus the One-Eyed and the Greeks', *Historia* 8, 385–409.
Smith, L. C.
   1961   'The Chronology of Books XVIII–XX of Diodorus Siculus', *AJPh* 82, 283–90.
Stengers, J.
   1990   'La Belgique', in J. J. Becker (ed.) *Les sociétés européennes et la guerre de 1914–1918*, Paris, 75–91.
Stewart, A.
   2014   *Art in the Hellenistic World. An Introduction*, Cambridge.
Strootman, R.
   2014a   '"Men to Whose Rapacity neither Sea nor Mountain Sets a Limit": The Aims of the Diadochs', in H. Hauben and A. Meeus (eds) *The Age of the Successors and the Creation of the Hellenistic Dynasties (323–276 BC)* (Studia Hellenistica 53), Leuven, 307–22.
   2014b   'Hellenistic Imperialism and the Ideal of World Unity', in C. Rapp and H. Drake (eds) *The City in the Classical and Post-Classical World: Changing Contexts of Power and Identity*, Cambridge, 38–61.
Walbank, F. W.
   1981   *The Hellenistic World*, Brighton.
Waterfield, R.
   2011   *Dividing the Spoils. The War for Alexander the Great's Empire*, Oxford.
Wehrli, C.
   1968   *Antigone et Démétrios*, Geneva.
Welles, C. B.
   1934   *Royal Correspondence in the Hellenistic Period. A Study in Greek Epigraphy*, New Haven.
Wheatley, P. V.
   1998   'The Date of Polyperchon's Invasion of Macedonia and Murder of Heracles', *Antichthon* 32, 12–23.
Will, É.
   1979²   *Histoire politique du monde hellénistique (323–30 av. J.C.)* I, Nancy.
Worthington, I.
   1984   'IG II² 370 and the Date of the Athenian Alliance with Aetolia', *ZPE* 57, 139–44.
Yardley, J. C.
   1994   (trad.), *Justin*. Epitome of the Philippic History of Pompeius Trogus (Classical Resources 3), Atlanta.
Yardley, J. C., Wheatley, P. and Heckel, W.
   2011   *Justin. Epitome of the Philippic History of Pompeius Trogus. Vol. 2, Books 13–15: The Successors to Alexander the Great*, Oxford.

Appendix: Overview of explicitly attested alliances and treaties among the Successors down to 279 BC

Year	Parties	Sources	Description	Reason	Breach
323/2	Ptolemaios and Antipatros	D. 18.14.2	κοινοπραγίαν συνέθετο	'he well knew that Perdiccas would attempt to wrest from him the satrapy of Egypt'	– (alliance renewed in 321/0; Antipatros † 319)
323/2	Antipatros and Leonnatos	D. 18.12.1, 14.4; P. E. 3.3; J. 13.5.14	ἐπηγγείλατο συμμαχήσειν	Lamian war/Leonnatos wants to seize Macedon	Leonn. † almost immediately after, breach was planned
323/2	Antipatros and Krateros	D. 18.12.1, 16.4; A. F1.12	Βοηθῆσαι // συμμαχόν	Lamian war	– (Krateros † 320)
c.323–1	Antipatros and Perdikkas	D. 18.23.1–3; A. F1.21; J. 13.6.5–7	κοινοπραγία		321/0
321	Antipatros, Krateros and Antigonos	D. 18.25.3; A. F1.24; J. 13.6.8–9	Auxilium ferebant	Perdikkas' chasing Antigonos and his ambitions on Macedonia	(Krateros † 320; Antipatros † 319; Antigonos was plotting breach)
321/0	Antipatros, Krateros and Ptolemaios	D. 18.25.4, 29.6	κοινοπραγία // συμμαχία	war against Perdikkas; they knew Ptol. was on their side	– (Krateros † 320, war ended in 320, Antipatros † 319)
320	Neoptolemos and Antipatros, Krateros	D. 18.29.4; A. F1.27; J. 13.8.3–5	συνθέμενος κοινοπραγίαν // πείθει τούτους ἐπὶ συμμαξίαν κατὰ Εὐμένους	'Neoptol. (...) was jealous of Eumenes'	– (Neoptol. and Krat. died within months, Antip. in 319)

A. = Arrian, *Succ.*; D. = Diodorus; J. = Justin; P. = Plutarch (E. = Eumenes; De. = *Demetrius*; Py. = *Pyrrhus*); Pa. = Pausanias

319	Kassandros and Ptolemaios	D. 18.49.3	τήν τε φιλίαν ἀνανεούμενος καὶ παρακαλῶν συμμαχεῖν αὐτῷ καὶ ναυτικὴν δύναμιν πέμψαι	War against Polyperchon	– (new alliance in 315)
319	Kassandros and Antigonos	D. 18.54.3	ἐπηγγείλατο πάντα συμπράξειν προθύμως αὐτῷ	War against Polyperchon	– (enemies after ultimatum of 315)
318	Antigonos and Eumenes	D. 18.50.4, 53.5; P. E. 12.1–2 (StV III 418)	παρακαλῶν (...) γενέσθαι δὲ φίλον καὶ σύμμαχον αὐτῷ // παρεκάλεσεν αὐτὸν πρὸς κοινοπραγίαν // φίλον ἔχειν καὶ συνεργὸν ἐπὶ τὰς πράξεις	Assistance in gaining the entire empire (P.)	immediate according to P., later that year according to D. 18.58.4
318	Polyperchon and Eumenes	D. 18.57.3	μετ' αὐτοῦ κοινοπραγῶν	War against Antigonos and Kassandros, presented as protecting the kings	– (Eumenes † winter 317/6)
318	Polyperchon, Kleitos, Arrhidaios	D. 18.72.1–2		War against Antigonos	– (Kleitos † soon after; Arrhidaios = ?)
318	All satraps east of Babylonia	D. 19.13.7–14.2	συνδεδραμηκέναι πρὸς ἀλλήλους	War against Peithon	–
317	Eumenes and the eastern satraps	P. E. 13.4; D. 19.15.1	συνεμίξαντο τὰς δυνάμεις	War against Antigonos	Winter 317/6: most desert Eumenes after the defeat at Gabiene
317	Antigonos, Seleukos and Peithon	D. 19.17.2	συνέθετο κοινοπραγίαν	War against Eumenes	Ant. kills Peith. in winter 317/6, chases Sel. in 316

Date	Parties	Source	Greek	Purpose	Notes
315	Ptolemaios, Kassandros and Lysimachos (and Seleukos)	D. 19.57.2; J. 15.1.4	συμμαχίαν πρὸς ἀλλήλους ποιησάμενοι // Ptolomeus et Cassander inita cum Lysimacho et Seleuco societate	War against Antigonos	– (but acts against the spirit of the treaty by Ptol. twice in 315 and Kass. in 312; initially separate peace for Kass. and Lys.)
315	Antigonos and Polyperchon, Alexander	D. 19.60.1, 61.1	φιλίαν συνέθετο	War against Kassandros and his allies	315: Alexander joins Kassandros
315	Asandros and Ptolemaios, Kassandros and Lysimachos (and Seleukos)	D. 19.62.2	συμμαχία		313: Asandros makes a treaty with Antigonos
315	Kassandros and Alexander	D. 19.64.4	συμμαχίαν ποιησάμενος	War against Antigonos	– (Alexander † soon after)
313	Asandros and Antigonos	D. 19.75.1 (*StV* III 425)	διελύσατο πρὸς Ἀντίγονον		313, μετ' ὀλίγας ἡμέρας (19.75.2)
311	Kassandros, Lysimachos, Ptolemaios, Antigonos	D. 19.105.1; *RC* 1/*OGIS* 5 (*StV* III 428)	διαλύσεις ἐποιήσαντο πρὸς Ἀντίγονον καὶ συνθήκας ἔγραψαν	Avoiding war on too many fronts or isolation	Ptolemaios in 310 (D. 20.19.3–4), Antigonids in 307 (20.45.1); both under guise of Greek freedom
310	Polemaios and Kassandros	D. 20.19.2	πρὸς δὲ Κάσσανδρον συμμαχίαν ἐποιήσατο		Pol. allies himself with Ptolemaios soon after
309	Polemaios and Ptolemaios	D. 20.27.3	πρὸς δὲ Πτολεμαῖον κοινοπραγίαν ἐτίθετο		Ptol. kills Pol. almost immediately
309	Kassandros and Polyperchon	D. 20.28.3	κοινοπραγῶν	Kassandros: to remove threat of Herakles,	– (Polyperchon † 308?)

Polyperchon: regaining former possessions, becoming general Peloponnese

309/8	Ptolemaios and Demetrios	Suid. s.v. Δημήτριος (Δ 431 Adler) (*StV* III 433)	ὡμολόγησαν φιλίαν σφίσιν ἔνσπονδον εἶναι	Avoiding war on several fronts simultaneously	306 (invasion of Cyprus) if not earlier
308	Ptolemaios and Kassandros	D. 20.37 (*StV* III 434)	πρὸς μὲν Κάσσανδρον εἰρήνην ἐποιήσατο	Lack of success in Ptolemaios' campaign; Antigonos' return west (?)	– (renewed in 302)
302	Kassandros and Lysimachos	D. 20.106.2	Λυσίμαχον ἐκ τῆς Θράκης μετεπέμψατο πρὸς τὴν τῶν ὅλων κοινοπραγίαν	War against Antigonos	– (Kassandros † 297)
302	Kassandros+Lysimachos, Ptolemaios, Seleukos	D.S. 20.106.3–5, 21.1.2; P. De. 28.1; J. 15.2.15–17 (*StV* III 447)	συνετάξαντο πρὸς ἀλλήλους βοηθεῖν δορᾷς δυνάμεσι // τὴν τῶν ὅλων κοινοπραγίαν // συνισταμένων ἐπὶ τὸν Ἀντίγονον // bellum communibus uiribus instruunt.	War against Antigonos, 'the danger was common to all' (D. 20.106.3; 'compelled by the fears each had for himself' (D. 21.1.2)	In practice immediately by Ptolemaios (cf. D. 21.1.5), and to some extent by Kassandros (D. 20.111.2)
302	Lysimachos and Dokimos	D. 20.107.4; Pa. 1.8.1	συμμαχεῖν	War against Antigonos	–
302	Kassandros and Demetrios	D. 20.111.2 (*StV* III 448)	πρὸς μὲν Κάσσανδρον διαλύσεις ἐποιήσατο	Demetrios' retreat to Asia for Ipsos	Never ratified by Antigonos, as was Dem.'s intention

300	Lysimachos and Ptolemaios	P. *De.* 31.3; J. 15.4.23–24			– (some indications of acting against spirit of alliance)
300	Seleukos and Demetrios	P. *De.* 31.3; J. 15.4.23–24	οἰκειότης	Marriage alliance between Ptolemaios and Lysimachos	288/7 (Sel. in alliance against Dem.; earlier antagonism, P. *De.* 32.4–33.1)
297	Demetrios and Ptolemaios	P. *De.* 32.3, *Py.* 4.3	φιλία, σύμβασις		294: Ptol. intervenes near Athens, reconquers Cyprus, P. *De.* 35.3)
c. 294?	Antipatros and Lysimachos	Euseb. *Chron.* 110 (Kraft); cf. J. 16.1.7			Lysimachos soon had Antipatros killed (J. 16.2.4)
294	Alexander and Pyrrhos	P. *De.* 36.1, *Py.* 6.2–3 (*StV* III 458)	συμμαχία	Quarrel between Alexander and his brother Antipatros	– (immediate fear, Alexander dies soon after)
294	Lysimachos and Demetrios	J. 16.1.19 (*StV* III 460)	pacem cum eo fecit	To have his hands free for the war with Dromichaites	292: Demetrios invades Thrace
288/7	Demetrios and Pyrrhos	P. *De.* 43.1, *Py.* 10.4	ὁμολογίαι	Demetrios wanted to avoid that Pyrrhus would invade Macedonia while he was campaigning elsewhere	287: Pyrrhos invades Macedon (P. *De.* 44.1, *Py.* 11.1)

135

288/7	Seleukos, Ptolemaios and Lysimachos, and Pyrrhos	P. *De.* 44.1; J. 16.2.1–2	Συνέστησαν ἐπὶ τὸν Δημήτριον	Demetrios' vast ambitions	287: Ptolemy makes peace with Demetrios and allows him to attack Lysimachos and Seleukos
287	Ptolemaios and Demetrios	*SEG* XXVIII 60, l. 32–40	εἰρήνη		– (Demetrios captured by Seleukos in 285)
287	Pyrrhos and Demetrios	P. *Py.* 12.5	πρὸς Δημήτριον εἰρήνην ἐποιήσατο		Pyrrhos soon re-opens hostilities (μετ' ὀλίγον χρόνον, P. *Py.* 12.5)
287/6	Lysimachos and Pyrrhos	P. *Py.* 12.1		Pyrrhos did not risk war yet, because he did not fully trust the Macedonians	286/5: Lysimachos attacks Pyrrhos (P. *Py.* 12.6; J. 16.3.1)
c. 282?	Seleukos and Ptolemaios II (?)	Pa. 1.7.3	συνθήκας πρὸς Πτολεμαῖον		c. 275? (Pa. 1.7.3)
280	Pyrrhos and Ptolemaios Keraunos	J. 17.2.15, 24.1.8	pacificatus; matrimonium (of Pyrrhos with Ptolemaios' daughter) // adfinitas	Removing all threats before crossing the Adriatic	– (Ptolemaios † 279)
280	Ptolemaios Keraunos and Antiochos	J. 24.1.8	Pacem cum Antiocho facit		– (Ptolemaios † 279)
279	Antiochos I and Antigonos Gonatas	Just. 25.1.1	'statuta pace'		–

PART III

ROYAL SELF-PRESENTATION
AND IDEOLOGY

7

THE ANIMAL TYPES ON THE ARGEAD
COINAGE: WILDERNESS AND MACEDONIA

Víctor Alonso Troncoso

'Perhaps in the leafy coverts
of Olympus where Orpheus, playing his lyre,
assembled the beasts of the wild.
Happy Pieria, ...

(Euripides, *Bacchae* 560–65; transl. D. Kovacs, Loeb).

Horses, goats, lions, eagles, dogs, wolves, boars, bulls, serpents and frogs appear on the coinage of the Argead kings, from Alexander Philhellene to Alexander the Great and Philip Arrhidaios. As far as I know, no other city or any other kingdom in the entire Greek world can offer such an extraordinarily diverse variety of animals on its coins, to put it in the words of Franke (1952/3, 106), at least during the same period. Conversely, the Antipatrids and the Antigonids did not appreciably expand the repertoire of zoological types on their coinage. Not even the bull, associated with the Antigonids as a game animal,[1] represented a novelty in the regal currency of Hellenistic Macedonia. Some species remained for several generations as long-term emblems of the dynastic identity, while other animals had only a short period of life, attached to one or two rulers, for instance the wolf under Archelaos. At least one animal seems to have achieved the status of royal icon, the lion, being exclusively related to the person of the sovereign or his house, but surely not all the zoology featured on the coin types represented the king's power nor did all beasts enjoy the same positive qualities. For instance, horses and dogs continued to be associated with the Argeads in different ways, although it remains difficult to gauge the extent to which these domestic species, without further qualifications,

137

can be labelled as specifically kingly emblems. Were they not symbols of aristocratic status in general? Moreover, the supernatural or numinous dimension of certain creatures, like the eagle or the goat, is not as clearly present in others.

It has often been noted that the earliest royal issues borrowed a lot from the so-called 'tribal' coinages of the Thraco-Macedonian area, as well as from the Greek *poleis* scattered along the coasts, regarding denominations, iconography and style.[2] Of course, Macedonian regal coinage did not emerge *ex nihilo* and did not evolve in isolation, but I think that these obvious influences should not obscure the peculiarities of the regal coinage, in particular the role played by the 'identity politics' of the Argeads when choosing some coin types instead of others. As noted repeatedly by Herodotos (5.22; 8.137–9), the Macedonian royal house boasted of descending from the Temenids of Argos, a claim that ultimately meant presenting themselves in the region as Hellenes among barbarians.

The kings and their animal types

To begin with, this is the case of Alexander I (c. 498/7–454) (later Philhellene), the first king of the dynasty to mint coins, sometime after the retreat of the Persians from Greece in 479.[3] As Raymond (*MRC* 85) observed, in his coinage three aims were embodied: 'it was to be readily exchangeable with the most influential currencies of the Aegean area; it was to be readily recognized as Macedonian; and it was to be unmistakably a regal issue'.

Alexander's currency presents three obverse and five reverse types. The first basic type of the obverse is the so-called Rider, holding reins and two spears, wearing a tunic and *chlamys*, with a *petasos* as headgear, and occasionally accompanied by a dog.[4] It must be noted that this device prevails on the larger denominations, octadrachms and tetradrachms, and it also appears on the heavy tetrobols. The second basic type consists of a horse with his horseman standing behind the animal, again carrying two spears and exhibiting the same dress.[5] This device appears on the octadrachms, which points to its importance, and on the octobols. The third obverse type is a horse unattended, and its minting is limited to lesser denominations and fractions.[6] A fourth obverse type that adds nothing new to the equine theme is the forepart of a horse, limited to the smallest fractions.[7] In the light of this iconography, it makes sense that Hesiod (F 7 Merkelbach, West) had written of Makedon, the mythological son of Zeus and Thyia, that 'he delighted in horses'.[8]

The type with the mounted horseman, however, presents three variations that are quite relevant for this investigation. In a series of octadrachms belonging to Raymond Group I (480/79–477/6), there appears an enormous frog below the horse,[9] which most probably alludes to the typical lakes and marshy landscapes of the country, e.g. in the Emathian and Strymonian plains and along the lower Axios river.[10] In a subsequent series of the same group we see a hound leaping up before the horse,[11] while in the third group of emissions (c. 460–451) the *canis* is probably a Maltese/Melitaean (Gaebler 1935, 152), perhaps a companion dog.[12] Clearly, the engraver has been very careful to capture the differences between the two breeds of dogs.

Out of the five reverse types designed by Alexander's engravers (and apart from the helmeted head, the crested helmet, and the caduceus), two feature animals in incuse square. One, the most important, presents the head or the forepart of a goat on tetradrachms (fig. 1), being paired in this case with the mounted horseman (fig. 2),[13] and also on light tetrobols of Group I, having here the horse unattended as obverse (*MRC* 68–9, 88, no. 34). The other type consists of the head of a lion showing its right paw, unique to the heavy tetrobols.[14] In reality, the caprine iconography constituted no novelty, as it had already appeared on earlier civic or tribal issues.[15] In the present case the primary meaning of the goat may refer to religious worship, possibly of Dionysus, if not Hermes (Westermark 1993, 20–1), though the cycle of legends about the foundation of the dynasty and its old capital, Aigai, must have provided an additional source of inspiration.[16] Famously, Alexander the Great would remind his compatriots

Fig. 1. Silver tetradrachm (rev.) of Alexander I (ANS, 1963.268.40)

Fig. 2. Silver tetradrachm (obv.) of Alexander I (ANS, 1963.268.40)

All photos are reproduced with the permission of the American Numismatic Society (New York)

that until the reforms of his father most of them lived in goat-hair cloaks and herded sheep upon the mountains (Arr. *An.* 7.9.2); and likewise the memory of 'a land of many flocks' (Diod. 7.16; cf. schol. Clem.Al. *Prot.* 2.11), as the Delphic oracle once put it (Parke, Wormell 2004, n° 226), had inspired in early times one of the most important stories about the Argeads' origins (Just. 7.1.7–2.1). Perdikkas, the founder king of the dynasty, shepherded lesser stock, unlike his two older brothers, who tended horses and oxen (Hdt. 8.137.2). In any case, the caprine device on Philhellene's coinage is no longer the magnificent kneeling goat on the obverse of the tribal issues, as Hammond (1979, 86) pointed out, but a protome or a mere head exhibited as a reverse type concurrently with the crested helmet.[17] For its part, the lion was initially used for the heavy tetrobols of Group I, having as obverse the same mounted man. The intermission of the heavy tetrobols left their reverse type, the lion, unused in Group II between 475/76 and c. 460, contrary to the goat, which remained on the tetradrachms during this period. At any rate, the heavy tetrobols returned with Group III, c. 460–451, carrying again the forepart of the feline. Since this is the only animal type used by Alexander that did not have a place in the tribal issues (*MRC* 59, 111), I wonder if the lion reflects, even better than the goat, the Macedonian ethnicity according to the Argead point of view.[18] The question is what the big cat means on this coinage.

It has been debated whether the feline head contains a remote reference to Herakles (so Franke 1952/3, 107), the ancestor of the Temenid dynasty, or whether 'that type has an uncompromising anonymity'.[19] Again, such a symbolic beast as the lion may have connoted various things, though in this case I incline to think that the allusion to its status as the prey (and contender) par excellence of royal hunting was inescapable. Herodotos (7.125–6), Xenophon (*Cyn.* 11.1), Aristotle (*HA* 6.31, 579a; 8.28, 606b), Pausanias (6.5.4–5; cf. 9.40.8–9), Pliny (*NH* 8.45) and Dio Chrysostom (21.1) report that lions existed in areas of Macedonia and surrounding regions in the classical period.[20] Most researchers agree that the extinction of this felid in all Greece happened in the second half of the 1st millennium BC or at the beginning of the Christian era.[21] Moreover, it cannot be by chance that the lion type has on the obverse of the coin the figure of the rider, perhaps suggesting the idea of hunting.[22]

If the denominations for export also served the Argead policy of promoting and raising the prestige of the dynasty beyond Macedonia, it is noteworthy that the chosen zoological imagery for the large denominations is equine and equestrian, in contrast to the prevalent bovine (oxen) devices of the neighboring tribes: the Edonoi of King Getas (*ACGC* nos. 482–83), the Orreskioi (*ACGC* no. 481; *SNG ANS* 7 nos. 977, 983–8), the Tyntenoi

(*ACGC* no. 485), the Ichnai (*SNG ANS* 7 nos. 939–43) and above all the Derrones (*SNG ANS* 7 nos. 927–36; *ACGC* nos. 486–8), with Hermes as the patron of the cattle-herders (*ACGC* 139–40; Hammond 1979, 82). These iconographic variations on the cattle theme cannot have been gratuitous, especially if we bear in mind that in ancient Greece animal husbandry and social power formed the fundamental structure of 'pastoral politics' (Howe 2008). Of course, pastoral politics could also involve identity strategies, since such variations and preferences often signalled ethnic boundaries from one tribe to another, or from one region (e.g., Macedonia) to another (Thrace or Illyria). For instance, if a connection really existed between the ox as symbol of kingship in Paionia (e.g., among the Derrones) and the ox cart of Gordios in Phrygia, this may explain why Alexander the Great undid the Gordian knot, bearing in mind the political advantages of doing so in terms of international legitimisation (Munn 2008); but his action should not lead us to the conclusion that for the Argeads both equines and bovines were on a par in the zoology of power. The former were far ahead. The omnipresence of the horse on the first Macedonian regal coinage is undeniable and meaningful, pointing to a 'hippocentric' ideology of kingship under Alexander I (Tripodi 1998, 33; cf. Franks 2012, 48). In particular, the political message of the monarch may well have included the vindication of the cavalry's role in the kingdom's army – note Thucydides' remark (2.100.6) on 'the good horsemen and cuirassiers' of Perdikkas II, comparable in their level of training to his father's forces (cf. Th. 2.100.2). Moreover, the reading of the rider in military terms was encouraged by the fact that the crested helmet was chosen as his reverse type on a series of tetradrachms (*MRC* nos. 8–13), apart from the long-lived helmet series of light tetrobols showing a standing equine on the obverse (*MRC* Groups I–III). That said, it must be recalled that it is not a rider in full armour who appears on these emissions, but rather someone equipped for hunting on horseback (so Borza 1990, 130), in particular to pursue big game, regardless of whether he stands for the king himself, for the idea of kingship or more generally for the Macedonian mounted elite.[23]

The son and successor of Alexander I, Perdikkas II (454–413), struck no large coins of silver, possibly due to the loss of control over the mining areas, and used the two tetrobol denominations, starting with the light tetrobols and finally ending with them;[24] the heavy tetrobols were struck at first concurrently with the light, then alone for about ten years, after which time they were abandoned.[25] It has generally been observed that Perdikkas did not introduce novelties in the iconography of the royal coinage, the boar aside, and 'except that the reverse of the light tetrobol is now simply

Fig. 3. Silver tetrobol (obv.) of
Perdikkas II (ANS, 1963.268.48)

Fig. 4. Silver tetrobol (rev.) of
Perdikkas II (ANS, 1963.268.48)

a helmet instead of a helmeted head, and that the horses, hitherto almost always walking, begin to gallop'.[26] This statement, however, overlooks a significant change in the zoological hierarchy as presented by the regal coinage. On the heavy tetrobols, in effect, the devices were inherited, but the rider (fig. 3) is now only combined on the reverse with the forepart (not just the head) of a lion showing the two legs (fig. 4), instead of the goat.[27] The latter disappears from the entire coinage in favour of the big feline, which is not only featured more frequently, its design achieving a better quality than Alexander's, but also becomes closer to the idea of hunting embodied, or at least suggested, by the cavalryman on the obverse. Many viewers, insiders and outsiders, may have reasonably concluded that the animal was taken to mean the royal prey par excellence, depicted roaring in an offensive and defensive position.[28] Finally, though this piece of information is usually unknown or forgotten, it is to be noted that Perdikkas' iconography maintained the representation of a dog in at least one issue of the second series of his heavy tetrobols, again a Maltese, accompanying the horseman (fig. 3).[29] Its reappearance reasonably suggests that this canine motif had not been a mere occurrence of Perdikkas' father and that Alexander the Great's love for dogs, beginning with Peritas (Plut. *Alex.* 61.3), was not a mere anecdote, but an inclination without precedents at the royal house (cf. Le Bohec-Bouhet 2011).

According to Raymond (*MRC* 163–4), Perdikkas' fractional pieces show four main combinations: a bridled horse tethered to a ring and a quadripartite incuse square;[30] a similar obverse, but with the reverse showing the forepart of a lion with the king's name in abbreviation, EP;[31] a head of Herakles in his lion-skin on the obverse and on the reverse his bow and club with the legend EP (Raymond 164 pl. XI, f); and, finally, the forepart of a horse galloping, on one side, and the forepart of a boar with faint traces of a club above, on the other, with the letters EP.[32] In fact, however, more varieties are attested in the catalogues, for instance, a bridled horse standing tethered to a ring and the forepart of a boar, a horse standing and the forepart of a lion, and a horse's head and a lion's head within incuse square, with EP.[33]

Again, a difference in emphasis regarding the lion motif and heroic hunting is to be mentioned. If the choice of the Heraklean type can be justified primarily by the Argive ancestry of the Argeads, here for the first time marked on the coins,[34] the fact remains that the hero appears wearing a hunting trophy, the head of the Nemean lion. Out of the twelve labors performed by Herakles, the issuing authority has opted for the epic fight against the great feline. As Carney has concluded (2002, 61), 'whether these images of Heracles purposefully resemble the current ruler, they certainly associate the monarchy with Heracles and lion hunting'. Moreover, the attribution of the fractional issue depicting a boar to Perdikkas II, instead of Perdikkas III, could be disputed, but probably the former is the best candidate, not least because the style of the half-horse on the obverse is very like that of the horses of the fourth series of light tetrobols, and because by the second quarter of the fourth century fractional pieces were regularly issued in bronze (*MRC* 164–5). The club over the boar with one leg bent may be an allusion to the fourth labor of Herakles, the capture of the Erymanthian beast (S. *Tr.* 1097; Diod. 4.12.1–2), rather than to the Kalydonian boar hunting, as Raymond (*MRC* 165) pretended (cf. Hammond 1983, 252). Like the lion, the boar appears on the royal coinage to reinforce the idea of the ancestor hero as a big-game hunter, that is, as a *paradeigma* for the entire Argead dynasty. No wonder that a royal cult to Herakles the hunter existed by Hellenistic times.[35]

The son and successor of Perdikkas, Archelaos (413–399), reformed the coinage, reintroducing the larger silver denominations that his father had abandoned and initiating for the first time the bronze issues (Price 1974, 20). As Westermark (1989, 302; 1993, 17) has pointed out, the coinage of this Argead is 'rich and varied'. In fact, the royal mint (Aigai or Pella) exhibits an arresting variety of zoological types, retaking the goat motif, generalising the boar, and incorporating the wolf and the eagle to the official iconography.

The king's new silver coin was struck at a lower weight than the tetradrachms of Alexander I, his larger denomination being the stater (10.90 g), issued in two types: Macedonian horseman (obv.) and forepart of a goat (rev.); young male head (most probably Apollo) wearing *taenia* (obv.) and bridled horse walking (rev.).[36] His second denomination, a light

Fig. 5. Silver obol (obv.) of Archelaos I
(ANS, 1944.100.12153)

Fig. 6. Silver obol (rev.) of Archelaos I
(ANS, 1944.100.12153)

tetrobol on the Thraco-Macedonian standard (Psoma 2000, 134), existed
in two varieties: one retained the old types, with rearing or galloping horse
(obv.) and helmet (rev.), which were previously used by Perdikkas II; the
other had the same obverse type but a new reverse, showing an eagle
standing with spread wings and head turned back,[37] an obvious reference
to Zeus and the idea of majesty, which from now onwards would be
revived by several Macedonian kings: Amyntas III, Perdikkas III and
Alexander the Great.[38] Herakles in the lion's skin reappears on the three
smallest silver fractions of Archelaos, the diobols, obols and hemiobols
(Psoma 2000, 131, 134). He is either unbearded or bearded (fig. 5), and his
main attribute, the club, is found on the reverses above the forepart of a
wolf devouring prey (fig. 6) or below the head of a wolf, and above or below
a lion's head.[39]

As regards the bronze coins of Archelaos, they are much rarer than the
small silver fractions, which at first was taken to mean that these specimens
began to be issued at the end of his reign (Westermark 1987, 181–2; 1989,
304), although an earlier chronology seems now more probable (Gatzolis
2013, 125). Their types are exclusively zoological, without any explicit
Heraklean symbol, alluding primarily to the local wild fauna: the lion, the
boar and, for the first time, the bull, a short-lived icon on the Argead
bronze coinage. Three series are known, struck in two denominations,
B and C: lion's mask facing (obv.) and forepart of a running bull with
APXE legend (rev.);[40] same obverse and forepart of a running boar, and
again APXE (rev.); same obverse and same reverse, with split legend
APXE.[41] The king's initials emphasise, to the last fraction, his personal

identification with the chosen imagery, in a conscious effort to point to the animal world as an essential element in the Argead ideology of kingship.

It was in effect a wild world, but also a world of domestic species, of farmers and herders. Thus, the pastoral theme now has a revival after being overlooked by Perdikkas II. In the present case the caprine motif could be related to the foundation legend of the Argead dynasty according to Euripides' version in *Archelaos*, c. 408/7 (Hammond 1979, 138; Borza 1990, 172). The Temenid hero, descendant from Herakles, fled from Thrace to Macedonia led by a goat, following an oracle from Apollo, and founded the city of Aigai, called after the animal.[42]

At the same time, the legend of Euripides' death in Macedonia bears witness to hunting as a practice of paramount importance at court during the reign of Archelaos (Tripodi 1998, 38–43). The king himself is said to have been accidentally killed by his *erōmenos* Krateros while he was on a hunt (Diod. 14.37.6), though Aristotle claimed, without giving its context, that the death was quite intentional and related to a love affair (*Pol.* 1311b, 8–16). If against this background the appearance of the boar in the regal issues comes as no surprise, the wolf introduces an iconographic novelty that requires an explanation. It was a rare and relatively peripheral device in the history of Greek numismatics,[43] with the exception of Argos (*ACGC* 96, no. 287; Flament 2009), where the wild canid enjoyed a privileged cult status due to its role in the myth of Danaos (the wolf) and Gelanor (the bull), and its association to Apollo Lykeios.[44] Because Argos was the legendary origin of the Argeads, this connection may account in part for the adoption of the wolf as a type by Archelaos (so Psoma 2002, 27), but probably other traditions and feelings inspired his choice as well. Contrary to the classical *polis*, where the wolf was basically seen in negative terms (Mainoldi 1984, 127–41, 213–5; Schnapp 1997, 38–46), the Homeric poems had given quite a positive image of the animal, serving as a metaphor for a warrior's force and aggressiveness (Mainoldi 1984, 97–103). The heroic way of life lived on in the Macedonian elite (Greenwalt 1985a, 156; Cohen 1995), and the packs of wolves moving and hunting freely in a geography that Archelaos himself began to make more accessible (Th. 2.100.2) may also have contributed to illustrating the permanence and poetic validity of the Homeric natural settings. Even the bull, if inspired in types from Thourioi (Westermark 1996, 293), formed part of the Macedonian landscapes, being a natural prey for lions, bears and wolves, as well as later for the Antigonid hunters.

Between Archelaos and Philip II the most important monarch was Amyntas III (394/3–370/69), and this is also valid for the numismatic evidence. Before him, under king Airopos (c. 398/7–395/4), only the lion gnawing a bone represented a new type in bronze (Westermark 1989, 305, 310, fig. 17), a realistic variation on an old theme. Amyntas III added to the zoological imagery the eagle devouring a snake in its claws (fig. 7), on one of his bronze denominations, thus persevering along the same lines of dynastic devotion to wilderness and celebration of nature.[45] The boar's head and the boar's forepart (fig. 9), with a bearded Herakles on the obverse (fig. 10), continued to appear on these bronze emissions for local use (Picard 2003, 77). However, his most important contribution to the visual tradition of the Argead coinage was a new horseman series of silver staters recreating the obverse type of Archelaos and depicting on the

Fig. 7. Bronze unit (rev.) of Amyntas III (ANS, 1944.100.12171)

Fig. 8. Bronze unit (obv.) of Amyntas III (ANS, 1944.100.12171)

Fig. 9. Bronze unit (rev.) of Amyntas III (ANS, 1944.100.12180)

Fig. 10. Bronze unit (obv.) of Amyntas III (ANS, 1944.100.12180)

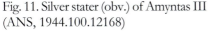

Fig. 11. Silver stater (obv.) of Amyntas III   Fig. 12. Silver stater (rev.) of Amyntas III
(ANS, 1944.100.12168)   (ANS, 1944.100.12168)

reverse a lion crunching a spear in its jaws.[46] The image would be adopted as a standard type on bronzes of Perdikkas III (365–360/59). Its meaning as a mounted huntsman on the obverse (fig. 11) with his quarry, a lion, on the reverse (fig. 12), was first understood by Babelon (1907, 491–2) and later accepted by Kraay (*ACGC* 144, no. 506), Picard (1986, 70), Greenwalt (1993, 515) and Tripodi (1998, 30), whereas Briant (1991, 238–9) has avoided taking a position on the issue. Perhaps it is no coincidence that the lion also appears in the landscape of Karanos' early Macedonia (Paus. 9.40.8–9), the kingdom's mythological founder introduced in the Argead king list precisely during the reigns of Amyntas II and Amyntas III (Greenwalt 1985b; Franks 2012, 111). Furthermore, the design of the stater certainly reinforces the interpretation that the Macedonian rider evoked *prima facie* a hunter (Greenwalt 1993, 515), but at the same time it could be claimed that the pairing of the emblematic figure on horseback with the great cat advertises the symbiosis between monarchy and wilderness, or nature and culture, according to the Argead ideology of power. In this regard, the continuity of Herakles as obverse type in many of these coins may point to his functioning not only as a role model of great hunter, but also as tamer and lord of the beasts, one of his attributes in Greek mythology (Burkert 1979, 78–98; cf. Cohen 1995, 493–4). For the rest, it is noteworthy that the eagle standing with reversed head on Amyntas' fractional silver (*SNG ANS 8* nos. 94–6; *SNG ABC* nos. 200–13) has an exact and contemporary parallel in twelve gilded silver eagles from Katerini (Pieria), from the second quarter of the 4th century, probably ornaments from a leather cuirass (Despini 1988, 279 no. 228).

Fig. 13. Bronze unit (rev.) of
Perdikkas III (ANS, 1944.100.12189)

Fig. 14. Bronze unit (obv.) of
Perdikkas III (ANS, 1944.100.12189)

There is not much to be said about Alexander II, unlike his brother and successor Perdikkas III (365–359). In contrast to the scarce silver, which incorporates the bull head on one of its fractions (Lykiardopoulou, Psoma 2000, 322, 5b), the bronze coins of Perdikkas are plentiful and maintain the usual variety of zoological icons on their obverses: the lion crunching a spear in its jaws (*SNG ANS 8* nos. 114–9), the butting bull (fig. 13) (*SNG ANS 8* nos. 120–1; *SNG ABC* no. 251) and the eagle standing (*SNG ANS 8* no. 113). They present the same obverse type as the silver, the young unbearded Herakles (fig. 14) (see too Westermark 1989, 309, 314–5; Picard 2003, 78).

It is my contention that Philip II (359–336) represented a turning point in the history of the Argead coinage. This exceptional king internationalised the iconography by emphasising the panhellenic dimension of the remaining animal type, the horse – 'suited to a vision of a pan-Hellenic Empire' (Price 1974, 22). The imaginative zoology of kingship, which had dominated the previous dynastic iconographies, now gave ground in favour of Zeus, the god of Olympia and Mount Olympus, and Apollo, the Delphic deity. To both sanctuaries the Argead was attached, both agonistically and politically. Philip's images maintain the larger theme of the horseman, but without hunting connotations. On his gold and silver currency the prevailing types are the disarmed cavalryman, in a pose of political or military triumph, the naked jockey on horseback holding a palm, and the chariot driver on a *biga*, in the latter two cases with agonistic denotations (Le Rider 1977, 364–9). The traditional equine type is now reinterpreted as a genuine panhellenic and Olympic emblem, an idea reinforced by the image of Zeus on the obverse. No other animals appear prominently on his gold and silver coinage, except the typical lion on the hemistaters from Pella and Amphipolis, paired with Herakles in lion headdress on the obverse (Le Rider 1977, 237–8, 248, 251). Philipp, therefore, imposes a more urbane and domestic iconographic program, far from the idea of wilderness and the regional exoticisms. Also the founder figure of the dynasty (Perdikkas, Archelaos or Karanos), probably featured on his hemidrachms, is relegated to pieces 'that were essentially destined to circulate in the interior of the kingdom' (Le Rider 1977, 368). Alexander the Great continued and even simplified his father's numismatic legacy. Only the eagle figures prominently in his emissions, both on the limited issues known as the 'eagle coinage', conventionally ascribed to the mint of Amphipolis (Price 1991, 103–4, pl. 143), and above all on his typical tetradrachms, forming a unitary image with the father of the gods. It should not be ruled out that this eagle could also be read as an emblem of the Macedonian geography and zoology, but I think that in Alexander's iconographic program the king of the birds of prey (*rex avium rapicum*, Polem.Phgn. 2.151) figures basically as a symbol of Zeus and, largely by implication, of monarchy and universal power (on which see Lerner 2009, 220–3; Bleakley 2000, 96).

Conclusions

Macedonian regal coins offer one of the widest repertoires of animals in the history of Greek numismatics, at least ten species, both domestic and wild, all issued during the Classical age. As far as I know, there is no other Greek city, federation or kingdom that developed such a zoological variety in the realm of monetary iconography. The exception may have been Kyzikos, with at least eleven animal varieties, although its emissions began in the sixth century.[47] The coinage of the neighboring Amphipolitans knew the goat, the eagle, the horse, the dolphin, the bull and the lion (*SNG ANS 7*, nos. 76–143), yet they did not match the Argead variations on the animal theme. Interestingly, the marine environment had no appeal for the Macedonian ideology (or zoology) of kingship: Could we link this disinterest in the sea to the subordinate role accorded to the navy in the military history of the Argead monarchy?

The richness of the animal iconography arose from the peculiar geography of Macedonia, in close symbiosis with wild nature. In my opinion, the experience of wilderness should be considered an essential element of the country's identity and self-representation as defined by the royal house, the Argeads.[48] The great variety of beasts depicted on the regal coinage was not a capricious invention of the designers and engraves, nor an artistic mimesis of the mythological landscapes of the heroic past, but reflected the real conditions of the land with its exuberant zoology and giant trees in heavily forested areas (Hammond 1972, 207–11; Borza 1995, 37–40). As Hatzopoulos (2011, 46) has recently recalled:

> Although lion and wild ox, once the favourite trophies of royal hunts, no longer haunt its hills and valleys, the deer, the lynx, the wolf, and the bear still resist the attacks of modern civilisation. Over the vast stretches of lakes Prespa and Begorritis fly swans, storks, and pelicans, while in their depths swarm freshwater fish (cf. also Thomas 2010, 70–1).

This 'un-Greek nature of the Macedonian terrain' (Hammond 1972, 210), its otherness, explains the fascination of Euripides for 'the leafy coverts of Olympus' and its 'wild beasts', in 'happy Pieria' (*Ba.* 561–5). Another artist, inspired by the same blend of exuberance and wildlife, decorated the Derveni krater with embossed panels depicting episodes of Dionysiac myth and a varied fauna of predators and prey (Bar-Sharrar 2008). As in the world of the epic, where 'the wilderness was not yet wholly on the defensive' (Anderson 1985, 253), the Macedonians of the classical period could experience the primary landscapes with all its beasts as a part of their culture – an experience no longer possible for many Greeks.[49] Still in Polybios' time the royal game parks showed the effects of hunting inactivity, when war prevented the Antigonids, offering 'an abundance of big game of every kind' (Plb. 31.29.4).

Intertextuality and intericonicity should now be borne in mind to explain the interdependent ways in which our images stand in relation to one another to produce meaning within the Macedonian cultural code. In fact, there is a broad homology and correspondence between the regal iconography of the coins, the funerary painting of Tomb II at Vergina and the hunting mosaics of Pella and Palermo regarding the animal repertoire. Lions and boars, the prey *par excellence* in the royal hunts, appear in the three artistic media, not to mention the ivory boar from one of the funeral couches found at Tomb II.[50] For their part, horses and dogs remain as the animal allies of human beings, domestic mediators between culture and nature, omnipresent in the entire Macedonian literary and visual tradition (Le Bohec-Bouhet 2011), including the contemporary funerary steles, for instance the grave stele of Xanthos (Pella, c. 400). The absence of the wolf and the eagle on the Vergina fresco is easily understandable, considering that both species were not game animals.[51] The bull is not present either, in spite of the fact that wild oxen, aurochs (*box primigenius*), infested the heavily forested high country, as Herodotos (7.126) knew (Hammond 1972, 194, 209; Lane Fox 2011, 14). Its lack of relevance on the coinage imagery confirms that this beast was not indispensable for the ideology of kingship, although Hammond (1983, 253) did not exclude the possibility that Archelaos' bull types were reminiscent of the royal hunts; this kind of hunting, however, seems to have flourished later, among the Antigonids and the Paionian kings (see above note 1).

Conversely, the bear and the deer were not chosen by the royal engravers, though this was not the case with other artists of the period, at least as regards the cervids. The Pella mosaic from the House of the Abduction of Helen and the Alexander Sarcophagus suggest that stags were not an infrequent motif in the representation of hunting (Cohen 2010, 30–8). The deer is the only game animal that appears twice on the fresco (Andronicos 1984, 102–4, figs. 58–60), probably male and female, occupying a whole section of the narrative.[52] The ursids, unlike the Near Eastern visual traditions (Palagia 2000, 177–8), were not found often in the contemporary Greco-Macedonian media, at least judging by the available evidence.[53] However, the presence of an exemplar of this family on the Vergina fresco (Andronicos 1984, 102–5, figs. 58–9, 63) is not without parallels in early Greece (Lane Fox 2011, 13–14), beginning with the references to it in heroic legend (Hom. *Od.* 11.609–12), while Achilles' *paideia* testifies to the beast's status as big game.[54] It is worth noting that Xenophon describes with admiration how Cyrus the Younger, a projection of the Greek political ideas of the author, had been scarred by a bear-bite (X. *An.* 1.9.4; Lane Fox 1996, 139), an accident that may have a parallel in a Macedonian hunting episode attributed to Peukestas in Asia, as a result of which he was seriously bitten while in pursuit of a bear along with his fellow-huntsmen (Plut. *Alex.* 41.2; Carney 2002, 63). Last but not least, the Vergina bear is biting a broken javelin, and this motif can be traced to previous Argead numismatic iconography, as Amyntas' stater illustrates (Palagia 2000, 193 n. 114).

All in all, the zoological repertoire of the Macedonian coinage was not intended as a full catalogue of hunting: it was more than that and less than that. It included domestic species (not only horses and dogs, but above all goats), thus pointing to the pastoral dimension of the Macedonian landscape, which was clearly excluded from the Vergina fresco (Franks 2012, 91); and it added apparently minor creatures, like the frog and the snake, apart from the eagle and the wolf, denoting a special taste for wildlife beyond its game exploitation.[55] Consequently, if it is true that the heroic hunt worked as a paradigm for the Macedonian aristocrats and kings in their self-fashioning (Franks 2012, 64–6), the fact remains that the numinous spaces canonised by myth, like Mount Pelion, Kalydon or Arkadia, did not actually inspire the designers of coin types, but Macedonia did, in its wild splendour. As much as an evocation of myths and dynastic legends, the numismatic visual tradition offered a genuine celebration of nature – of the country's geography and nature. Thus, it is no coincidence that the natural and real landscape, as seen in the Hunting Frieze, constituted an essential element of pictorial representation, testifying to a major artistic achievement of this period.[56] At any rate, no less than of Orpheus, we can say of the Vergina painter and of the die engravers that they assembled the beasts by their art, they 'assembled the beasts of the wild'.

Finally, it should be underlined that the official coin design remained true to its own tradition all the time, inspired by a remarkable sense of realism and by a rejection of Hellenistic exoticism from the Orient. For instance, the elephant emerged during the reign of Alexander the Great and the Diadochoi as an image of royal power, and we have a whole series of iconographies devoted to this animal by Perdikkas, Ptolemy and Seleukos (Alonso 2013). We know that prominent generals and monarchs from Macedonia, like Philip IV, Polyperchon, Kassandros, or Ptolemy Keraunos, put to good use this formidable weapon on the battlefield, but there is no trace of the pachyderm on the coinage of the two last Argeads, or of the Antipatrids and Antigonids, as far as we know. The griffin could also be invoked to this effect. This mythic beast was very much present in the Macedonian artistic imagination, as mosaics and funerary paintings show (Cohen 2010, 93–105), and it was the main device of the neighbouring Abdera since at least the beginning of the classical age. But it does not appear on the regal coinage, not even as a mint symbol of reduced size.

Acknowledgements

The present paper was partially written at the Institute for the Study of the Ancient World (New York University), in 2013, during my stay as visiting research scholar. I would like to express my gratitude to the Spanish *Ministerio de Educación, Cultura y Deporte*, for generously financing my research stay in NY (PRX12/00110), and to ISAW and the Leon Levy Foundation for their hospitality. Moreover, my thanks go to the American Numismatic Society (particularly to Robert W. Hoge) for the facilities given to work at its library and to see the collection of Argead coins.

Abbreviations

ACGC: Kraay, C.M., *Archaic and Classical Greek Coins*, Berkeley and Los Angeles 1976.

MRC: Raymond, D., *Macedonian Regal Coinage to 413 BC*, New York 1953.

SNG DNM: *Sylloge Nummorum Graecorum. The Royal Collection of Coins and Medals Danish National Museum. Macedonia. Part II: Alexander I – Alexander III*, N. Breitenstein (cur.), Copenhagen 1943.

SNG ABC: *Sylloge Nummorum Graecorum. The Alpha Bank Collection. Macedonia I:*
           Alexander I – Perseus, S. Kremydi-Sicilianou (cur.), Athens 2000.
SNG ANS 7: *Sylloge Nummorum Graecorum. The Collection of the American Numismatic*
           Society. Part 7. Macedonia I: Cities, Thraco-Macedonian Tribes, Paeonian
           Kings, N. M. Waggoner (cur.), New York 1987.
SNG ANS 8: *Sylloge Nummorum Graecorum. The Collection of the American Numismatic*
           Society. Part 8. Macedonia II: Alexander I – Philip II, H. A. Troxell (cur.),
           New York 1994.

Notes

[1] *Anth.Pal.* 6.114–6; cf. Edson 1934, 213–32; Tripodi 1998, 127–40; Carney 2002, 68.

[2] *MRC* 43; Hammond 1979, 104–15; Greenwalt 1997, 121–2; Dahmen 2010, 50; Kremydi 2011a, 161–2.

[3] *MRC* 57, 85; Hammond 1979, 84, 104; Kremydi 2011a, 161.

[4] *MRC* 79–83, 126–7, 140–7, nos. 1–33c, 60–3, 108–21, 176–244; *ACGC* nos. 494, 496–500; *SNG ANS 8* nos. 1–5, 7–17, 24–6, 33–4; *SNG ABC* nos. 1–14, 16–25, 45–7, 55–6, 72–4.

[5] *MRC* 100–1, 103–4, nos. 45–57, 66–75; *ACGC* no. 495; *SNG ANS 8* nos. 22–3, 27; *SNG ABC* no. 48.

[6] *MRC* 84–5, 104–7, 128–9, 136–40, nos. 34–44, 76–107, 122–30; *ACGC* no. 501; *SNG ANS 8* nos. 18–21, 28–32; *SNG ABC* nos. 15, 26–7, 49–53, 57–61, 75–80.

[7] *SNG ANS 8* no. 36; *SNG ABC* nos. 28–44.

[8] For a discussion on the cavalryman and its meaning on the early Argead coinage, whether a hunter or a warrior, see Picard 1986 and above all Tripodi 1998, 13–34, who defends the polysemy or cumulative nature of the image, as Carney 2002, 60–1 does. Along similar lines, Seyer 2007, 72–4; and Franks 2012, 53–7, interpreting the horseman as a synthetic icon of the Macedonian kingship (cf. already Price 1974, 10). For Greenwalt 1993, 516; 1997, the rider would be the Macedonian version of the Thracian Hero. It is more difficult to follow Poulios 1988, 110, who identifies him with a warrior, Ares or Karanos (cf. Le Rider 1977, 365).

[9] Svoronos 1919, 112, pl. XIII 3; Gaebler 1935, 152, no. XXVIII 3; *MRC* 78, 89, no. 4 (= pl. III 4).

[10] On these ecological conditions, see Hammond 1972, 160, 205–6; Borza 1995, 58, 71–3. Cf. too Hammond 1979, 81, 110, and Svoronos 1919, 86.

[11] Svoronos 1919, 112, pl. XIII 4; *MRC* 78, 89, no. 5.

[12] *MRC* 126, 130, nos. 109–11; *ACGC* no. 496; *SNG ABC* no. 72. See Tripodi 1998, 23, followed by Carney 2002, 60–1; Seyer 2007, 73; Le Bohec-Bouhet 2011, 494, 498. Contra, Raymond (*MRC* 130) and Hammond 1979, 106, 109, in favour of a Molossian. The anatomy of this hound is similar to that of its contemporary on Sermylia's tetradrachms (*SNG ANS 7* no. 721), cf. Psoma 2002, 25–6 (fig. 3).

[13] *MRC* 79–82, 102–3, 126–7, nos. 14–21, 58–65, 112–7; *ACGC* nos. 498–9; *SNG ANS 8* nos. 12–15, 24–6, 33–4; *SNG ABC* nos. 19–20, 45–7, 73–4.

[14] *MRC* 82–3, 88, 129–31, nos. 23–33, 118–21; *SNG ANS 8* nos. 16–17; *SNG ABC* nos. 21–5.

[15] Assigned either to some tribes (from Bisaltia, Krestonia or Migdonia) or tentatively to the city of Galepsos: see Hammond 1979, 86–9; more recently, Dahmen 2010, 48, with the discrepant bibliography (including Lorber 2000). For the Greek world in general, Plant 1979, 1090–118.

[16] So, e.g., Babelon 1907, 1080–1; *ACGC* 141, 143; Hammond 1979, 8; Poulios 1995, 87; Kremydi 2011b, 207; and Franks 2012, 44, 109, who soundly points to the polysemy of the goat device. The evidence for the role of goats and sheep in the Argead ideology of kingship has been collected and discussed by Ogden 2011, 58–63, 68.

[17] The whole-body animal would only appear on the reverse of an octadrachm series accepted by the Copenhagen authorities (*SNG DNM* no. 493), but rejected by Raymond (*MRC* 79, no. 7) as a forgery.

[18] Linked to this is the question as to whether the mythical correlate of the lion at this very moment was Ares, rather than Herakles. On the latter possibility, see *MRC* 44, 60 and Borza 1990, 130 n. 74.

[19] *MRC* 164. On the current state of our knowledge about the (Argive?) origins of the Argeads, see Seyer 2007, 68–9.

[20] Cf. Helly 1968; Hammond 1972, 182, 194, 209, 267; Sallares 1991, 401 with n. 18; Hatzopoulos 1993, 19–20; Richer 2010, 11 with n. 140. On the real possibility of royal lion hunting in Macedonia before Alexander, see Anderson 1985, 4, 80; Lane Fox 1996, 137–8; 2011, 10–13; Etienne 2000, 75; Carney 2002, 61; Brécoulaki 2006, 106 n. 3; Kremydi 2011b, 207; Cohen 2010, 68–71; Franks 2012, 36–42. Note also Greenwalt 1993, 514–6. Undecided: Briant 1991, 236–43 and Sawada 2010, 401. *Contra*: Borza; Palagia 2007, 95–6.

[21] See above n. 20, and Strawn 2005, 32, with Map 2.1.

[22] Leontophoric names are found in Argead Macedonia (Leonnatus, Pantaleon), although apparently in a lower proportion than in Sparta: on the latter, see Richer 2010, 12–13.

[23] On the traditional relationship between large wild game and horsemanship among the Argeads, see Hammond 1990, 262; Greenwalt 1993, 515, 518; Lane Fox 1996, 141; Tripodi 1998, 48; Carney 2002, 62 with n. 49. Cf. also Franks 2012, 41–2. *Contra*, Palagia 2000, 177, though note Borza, Palagia 2007, 90, on Archelaos. Furthermore, it has been observed that the *petasos* is a travelling hat (Franks 2012, 44, 134 n. 124), rather than an element of huntsman's clothing, in the same way that the Maltese would be a dog for company, rather than for hunting (so Borza 1990, 130 n. 73; Tripodi 1998, 23–4; Seyer 2007, 73); but the fact is that this type of headdress appears in the visual tradition of the Macedonian hunter, as the Gnosis Mosaic at Pella proves: see Cohen 2010, 31.

[24] *MRC* 151; *SNG ANS 8* nos. 37–46; *SNG ABC* nos. 82–105.

[25] *MRC* 151; *SNG ANS 8* nos. 47–62; *SNG ABC* nos. 106–26.

[26] *ACGC* 144, no. 502. Cf. too Poulios 1988, 110. See more accurately Hammond 1983, 252; 1979, 120.

[27] Hammond 1979, 120 n. 1; 1983, 252, remarked that the mounted man is not the same as that on Alexander's coins and may represent Perdikkas (it is only on tetrobols of weight C).

[28] Kraay's (*ACGC* 143) supposition that the feline might refer here to Apollo is unwarranted.

[29] *SNG ANS 8* no. 53; *SNG ABC* no. 116.

[30] *MRC* 163 pl. XI,d; *SNG ANS 8* no. 63; *SNG ABC* nos. 127–128; Psoma 2000, 131.

[31] *MRC* 163 pl. XI,e. *SNG ABC* gives no. 129 as the equivalent, but in fact its reverse is a boar, not a lion, therefore implying a new variety.

[32] *MRC* 164 pl. XI, g; *SNG ABC* nos. 131–3; Psoma 2000, 131. Contrary to Raymond (*MRC* 164), who claims that the last two devices must have been struck near the end of Perdikkas' life, Hammond 1979, 120–1, argues that the stress on the connection between the royal house, Herakles, and Argos was particularly relevant during the Peace of Nicias, when it became politically effective, placing them in 417/16.

[33] *SNG ABC* no. 129 (see above n. 31), 130, 134. Add Psoma 2000, 131, for two other combinations.

[34] *MRC* 60; Hammond 1979, 121; Greenwalt 1985, 257; Franks 2013, 72–3.

[35] On the heroic hunt and Herakles Kynagidas as paradigm for the Argeads, see Seyer 2007, 69–71; Franks 2012, 64, 99.

[36] Respectively, *SNG ANS 8* no. 64; *SNG ABC* nos. 135–7 and Westermark 1989, fig. 1; *SNG DNM* no. 503; *SNG ANS 8* nos. 65–70; *SNG ABC* nos. 138–48 and Westermark 1989, fig. 2. See too Westermark 1993, 18; Lykiardopoulou, Psoma 2000, 321.

[37] Respectively, *SNG DNM* no. 504; *SNG ANS 8* no. 71; *SNG ABC* nos. 149–52 and Westermark 1989, figs. 3–4; *SNG DNM* no. 505; *SNG ABC* no. 153 and Westermark 1989, no. 5.

[38] An eagle, but holding a serpent in the beak, had already appeared on the coins of the Derroni after 475 (Tačeva 1992, 70) and before 432 on Olynthus' tetrobols as reverse type (Head 1879, 87 nos. 2–4; *ACGC* no. 476; *SNG ANS 7* nos. 464–7), as well as on the bronzes of the autonomous city of Pydna (Head 1879, 101 no. 1). Cf. too Tačeva 1992, 70–1; Psoma 2002, 30; Franks 2012, 43, 49.

[39] Respectively, *SNG DNM* no. 506; *SNG ANS 8* nos. 72–4; *SNG ABC* nos. 154–61 and Westermark 1989, fig. 6; *SNG DNM* no. 507; *SNG ABC* nos. 162–3 and Westermark 1989, fig. 7; *SNG DNM* no. 508; *SNG ANS 8* no. 75; *SNG ABC* nos. 164–70 and Westermark fig. 8.

[40] Westermark 1996, 291 pleads for the lion type of Rhegion as prototype. The lion, however, is pervasive on the coinage of neighbouring Acanthus, including the head and neck of a lioness seen from above, c. 525–470 (*SNG ANS 7* nos. 27–9), with a visual effect not very unlike Archelaos' frontal type.

[41] Respectively, *SNG ABC* no. 171 and Westermark 1989, fig. 8; Westermark 1989, fig. 9; Westermark 1989, fig. 10. See Hammond 1979, 138; Picard 2003, 76.

[42] Cf. Harder 1985, 125–39, 174–5, test. 7, l.13–14; Ogden 2011, 67–70.

[43] See Plant 1979, nos. 1063, 1069, 1079, 1082, 1428, 1443.

[44] Paus. 2.19.3–4; Plut. *Pyrrh.* 32.4–5. Cf. Mainoldi 1984, 24–6, and note that Pelasgos reigned over Macedonia too (Aesch. *Supp.* 250–9). For Lyttos in Crete, which claimed Argive ancestry and also included the heraldic animal on its coins, see Le Rider 1966, 179 n. 5, pl. I 8–12; Plant 1979, no. 197.

[45] *SNG ANS 8* nos. 100–9; *SNG DNM* nos. 513–5, 517–8; Westermark 1989, 307, 312, fig. 34. The coin carries a beardless Herakles on the obverse (fig. 8). As Palagia 2000, 170, has recalled, the eagle carrying a snake in its claws is a well-known omen of victory (Hom. *Il.* 200–7; Plut. *Timol.* 26.6).

[46] *ACGC* no. 506; *SNG DNM* no. 516; *SNG ANS 8* no. 99.

[47] This is its list of animals: crab, lion, boar, tunny-fish, bull, goat, ram, dog, horse, cock and eagle: see www.sylloge-nummorum-graecorum.org, under 'Cyzicus'. I am grateful to Catherine Lorber for calling to my attention the coin types of this *polis*.

[48] On this, see in more detail Alonso 2014a, recognising the seminal influence of Nash 1982. In this regard, the comparison between ancient Macedonia and modern USA or pre-industrial Europe, *mutatis mutandis*, might be productive: cf. a first approach to the subject in Alonso 2014b, 188–94.

[49] Nor for most Europeans today. Note, on the contrary, the words of Theodore Roosevelt, an American president very conscious of his cultural roots in the New World: 'There are no words that can tell the hidden spirit of the wilderness, that can reveal its mystery, its melancholy, and its charm' (American Museum of Natural History, New York). Cf. Nash 1982, 68. It is in this context, I think, that the crude description of the Macedonians as 'a great herd of wild beasts' (by Eumenes of Kardia: Plut. *Eum.* 16.2) would make sense. Alexander himself was probably aware of such opinions about his people: Plut. *Alex.* 51.4.

[50] Graekos 2011, fig. 61 (Cat. no. 485). A group of a hunter with dog and a boar comes perhaps from the gymnasium at Pella: see Graekos 2011, fig. 63.

[51] Psoma 2002, 27, seems to suggest that the wild canid was a game target. Probably, but the evidence does not point to royal hunts.

[52] The deer connoted cowardice according to the Greek aristocratic scale of values (cf. Cartmill 1993, 37 with n. 37), as Achilles had shown when insulting Agamemnon, 'with the front of a dog but the heart of a deer' (Hom. *Il.* 1.225). No doubt, the Macedonian elite knew Achilles' words, and perhaps the cervid could not fit in the Argead catalogue of animal types inspired by the wild, conceptually males and strong, if not predators (note X. *Cyr.* 1.4.7).

[53] Anderson 1985, 15; Etienne 2000; cf. Bevan 1987, for the scarcity of bear-dedications in Greek sanctuaries, and *ACGC* 96 no. 285, for the unusual type of a bear on the Mantinean coins of the fifth century.

[54] Statius, *Achilleis* 2.121–5; Apoll. *Bibl.* 3.13.6; cf. Anderson 1985, 4; Étienne 2000, 74–5, and Franks 2012, 64–7.

[55] The wild canid had never been hunted for sport by heroes: see Anderson 1985, 15.

[56] See Brécoulaki 2006, 112, 116–8; 2007, 87, 90; Saatsoglou-Paliadeli 2007, 49, 51, 54.

Bibliography

Alonso Troncoso, V.

2013 'The Diadochi and the Zoology of Kingship: the Elephants', in V. Alonso Troncoso, E. M. Anson (eds) *After Alexander: The Time of the Diadochi*, Oxford, 254–70.

2014a 'The Zoology of Kingship: From Alexander the Great to the Epigoni', *Anabasis. Studia Classica et Orientalia* 5, 52–74.

2014b 'El golfo Ártabro: paisaje prehistórico y teatro de historia (c. 900 – 61 a.C.)', in V. Alonso Troncoso, A. R. Colmenero, A. Goy (eds) *El golfo Ártabro. Fragmentos de historia litoral y patrimonio*, La Coruña, 152–207.

Anderson, J. K.

1985 *Hunting in the Ancient World*, Berkeley.

Andronicos, M.

1984 *Vergina: The Royal Tombs and the Ancient City*, Athens.

Babelon, E.

1907 *Traité des monnaies grecques et romaines*, 2ème Partie, tome 1, Paris.

Barr-Sharrar, B.

2008 *The Derveni Krater: Masterpiece of Classical Greek Metalwork*, Princeton.

Bevan, E.

1987 'The Goddess Artemis and the Dedications of Bears in Sanctuaries', *ANBSA* 82, 17–21.

Bleakley, A.

2000 *The Animalizing Imagination: Totemism, Textuality and Ecocriticism*, London and New York.

Borza, E. N.

1990 *In the Shadow of Olympus: The Emergence of Macedon*, Princeton.

1995 *Makedonika*, Claremont, CA.

Borza, E. N. and Palagia, O.

2007 'The Chronology of the Macedonian Royal Tombs at Vergina', *JDAI* 122, 81–125.

Brécoulaki, H.

2006 *La peinture funéraire de Macédoine. Emplois et fonctions de la couleur, IVᵉ – IIᵉ s. av. J.-C.*, vol. I, Athens.

2007 'Suggestion de la troisième dimension et traitement de la perspective dans la peinture ancienne de Macédoine', in S. Descamps-Lequime (ed.) *Peinture et couleur dans le monde grec antique*, Milan – Paris, 81–93.

Briant, P.

1991 'Chasses royales macédoniennes et chasses royales perses : le thème de la chasse au lion sur la chasse de Vergina', *DHA* 17, 211–55.

Burkert, W.

1979 *Structure and History in Greek Mythology and Ritual*, Berkeley and Los Angeles.

Carney, E.

2002 'Hunting and the Macedonian Elite: Sharing the Rivalry of the Chase (Arrian 4.13.1)', in D. Ogden (ed.) *The Hellenistic World: New Perspectives*, Swansea and London, 59–80.

Cartmill, M.
1993   *A View to a Death in the Morning: Hunting and Nature through History*, Cambridge, MA.

Cohen, A.
1995   'Alexander and Achilles – Macedonians and "Mycenaeans"', in J. B. Carter, S. P. Morris (eds) *The Ages of Homer: A Tribute to Emily Townsend Vermeule*, Austin, 483–505.
2010   *Art in the Era of Alexander the Great: Paradigms of Manhood and their Cultural Traditions*, Cambridge.

Dahmen, K.
2010   'The Numismatic Evidence', in J. Roisman and I. Worthington (eds) *A Companion to Ancient Macedonia*, Malden, MA, 41–62.

Despini, K.
1988   '228. Δώδεκα ασημένιοι επίχρυσοι αετοί / Twelve Gilded Silver Eagles', in L. Braggiotti (ed.) / *Ancient Macedonia*, Athens, 279.

Edson, C. F.
1934   'The Antigonids, Heracles, and Beroea', *HSPh* 45, 213–46.

Étienne, R.
2000   'La chasse à l'ours', in A. Avram, M. Babes (eds) *Civilisation grecque et cultures antiques périphériques. Hommage à Petre Alexandrescu*, Bucarest, 68–76.

Flament, C.
2009   'Classement stylistique et essai de périodisation des monnaies au loup d'Argos', *RN* 165, 81–105.

Franke, P. R.
1952/3 'Geschichte, Politik und Münzprägung im frühen Makedonien', *JNG* 3/4, 99–111.

Franks, H. M.
2012   *Hunters, Heroes, Kings: The Frieze of Tomb II at Vergina*, Princeton.

Gaebler, H.
1935   *Die antiken Münzen von Makedonia und Paionia* (*Die Antiken Münzen Nord-Griechenlands, III 2*), Berlin.

Gatzolis, C.
2013   'New Evidence on the Beginning of Bronze Coinage in Northern Greece', in C. Grandjean, A. Moustaka (eds) *Aux origines de la monnaie fiduciaire*, Paris, 117–28.

Graekos, I.
2011   'War and Hunting: The World of the Macedonian King and his Companions', in *Heracles to Alexander the Great: Treasures from the Royal Capital of Macedon, a Hellenic Kingdom in the Age of Democracy*, Ashmolean Museum Exhibition, Oxford, 75–92.

Greenwalt, W. S.
1985a Studies in the Development of Royal Authority in Argead Macedonia, Diss. University of Virginia.
1985b 'The Introduction of Caranus into the Argead King List', *GRBS* 26, 43–49.

1993   'The Iconographical Significance of Amyntas III's Mounted Hunter Stater', *Ancient Macedonia* 5, 509–19.

1997   'Thracian Influence on the Ideology of Argead Kingship', in *Actes 2e Symposium International des Études Thraciennes*, vol. 1, Komotini, 121–33.

Hammond, N. G. L.

1972   *A History of Macedonia. I: Historical Geography and Prehistory*, Oxford.

1983   'The Lettering and the Iconography of Macedonian Coinage', in W. G. Moon (ed.) *Ancient Greek Art and Iconography*, Madison, WI, 245–58.

1990   'Royal Pages, Personal Pages, and Boys trained in the Macedonian Manner during the Period of the Temenid Monarchy', *Historia* 39, 261–90.

Hammond, N. G. L. and Griffith, G. T.

1979   *A History of Macedonia. Volume II: 550–336 BC*, Oxford.

Harder, A.

1985   *Euripides' Kresphontes and Archelaos: Introduction, Text and Commentary*, Leiden.

Hatzopoulos, M. B.

1993   'The Natural and Human Resources', in R. Ginouvès (ed.) *Macedonia from Philip II to the Roman Conquest*, Athens, 19–23.

2011   'Macedonia and Macedonians', in R. Lane Fox (ed.) *Brill's Companion to Ancient Macedon. Studies in the Archaeology and History of Macedon, 650 BC– 300 AD*, Leiden, 43–9.

Head, B. V.

1879   *A Catalogue of the Greek Coins in the British Museum. Macedonia, etc.*, London.

Helly, B.

1968   'Des lions dans l'Olympe!', *REA* 70, 271–85.

Howe, T.

2008   *Pastoral Politics: Animals, Agriculture and Society in Ancient Greece*, Claremont, CA.

Kremydi, S.

2011a   'Coinage and Finance', in R. J. Lane Fox (ed.) *Brill's Companion to Ancient Macedon: Studies in the Archaeology and History of Macedon, 650 BC–300 AD*, Leiden, 159–78.

2011b   'Macedonian Coinage before Alexander', in *Heracles to Alexander the Great: Treasures from the Royal Capital of Macedon, a Hellenic Kingdom in the Age of Democracy*, Exhibition Catalogue, Oxford, 205–8.

Lane Fox, R.

1996   'Ancient Hunting from Homer to Polybios', in G. Shipley, J. Salmon (eds) *Human Landscapes in Classical Antiquity: Environment and Culture*, London and New York, 119–53.

2011   'Introduction: Dating the Royal Tombs at Vergina', in R. J. Lane Fox (ed.) *Brill's Companion to Ancient Macedon: Studies in the Archaeology and History of Macedon, 650 BC–300 AD*, Leiden, 1–34.

Le Bohec-Bouhet, S.

2011   'Les chiens en Macédoine dans l'Antiquité', in N. Badoud (ed.) *Philologos Dionysios. Mélanges offerts au professeur Denis Knoepfler*, Geneva, 491–515.

Le Rider, G.
  1966   *Monnaies crétoises du Ve au Ier siècle av. J.-C.*, Paris.
  1977   *Le monnayage d'argent et d'or de Philippe II frappé en Macédoine de 359 à 294*, Paris.

Lerner, J.
  2009   'Animal Headdresses on the Sealings of the Bactrian Documents', in F. de Blois, A. Hintze, W. Sundermann (eds) *Exegisti monumenta. Festschrift in honour of Nicholas Sims-Williams*, Wiesbaden, 215–26.

Lorber, C.
  2000   'The Goats of Aigai' in S. Hurter, C. Arnold-Biucchi (eds), *Pour Denyse: Divertissements numismatiques*, Berne, 113–33.

Lykiardopoulou, M. and Psoma, S.
  2000   'Ἡ αργυρή Βασιλική νομισματοκοπία των Τημενιδών της Μακεδονίας από τα τέλη της Βασιλείας του Περδίκκα Β΄ έως το θάνατο του Περδίκκα Γ΄ (413–360). Τεχνολογία κατασκευής, ανάλυση μετάλλου, ιστορική προσέγγιση', Οβολός 4, 321–38.

Mainoldi, C.
  1984   *L'image du loup et du chien dans la Grèce ancienne d'Homère à Platon*, Paris.

Munn, M.
  2008   'Alexander, the Gordian Knot, and the Kingship of Midas', in T. Howe, J. Reames (eds) *Macedonian Legacies: Studies in Ancient Macedonian History and Culture in Honor of Eugene N. Borza*, Claremont, CA, 107–43.

Nash, R.
  1982   *Wilderness and the American Mind*, 3rd ed., New Haven and London.

Ogden, D.
  2011   *Alexander the Great: Myth, Genesis and Sexuality*, Exeter.

Palagia, O.
  2000   'Hephaestion's Pyre and the Royal Hunt of Alexander', in A. B. Bosworth, E. J. Baynham (eds) *Alexander the Great in Fact and Fiction*, Oxford, 167–206.

Parke, H. W. and Wormell, D. E. W.
  2004   *The Delphic Oracle*, II, Chicago.

Picard, O.
  1986   'Numismatique et iconographie : le cavalier macédonien', in L. Kahil, Ch. Augé, P. Linant (eds) *Iconographie classique et identités régionales*, Paris, 67–76.
  2003   'Remarques sur le monnayage de bronze macédonien avant Philippe II', *BSFN* 58.5, 73–8.

Plant, R.
  1979   *Greek Coin Types and their Identification*, London.

Poulios, V.
  1988   'Macedonian Coinage from the 6th century to 148', in L. Braggiotti (ed.) *ΑΡΧΑΙΑ ΜΑΚΕΔΟΝΙΑ / Ancient Macedonia*, Athens, 107–13.

Price, M. J.
  1974   *Coins of the Macedonians*, London.

1991 *The Coinage in the Name of Alexander the Great and Philip Arrhidaeus*, I–II, Zurich and London.

Psoma, S.
2000 'Τὰς παλαιὰς πεντεδραχμίας. Un strategème de Polyen et le monnayage d'argent des rois de Macédoine de 413 à 360 av. J.-C.', *RN* 155, 123–136.
2002 'Τὸ βασίλειο των Μακεδόνων πριν από τον Φίλιππο Β': Νομισματική και ιστορική προσέγγιση', in Η ιστορική διαδρομή της νομισματικής μονάδας στην Ελλάδα, Athens, 25–45.

Richer, N.
2010 'Elements of the Spartan Bestiary in the Archaic and Classical Periods', in A. Powell, S. Hodkinson (eds) *Sparta: The Body Politic*, Swansea, 1–84.

Saatsoglou-Paliadeli, C.
2007 'La peinture de la Chasse de Vergina', in S. Descamps-Lequime (ed.) *Peinture et couleur dans le monde grec antique*, Milan-Paris, 47–55.

Sallares, R.
1991 *The Ecology of the Ancient Greek World*, Ithaca, NY.

Sawada, N.
2010 'Social Customs and Institutions: Aspects of Macedonian Elite Society', in J. Roisman, I. Worthington (eds) *A Companion to Ancient Macedonia*, Malden, MA, 392–408.

Schnapp, A.
1997 *Le chasseur et la cité. Chasse et érotique en Grèce ancienne*, Paris.

Seyer, M.
2007 *Der Herrscher als Jäger. Untersuchungen zur königlichen Jagd im persischen und makedonischen Reich vom 6. – 4. Jahrhundert v. Chr. sowie unter den Diadochen Alexanders des Großen*, Vienna.

Strawn, B. A.
2005 *What is Stronger than a Lion? Leonine Image and Metaphor in the Hebrew Bible and the Ancient Near East*, Fribourg.

Svoronos, J.
1919 *L'hellénisme primitif de la Macédoine prouvé par la numismatique*, Paris–Athènes.

Tačeva, M.
1992 'On the Problems of the Coinages of Alexander I Sparadokos and the So-Called Thracian-Macedonian Tribes', *Historia* 41, 58–74.

Thomas, C. G.
2010 'The Physical Kingdom', in J. Roisman, I. Worthington (eds) *A Companion to Ancient Macedonia*, Malden, MA, 65–80.

Tripodi, B.
1998 *Cacce reali macedoni tra Alessandro I e Filippo V*, Messina.

Westermark, U.
1987 'Notes on Macedonian Bronze Coins', in T. Caruso (ed.) *Studi per Laura Breglia (Bollettino di Numismatica*, Suppl. to no. 4), Rome, 179–87.

1989   'Remarks on the Regal Macedonian Coinage ca. 413–359 BC', in G. Le Rider *et al.* (eds) *Numismatic Studies in Memory of C. M. Kraay and O. Mørkholm*, Louvain-la-Neuve, 301–15.

1993   'The Staters of Archelaus: A Die Study', in M. J. Price, A. Burnett, R. Bland (eds) *Essays in honour of Robert Carson and Kenneth Jenkins*, London, 17–30.

1996   'Influences from South Italy on Early Macedonian Bronze Coins', in W. Leschhorn, A. V. B. Miron, A. Miron (eds) *Hellas und der griechische Osten. Festschrift P. R. Franke*, Saarbrücken, 291–9.

ALEXANDER AS ACHILLES: ARRIAN'S USE OF HOMER FROM TROY TO THE GRANIKOS

Hugh Bowden

The idea that Alexander was inspired by the figure of Achilles goes back to antiquity. The debt that Arrian owed to Homer has also been well recognised. However, the assumption that Alexander consciously modelled himself on Achilles has made it more difficult for scholars to identify how far the presentation of Alexander as a 'Homeric hero' was a reflection of historical reality and how far it was a literary creation. In this chapter I will focus on one section of Arrian's account, running from Alexander's arrival at Troy to his victory at the Granikos (1.11.6–16.7), and argue that it is modelled on a specific section of the *Iliad* (Books 19–21) – while also drawing on other parts of that work. I will show that some of the decisions Arrian makes in the construction of his narrative were influenced by what he knew from Homer. While this analysis does not offer definitive answers to long-debated questions such as how the Battle of the Granikos was fought, it does suggest that more weight should be given to literary considerations when reading the accounts of the battle and the surrounding events than has been given hitherto.

Alexander and Achilles

We must start by establishing some of the limits of our knowledge. It is taken for granted by most scholars that Alexander consciously imitated Achilles, and took him as a role model.[1] All the Alexander historians tell stories about this imitation.[2] However, demonstrating that these stories go back to the time of Alexander himself is not easy. The episode most often taken to show Alexander's devotion to Homer concerns the 'Casket *Iliad*'. Plutarch mentions this item twice. In the second story, which he attributes to 'many reliable sources' (οὐκ ὀλίγοι τῶν ἀξιοπίστων), he says that a small and very valuable casket (κιβώτιον) was found in Darius' possessions and brought to Alexander. Alexander asked his friends what he should keep in it, and then decided that he would keep a copy of the *Iliad* in it.[3] Strabo also describes how Alexander kept a copy of the Iliad in a valuable casket, and calls it the 'Casket Rescension' (διόρθωσις...ἡ ἐκ τοῦ νάρθηκος).[4] Plutarch himself uses this phrase the first time he mentions Alexander's personal *Iliad*, when he says that he always kept it under his pillow (προσκεφάλαιον) alongside a dagger, a story that he attributes to Onesikritos.[5] However, it is recognised that a casket containing the text of the *Iliad* would be far too large to fit under any pillow,[6] and Chares of Mytilene states that the 'King's pillow' (προσκεφάλαιον βασιλικόν) was actually a treasury next to the King's bedroom.[7] Onesikritos, deliberately or not, has misrepresented Alexander's relationship with the *Iliad*.[8] Once the idea that Alexander kept a copy of the *Iliad* with him every night is removed, we are left with the information reported by both Plutarch and Strabo, that Alexander discussed the text of the *Iliad* with his advisers, and considered it 'a guide to military excellence' (τῆς πολεμικῆς ἀρετῆς ἐφόδιον). This is not a particularly surprising idea, and it does not necessarily imply that Alexander sought to emulate any particular figure within the work.

Although Alexander may not have identified himself with Achilles, it is likely that the identification was made soon after his death. Indeed Alexander's early death was one of the most obvious points of parallel between the two figures.[9] But it would not only have been Alexander's near contemporaries who would have wanted to make the comparison. We can now turn to Arrian's account: he will have been well aware of earlier comparisons between Alexander and Achilles, but that does not mean that he would not have considered their relationship for himself.[10]

The *Anabasis* and the *Iliad*

Arrian refers to Achilles at two points in his narrative: the second is when he describes the death of Hephaistion, and Alexander's reaction to it;[11] the first is when Alexander visits Achilles' tomb at Troy, while Hephaistion visits that of Patroklos.[12] It is clear that Alexander's arrival at Troy marks a second beginning to Arrian's *Anabasis*, leading as it does into the 'second preface' (1.12.2–5), but the focus on the tombs of Achilles and Patroklos suggests that Arrian is drawing a parallel with another new beginning, Achilles' single day of fighting in the *Iliad*. Achilles plays no part in the military action in the *Iliad* before the day that dawns at the start of Book 19. That book begins with his receiving from Thetis his new armour, made by Hephaistos, and his reconciliation with Agamemnon, so that the Greek army is once more united. Briseis' mourning for Patroklos, and preparation for battle, then follow. Book 20 starts with Zeus sending the other Olympian gods to join the battle, and then describes Achilles' encounter with Aeneas, and then his first attempt to fight Hektor, from which, with Apollo's help, Hektor escapes. Then Achilles begins to kill the Trojans in earnest. Book 21 takes him to the banks of the Skamandros (Xanthos), and into the river itself, which turns on him, and Achilles is only rescued by Athena and Poseidon, before Hephaistos forces it back to its bed. Achilles then drives the Trojans back to the city, but is kept at bay by the Trojan Agenor, aided by Apollo. Book 22 describes the climactic combat between Achilles and Hektor, ending in Hektor's death.

While it would be wrong to try to make detailed comparisons between the narrative in the *Iliad* and Alexander's campaign in Asia as described by Arrian, there are important similarities. The real *anabasis* of Alexander begins with his arrival at Troy, and his campaigns in Europe are to be understood as a prelude to the war against Darius.[13] Just as Achilles meets Hektor twice in battle, so Alexander is to meet Darius twice, the second time at Gaugamela close to the Achaemenid centres of Babylon and Susa.[14] And, as we will see, Achilles' battle against a river can be matched to Alexander's experience. And to reinforce these parallels in his readers' minds Arrian draws attention to the work of Homer both explicitly in the so-called 'second preface' and by clear allusions elsewhere.

Troy and the 'Second Preface'

Arrian's account of Alexander's actions crossing the Hellespont and at Troy itself are inevitably rich in references to the story of the Trojan War. These include his sacrifices to Protesilaos (so that Alexander might be more fortunate than he was),[15] and to Priam (so that he would not be angry with the descendants of Neoptolemos).[16] These two sacrifices, one relating to the very beginning of the Trojan War and one to its very end, encapsulate the whole story of the first Greek war in Asia.[17] But Arrian explicitly refers to the *Iliad* when he notes that 'as the story goes (ὡς λόγος) Alexander called Achilles fortunate since he had Homer as herald to pass on the memory of his deeds to posterity.'[18]

At this point Arrian places the 'second preface'. It is here that, as has been recognised, the historian claims the right to be considered a new Homer.[19] He goes on to talk about his ancestry in terms that have also been seen as distinctly Homeric.[20] But Arrian's depiction of Alexander does not correspond fully to Homer's depiction of Achilles. Achilles is of course absent from much of the action in the *Iliad*, in his tent, while Alexander is constantly active throughout the *Anabasis*. On those occasions later in the campaign when Alexander does briefly withdraw to his tent, after the 'mutinies' at the Hyphasis and at Opis,[21] Arrian draws no parallels with Achilles, and no other writers do.[22] Arrian's Alexander does not evoke the hero who is so concerned for his honour that he will sit out the action while others die; he resembles instead Achilles the invincible warrior, and also perhaps the introspective Achilles who mourns the death of his companion and is conscious of his own mortality. This is the Achilles presented in Books 19–21 of the *Iliad*.

From Troy to the Granikos

There are other ways in which Arrian evokes the *Iliad* at this point in the narrative. In the 'Trojan catalogue' Homer lists the allies of Troy who came from the area to the northeast of the Trojan plain:

> Those who lived around Perkote and Praktion,
> And held Sestos and Abydos and noble Arisbe,
> They were led by the son of Hyrtakos, Asios, leader of men,
> Asios, son of Hyrtakos, who had ridden from Arisbe on his horses,
> Tall and chestnut, from the river Selleis (*Il.* 2.835–9).[23]

Arrian has already mentioned Sestos and Abydos as the points between which Parmenion crossed with the main part of the army;[24] in his account of Alexander's advance from Troy to the Granikos he has Alexander camp at each of the other places listed here, Arisbe, Perkote and the Praktios (a river, not a city).[25] Bosworth has pointed out that the Praktios, as identified by Strabo at least, is too close to Perkote for this to be a consistent progress, and suggests that Alexander actually encamped on the third night by the river Paisos.[26] Arrian's slip may well have been deliberate, to remind his readers of the Homeric catalogue as he takes his hero through the territory of Achilles' enemies.

Meanwhile the Persian generals were encamped at another city mentioned in the Trojan catalogue, Zeleia.[27] The inhabitants of that city are described by Homer as 'wealthy' (ἀφνειοί), and their leader, Pandaros, plays a treacherous role in the poem. He is responsible for breaking the truce arranged to settle the war, by shooting and wounding Menelaos, and is subsequently killed by Diomedes.[28] Thoughts of Pandaros would come to the mind of Arrian's readers when he describes the Persian satrap Arsites refusing to countenance the proposal of Memnon of Rhodes that the Persians employ a scorched earth policy against Alexander, and his subsequent ignominious death.[29]

The Granikos itself is mentioned once in the *Iliad*, as one of the eight rivers redirected by Poseidon and Apollo to destroy the Greek defensive wall after the fall of Troy.[30] This is an obvious contrast to Alexander's dismissal of the river as 'a little stream' (σμικρὸν ῥεῦμα),[31] but it is a different Homeric river that impacts upon Arrian's narrative at this point, the Skamandros.

Fighting a river

In his account of Alexander's journey down the Indus valley, Diodoros reports how Alexander was nearly drowned in the rapids at the confluence of the Hydaspes and the Akesines. He survived, and sacrificed to the gods 'as one who had survived the greatest dangers and had, like Achilles, fought a river'.[32] Arrian, who also mentions this episode,[33] does not make the connection with Achilles, but this is perhaps because he has already drawn a connection between Achilles fighting the river Skamandros and Alexander's campaign.

The encounter between Achilles and the river Xanthos, or Skamandros, is the most extended episode in the sequence of combats that Achilles fights in the course of his day of battle.[34] Once he has got past the river, the way is open for him to Troy, and his climactic duel with Hektor. So it is appropriate that Arrian's Alexander should also fight with a river flowing from Mount Ida on his way to his encounters with Darius III, and the battle of the Granikos provides this opportunity. It is therefore important to examine how far Arrian shapes the narrative to fit this pattern.

Arrian had at least two accounts of the battle available to him, and these are known to us through the narratives of Plutarch and Diodoros.[35] Although it is generally claimed that these are very different versions of events,[36] and that Plutarch's account is close to that of Arrian, it can be argued that the differences are less fundamental than might be thought, and that it is Arrian's that is most distinctive. Diodoros has Alexander reach the Granikos and encamp opposite the Persians, who are on the far side of the river, occupying the higher ground (τὴν ὑπώρειαν κατειλημμένοι), ready to descend on the Macedonian forces as they cross the river.[37] Alexander avoids this danger by crossing at dawn, before the Persians are ready to move against him. The subsequent battle then takes place on dry land on the Persian side of the river. In Plutarch's version Alexander launches his attack almost as soon as he reaches the river, having dismissed various objections from his officers, and responded to Parmenion's concern that it was too late in the day by saying that 'the Hellespont would be ashamed if, having already crossed that, he should be afraid of the Granikos'.[38] What happens next needs to be clarified. According to Plutarch, Alexander crosses the river with his cavalry under missile fire, gains the opposite bank, and at that point immediately (εὐθὺς) joins battle with the Persian cavalry before he can get his troops into good order.[39] Subsequently the Macedonian infantry cross the river and in turn, having emerged on the other side, engage the Persian infantry (that is the Greek mercenaries).[40] Therefore Plutarch, like Diodoros, has the battle take place on dry land on the far side of the river. Both accounts then have more or less the same sequence of events: Alexander is struck by a javelin, but not wounded; he is attacked by two brothers (Spithrobates and Rhosakes, or Spithridates and Rhoisakes), one of whom is killed; the other lands a blow on his helmet which shears off the crest, and then when he is about to strike again, has his arm cut off by Kleitos.[41] This is followed soon after by the flight of the Persian cavalry and then the defeat of the infantry.

Arrian's account, which has much more detail, takes elements from both these versions, but deploys them in very different ways. In his version, Diodoros' description of the dawn crossing of the river is outlined as a plan by Parmenion that is rejected by Alexander.[42] From the version we know from Plutarch Arrian takes the story of Alexander's response to Parmenion, and the idea that Alexander launched his attack on the day he reached the river. But the depiction of the battle itself is rather different. He has much of the battle take place in the river, describing a shoving (ὠθισμός) by the cavalry as the Macedonians tried to get out of the river and the Persians tried to keep them there.[43] This was a normal feature of hoplite infantry battles, not cavalry ones, as Arrian later suggests.[44] Arrian does not make it clear at what point the battle moved from the river to the farther shore, although his account implies that it did. He describes the initial Macedonian charge as unsuccessful, and the survivors falling back to where Alexander was (by implication still in the river); then a fight developed around Alexander, but meanwhile the Macedonian units were finding it easier to cross; but Arrian then returns to his account of the Persians barring the Macedonians from coming ashore.[45] He then notes that those with Alexander 'were gaining the advantage' (ἐπλεονέκτουν), and it may be that he is using this rather vague term to suggest that Alexander had made it to the other side.[46] From this point on, with a few additions, Arrian's account follows the same lines as those of Diodoros and Plutarch, with the encounter with Spithridates and Rhoisakes preceded by a story of Alexander breaking his spear and borrowing one from a companion.[47] This is followed by the flight of the cavalry and the destruction of the infantry.[48]

The most important addition Arrian makes to the earlier accounts we have is the description of the fighting in the river.[49] In this account Alexander, like Achilles,[50] finds himself struggling to escape from the water, but at last succeeding, and being able to take his fight to the enemy. After the struggle with the river, Arrian describes Alexander picking out Darius' son-in-law Mithridates, and dispatching him in single combat, in typical Homeric fashion.[51] The closeness of Arrian's description of this battle to Homer has been noted by others.[52] Inevitably, after the battle, as Alexander moves south into Lydia, the Homeric elements of the landscape, and of Arrian's account, disappear.

Quellenforschung and the Granikos

The account of the battle of the Granikos takes up a large part of the section of Arrian which we are examining. Discussions of the battle, and attempts to reconstruct it, have long preoccupied scholars.[53] The traditional approach has been to go in search of the original eye-witness sources on which the surviving accounts are based.[54] In this case the candidates are Kallisthenes, Ptolemy, Aristoboulos and whatever source Kleitarchos is taken to have used in his account, which is assumed to lie behind Diodoros'.[55] The differences between Arrian's account and Plutarch's are to be explained entirely in terms of their access to earlier sources.[56] There are two problems with this approach: it assumes that it is possible to get back to an accurate account at all, and it effectively denies the authors of the surviving narratives any credit for the stories they tell.

The first of these problems has been described by Michael Whitby as the 'fallacy of military knowledge' in a study that pays particular attention to the accounts of the Granikos.[57] For Whitby it is Alexander himself who is responsible for much of the difficulty: 'Alexander's determination to maximise his personal heroic glory, especially early in his career, may have distorted accounts of the Granicus beyond all expectations.' This may be to put too much stress on influences from the time of the battle, and too little on later issues, and it makes assumptions about Alexander's character and motivations that are based on the same problematic evidence.[58] Nonetheless Whitby's caution is sensible, and he goes on to raise questions about the reliability of the assumed sources for the surviving account.

The difficulty that participants in a battle would have in trying to work out what was actually happening was identified by Thucydides, in his description of the night battle at Epipolai:

> The whole army was soon in utter confusion, and the perplexity was so great that from neither side could the particulars of the conflict be exactly ascertained. In the daytime the combatants see more clearly; though even then only what is going on immediately around them, and that imperfectly – nothing of the battle as a whole. But in a night engagement, like this in which two great armies fought – the only one of the kind which occurred during the war – who could be certain of anything?[59]

This suggests that of the four postulated sources for the account of the Granikos, Ptolemy, although a participant and therefore an eyewitness, was not likely to be able to produce a reliable account of the battle. Indeed it is argued that he did not try to do so, but relied on Kallisthenes' narrative, not only at Granikos, but also at Issos and Gaugamela; and it is suggested that Aristoboulos did the same. Both these writers are assumed to have written decades after the events they described.[60] Kallisthenes, assumed to be an eye-witness but not a participant, was potentially in a better position to describe the battle, but his reputation as a flatterer has made his reliability suspect.[61]

It has been argued that Diodoros' account (whether or not deriving from Kleitarchos), 'contains elements of the "official" version as well as details that are unlikely to be true',[62] and therefore cannot be accepted as an independent account. If Ptolemy and Aristoboulos used Kallisthenes' details for their account, then rather than having four sources for the battle we may in fact have only one.[63] But as we have seen, the description of the battle proper, consisting as it does of Alexander engaging in single combat, followed by the flight of the Persians, is more or less the same in the three surviving versions. It is only in the details of when and how the river was crossed that there are differences between the three accounts, and these are best explained in other ways.

The two accounts that have Alexander crossing the Granikos as soon as he reaches it include Alexander's remark to Parmenion about the shame if, having crossed the Hellespont, he should be held up by the Granikos.[64] Diodoros does not record this anecdote, and it is clear that the story of the contested river crossing and Alexander's remark are interdependent. This is not the only example of Alexander making a witty remark before a battle. Before Gaugamela Alexander spoke what Plutarch refers to as the memorable (μνημονευόμενον) words: οὐ κλέπτω τὴν νίκην ('I will not steal the victory'); Arrian (but not Plutarch) presents this as a response to a suggestion of Parmenion.[65] This is part of a wider pattern of exchanges between the two men: Plutarch's *Life of Alexander* and Arrian each have five examples, Diodoros three, and Plutarch's *Sayings of Kings and Commanders* adds a further one.[66] It has been argued that these stories were originally told by Kallisthenes to belittle the achievement of Parmenion.[67] But this view downplays the broader historiographical context of such exchanges.[68] As has been noted, but not examined more closely, these episodes belong in the tradition of the 'wise adviser story', a pattern that is most clearly noted in Herodotus, but which goes back at least to Homer.[69] In their usual form, these stories have an older, experienced man giving advice to a young ruler: thus Croesus advises Cyrus, and Artabanos and Demaratos advise Xerxes. A wise ruler like Cyrus heeds the advice, and succeeds, while a foolish one like Xerxes ignores it, and ultimately fails. A clear example in the Alexander historians is the conversation in Curtius between Darius III and the Athenian exile Charidemos,[70] where Darius asks whether his army will destroy Alexander's much smaller force, and Charidemos sings the praises of Macedonian discipline. This episode is modelled directly on Herodotus' story of a discussion between Xerxes and Demaratos at the start of Xerxes' invasion of Greece.[71] But while this story follows the standard pattern, the Alexander-Parmenion exchanges clearly play with the tradition. To appreciate what is going on it is important to recognise that Parmenion does not give bad advice. His proposals are always sensible and ought, under normal circumstances, to have been followed. But Alexander is no ordinary ruler, and this is what the Parmenion stories are supposed to reveal: Alexander uniquely can ignore his wise adviser, and still turn out to be right.[72] Such stories can float free of their original context, as is indicated by the existence of collections like Plutarch's *Sayings of Kings and Commanders*.[73] This suggests that the exchange reported by Arrian and Plutarch as happening before the battle of the Granikos, whatever its actual origins, may not have been found by them in a narrative account of the battle. Rather it may have been told for its own sake, and have been integrated into the battle narrative by Plutarch and Arrian.

This brings us to the second problem with the *Quellenforschung* approach, the assumption that the surviving narratives contain little that is original to their authors. Arrian's *proem* may be seen to encourage this approach, since the author chooses there to emphasise his reliance on earlier texts. However, it is not necessary to take an author at face value when he makes claims like this.[74] Arrian's assertions of his own merit as an author, in particular in the 'second preface', indicate that he intends to be better than his sources.[75] As Bosworth puts it: 'Arrian makes historical aims clear. His history is intended to be a literary showpiece, to do for Alexander what Homer did for Achilles and Pindar for the Deinomenid tyrants.'[76] Under these circumstances we should not be surprised to see Arrian bringing his knowledge gathered from elsewhere into his account of Alexander's activities. The description of Alexander's crossing of the Granikos is one such example.

As we have seen, Arrian's account includes an extended description of the Macedonian forces crossing the Granikos, and the Persians attempting, with some success, to keep them from coming ashore. He describes how Alexander extended his troops obliquely as he crossed, so that he could attack the Persians in deep formation as he emerged.[77] Beyond this however the passage is short of specific detail, and is rather repetitive.[78] There is nothing there to indicate that Arrian had access to a significant alternative account to those lying behind the accounts of Plutarch and Diodoros. The description of Alexander's cavalry formation could have been deduced from the circumstances, given Arrian's own understanding of military tactics.[79]

According to Hammond, Arrian's account of the battle 'is not romantic but factual... The account is a careful record, derived from Ptolemy, who had the *King's Journal* to draw on.'[80] My argument has been that it is actually the opposite: it is constructed from a disparate range of elements, including a contemporary account (most likely Kallisthenes), Arrian's own military understanding, and Homer. Arrian's interest here is in the presentation of Alexander as a heroic individual, not in accurately reporting the details of the engagement.[81]

If Arrian's account shows his own input in matters of detail, there is no reason to doubt that he was also concerned to shape the narrative on a larger scale. It is clear that elsewhere he organises his material to draw out particular themes. Attention has been drawn to the 'Great Digression' (Arr. *Anab.* 4.7–14), where Arrian gathers together a series of stories showing Alexander in a less attractive light than normal, taking them out of chronological context.[82] A similar process is visible here. In his discussion of the 'second preface', Marincola notes:

> Alexander's actions in Greece were by no means negligible but Arrian gives them brief treatment, seeing in the campaign against Asia the true starting point of his work. And at the true starting point he gives a 'true' proem.[83]

And having evoked Homer in that 'true' proem, Arrian continues to evoke him in the narrative that follows.

The period from Alexander's first landing in Asia to his first victory over the Persians was crucial for the success of his campaign as a whole. It was an opportunity for Arrian to characterise his hero in a way that would let his readers understand what kind of a leader and a warrior Alexander was. His method was to draw attention to the parallels between Alexander and Achilles – both the greatest warriors of their time, and both fated to die young[84] – by shaping the narrative to echo the pattern of Achilles' actions when he goes in pursuit of Hektor after the death of Patroklos. Any minor distortions that this may have introduced into Arrian's account of Alexander's route, or the details of the battle, would have been seen as a price worth paying, if it allowed Arrian to achieve his goal of 'making clear to men the deeds of Alexander'.[85]

Notes

[1] E.g. Lane Fox 1973, 59–63; Ameling 1988; Bosworth 1988, 281; Cohen 1995; Carney 2000, 274–85.

[2] Diod. 17.97.3; Curt. 4.6.29; Plut. *Alex.* 5.5; Arr. *Anab.* 7.14.4. On this subject more generally, see Maitland 2015.

[3] Plut. *Alex.* 26.1.

[4] Strab. 13.1.27.

[5] Plut. *Alex.* 8.2 = *FGrH* 134 F 38.

[6] Boyd 1995, 39 n. 13.

[7] Athen. 12.514e–f = *FGrH* 125 F 2. I owe this reference to the abstract of an unpublished paper by Christopher Brunelle: https://classicalstudies.org/annual-meeting/146/abstract/alexanders-persian-pillow.

[8] Cf. Plut. *Alex.* 46.4 = *FGrH* 125 F 12 for another story told by Onesikritos that was regarded as unreliable.

[9] Heckel 2005, 67; 2015, 30.

[10] Burlinga 2013, 104–6.

[11] Arr. *Anab.* 7.14.4, 7.16.8.

[12] Arr. *Anab.* 1.12.1–2.

[13] Marincola 1989, 187–8.

[14] Alexander's arrival in Babylon and Susa is reported rapidly after the account of the battle: Arr. *Anab.* 3.16.3–7.

[15] Arr. *Anab.* 1.11.5.

[16] Arr. *Anab.* 1.11.8.

[17] See Bosworth 1980–95, 1.99–100.

[18] Arr. *Anab.* 1.12.1. cf. Cic. *Arch.* 24.

[19] Stadter 1981, 162; Moles 1985, 163.

[20] Arr. *Anab.* 1.12.5 echoes Hom. *Il.* 6.150–1, 20.203–4: Moles 1985, 165; cf. Marincola 1989.

[21] Arr. *Anab.* 5.28.3, 7.11.1.

[22] But see Maitland 2015, esp. 12–14, and from a different perspective Carney 2000, 276.

[23] For a summary of what is known about these places see Latacz 2003, 273.

[24] Arr. *Anab.* 1.11.6.

[25] Arr. *Anab.* 1.12.6. The manuscript gives προσακτίῳ, corrected by almost all commentators to Πρακτίῳ. See Bosworth 1980–95, 1.108, followed by Sisti 2001, 350.

[26] Bosworth 1980–95, 1.108–9 with Strab. 13.1.21.

[27] Hom. *Il.* 2.824–7.

[28] Hom. *Il.* 4.85–140 (where Zeleia is mentioned twice: 103 and 121); 5.280–96.

[29] Arr. *Anab.* 1.12.10, 1.16.3.

[30] Hom. *Il.* 12.21.

[31] Arr. *Anab.* 1.13.6.

[32] Diod. 17.97.3. Curtius' report of the same incident (9.4.14) also refers to Alexander fighting the river (*cum amne bellum fuisse crederes*), but does not mention the comparison with Achilles. See Heckel 2015, 30–31.

[33] Arr. *Anab.* 6.5.1–4.

[34] Hom. *Il.* 21.211–382.

[35] Plut. *Alex.* 16; Diod. 17.19–21.

[36] E.g. Hammond 2001, 73–4; Matthews 2008, 166.

[37] Diod. 17.19.2. Bosworth (1980–95, 1.116) identifies this higher ground as 'the hills running parallel to the river bank at an interval of 1½–2 km'.

[38] Plut. *Alex.* 16.2.

[39] Plut. *Alex.* 16.3.

[40] Plut. *Alex.* 16.6.

[41] Diod. 17.20; Plut. *Alex.* 16.4–5.

[42] Arr. *Anab.* 1.13.3. Sheppard (2008, 117) implausibly suggests that Diodoros' account was based on this plan, 'as if Alexander accepted Parmenio's advice'. How and why a piece of advice made presumably in the restricted context of a meeting of the high command, and there rejected, should makes its way into the historical tradition, is not explained.

[43] Arr. *Anab.* 1.15.2.

[44] Arr. *Anab.* 1.15.4: 'And although the fight was on horseback, it seemed rather more like an infantry battle.'

[45] Arr. *Anab.* 1.15.2–4.

[46] Arr. *Anab.* 1.15.5.

[47] Arr. *Anab.* 1.15.6–8.

[48] Arr. *Anab.* 1.16.1–3.

[49] Arr. *Anab.* 1.14.5–15.5.

[50] Hom. *Il.* 21.233–304.

[51] Green 1991, 178: 'It is all remarkably like a battle-scene from the *Iliad*.' Similar comments have been made about Diodoros' account: Heckel 2015, 31–2.

[52] Devine 1994, 94: 'Certainly the individual glorification of Alexander – by means of a full-blown *aristeia* (1.14.6–7, 1.15.5–8) – is much more prominent here in relation to hard tactical detail than in Arrian's accounts of the later battles.'

[53] A selection: Judeich 1908; Lehmann 1911; Fuller 1958, 147–54; Lane Fox 1973, 118–25; Davis 1964; Nikolitsis 1974; Foss 1977; Badian 2012/1977; Hammond 1980; Devine 1986; Bosworth 1988, 35–44; Devine 1988; Harl 1997; Sabin 2007, 129–33; Thompson 2007; Heckel 2008: 45–51; Matthews 2008; English 2011. Games should also be included amongst attempts to reconstruct the battle: see Sabin 2009.

[54] E.g. Hammond 1976, 236: 'As in all matters which concern the activities of Alexander one has to decide as far as one can what is the ultimate source of our information and which author or authors have transmitted that source most accurately.'

[55] Matthews (2008, 9) is the latest to resurrect the theory that Kleitarchos 'spoke to at least one of the Greek mercenaries who had fought on the Persian side during the Granickos campaign', a suggestion of Tarn refuted by Brunt 1962.

[56] Hammond 1993, 36: 'The simplest explanation is that Plutarch was following Aristoboulos, who wrote from memory, and that Arrian was following Ptolemy, who had access to A's *Royal Journal*, in which details of A's actions and of Macedonian losses were recorded.'

[57] Whitby 2008, 62–3.

[58] Whitby 2008, 59: 'Alexander the Great's devotion to Homer is well attested, and his actions were given an epic gloss by his court historian Callisthenes, but he also deliberately modelled his behaviour on Homeric heroes, especially his ancestor Achilles, so that the distinction between 'reality' and representation is bound to be complex.' This paper seeks to demonstrate that Arrian, rather than Alexander, may be responsible for some of the characterization of Alexander as Homeric.

[59] Thuc. 7.44.1 (Jowett's translation). See also Whatley 1964, 119: 'Battles of all

periods are difficult things to reconstruct. In battle many and different events happen simultaneously and changes are rapid. The actors are in a state of excitement and extreme nervous tension-the worst possible condition for viewing a situation with a proper sense of proportion. It is impossible for anyone to know what is happening in every part of an engagement and there is unlikely to be the occasion, even if there is the desire, for an impartial inquiry and examination of representative witnesses while the battle is recent and its memory fresh.'

[60] Devine 1994; cf. Brunt 1976–83, 2.546, for the suggestion that Aristoboulos also used Kallisthenes.

[61] Polyb. 12.12b; Strab. 17.1.43. But see Milns 2006/7.

[62] Heckel 2008, 48. What is meant by 'the "official" version', or 'official propaganda' (177 n. 11) is not made clear. Does it mean Kallisthenes, or the *Royal Journal* mentioned by Hammond (1993, 36)?

[63] Presumed to be Kallisthenes (Devine 1994).

[64] Plut. *Alex.* 16.2 has the Hellespont being ashamed; in Arr. *Anab.* 1.13.6 it is Alexander himself. The accounts differ too in what Parmenion says to prompt it.

[65] Plut. *Alex.* 31.7. Cf. Arr. *Anab.* 3.10.2 (in reported speech).

[66] Plut. *Alex.* 16.2, 19.3, (21.4), 29.4, 31.5–7, 32.1–2; Arr. *Anab.* 1.13.3–7, 2.4.9–10, 2.25.2, 3.10.1–2, 3.18.11; Diod. 17.16.2, 17.54.4–5, 17.56.2–3; Plut. *Mor.* 180b (referring to the Granikos).

[67] E.g. Bosworth 1980–95, 1.137; Hamilton 1999, 89; Green 1991, 175: 'From now on, it has been observed, Callisthenes never misses an opportunity, in his official record, of reporting occasions when Parmenio supposedly gave the king bad advice. This advice, needless to say, was always ignored – to the benefit of everyone concerned.'

[68] See Carney 2000, 264–73.

[69] Bischoff 1932; Lattimore 1939; more recently Gray 1986; Shapiro 1994; Chaplin 2011. For Thucydides, Pelling 1991.

[70] Curt. 3.2.10–19.

[71] Hdt. 7.101–5. Atkinson 1980, 101–2.

[72] Lane Fox 1973, 121: 'This conversation with Parmenion is probably fiction, for Parmenion appears suspiciously often as Alexander's 'adviser', not only in his officer's histories but also in legend, whether Greek or Jewish, where he is usually refuted and so serves to set off his master's daring and intelligence.'

[73] On the notion of 'transferable stories' in relation to Alexander see also Bowden 2013, 66–7.

[74] See for example the analysis of Thucydides' self-presentation in Rood 2012, esp. 249: 'The tensions in modern responses to Thucydides' narrational persona and in Thucydides' own construction of that persona both reflect the fact that that persona is not a single entity, but itself formed by his armory of narrational techniques.' It is worth noting that modern responses to Arrian have not yet got as far as having significant 'tensions', and that there is much still to explore of Arrian's narrational techniques.

[75] Arr. *Anab.* 1.12.2–5, following on from *proem* 3.

[76] Bosworth 1980–95, 1.104.

[77] Arr. *Anab.* 1.14.7.

[78] In chapter 15, we are twice told about pushing and shoving (§2 and §4), and twice told that the initial Macedonian assault was beaten back (§2 and §3).

[79] Cf. Arr. *Tact.* 16–17. Although the *Tactica* was probably written later than the *Anabasis*, there is no reason to suppose that Arrian did not have the relevant understanding when writing the earlier work. On Arrian's tactical writings see Bosworth 1993, 253–72.

[80] Hammond 2001, 73.

[81] See Burlinga 2013 for an analysis of how Arrian intends to present Alexander.

[82] Brunt 1976–83, 1.532–44; Bosworth 1980–95, 2.45–7; Bowden 2013, 62–6.

[83] Marincola 1989, 187–8.

[84] Achilles is warned of his forthcoming death before he sets out after Hektor: ἀλλά τοι ἐγγύθεν ἦμαρ ὀλέθριον (Hom. *Il.* 19.409); Arrian uses a strikingly similar phrase about Alexander near the end: ἀλλὰ γὰρ αὐτῷ ἤδη Ἀλεξάνδρῳ ἐγγὺς ἦν τὸ τέλος (Arr. *Anab.* 7.24.1).

[85] Arr. *Anab.* 1.12.4.

Bibliography

Ameling, W.
1988   'Alexander und Achilleus: Eine Bestandsaufnahme', in W. Will and J. Heinrichs (eds) *Zu Alexander der Grosse: Festschrift G. Wirth zum 60. Geburtstag am 9.12.86*, Amsterdam, 657–92.

Atkinson, J. E.
1980   *A Commentary on Q. Curtius Rufus' Historiae Alexandri Magni Books 3 and 4*, Amsterdam.

Badian, E.
2012   'The Battle of the Granicus: A New Look', *Collected Papers on Alexander the Great*, London, 224–43.

Bischoff, H.
1932   *Der Warner bei Herodot*, Marburg.

Bosworth, A. B.
1980–95 *A Historical Commentary on Arrian's History of Alexander*, 2 vols., Oxford.
1988   *Conquest and Empire: The Reign of Alexander the Great*, Cambridge.
1993   'Arrian and Rome: The Minor Works', *ANRW* 2.34.1, 226–75.

Bowden, H.
2013   'On Kissing and Making up: Court Protocol and Historiography in Alexander the Great's "Experiment with *Proskynesis*"', *BICS*, 56, 55–77.

Boyd, T. W.
1995   '*Libri confusi*', *CJ* 91, 35–45.

Brunt, P. A.
1962   'Persian Accounts of Alexander's Campaigns', *CQ* 12, 141–55.
1976–83 *Arrian, History of Alexander and Indica*, 2 vols., Loeb Classical Library, Cambridge, MA.

Burlinga, B.
  2013   *Arrian's* Anabasis: *An Intellectual and Cultural Story,* Gdańsk.
Carney, E. D.
  2000   'Artifice and Alexander History', in A. B. Bosworth and E. J. Baynham,
          (eds) *Alexander the Great in Fact and Fiction*, Oxford, 263–85.
Chaplin, J. D.
  2011   'Conversations in History: Arrian and Herodotus, Parmenio and
          Alexander', *GRBS* 51, 613–33.
Cohen, A.
  1995   'Alexander and Achilles – Macedonians and "Mycenaeans"', in J. B.
          Carter and S. P. Morris (eds) *The Ages of Homer: A Tribute to Emily
          Townsend Vermeule*, Austin, 483–505.
Davis, E. W.
  1964   'The Persian Battle Plan at the Granicus', *James Sprunt Studies in History
          and Political Science* 46, 34–44.
Devine, A. M.
  1986   'Demythologizing the Battle of the Granicus', *Phoenix* 40, 265–78.
  1988   'A Pawn-Sacrifice at the Battle of the Granicus: The Origins of a
          Favorite Stratagem of Alexander the Great', *AncW* 18, 3–20.
  1994   'Alexander's Propaganda Machine. Callisthenes as the Ultimate Source
          for Arrian, *Anabasis* 1–3', in I. Worthington (ed.) *Ventures into Greek
          History*, Oxford, 89–104.
English, S.
  2011   *The Field Campaigns of Alexander the Great*, Barnsley.
Foss, C.
  1977   'The Battle of the Granicus: A New Look', *AM* 2, 495–502.
Fuller, J. F. C.
  1958   *The Generalship of Alexander the Great*, London.
Gray, V. J.
  1986   'Xenophon's *Hiero* and the Meeting of the Wise Man and Tyrant in
          Greek Literature', *CQ* 36, 115–23.
Green, P.
  1991   *Alexander of Macedon, 356–323 BC: A Historical Biography*, Berkeley.
Hamilton, J. R.
  1999   *Plutarch, Alexander: a Commentary*, 2nd ed., Bristol.
Hammond, N. G. L.
  1976   review of Nikolitsis, *The Battle of the Granicus*, *CR* 26, 235–6.
  1980   'The Battle of the Granicus River', *JHS* 100, 73–88.
  1993   *The Sources for Alexander the Great*, Oxford.
  2001   *Alexander the Great: King, Commander and Statesman*, 3rd ed., Bristol.
Harl, K.
  1997   'Alexander's Cavalry Battle at the Granicus', in C. D. Hamilton and
          P. Krentz (eds) *Polis and Polemos. Essays on Politics, War, and History in
          Ancient Greece in honor of Donald Kagan*, Claremont, CA, 303–26.
Heckel, W.
  2005   *The Marshals of Alexander's Empire*, London.

2008   *The Conquests of Alexander the Great*, Cambridge.
2015   'Alexander, Achilles, and Heracles: Between Myth and History', in P. Wheatley and E. Baynham (eds) *East and West in the World Empire of Alexander: Essays in honour of Brian Bosworth*, Oxford, 21–33.

Judeich, W.
1908 'Die Schlacht am Granikos', *Klio* 8, 372–97.

Lane Fox, R.
1973   *Alexander the Great*, London.

Latacz, J.
2003   *Homers Ilias Gesamtkommentar. Band II. 2. Gesang. Faszikel 2: Kommentar,* Leipzig.

Lattimore, R.
1939   'The Wise Adviser in Herodotus', *CP* 34, 24–35.

Lehmann, K.
1911   'Die Schlacht am Granikos', *Klio* 11, 230–44.

Maitland, J.
2015   'ΜΗΝΙΝ ΑΕΙΔΕ ΘΕΑ: Alexander the Great and the Anger of Achilles', in P. Wheatley and E. Baynham (eds) *East and West in the World Empire of Alexander: Essays in honour of Brian Bosworth*, Oxford, 1–20.

Marincola, J.
1989   'Some Suggestions on the Proem and "Second Preface" of Arrian's *Anabasis*', *JHS* 109, 186–9.

Matthews, R.
2008   *Alexander at the Battle of the Granicus: A Campaign in Context*, Stroud.

Milns, R. D.
2006/7 'Callisthenes on Alexander', *Mediterranean Archaeology*, 19–20, 233–7.

Moles, J.
1985   'The Interpretation of the "Second Preface" in Arrian's *Anabasis*', *JHS* 105, 162–8.

Nikolitsis, N. T.
1974   *The Battle of the Granicus*, Stockholm.

Pelling, C.
1991   'Thucydides' Archidamus and Herodotus' Artabanus', in M. A. Flower and M. Toher (eds) *Georgica. Greek Studies in honour of George Cawkwell*, London, 120–42.

Rood, T.
2012   'Objectivity and Authority: Thucydides' Historical Method', in A. Rengakos and A. Tsakmakis (eds) *Brill's Companion to Thucydides*, Leiden, 225–49.

Sabin, P.
2007   *Lost Battles: Reconstructing the Great Clashes of the Ancient World*, London.
2009   'Recent Reconstructions of the Battle of the Granicus: A Case Study in Varying Standards of Scholarship', *Slingshot* 263, 14–16.

Shapiro, S. O.
1994   'Learning through Suffering: Human Wisdom in Herodotus', *CJ* 89, 349–55.

Sheppard, R.
    2008   *Alexander the Great at War: His Army – His Battles – His Enemies*, Oxford.
Sisti, F.
    2001   *Arriano, Anabasi di Alessandro*, vol. 1, Milan.
Stadter, P.
    1981   'Arrian's Extended Preface', *Illinois Classical Studies* 6, 157–71.
Thompson, M.
    2007   *Granicus 334 BC: Alexander's First Persian Victory*, Oxford.
Whatley, N.
    1964   'On the Possibility of Reconstructing Marathon and Other Ancient Battles', *JHS* 84, 119–39.
Whitby, M.
    2008   'Reconstructing Ancient Warfare' in P. Sabin, H. van Wees and M. Whitby (eds) *Cambridge History of Ancient Greek and Roman Warfare*, Cambridge, 54–81.

9

THE GRAND PROCESSION, *GALATERSIEG*, AND PTOLEMAIC KINGSHIP

Paul Johstono

The Ptolemaic dynasty of Hellenistic Egypt has a reputation more for opulence, or τρυφή, than for any particularly praiseworthy quality of monarchs: wisdom, charity, stability, bravery, and the like. Athenaios, in his *Deipnosophistae*, could reliably dip into the Egyptian well for images of extravagance, producing accounts of super-ships that were all show, luxury barges that presaged the modern cruise ship, and a parade – the Grand Procession – with more gold, more exotic animals, and more laughably large phalli than anyone could scarcely have imagined. Austere Romans were appalled by Ptolemaic extravagance, and dour Polybios likewise found it both distasteful and deleterious to the fortunes of a state.[1] For the Ptolemies, however, manifestations of wealth were performative politics, and enhanced the fortunes of their state.

Ptolemy II Philadelphos was the most successful of the dynasty at converting wealth, through opulent display, into legitimacy and prestige, and was known as the most formidable, most lavish, and most magnificent of Hellenistic kings.[2] Many studies have drawn attention to the second Ptolemy's capital-intensive strategy for securing his personal rule over his father's empire.[3] His strategy worked well enough but marked a departure from traditionalist royal authority. His father and each of their contemporaries won acclamations from soldiers on battlefields before their coronations or as confirmation to their accession. Philadelphos has thus gained a reputation as rather more a lover than a fighter. Yet this is not entirely correct.[4] The trophies of a major military victory figured prominently in the Ptolemaic festival – probably the Ptolemaia – that featured Athenaios' Grand Procession, a lengthy parade early in Philadelphos' reign that has often occupied pride of place in the pantheon of gaudy displays. Recognizing the nature and purpose of these trophies requires adjusting the customary date for the Grand Procession and contributes to our understanding of Ptolemaic kingship.

Ptolemy II ruled Egypt and far-flung Mediterranean domains from 282 to 246 BC. His father had been one of Alexander's generals, and cultivated his association with the conqueror through the remainder of his life. Ptolemy I waged numerous campaigns against other Successors and gained several noteworthy victories, conforming to the rapidly developing and enduring model of Hellenistic kingship.[5] Soldiers supported leaders who, through victories and conquests, were likely to gain them plunder and bring them home alive. His soldiers acclaimed him as king following his able defense of Egypt against Antigonos the One-Eyed – and the largest army assembled since Alexander's Indian campaign – in 305. Considering the natural wealth and defenses of Egypt, Ptolemy I wisely avoided the aggressive, gambling campaigns that characterised the Successor Wars (321–281). For that reason, his son did not grow up in the saddle in the way the second and third generations of Seleukid and Antigonid kings did.[6] When Ptolemy II became king, he had little to no military experience.

Until some famous victory afforded itself to him, the best strategy Philadelphos could adopt was to emphasise his association with his father and to further his father's ideological mission. Like his father, he cultivated the arts, and his patronage yielded numerous works that celebrated the budding dynasty and crafted multiple mythic associations between the Lagids and the divine. As Alexander had been deified following his death, Ptolemy II ensured his own father was deified soon after his passing. On the fourth anniversary of his father's passing, and as a poignant expression of his filial piety, he established a festival called the Ptolemaia.[7] It honoured his deified father and further forged the mythologies surrounding his family and their right to rule. The Ptolemaia was established as an athletic, dramatic, and equestrian competition (ἀγῶνα ἰσολύμπιον γυμνικὸν καὶ μουσικὸν καὶ ἱππικόν) held once per Olympiad, accompanying sacrifices to the deified Ptolemy I and Berenike I.[8] With the wealth of Egypt at his disposal, Ptolemy developed the competition into a spectacle and event practically on par with the Olympics. The Ptolemaia incorporated features that reinforced Ptolemaic ideology: aspects of religious festival, royal cult, military review, and diplomatic embassy found places alongside the competitions. Embassies of *theōroi* from the Aegean world came to the Ptolemaia to enjoy the Ptolemies' lavish hospitality and the Ptolemaia's unmatched spectacle. *Theōroi* hailed, in particular, from those states that had benefited, or hoped to benefit, from royal patronage.[9] From the beginning it featured a grand procession, or *pompē*, an elaborate parade through the city of Alexandria.[10]

The opulence of one of these parades surpassed all the others, and became, along with the banquet pavilion from the same festival, the subject of a lengthy description by Kallixeinos of Rhodes.[11] Kallixeinos' career is not securely dated, but probably wrote about the middle of the second century

BC.[12] His chief source, as referenced in his text, was *The Penteteric Records*.[13] His account of what is now generally known as *the* Grand Procession was quoted at length by Athenaios (5.196–203) as one of the chief examples of Ptolemaic wealth and display and is known only through those selections. The parade route covered approximately three and a half miles through the city, but the Procession was many miles greater in length. It featured hundreds of massive, elaborate floats, thousands of costumed actors, a host of exotic animals, a full military review, golden crowns, gold-plated and larger-than-life-sized armour, and symbolism in spades. Prominent were symbols of Ptolemaic authority across the Hellenic world, and associations between Ptolemy I and Zeus and between Ptolemy II and Dionysos, the conquering reveler, were common. In addition to the procession, the royal pavilion, a banquet site on the palace grounds where the king hosted the most distinguished guests, was made up with similar pomp. Within the scarlet tent elite Greco-Macedonian diners relaxed on 130 couches, surrounded by the finest works of the day, served from dishes of gold and silver many talents in weight, as trophies overhead silently but powerfully proclaimed the prowess of king Ptolemy.

The Historiography of the Grand Procession

Historians and Classicists have bickered for decades over the date of the Grand Procession and attendant Ptolemaia. The first Ptolemaia was indisputably celebrated in the winter of 279/8 BC.[14] For nearly 100 years the preponderance of scholars have identified the Grand Procession with this first Ptolemaia. Others have leaned toward the second in 275/4, the third in 271/0, the fifth in 263/2, or questioned the association between the Procession and any Ptolemaia. Tarn reasoned that the absence of Arsinoe II in the Procession narrative could be resolved most easily with a date before her arrival in Egypt, and on the basis of this argument from silence associated the Grand Procession with the inaugural celebration of the event.[15] The earliest date has remained the standard (although not necessarily fixed) date in most coverage of Ptolemaic or Hellenistic history.[16] While Fraser, in his study of Alexandria, questioned the association between the Ptolemaia and the Procession, he nonetheless settled for a date between 280 and 275, for largely the same reasons Tarn preferred 279/8. Fraser's pupil Rice, who composed the largest study to date of the Grand Procession, left both its association with the Ptolemaia and its date open questions, but preferred the same date range.[17] Walbank, and more recently Thompson, have argued strongly – and to many, persuasively – for association with the Ptolemaia and for the 279/8 date.[18] This paper will demonstrate that a date for Kallixeinos' Grand Procession in 279/8 is impossible.

Support for a later date has tended to settle around 275/4.[19] While this date risks some entanglements with the absence of Arsinoe II, some have resolved the difficulty by locating the sibling marriage later than mid-winter 274.[20] Foertmeyer offered the first determined proposal for dating the Grand Procession to 275/4, and specifically to December–February, on the basis of astronomical indications within the description.[21] Foertmeyer's hypothesis has received little support, but her date has received backing from two directions: from those who employ the positive evidence of Africans and African beasts in the Procession to date it subsequent to Ptolemy II's Nubian War and from those who see the substantial military review as indicative of an imminent war, namely, the First Syrian War.[22] Others have preferred to see the military review as celebration of Ptolemy's (inflated) military victory in the same war and have dated the Procession to 271/0.[23] The latest suggested date is that of Hazzard – January 262 – for whom the Grand Procession figures as a key component in a major ideological program Ptolemy II undertook that year to revitalise the monarchy.[24] Unfortunately, Hazzard's suggestion has not acquired much support.

The date of the Procession remains open in large part for lack of testimony that provides more specific evidence. A woman, clad in scarlet costume, played the role Πεντετηρίς in the Grand Procession (198b), leaving little doubt the context was a Ptolemaia. The Arsinoe II question is rather complicated. Not only is it an argument from silence, Athenaios (or Kallixeinos) admits to describing only selected portions of a parade that featured many divisions (197d). Further, the second division was dedicated the parents of the kings (τοῖς τῶν βασιλέων γονεῦσι), where the plural could be construed as a reference Arsinoe II.[25] The Nubian or Ethiopian details have limited utility, both because the date of Ptolemy's campaign against Meroë is hardly set more firmly than the Procession and because the African elements in the Procession could have been accessible without a military campaign. Without a more specific date, any attempt to read the Procession for Ptolemaic royal ideology will be either faulty or, at minimum, generalised. Thus the details end up fitting a kingdom ramping up for war, and the Grand Procession resembles the autumn of 1914, or celebrating a victory after the war; the Procession can be the politics of a king newly-crowned, or of a king reinventing himself and his rule. I suggest we can do better, and in hopes of such, turn away from the Procession itself and toward the Royal Pavilion.

The Royal Pavilion
While the Procession was the grandest spectacle of the occasion Kallixeinos described, Ptolemy hosted his elite guests in a pavilion that was 'beautiful

to extremes and worth hearing about' (καλὴ εἰς ὑπερβολὴν ἀξία τε ἀκοῆς: 196a). The large structure he described shared some features with modern-day athletic arenas, although on a smaller scale, and of less permanent construction.[26] It was located within the palace neighbourhood, and almost certainly within gardens on the landward side of Lochias.[27] The best guests were hosted on 130 couches in the middle of the tent, beneath a rectangular canopy, dyed in Tyrian purple with white fringe, suspended from ten fifty-cubit-tall columns. Additional beams helped support the whole structure, which was enclosed by a covered, colonnaded peristyle on three sides. The peristyle may have been a permanent structure in the palace complex. Along the colonnade were a hundred marble sculptures of animals (ζῷα μαρμάρινα), one beside each column, with Sikyonian paintings or curtains embroidered with dynastic and mythic images in the spaces between (196e–f). Above the colonnade, the sculptures, and the artworks was the entablature, 'covered the whole way round with shields alternating silver and gold' (θυρεοὶ περιέκειντο ἐναλλὰξ ἀργυροῖ τε καὶ χρυσοῖ: 196f). The shields have not received the attention they merit. A recent description of the pavilion referred to the 'beautifully elaborate cloaks, armor, and shields' along its sides, when armor does not actually appear in the description.[28]

Shields were placed in public and celebratory spaces like this pavilion as trophies, monuments to victories won. Among the civilizations of the ancient Mediterranean, victory brought honor and glory to the victor, but 'there could be no honor without public proclamation; and there could be no publicity without the evidence of a trophy'.[29] Trophies, often the shields and armor of the defeated army, occupied public spaces and silently proclaimed a legacy of triumph. Hellenistic monarchs, and even Roman generals operating in the Greek world, used the glory from military victories, sustained over time through trophies, to establish and buttress their legitimacy.[30] Here is evidence, then, of Ptolemy II's participation in contemporary monarchic culture, fulfilling conventional expectations by demonstrating martial prowess.

The menacing trophies of King Ptolemy

While it was not unusual that shields should appear prominently in a central location at a major royal festival, the type of shield, and the presence of a victory monument, merit remark. Kallixeinos recorded that the shields were θυρεοί. This particular detail is crucial, but technical, and so its significance has not often been appreciated. The Greeks used two types of shields traditionally: the ἀσπίς and the πέλτη, and the former in particular stood generically for shields. Both were concave, round shields. Greeks used exclusively those two shields well into the Hellenistic period.[31]

The θυρεός, on the other hand, was not a Greek shield at all. In fact, the word θυρεός, for a type of shield, was unknown in Classical Greece, and was coined in the Hellenistic period. In the Hellenistic period its reputation was as the national shield of the Galatians, not the Greeks.[32] It was a flat, elongated shield, usually oval in shape, with a prominent rib running across it from top to bottom. In addition to its use by the Galatians and other European tribes, it was a very popular shield in Italy, and was probably developed there during the fifth century before becoming the standard shield in the La Tène, Celtic world. The word θυρεός, which plays on the large wooden shield's similarity to a door, probably originated in Magna Graecia, and may have crossed into Greece with Pyrrhos' returning armies in 275/4.[33] The earliest reasonably secure use of the word is in Pyrrhos' dedication of spoils at the temple of Athena Itonis in 274.[34] A few years earlier, an Aitolian inscription concerning shields deposited at Delphi referred to 'the weapons from the Galatians' (τὰ ὅπλα ἀπὸ Γαλατᾶν). And about the time of Pyrrhos' inscription, Kallimachos of Kyrene, writing in Alexandria, referred to the Galatians' 'hated shields' (ἐχθομένας ἀσπίδας).[35]

Why were Galatian shields so prominently displayed at the Ptolemaia? Why were the shields, made of wood, decorated in silver and gold? The Galatians were a Celtic people from Central Europe who invaded Greek territories in Greece and Asia Minor beginning in 280 BC.[36] The Galatian invasions were a terrifying period in Hellenistic history: they routed armies, burned towns, committed massacres. Their warriors were known for their ferocious charge, for their distinctive shield, and for plunging into battle stark naked. After slaying Ptolemy Keraunos, half-brother to Philadelphos, their great host plundered Macedonia and Thessaly with impunity, battled the Greeks at Thermopylai, and sacked the sacred site of Delphi in 278. It was only then, in the rough ground around Parnassos, they finally met reverses. The threat posed by the Galatians was so terrifying and severe the Greeks attributed their delivery and the invaders' defeat to divine intervention. The narrative paired Greek efforts and 'the manifestation of the gods' (τήν τε ἐπιφάνειαν τῶν θεῶν) in a joint venture that saw the Galatians routed, scattered, and slaughtered, pursued by bands of light infantry, hail, snow, and tumbling rocks.[37]

The Galatians were defeated at Delphi, but continued to terrorise the Greek world by their actual or threatened presence throughout the 270s. City-states and kings who saved others from the Galatian terror – particularly if by *Galatersieg*, defeating them in battle – won acclaim, legitimacy, and a place in the narrative of divine salvation. The Galatian Invasion, an event that actually happened, assumed within the Hellenistic imagination nearly apocalyptic significance. Therefore the saviors of civilization naturally profited from their saving. The Aitolians profited first, having suffered one of the worst losses of the war when the Galatians sacked Kallion, but also having contributed to the defense of Delphi. Although the Phokians seem to have played the key role in the fighting there (Paus. 10.8.3), the Aitolians crafted the event's memory. They dedicated at the temple of Pythian Apollo shields they plundered and led the way in establishing the Soteria, a festival dedicated to the gods and men who defended Greece against the barbarians.[38]

Of *Galatersieg* and Hellenistic legitimacy

The Galatian invasion accomplished for the Aitolians what the Successors had been labouring to engineer for themselves for a generation: to be seen as defenders, saviors, and benefactors of the Greeks, associated with the gods, and recognised for their piety. Participation in the defense of Greece against the Galatians was the most promising path to legitimacy, loyalty, and acclaim since Alexander vanquished the Persians.[39] Not to be left out, the Hellenistic kings soon acquired their own victories over Galatians. Antigonos Gonatas defeated a force of Galatians near Lysimachia. He did so by a ruse, but gained enough credit from his *Galatersieg*, which he trumpeted on coinage for years, to regain control of Macedonia.[40] An inscription at Athens praised him for campaigning 'for the salvation of the Greeks' (ὑπὲρ τῆς τῶν Ἑλλήνων σωτηρίας).[41] After a large body of Galatians had crossed to Asia Minor and terrorised the country, Antiochos defeated them in what came to be known as the Battle of the Elephants. The beasts bested the barbarians, and his Macedonians hailed Antiochos as both king and Savior (Σωτῆρ).[42]

Ptolemy II's position in Egypt shielded him from Galatian plunderers, but also from the glory of a *Galatersieg*. After the Galatians crossed to Asia Minor, there were only short skirmishes in Ionia and Lycia between Ptolemaic forces and Galatians; perhaps two small encounters out of years of violence.[43] Lacking a clear path, he forged his own: he contracted a body of Galatians as mercenaries when his half-brother Magas, ruler of Kyrene, rebelled.[44] When they got to Egypt, so Ptolemy's official narrative goes, the greedy barbarians began eyeing the wealth of Alexandria and Egypt, and plotted to turn on and plunder their employer. Outsmarting the traitors, Ptolemy led them on an exercise into the Nile Delta, trapped them on an island, and oversaw their destruction.[45] The court poet Kallimachos narrated that final act from the perspective of the Galatians' shields, which 'having beheld their bearers expire in the fire by the Nile, became prizes for the king' (ἐπὶ Νείλῳ ἐν πυρὶ τοὺς φορέοντας ἀποπνεύσαντας ἰδοῦσαι, κείσονται βασιλῆος ἀέθλια; *Hymns* 4.186–7). Kallimachos, in using the shields to view the fate of the Galatians, emphasised and even enhanced their cultural power as witnesses to Ptolemy's victory. The θυρεός shields on the entablature at the Royal Pavilion were unmistakably those of the slaughtered Galatian mercenaries.[46] They invited the banqueters, prominent men from the Aegean world, to view them, and in doing so, to witness Ptolemy's *Galatersieg* and to recognise his participation in the salvation of the Greeks. Many of the banqueters would have seen the shields arrayed at Delphi, some would have encountered the Galatians themselves, and they could not have missed the significance of the monument or the equivalence it attempted to forge with Delphi.

Ptolemy deployed the θυρεός shield, representing the defeated Galatians, as a symbol of his personal right to rule, a symbol of victory and authority that was not inherited from his father or engineered by opulence. Never mind that the victory came by tricking his own (seditious) mercenaries, or that the Galatians were only in Egypt because he first hired them. The renowned perfidiousness of the Galatians shielded Ptolemy II from much skepticism, and when Magas' campaign ground to a halt, allowed Ptolemy II both not to pay his mercenaries and, by killing them, to write his own chapter in the grand narrative of Greek salvation from an apocalyptic terror. Ptolemy deployed the victory in court propaganda as if he had personally defended Delphi. Through court poetry the Galatians became 'latter-born Titans' (ὀψίγονοι Τιτῆνες; *Hymns* 4.174); Ptolemy bore comparison with Apollo and his victory at Delphi, and through the Procession Ptolemy proclaimed a proven record and promising future as a victor and benefactor in the tradition of Dionysos.

The Galatian shield trophies were sufficiently significant for Ptolemy's legitimacy that he had them inlaid with gold and silver. This was not unusual. The Aitolians decorated Galatian shields with gold inlay before dedicating them at the temple of Pythian Apollo.[47] Antiochos I did the same thing in the later 270s, dedicating a single, silver-inlaid θυρεός on Delos.[48] Ptolemy also used the θυρεός on his coinage after the victory, on bronze and silver issues until the currency reform around 265/4, and after the reform on his famous ΑΔΕΛΦΩΝ ΘΕΩΝ gold issues. As a badge on his coinage the shield proclaimed the same propaganda promulgated by the pavilion's encircling shields: Ptolemy as barbarian-conquering, freedom-preserving hero.[49] That this badge remained on his coinage so long suggests that Philadelphos' attempt to exploit the Galatian crisis for his own political ends was fairly successful.

The θυρεός shields in the Royal Pavilion were used, eventually, 'to adorn the general arena' (ξυνὸν ἀγῶνα ἔσεσθαι), according to a scholiast's comment on Kallimachos' ἀέθλια.[50] Their permanent fixture in a major public space improved their visibility to the citizens of Alexandria. θυρεός acquired impressive currency in Alexandrian vocabulary in the decades after the Galatian invasion, a possible indicator of Ptolemy's propagandistic success. In many ways its use reinforced royal ideology. Poseidippos of Pella declared a grand ocean rock 'more terrifying than Polyphemos' shield' (τοῦ Πολυφημείου σκαιοτέρην θυρεοῦ), reflecting both the abiding negative associations with the shield and the mythic tradition that the Galatians were Polyphemos' progeny.[51] Euclid, in seeking to describe an ellipse, likened it to the word θυρεός as a shape the reader would comprehend.[52] In the Septuagint's *Psalms* 45.10.3, Jehovah 'burns their shields in fire' (θυρεοὺς κατακαύσει ἐν πυρί). Here, the Greek translation replaced Hebrew 'chariots' with 'Galatian shields', a change that references Ptolemy's victory and Kallimachos' hymn. The shields themselves could be desirable as well. An acquaintance of Zenon, the well-known estate manager for Philadelphos' διοικητής Apollonios, sent him five of his 'much-prized shields' (θυρεοὺς πεφιλοτιμημένους), which he claimed had no like even in Aitolia.[53] It is difficult to parse either the honor paid these shields, or the reference to Aitolia, unless they, too, were being used as trophies.

Conclusion

One result of this study is that it sets the massacre of the Galatian mercenaries as a *terminus post quem* for Kallixeinos' Grand Procession. Most significantly, the first Ptolemaia, so often reckoned as the occasion for the Grand Procession, should be eliminated from consideration entirely. The second Ptolemaia, in the winter of 275/4, may just barely fit the chronology. The Galatian affair followed Magas' rebellion, which Pausanias described as an immediate consequence of Ptolemy II's marriage to Arsinoe II.[54] Their marriage could be dated anywhere from early 276 to sometime before November 274, and so Magas' rebellion and Ptolemy's *Galatersieg* could date as late as 274/3.[55]

The trophies may well have decorated Royal Pavilions at several festivals, although one might expect that, once they acquired a permanent home at an Alexandrian arena, they would stay there. The proximity to the victory increased its utility in promoting the legitimacy of Ptolemy II: a king, even an effete, Egyptianising king, still wins victories, and it was all the better for Ptolemy that his victory was over the bogeymen of the Hellenistic Age. The trophies, Galatian shields, were reminders of the terrible threat recently weathered, and accorded well with the court propaganda of Ptolemy's reign: like Octavian centuries later, he was introducing a Golden Age of wealth and order. Just as he neutralised the Galatian threat with fire and sword, he neutralised the threat memorialised in their shields with gold

189

and silver inlay. Monuments to his military prowess and abundant wealth, they proclaimed his eminent suitability as a defender and benefactor of the Greek world.

The prominence of the victory monument at the festival indicates that martial prowess was integral, rather than irrelevant or counter, to Ptolemaic τρυφή or opulent display. To historians from the Roman supremacy or to those in the present day, Ptolemaic τρυφή both reflected and contributed to the 'softening and feminizing' of the dynasty.[56] This interpretation may rest less on the character of Philadelphos' royal ideology or royal program and more on later dynasts' dearth of the sort of martial successes that could have validated dynastic τρυφή. Major victories authorised Roman triumphs and validated accompanying spectacle, even if their extravagance sometimes elicited concern from contemporaries and, later, condemnation, for contributing to the moral decline of the Republic.[57] The orchestration of lavish spectacle was even set on par with the virtues of capable military command.[58] While Philadelphos' victory over the Galatians may have been manufactured, it was nevertheless one of the primary points of reference from which Greek attenders in the late 270s would have evaluated the king's Grand Procession, his character, and the program of his monarchy.

This suggests conceptualizing the expression of Ptolemaic royal ideology as a combination of transcendental omnipotence and negotiated partnership. Hellenistic royal ideology trumpeted the permanent transcendence of the king and cast festivals and processions as rituals of gracious euergetism. However, Ptolemy's emulation of existing models for celebrating victories over Galatians reveals the monarch's intent to recruit foreign capital, manpower, and goodwill. Philadelphos could be seen, then, not as presiding over the Ptolemaic Golden Age, but forging it. The Ptolemaia festivals, the Grand Procession, and the Royal Pavilion were both venues for 'expressing monarchic power' and for constructing it.[59] The witnesses to the Procession and to the shields were also, in this sense, more than spectators of elaborate spectacle. Ptolemy II's ability to project power in the Greek world correlates with the extent to which these attenders legitimised Ptolemaic τρυφή as benefaction and accepted Ptolemy's attempt to insinuate himself into the narrative of Greek salvation from the Galatian menace.

Notes

[1] Diod. 33.28; Plut. *Mor.* 200f–201b; Plb. 5.34.10, 39.7.7, with discussion at Heinen 1983, 116–28; Eckstein 1995, 74–6; Ager 2005, 22–7.

[2] App. *Praef.* 10.

[3] On Ptolemaic royal ideology, τρυφή as Ptolemaic virtue, and the role of expenditure in Ptolemaic authority, see Heinen 1983; Koenen 1983, 143–90;

Mooren 1983, 205–40; Samuel 1993, 168–210; Hazzard 2000; Thompson 1997, 242–57; Murray 2008, 9–25.

[4] Tarn provided the baseline (1913, 216–7) for the modern narrative of an 'Oriental' despot 'opposed to war', his weak morals further exhibited by his devotion 'to pleasure in all its forms'.

[5] Austin 1986, 450–66; Samuel 1989, 72–3; Préaux 1978, 183; Chaniotis 2005, 55–77.

[6] Not that a martial upbringing assured a smooth succession. Parts of the Syrian Seleukis rebelled against Antiochos I after his father's death (*OGIS* 219), and Antigonos II Gonatas needed victories over both Galatians (in 277 or 276) and Pyrrhus (in 272) to truly secure Macedonia.

[7] On the importance of filial piety (a major component of the virtue *eusebeia*) in Hellenistic kingship, and its expression in the Ptolemaia, see Dunand 1981, 22–4.

[8] From *SIG* I³ 390.

[9] *Theōroi* are known from Athens (*IG* I³ 390), the Nesiotic League (*SIG* I³ 390), Samos (*SEG* 1.366), the Delphic Amphictyony (*CID* 4.40), and Xanthos (*SEG* 36.1218), but likely hailed from most Aegean states.

[10] Athenaios (10.7.415a–b) relates an anecdote that at the first of the Grand Processions a female trumpeter of unmatched appetites, the subject of an epigram of Poseidippos, played the processional.

[11] Kallixeinos, *FGrH* 627 F 2.

[12] He certainly wrote during or after the reign of Ptolemy IV, whose pleasure barge he described, but Kallixeinos has been tentatively associated with the possessor of a large *dōrea* in the Arsinoite nome attested in 156 or 145 (*SB* 20.15150), and the father of a priestess in the royal court in 160/59 (*BGU* 14.2390).

[13] Kallixeinos (=Ath. 5.27.197d) referred interested readers to the more complete accounts available in τὰς τῶν πεντετηρίδων γραφάς.

[14] *IG* XII 7, 506, a decree of the Nesiotic League recognizing the establishment of the Ptolemaia, and *SEG* 28.60, honors decreed by the Athenians for Kallias of Sphettos, secure a date in 279/8 (Shear 1978). The description of the Royal Pavilion specifies that the season was mid-winter (Athen. 5.26.196d).

[15] Tarn actually suggested the Ptolemaia for 275/4 in *Antigonus Gonatas*, and was followed by Bevan (1923, 127–8) but later argued for the first Ptolemaia (1928, 703 and 1933, 59–60).

[16] As, for example, in Coarelli 1990, 225–51; Walbank 1996, 119–30; Thompson 2000, 381–8; Manning 2003, 138; Marquaille 2008, 49–56; Salmenkivi 2008, 189; Weimer 2009, 119–22; and Strootman 2014, 77, among others.

[17] Fraser 1972, 1.228–32; Rice 1983, 135–50, 182–7. The absence of evidence for Arsinoe II figures prominently in Rice's attempt to triangulate dates.

[18] Walbank's 1984, 52–4 and *op. cit.*, Thompson *op. cit.*

[19] Some prefer to leave the question open as to which of the first two or three Ptolemaiai saw the Grand Procession described in Kallixeinos, e.g. Buraselis 2008, 300; Huss 2001, 323 (although with some preference for 275/4 on p. 292); Müller 2009, 179–81.

[20] They were married no later than about November 274. The Pithom stele, line 15, refers to the royal couple traveling together in Thoth of year 12.

Ptolemy II's regnal years counted from his co-rule with Ptolemy I, which began in 285.

[21] Foertmeyer 1988, 90–104. The argument, that the association of the first and last phases of the multiple-day parade with the Morning Star and Evening Star indicates the appearance of Venus in the morning and night sky at the time of the multi-day Procession, is discussed and rejected in Hazzard and Fitzgerald 1991, 6–23 and Walbank 1996, 121–2.

[22] Imminent war: Stewart 1993, 252–62, with Hölbl 2001, 39 for the Procession as both celebrating victories in Nubia and over Magas as well as anticipating the First Syrian War, and Lehmann 1988, 146–7; Török 2011, 106; Burstein 2008, 139–45 suggests comfort with a date c. 275/4 or 271/0, see esp. 140, n. 28: 'Aithiopians and Aithiopian goods in the procession...are difficult to reconcile with a date prior to Ptolemy II's Nubian campaign.' Hölbl 2001, 55 dates the Nubia campaign to approximately 275, and it is at least likely to have come before Theokritos' *Idyll* 17 (line 85 refers to command of parts of Nubia), cf. Agatharchides, *FGrH* 86 F19 ll. 202–8.

[23] Otto 1931, 414; Will 1979, 1.150; Dunand 1981, 13–40; Heinen in *CAH* VII² 1.417.

[24] Hazzard 2000, 28–32, 60–6. The argument leans heavily on reading in the processional symbolism the proclamation of a new dynastic era, the Soter era, based on the presence of a figure Ἐνιαυτός, but that figure need not symbolise anything more specific than penteteric eras.

[25] Hazzard 2000, 30–1 takes this reference to mean Ptolemy the Son before his rebellion. 'Kings' could also refer to Ptolemy II and his deceased father.

[26] Approximately 50–75 feet tall under the central canopy, and rectangular in shape, the pavilion's long walls could fit one hundred couches each (197a), and so were perhaps three hundred feet long or more, while the short wall (the facing short side was left open as the entryway) was approximately one-third shorter (196f), so still perhaps two hundred feet.

[27] For it, see Strootman 2014, 77; Müller 2009, 181–9; and especially Calandra 2011; Studniczka 1914. The garden location is based on the myrtles and laurels surrounding the pavilion (196d).

[28] Strootman 2014, 77.

[29] Finley 1956, 132. See also Pritchett 1974, 249–73 for a collection of examples.

[30] Pyrrhos of Epeiros, Hieron of Syracuse, and Philip V of Macedon dedicated spoils at Lindos (*I.Lindos* 2.2.C.114–31), while πέλτας and ἀσπίδας, either ἐπιχάλκους or Μακεδονικάς, appear frequently as spoils at Athens, e.g. *IG* II² 1487, and Attalos made dedications of spoils at Pergamon (*OGIS* 285). The Romans followed suit, as Paulus displayed Macedonian bronze shields (*clupeis aereis*) in his games at Amphipolis before taking them to Rome (Liv. 45.33.1), and Mummius displayed shields at Olympia (Paus. 5.10.2).

[31] For a proximate example, the ἀσπίς, covered in gold or several times life-size, appeared in the Grand Procession among the weapons of the gods (Kallixeinos, *FGrH* 627 F2 ll. 373–4).

[32] E.g. Paus. 10.20.8, which refers to 'the shields, their customary *thyreoi*' (τὰ ὅπλα, τοὺς ἐπιχωρίους θυρεούς), or Polyb. 2.30.3 on 'the Gallic shield' (τοῦ Γαλατικοῦ θυρεοῦ).

They were eventually used by some soldiers in many Greek armies, beginning about the middle of the third century, as among the Boeotian League (*IG* VII 985 and 2716). Its use among Successor soldiers is not securely attested until the last quarter of the 3rd century, during Molon's rebellion in Mesopotamia (Polyb. 5.53–4).

[33] Its earliest use may lie in a passage of Timaios (*fl.* first quarter of the 3rd century) paraphrased by Diodoros (*FGrH* 366 154.354 = Diod. 5.18.3), but Timaios' date of writing is not firmly established. Timaios may well have written the passage – which concerns Balaeric slingers – from Athens, after the Galatian invasion. The word also appears once among the surviving fragments of Fabius Pictor (*Fragmenta* 4c.4). A passage of Clement (*Strom.* 1.16.75.7) attributed to Skamon of Mytilene (4th c.) attributes the first θυρεός to Itanos, a Samnite, but the passage could easily have come from Philostephanos and the mid-3rd c. On the arrival of the θυρεός in the Greek world, see Gunby 2000: 359–62.

[34] Paus. 1.13.2–3 and Plut. *Pyrr.* 26.5 report the inscription at the temple: 'the Molossian, Pyrrhos, made a gift of these shields, which he took from the fierce Galatians, to Athena Itonis' (τοὺς θυρεοὺς ὁ Μολοσσὸς Ἰτωνίδι δῶρον Ἀθάνᾳ Πύρρος ἀπὸ θρασέων ἐκρέμασεν Γαλατᾶν).

[35] Delphi: *BCH* 102, 571–80. Kallimachos: *Delos* 183–4.

[36] Nachtergael 1977 is still the most prominent source on the Galatian invasions, particularly in Greece.

[37] Citation from *FD* III 1, 483 from Delphi, see similar language in *Syll*³ 398, from Kos. Diod. 22.9.5 and Just. 24.8 record a tradition of the physical appearance of Apollo, Artemis, and Athena, while Paus. 10.23.1–2 records a local tradition where five Phokian or Delphian heroes appeared to defend the shrine.

[38] *FD* III 1.815, lines 5–6: τιθέναι τὸν ἀγῶνα τῶν Σωτηρίων. *Syll*³ 398, from Kos, records that the shrine ἐπικεκοσμῆσθαι τοῖς ὑπὸ τῶν ἐπιστρατευσάντων ὅπλοις, was decorated with the weapons of the barbarians. *IG* II² 680, from Athens, c. 275/4, incorporates Athens' contribution to the defense of Greece into the Aitolian = dominated narrative and Aitolian-dominated Soteria, praises the Aitolians for their εὐσέβειαν. See Champion 1995, 315–28 and Scholten 2000, 1–28 on Aitolian propaganda, and Koehn 2007, 75–135 for the prominence of the Galatian foe in the military and political projects of second-tier Hellenistic states like the Aitolians and Attalids.

[39] The importance of early victories, particularly those gained against the Galatians, was studied, with reference mainly to the Aitolians and Antigonos Gonatas, in Nachtergael 1977. See Barbantani 2011, 178–200 and Müller 2009, 355: 'ein Galatersieg fur das militarische Prestige eines hellenistischen Herrschers viel zahlte,' related to Ptolemy in particular, but also Will 1979, 1.105–9; Hammond and Walbank 1988, 252–9; Strobel 1994, 67–96; Strootman 2005, 101–41; and Boteva 2010, 33–50 for the importance to the second (or third in the case of Gonatas) generation of Hellenistic kings to establish legitimacy of their own.

[40] Justin 25.1. He then hired many of them into his own army, according to Polyaen. 4.6.17. The bronze coinage of Antigonos showed helmeted Athena on the obverse, and on the reverse, Pan raising a trophy with Galatian gear.

[41] *IG* II² 677. See also Diog.Laert. 2.141–2 for a tradition of a similar proclamation at Eretria.

[42] App. *Syr.* 65, Lucian, *Zeuxis* 9. He was, of course, already king, but the victory over the Galatians was his first major success as king, and the body of Macedonians may well have included men who had participated in the rebellion in the Seleukis after his father's death.

[43] Steph. Byz. 1.33.5–10. The passage quotes from Apollonios' lost *Histories of Karia* (*FGrH* 740 F 14), describing a Galatian attack in Lycia and plunder of several Ptolemaic naval vessels. At least one Ptolemaic possession in Asia Minor, Erythrai in Ionia, also encountered the Galatians. *Syll.²* 210 (279/8) confirms it was Ptolemaic at the time of the attack. The text may even contain references to Ptolemaic forces (line 18: –μαϊκοῖς), and the mercenary troops (line 18–19: [μισθο]φόροις) may also have been from a Ptolemaic garrison.

[44] Narratives can be found in Kallimachos, *Hymn to Delos* lines 175–87 (Kallimachos *Hymns* 4), *Scholia in Callimachum* 4.175–87 ('Antigonos, a Friend of Ptolemy Philadelphos, recruited them for him as mercenaries': Ἀντίγονός τις φίλος τοῦ Φιλαδέλφου Πτολεμαίου προξενεῖ αὐτοὺς αὐτῷ ὥστε ἐπὶ μισθῷ στρατεύεσθαι), and Pausanias 1.7.2, where the number of Galatians is given as 4,000. For the *Hymn to Delos* (Kallimachos *Hymns* 4), see Barbantani 2011, 193–8. A fragmentary encomium, *SH* 958, seems to concern the Galatian Invasions, and likely the Galatian mutiny in Egypt in particular, for which see Barbantani 2001, 116–79.

[45] By fire, or flood, or ritual suicide, depending on the source.

[46] *contra* Barbantani 2011, 198, who proffers that the shields at the Pavilion 'probably do evoke the Celtic shields'.

[47] Paus. 10.19.4: ὅπλα δὲ ἐπὶ τῶν ἐπιστυλίων χρυσᾶ.

[48] *SEG* 34 778.122: θυρεὸν ὑπάργυρον Ἀντιόχου. And if there, surely at other locations, all related to his victory in the Battle of the Elephants.

[49] Instead, the badge has frequently been taken for a reference to the tradition that Lagos was discovered as a babe upon a shield (*Suda* L'25 Λάγος), but this interpretation only further highlights the inattention to martial details on the part of Classicists; the *Suda* relates that Lagos was discovered upon a bronze round shield (ἐπ' ἀσπίδος χαλκῆς), that is, the national shield of the Macedonians under Philip II. Yet this mistake appears in Svoronos 1904–8, 79–85, nos. 558–602; Barbantani 2011, 198; Müller 2009, 355.

[50] *Scholia in Callimachum,* 4.187.

[51] Poseidippos, *Lithika* 19–20, line 6.

[52] Euclid, *Phaenomena* Pref. 58.

[53] *P.Lond.* 7.2057.2–6: τοὺς πέντε θυρεοὺς πεφιλοτιμημένους ὑπ ἐ[μο]ῦ ὥστε μηδὲ ἐν τῆι Αἰτωλίαι εἶναι τοιούτους. The sender is Philinos, whose correspondence with Zenon ranged 252–242.

[54] Paus. 1.7.1: οὗτος ὁ Πτολεμαῖος Ἀρσινόης ἀδελφῆς ἀμφοτέρωθεν ἐρασθεὶς ἔγημεν αὐτήν, Μακεδόσιν οὐδαμῶς ποιῶν νομιζόμενα...τότε δὴ οὗτος ὁ Μάγας ἀποστήσας Πτολεμαίου Κυρηναίους ἤλαυνεν ἐπ' Αἴγυπτον ('This Ptolemy, after falling in love with his full sister, Arsinoe, married her, flaunting the customs of the Macedonians...at that very time Magas rebelled against Ptolemy and drove the Cyrenians against Egypt.') On Magas and his short revolt, see Paus. 1.7.1–3 and Polyaen. 2.28. Carney (2013, 73) questions the legitimacy of Pausanias' narrative of Macedonian disgust at the sibling marriage; the only attested critic was the poet Sotades.

[55] The Pithom Stele (CCG 22183) line 15. For the stele, see translation at Mueller 2006, 192–9. The date in November 274 relies on inclusive co-regnal years, which seem to be used throughout the document; if not, the *terminus ante quem* is November 272. See Carney 2013, 70–4 on the marriage; she accepts a date range from 276 to 272, but most likely 275.

[56] Quoted from Ager 2005, 27. On Athenaios' association of luxury and the decline of states, see Gorman and Gorman 2007, 47–54, and on Ptolemy in particular, Athen. *Deip.* 12.536e.

[57] Witness, for example, the debate over Cn. Manlius Vulso's request for a triumph at Livy 38.45–9, and Livy's condemnation of the spectacle of Vulso's triumph at 39.6.7–8. The most direct comparison may be with Aemilius Paulus, who displayed Macedonian bronze shields during his victory games at Amphipolis (Livy 45.33.1), which games Livy said emulated Hellenistic monarch's festivals (45.32.7–11). Paulus then displayed many spoils and made enormous expenditures during his three-day triumph (45.40, Plut. *Aem.* 32–4; Diod. 31.8.9–13). For these displays he received no censure in later authors, due in part to the untimely deaths of his sons, in part to the magnitude of his victory. On the elements of spectacle within Roman triumphs, their relation to Hellenistic processions, and the corrupting influence of Hellenistic luxury items and wealth delivered through triumphs to the Roman people, and even effecting the conduct of the triumph, see Pelikan Pittenger 2008 in particular, with Beard 2009, 147–9, 287–329; Erskine 201, 53–5; McDonnell 2006, 68–90; Sumi 2002, 414–32; Lintott 1972, 626–38 for the triumph as a symbol or *exemplar* for Romans of broader cultural and moral changes related to Roman imperial expansion into the Greek east.

[58] A proverb to such effect was attributed to Aemilius Paulus, and versions of it appear in Polybios (30.14) and Diodoros (31.8.13). The Polybian version goes: ὅτι τῆς αὐτῆς ψυχῆς ἐστιν ἀγῶνάς τε διατίθεσθαι καλῶς καὶ παρασκευὴν καὶ πότον μεγαλομερῆ χειρίσαι δεόντως καὶ παρατάξασθαι τοῖς πολεμίοις στρατηγικῶς ('For the same spirit is revealed in preparing the games well and arranging for magnificent banquets, as in wisely arraying one's forces against the foe').

[59] Quoted from Erskine 2013, 55. The performance of permanence and independent sufficiency in Hellenistic processions was not an expression of reality or even potentiality, but part of the negotiation of authority, legitimacy, submission, and collaboration.

Bibliography

Ager, S.
    2005   'Familiarity Breeds: Incest and the Ptolemaic Dynasty', *JHS* 125, 1–34.
Austin, M. M.
    1986   'Hellenistic Kings, War, and the Economy', *CQ* 36, 450–66.
Barbantani, S.
    2001   *PHATIS NIKEPHOROS. Frammenti di elegia encomiastica nell'età Guerre Galatiche*, Milan.
    2011   'Callimachus on Kings and Kingship', in B. Acosta-Hughes et al. (eds) *Brill's Companion to Callimachus*, Leiden, 178–200.

Beard, M.
2009   *The Roman Triumph*, Cambridge, MA.
Boteva, D.
2010   'The Ancient Historians on the Celtic Kingdom in South-Eastern Thrace', in L. Vagalinski (ed.) *In Search of Celtic Tylis in Thrace (IIIC BC)*, Sofia, 33–50.
Buraselis, K.
2008   'The Problem of the Ptolemaic Sibling Marriage: a Case of Dynastic Acculturation?', in P. McKechnie and P. Guillaume (eds) *Ptolemy II Philadelphos and his World*, Leiden, 291–302.
Burstein, S.
2008   'Elephants for Ptolemy II: Ptolemaic Policy in Nubia in the Third Century BC', in P. McKechnie and P. Guillaume (eds) *Ptolemy II Philadelphos and his World*, Leiden, 135–48.
Calandra, E.
2011   *The Ephemeral and the Eternal: the Pavilion of Ptolemy Philadelphos in the Court of Alexandria*, Athens.
Carney, E.
2013   *Arsinoe of Egypt and Macedon: A Life*, New York.
Champion, C.
1996   'Polybius, Aetolia, and the Gallic Attack on Delphi (279)', *Historia* 45, 315–28.
Chaniotis, N.
2005   *War in the Hellenistic World: A Social and Cultural History*, Oxford.
Coarelli, F.
1990   'La <pompé> di Filadelfo e il mosaico di Palestrina', *Ktemá* 15, 225–51.
Dunand, F.
1981   'Fête et propagande à Alexandrie sous les Lagides', in F. Dunand (ed.) *La fête pratique et discours*, Paris, 13–40.
Eckstein, A. M.
1995   *Moral Vision in the Histories of Polybius*, Berkeley.
Erskine, A.
2013   'Hellenistic Parades and Roman Triumphs', in A. Spalinger and J. Armstrong (eds) *Rituals of Triumph in the Mediterranean World*, Leiden, 37–55.
Finley, M.
1956   *The World of Odysseus*, London.
Foertmeyer, V.
1988   'The Dating of the Pompé of Ptolemy II Philadelphus', *Historia* 37, 90–104.
Fraser, P. M.
1972   *Ptolemaic Alexandria*, Oxford.
Gorman, R. and Gorman, V.
2007   'The *tryphe* of the Sybarites: A Historiographical Problem in Athenaeus', *JHS* 127, 38–60.

Gunby, J.
2000   'Oval Shield Representations on the Black Sea Littoral', *OJA* 19, 359–65.

Hammond, N. G. L. and Walbank, F. W.
1988   *A History of Macedonia, vol. III: 336–167 BC*, Oxford.

Hauben H.
1989   'Aspects du culte des souverains à l'époque des Lagides', in L. Criscuolo and G. Geraci (ed.) *Egitto e storia antica dall'ellenismo all'età araba*, Bologna, 441–67.

Hazzard, R. A.
2000   *Imagination of a Monarchy: Studies in Ptolemaic Propaganda*, Toronto.

Hazzard, R. A. and Fizgerald, M. P. V.
1991   'The Regulation of the Ptolemeia', *Journal of the Royal Astronomical Society of Canada* 85, 6–23.

Heinen H.
1983   'Die Tryphè des Ptolemaios VIII. Euergetes II', in H. Heinen (ed.) *Althistorische Studien Hermann Bengtson*, Wiesbaden, 116–28.
1984   'The Syrian-Egyptian Wars and the New Kingdoms of Asia Minor', *CAH* VII² 1, 412–45.

Hölbl, G.
2001   *A History of the Ptolemaic Empire*, London.

Huss, W.
2001   *Ägypten in hellenistischer Zeit 332–30 v. Chr.*, Munich.

Koehn, C.
2007   *Krieg – Diplomatie – Ideologie. Zur Aussenpolitik hellenistischer Mittelstaaten*, Stuttgart.

Koenen, L.
1983   'Die Adaptation ägyptischer Königsideologie am Ptolemäerhof', in E. van't Dack *et al.* (eds) *Egypt and the Hellenistic World: Proceedings of the International Colloquium, Leuven, 24–26 May 1982*, Leuven, 143–90.

Lehmann, G.
1988   'Der "Lamische Krieg" und die "Freiheit der Hellenen": Überlegungen zur Hieronymianischen tradition', *ZPE* 73, 121–49.

Lintott, A. W.
1972   'Imperial Expansion and Moral Decline in the Roman Republic', *Historia* 21, 626–38.

Manning, J. G.
2003   *Land and Power in Ptolemaic Egypt*, Cambridge.

Marquaille, C.
2008   'The Foreign Policy of Ptolemy II', in P. McKechnie and P. Guillaume (eds) *Ptolemy II Philadelphos and his World*, Leiden, 39–64.

McDonnell, M.
2006   'Roman Aesthetics and the Spoils of Syracuse', in S. Dillon and K. E. Welch (eds) *Representations of War in Ancient Rome*, Cambridge, 68–90.

Mooren, L.
1983   'The Nature of the Hellenistic Monarchy', in E. van 't Dack *et al.* (eds) *Egypt and the Hellenistic World*, Leuven, 205–40.

Mueller, K.
2006   *Settlements of the Ptolemies. City Foundations and New Settlement in the Hellenistic World*, Leuven.

Müller, S.
2009   *Das Hellenistiche Königspaar in der medialen Repräsentation, Ptolemaios II. und Arsinoe II*, Berlin.

Murray, O.
2008   'Ptolemaic Royal Patronage', in P. McKechnie and P. Guillaume (eds) *Ptolemy II Philadelphos and his World*, Leiden, 9–25.

Nachtergael, G.
1977   *Les Galates en Grèce et les Sôtéria de Delphes,* Brussels.

Otto, W.
1931   'Zu den syrischen Kriegen der Ptolemäer', *Philologus* 86, 407–25.

Pelikan Pittinger, M.
2008   *Contested Triumphs: Politics, Pageantry, and Performance in Livy's Republican Rome*, Berkeley.

Préaux, C.
1978   *Le Monde Hellénistique: La Grèce et l'Orient de la mort d'Alexandre à la conquête romaine de la Grèce, Tome 1*, Paris.

Pritchett, W. K.
1974   *The Greek State at War, Part III*, Berkeley.

Rice, E. E.
1983   *The Grand Procession of Ptolemy Philadelphus*, Oxford.

Salmenkivi, E.
2008   'Herakleopolis Magna under Philadelphus', in P. McKechnie and P. Guillaume (eds) *Ptolemy II Philadelphos and his World*, Leiden, 183–91.

Samuel, A. E.
1993   'The Ptolemies and the Ideology of Kingship', in P. Green (ed.) *Hellenistic History and Culture*, Berkeley, 168–210.

Scholten, J. B.
2000   *The Politics of Plunder: The Aetolians and their Koinon in the Early Hellenistic Era, 279–219 BC*, Berkeley.

Shear, T. L.
1978   *Kallias of Sphettos and the Revolt of Athens in 286 BC*, Princeton.

Stewart, A. F.
1993   *Faces of Power: Alexander's Image and Hellenistic Politics*. Berkeley.

Strobel, K.
1994   'Keltensieg und Galatersieger', in E. Schwertheim (ed.) *Forschungen in Galatien*, Bonn, 67–96.

Strootman, R.
2005   'Kings against Celts: Deliverance from Barbarians as a Theme in Hellenistic Royal Propaganda', in K. Enenkel and I. Pfeiffer (eds) *The Manipulative Mode: Political Propaganda in Antiquity*, Leiden, 101–41.
2014   *Courts and Elites in the Hellenistic Empires: The Near East After the Achaemenids, c. 330 to 30 BCE*, Oxford.

Studniczka, F.

1914   *Das Symposion Ptolemaios II. nach der Beschreibung des Kallixeinos*, Leipzig.

Sumi, G. S.

    2002   'Spectacles and Sulla's public image', *Historia* 51, 414–32.

Tarn, W. W.

    1913   *Antigonos Gonatas*, Oxford.

Thompson, D. J.

    1997   'Infrastructure of Splendor: Census and Taxes in Ptolemaic Egypt', in P. Cartledge *et al.* (eds) *Hellenistic Constructs: Essays in Culture, History, and Historiography*, Berkeley, 242–57.

    2000   'Philadelphus' Procession: Dynastic Power in a Mediterranean Context', in L. Mooren (ed.) *Politics, Administration and Society in the Hellenistic and Roman World: Proceedings of the International Colloquium, Bertinoro 19–24 July 1997*, Leuven, 365–88.

Török, L.

    2011   *Hellenizing Art in Ancient Nubia 300 BC–AD 250 and its Egyptian Models: A Study in 'Acculturation'*, Leiden.

Walbank, F. W.

    1984   review of Rice, *The Grand Procession of Ptolemy Philadelphus*', *Liverpool Classical Monthly* 9, 52–54.

    1996   'Two Hellenistic Processions: A Matter of Self-Definition', *Scripta Classica Israelica* 15, 119–30.

Weimer, H.-U.

    2009   'Bild der Polis oder Bild des Königs? Zur Repräsentationsfunktion städtischer Feste im Hellenismus', in A. Matthaei and M. Zimmerman (eds) *Stadtbilder im Hellenismus*, Heidelberg, 116–31.

Will, É.

    1979   *Histoire politique du monde hellénistique (323–30 avant J.-C.)*, Tome 1, 2nd ed., Nancy.

PART IV

THE MEMORY OF ALEXANDER

10

LEGENDS OF SELEUKOS' DEATH, FROM OMENS TO REVENGE

Daniel Ogden

This paper surveys and offers observations about the series of legendary traditions bearing upon the death of king Seleukos. Some of these traditions are explicitly reflected in the extant sources; others must, with an inevitable degree of conjecture, be reconstructed. These traditions focus on, in the order in which we shall approach them: first, the time and place of Seleukos' murder; secondly, a supposed retirement by Seleukos shortly before his death; thirdly, a pair of omens foretelling his death; and, fourthly, the revenge of Seleukos' ghost upon his murderer.

The murder of Seleukos

So far as we are able to tell, the accounts of Seleukos' death in 281 BC by Memnon of Herakleia (first century AD, recycling the work of the third-century BC Nymphis of Herakleia) and Pausanias for the most part cleave closely to the historical events.[1] As we pick up the narratives, Seleukos, after defeating Lysimachos at Koroupedion and thereby acquiring title to his empire, has spent some months incorporating the Asian sector into his administration, and is now crossing the Hellespont to continue the process with Thrace and Macedon itself:[2]

> Seleukos, fired up by the success of his campaign against Lysimachos, had rushed to cross over [sc. the Hellespont] into Macedonia, with a longing [*pothos*] for the fatherland out of which he marched with Alexander, and to spend the remainder of his life there. For he was by now an old man, and it was his intention to hand Asia over to his son Antiochos. However, since Lysimachos' possessions had fallen to Seleukos, Ptolemy Keraunos was now himself part of his team. He was not treated scornfully as a prisoner of war, but accorded honour and respect as the son of a king. He was puffed

up by the promises that Seleukos had made to restore him to Egypt, his patrimonial empire, whenever his father died. Such was the consideration he had been accorded. But these benefactions failed to make the wicked man any better. He hatched a plot, fell upon his benefactor and killed him. Then he mounted a horse and fled to Lysimacheia, where he donned the diadem and went down to the army accompanied by a magnificent bodyguard. The men of the army, hitherto in service with Seleukos, accepted him by necessity, and proclaimed him king (Memnon *FGrH* 434 F 1.8).[3]

After he had succeeded in these things and shortly afterwards had acquired Lysimachos' empire, he handed over the entirety of his Asian empire to his son Antiochos, whilst he himself made a dash for Macedon. He had an army of Greeks and barbarians. Ptolemy, the brother of Lysandra, had fled to his court from Lysimachos'. He was a man of vigorous audacity, and for that reason called 'Thunderbolt.' When Seleukos' army was approaching Lysimacheia, this man killed Seleukos by ambush, permitting the kings to seize his money for themselves, and made himself king of Macedonia, until becoming the first of the kings we know of to have the audacity to face the Galatians in pitched battle and to be killed by the barbarians. Antigonos [II Gonatas] the son of Demetrios [I Poliorketes] recovered the kingdom (Paus. 1.16.2).[4]

Before we speak of legends, let us first note the tragic beauty of the events themselves. In 316 BC Seleukos had been reduced to owning nothing but the horse upon which he fled from Babylon,[5] but now at the point of his death he could be seen to be on the very verge of reconstructing the entirety of Alexander's empire, with the exception of the two satrapies he had ceded, in seemingly honourable fashion, to Chandragupta.[6] He had just won Lysimachos' empire by the spear and so gained titular control at least of what he must have considered the ultimate prize, above and beyond any homesickness: Macedon itself. Whether he would in fact have had any chance of bringing the Ptolemaic empire under his control one can only guess, but in Ptolemy Keraunos he had in his possession the single most powerful tool for doing so, an heir to the throne of Egypt who could make as legitimate a claim to it as Ptolemy Soter's chosen heir, Philadelphos, and in many eyes no doubt a rather stronger one.[7]

'...for the most part cleave closely to the historical events': but there are some manipulations in Memnon's account at any rate, and notably in his strong implication that Seleukos set foot in Macedon itself. As is revealed by the setting of the action close to Lysimacheia in the accounts of both Memnon himself and Pausanias, and as becomes clear too from Appian's more geographically detailed account of Seleukos' death (quoted below), Seleukos had not yet got anywhere near Macedon itself. He had not yet progressed beyond the eastern extremity of Thrace.[8] The sleight-of-hand is just about permissible because under Lysimachos Macedon and Thrace had been united into a single empire, and it was into the first European lands of this empire that Seleukos was now stepping. Perhaps it seemed a better story to Memnon to have Seleukos die at the very point at which he set foot in his homeland. It is not clear how much weight we should give here to the Babylonian *Seleucus I Chronicle*, which reads:

> The thirtieth year: In the month Sivan... his troops he mustered and marched to the land of...the Greeks... The thirty-first year:...his troops from Sardis he mustered and took across the sea with him to Macedonia, his land... from the troops... They rebelled against him... (*Seleucus I Chronicle*, Grayson 1975 no. 12: obv. 3–5 and rev. 1–2, Grayson trans.).[9]

It is hard to believe that this chronicle is playing a similar game to Memnon in taking Seleukos all the way to Macedon before killing him: from the perspective of Babylon and the Babylonians, Macedon and Thrace probably seemed to be pretty much the same thing. One appreciates Memnon's efforts, but one might nonetheless insist that the historical events themselves make a more exquisitely poignant story, to the effect that Seleukos should have acquired technical possession of Macedon, and should have come as close to it as the adjacent land, but should not have been able actually to set foot in it again. One thinks of Moses being permitted only to glimpse the Promised Land from the summit of Mt. Nebo before his death.[10]

The retirement that never was

Memnon asserts that Seleukos planned to retire to Macedon with the notion of retaining for himself the supposedly light task of ruling it (sc. together with Thrace), whilst leaving the entirety of Asia in the hands of his son Antiochos. This would now represent a very different division of territories with his son to that made after the handover to him of his wife Stratonike in 294–3 BC, when he established the new couple at Seleukeia-on-the-Tigris in Babylonia and set them over the Upper Satrapies.[11] Memnon is not the only source to talk in these terms. Pausanias also speaks of Seleukos entrusting the entirety of his Asian empire to his son Antiochos, whilst he himself made a dash for Macedonia. The notion of Seleukos' retirement also manifests itself, in a much transformed fashion, in Lucian's account of the off-repeated tale of Antiochos and Stratonike. Lucian concludes his telling with the brief details that Seleukos relinquished his wife and his kingdom *tout court* to his son, whilst he himself went off to Babylonia where he founded a city on the *Euphrates* named for himself – i.e., presumably, Seleukeia-on-the-*Tigris* – and died there. Lucian here seems to meld the notion of Seleukos retiring and bequeathing his Asian empire to Antiochos *inter vivos* with the notion of one of the (now two) kings going off to Babylonia and basing himself there.[12] Perhaps too the brief but strange ending that Julian gives to his account of the Antiochos and Stratonike tale derives from a syncopation of the Stratonike-handover with the notion of Seleukos' retirement: he tells that Antiochos refused to accept his father's offer of Stratonike, but did go on to marry her when his father died shortly afterwards (μικρὸν ὕστερον). The 'shortly afterwards' seems to speak of the gap between Seleukos leaving Antiochos in charge of Asia and then meeting his end near Lysimacheia, rather than the historical, decade-long gap between the actual handover of Stratonike and death of the king.[13]

The tradition to which Lucian refers in puzzlingly taking Seleukos off for a retirement and seemingly peaceful death in Seleukeia-on-the-Tigris may find corroboration of sorts in the notoriously unquantifiable work of the sophisticated second-century AD semi-fantasist Ptolemy Chennos. Photios' summary informs us that his miscellany, the *Strange History*, told as follows:[14]

> When Demetrios of Skepsis died, Tellis' book was found beside his head. They say that *The Diving Girls* of Alkman was found beside the head of Tyronichos of Chalkis, the *Abusers of Justice* of Eupolis by the head of Ephialtes, the *Eunidae* of Kratinos by the head of Alexander, king of the Macedonians, and the *Works and Days* of Hesiod by the head of Seleukos Nicator. Kerkidas, the lawmaker of the Arcadians, however, he tells, ordered that the first and second books of the *Iliad* should be buried with him (Ptolemy Chennos, *Strange History* 5, *apud* Photios, *Bibl.* cod. 190, 151a).

We should not, I think, be misled by the final claim quoted here, about Kerkidas, into thinking that Ptolemy is speaking of the circumstances of burial in the prior examples he gives. We are not dealing here with books discovered in coffins when these various luminaries were disinterred (though Alexander's own body was evidently disturbed on a frequent basis), nor are we talking about any mysterious epiphanies of books in the places in which they fell.[15] Rather, as the initial example of Demetrios of Skepsis implies by default, Ptolemy is telling us about books supposedly found on the pillows of great men that died in their beds, as Alexander did,[16] in other words, about the books in which the great men had found some sort of meaningful solace in what they knew to be their final moments (or otherwise the books through which fate chose to give the world a final message about these great men). This accordingly implies that Seleukos too died peacefully in his sleep, rather than by being cut down at some opportune random moment by Ptolemy Keraunos. The same violence is done to history as it is in the case of Ephialtes, who was also assassinated either by persons unknown or by Aristodikos of Tanagra.[17]

Even if all these details are the invention of Ptolemy Chennos (and his *modus operandi* would indicate that they are unlikely to be complete inventions *ex nihilo*), an emphatic typological link is of course forged between Alexander and Seleukos: they both died reading abed. But the significance of the solace they both found in reading their respective last books must elude us. If the significance of Kratinos' comic play *Eunidae* for Alexander is baffling enough, the significance for Seleukos of Hesiod's ancient hexameter farming manual *Works and Days* is hardly less so. Seleukos had not the name of a farmer, for all the new land he must have had brought under cultivation in connection with his many new foundations. Perhaps Ptolemy Chennos' choice of text (if it is indeed his) is arbitrary, or perhaps there lurks here some obscure and (to us) irrecoverable Second Sophistic joke.

Omens of Death

Appian offers the following account of the Seleukos' death and the omens attaching to it:

> **329.** He waged his final war against Lysimachos for Hellespontine Phrygia. He conquered Lysimachos, who fell in battle, and then crossed the Hellespont. He was killed as he went up to Lysimacheia. **330.** The man who killed him was one of his own retinue, the Ptolemy surnamed Keraunos ['Thunderbolt']. This Keraunos was the son of Ptolemy Soter and Eurydike the daughter of Antipater. He had fled Egypt through fear, when Ptolemy formed the notion to give the rule to his youngest son [sc. Philadelphos]. Seleukos had received him as the unfortunate son of a friend. He maintained him and took him round everywhere with him, his own murderer.
>
> **63.331.** And so it was that Seleukos died, after living for seventy-three years, and having ruled for forty-two of them. That same oracular response of his [sc. as the one mentioned at 56.283 seems to me to have been referring to this, the one running, 'Hurry not to Europe; Asia is much better for you.' For Lysimacheia is in Europe, and that was the first time he had crossed to Europe since his expedition with Alexander.[18] **332.** And it is said that once when he was making consultation about his actual death the response was given, 'If you avoid Argos, you will come to your destined year. But if you approach Argos, then you may perish before your time.' **333.** Seleukos searched out all the Argoses and kept well clear of them: Peloponnesian Argos, Amphilochian Argos, Argos in Orestia (whence derive the Macedonian Argeads), and the Argos on the Ionian [i.e. Adriatic] Sea, of which it is said that Diomede founded it in the course of his wanderings, and anywhere else in the world that was called Argos.[19] **334.** But as he was on his way up to Lysimacheia from the Hellespont there hove into view a huge and spectacular altar. This was set up either by the Argonauts as they sailed past en route for Kolchis, or by the Achaians as they made for Troy, and the locals called the altar Argos, either in tribute to the ship (albeit corrupting its name), or in tribute to the homeland of the Atreids. Seleukos was killed as he was still being told all this, Ptolemy falling upon him from behind. **335.** Philetairos, the dynast of Pergamon, secured

his body from Keraunos at the cost of a great deal of money, burned it, and sent the ashes to his son Antiochos. **336.** He laid them to rest in Seleukeia-by-the-sea [i.e. Seleukeia-in-Pieria], established a temple for him and made a sacred precinct around it. The precinct is called the Nicatoreum (App. *Syr.* 62.329–63.336).[20]

The Europe-Asia prophecy broadly corresponds with Memnon's (Nymphis') presentation of Seleukos as longing to return to the land of his birth and again helps to construct a particularly tragic and poignant demise for the king.[21] It is such an effective detail, in fact, that we are moved to ask not whether the prophecy was truly given (surely not), but whether it was indeed the case that Seleukos had not set foot on the continent of Europe since leaving it with Alexander for his Asian campaign. No source tells us that he had done so, but he would have had easy opportunity to do so, had he wished to take it, in the years between 315 and 312 BC when, after his ejection from Babylon, he operated as Ptolemy's admiral in the regions of Cyprus and the Aegean. For his movements during this time we are wholly dependent upon Diodoros, and he does not aspire to give us a complete record of them.[22] We hear of him sailing with his initial hundred ships past Antigonos' camp at Old Tyre, thereby demoralising his troops;[23] laying siege to Erythrai on the coast of Asia Minor;[24] waging war against the allies of Antigonos in Cyprus;[25] and conferring with Cassander's general Aristotle on Lemnos and thence moving on to Cos.[26] Diodoros may imply that he was still in the region when Asander, the ruler of Karia, approached 'Ptolemy and Seleukos' for help against Antigonos,[27] but otherwise we hear nothing of his movements until he was back at Ptolemy's side making preparations for the Battle of Gaza (312 BC).[28] Within this three-year span, it must be conceded, there would have been many opportunities for Seleukos to scoot across to the Greek or Macedonian mainland.

Many of the more obviously fictive elements of the Seleukos tradition serve to bring it into harmony or dialogue with the Alexander tradition, as we have observed with Ptolemy Chennos' notes on deathbed books. A further case in point is the *pothos*, the 'longing', that Memnon ascribes to Seleukos to return home. This nicely corresponds with, but inverts, Alexander's famous *pothos* ever to press on further with his campaign and his journey of discovery.[29] So it is too with Seleukos' death omens, which find a great many counterparts in the Alexander tradition and in the *Alexander Romance* above all. It is the first of the death omens the *Romance* gives for Alexander that is of the greatest interest here. In this a bird lays an egg on Philip's lap, only for it to roll off onto the floor and break open, whereupon a tiny serpent (*drakontion*) emerges, circles around the egg and dies as it tries to return within. This foretells Alexander's encirclement of the world but also his death 'before he lays his head down in the fatherland that gave him birth.'[30] This has a marked affinity with Seleukos' Europe-Asia omen. Both omens combine a prediction of great conquests with one of death before a return to Macedon. Indeed it is noteworthy that in dying in the act of returning home the serpent describes the historical fate of Seleukos rather better than it does that of Alexander himself.

The Argos oracle conforms to a much more broadly attested variety of death-omen, albeit not one attested in the *Alexander Romance*, in which the subject accidentally finds himself in a place bearing the name he has been warned to avoid.[31] Indeed earlier in this same work Appian tells the story of Hannibal, who was poisoned in Bithynia by Prousias on the orders of Flamininus. Hannibal had believed he was safe, because he was destined to die only in Libya, for an oracle had told him that 'A Libyssan clod shall conceal the body of Hannibal'. He had not realised that there was a Libyssa in Bithynia too, namely the country adjacent to its river Libyssos.[32] Many other such stories were told from Herodotos onwards,[33] and Argos itself featured in an oracle-story with a broadly similar twist: Delphi promised the Spartan king Kleomenes I that he would take Argos; he realised he was destined never to take the city upon discovering that Argos was also the name of a grove of trees he had burned down.[34]

Appian's explanations as to why the altar should be named 'Argos' admittedly seem contrived and unsatisfactory. One can accordingly sympathise with Mehl when he guesses that the oracle was originally contrived to refer to the Macedonian Orestian Argos named here by Appian, and therefore to function, like the Europe-Asia oracle, as a *post factum* warning to Seleukos not to return home. But the difficulties with this hypothesis are surely insuperable: Orestian Argos was not Seleukos' home town,[35] and Seleukos did not die there. It is surely too much of a strain for us to read (Orestian) 'Argos' first as a metonymy for Macedon as a whole, and then as metonymy for the entirety of Lysimachos' Macedonian-Thracian empire.[36]

Seleukos' revenge

We are comforted to know that Seleukos had his revenge, his ghost harassing Ptolemy Keraunos in a striking vignette, or more probably a pair of them. In a passage that may or may not be corrupt, Plutarch tells:

> The friends of Ptolemy Keraunos would see that he was being called before a court by Seleukos, the jurors consisting of vultures and wolves, and that he was distributing large quantities of meat to his enemies (Plut. *The Late Vengeance of the Gods, Mor.* 555b–c).

Comparison of the first part of Plutarch's sentence here with a note in Proklos makes the meaning clearer:

> Ptolemy Keraunos called out to his friends, who thought he was being called
> before a court by Seleukos in his dreams, and that vultures and wolves were
> sitting there as jurors (Proklos, *De decem dubitationibus circa providentiam* 57.30–3
> Boese).

It is not absolutely necessary, however, to assume that text has dropped out
from or has been corrupted in Plutarch's corrresponding phrases.[37] The
context of Plutarch's report in *The Late Vengeance* makes it clear enough
what is going on: it falls between the example (uniquely found here) of the
tyrant Hipparchos dreaming shortly before his death that Aphrodite was
throwing a bowl of blood into his face and the example (found more
widely) of the ghost of Kleonike, who had been killed by the regent
Pausanias, hounding him and driving him back to Sparta, where his own
death awaited him.[38]

Of greater difficulty is the second part of Plutarch's sentence. As it
stands Ptolemy sees himself distributing meat to his enemies, but Reiske
suggested an emendation to have Plutarch mean rather that the vulture-
and wolf-jurors were distributing the meat.[39] This produces an over-
complex metaphor. It seems preferable to understand that Plutarch is
reporting two distinct dreams or visions that each separately prophesy
Ptolemy's death with different metaphors that nonetheless share a central
conceit. In the second vision Ptolemy sees himself distributing meat that
is evidently representative of his own flesh (and perhaps too that of his
army) to his enemies, whereas in the first vision the vulture- and the wolf-
jurors themselves represent Ptolemy's enemies, who will tear his flesh apart
between them.[40]

Plutarch goes no further, but we must infer again from the immediate
context in which Plutarch cites this tale, and indeed from the subject of
The Late Vengeance as a whole, that the dreams immediately preceded
Ptolemy's death at the hands of the Galatian army and referred specifically
to that. And indeed the imagery of his flesh being torn apart precisely
anticipates both the Galatians' massacre of his army and, more specifically,
their dismemberment of his own body, which Justin compatibly represents
as the consequence of divine vengeance:

> Nor did Ptolemy's crimes go unavenged, for shortly afterwards the immortal
> gods punished all his forsworn oaths and his bloody murders of his kin. He
> was stripped of his kingdom by the Gauls, and gave up his life to the blade,
> as he deserved...[41] A few days later battle [sc. with the Galatians under
> Belgius] was joined, [6] and the Macedonians were conquered and cut down.
> Ptolemy was captured after receiving many wounds. His head was chopped
> off, fixed onto a spear and carried round the whole of the battlefield[42] to
> instil terror into the enemy (Just. 24.3.10 and 24.5.5–6).

And Pausanias, returning to the subject of Seleukos and Keraunos towards the end of his work:

> This was the Ptolemy that ambushed and killed Seleukos the son of Antiochos, despite having fled to him for refuge as a suppliant, and he had the surname 'Thunderbolt' by reason of his excessive audacity. This same Ptolemy was killed in the battle [sc. against the Galatian Bolgius] and there was an enormous slaughter of Macedonians (Paus. 10.19.7).

The ghost of Seleukos was evidently working in cahoots with the Galatians. Keraunos' deprivation of burial – and from Homer onwards deprivation of burial is most graphically realised in the casting out of a body for 'dogs and birds' to devour[43] – contrasts starkly with the grand *heroon* in which Seleukos was himself to reside, the Nicatoreum at Seleukeia-in-Pieria.[44]

Conclusions

The variety and the colourfulness of these traditions is striking. Taken together, and taken with the many other traditions bearing upon the life and adventures of Seleukos, they reveal that the figure of the king thrived in the imaginations of Greeks and Romans with almost as much vigour as did that of his distinguished predecessor and analogue Alexander. And this was, after all, only the due of the historical individual, who had constructed an empire almost as great, from a much poorer start, and who, with his city foundations and the creation of an initially successful dynasty, did rather more to establish Hellenism across western Asia, across, that is, the 'Greek East.'

Abbreviations

CPG Leutsch and Schneidewin 1839–51
FGrH Jacoby *et al.* 1923–

Notes

[1] For discussions of the circumstances of Seleukos' murder, see Heinen 1972, 50–3, 61–3 (from the perspective of Ptolemy Keraunos); Mehl 1986, 318–22; Grainger 1990, 187–91.

[2] For discussion of Seleukos' strategic motives in crossing the Hellespont, see Mehl 1986, 317–18; Grainger 1990, 188–9.

[3] Cf. Memnon *FGrH* 434 F 1.5, where Memnon notes that after Lysimachos' death (from a spear thrown by one Malakon of his own Herakleia), his kingdom was merged into Seleukos'. Discussion now at Primo 2009, 105–15.

[4] Cf. also Nepos *Reg.* 3.2; Strabo 13.4.1 (C623); Paus. 10.19.7 (quoted below); Eusebius Arm. *Chron.* p.89 Aucher = Porphyry *FGrH* F 60 F 3.8–9; Jerome

(i.e. Eusebius) *Chronicle* p.130.2–4 Helm; *Sibylline Oracles* 5.336–8 Geffcken ('O unfortunate Hellespont, ...an Egyptian king captures Macedonia').

[5] Diod. 19.55–6; App. *Syr.* 53.266–9; Lib. *Or.* 11.80–2 (*Antiochicus*); John Malalas, *Chronicle* 202 = Pausanias of Antioch *FGrH* 854 F 10.7.

[6] *Babylonian Chronicle Fragment of the Seleucid Period* (Grayson 1975 no. 13a); Just. 15.4.12–21; Pliny *NH* 2.167, 6.68, 16.135; Strabo 15.1.10 (C689), 15.2.9–10 (C724–5); Plut. *Mor.* 542d, 823c, *Alex.* 62; App. *Syr.* 55.282; Polyaen. *Strat.* 4.9.3, Ael. *NA* 9.58 = Juba of Mauretania *FGrH* 275 F 49; Ath. 1.18d; Oros. 3.23.46. Discussion: Mehl 1986, 158–93; Grainger 1990, 104–12; Capdetrey 2007, 43–50; Wheatley and Heckel at Yardley *et al.* 2009, 273–97 (with extensive bibliography); Kosmin 2014, 31–58; Wheatley 2014.

[7] See Ogden 1999, 68–73, with sources.

[8] For all that Seleukos was taking possession of Lysimachos' former kingdom, which had included Macedonia, he cannot be said to have 'invaded Macedon', *pace* Shipley 2000, 118 (and cf. 566, 'in Macedonia'), who seems to have been misled by the simplifications of the *Seleucus I Chronicle*.

[9] I have slightly edited Grayson's translation, and I have taken his supplements as read: they are not material to the current argument.

[10] Deuteronomy 34.1–8.

[11] Plut. *Dem.* 38, App. *Syr.* 59–6, etc. For discussion see Mesk 1913; Breebart 1967; Fraser 1969; Landucci Gattinoni 1978; Marasco 1982, 104–14; Mastrocinque 1983, 11–38; Brodersen 1985, 1989, 168–77; Mehl 1986, 230–67; Kuhrt and Sherwin-White 1991; Pinault 1992, 61–77; Lightfoot 2003, 373–84.

[12] Lucian, *De dea Syria* 17–18

[13] Julian *Mis.* 17–18 = 347a–348a.

[14] For Ptolemy Chennos and the nature of his work, see Chatzis 1914; Tomberg 1968; and most recently Hartley 2014.

[15] See Saunders 2006 *passim*.

[16] Arr. *An.* 7.25–7, etc.

[17] Antiphon 5.68; *Ath. Pol.* 25.4.

[18] Goukoswsky 2007, 161 n.796 suggests, after Meinecke, that Seleukos' birth-town of 'Oropos' (Ὀρωπόν) had been corrupted into 'Europe' (Εὐρώπην). But whilst there may have been an intimation of 'Oropos', the oracle works better with 'Europe' in the context in which Appian gives it us here, for it is at the point that Seleukos steps into Europe, not Oropos, that he is killed.

[19] For the various Argoses enumerated by Appian at this point, see Brodersen 1989, 182–4.

[20] The latest contribution (not necessarily the most secure) to the discussion of the baffling *Quellenforschung* for Appian's so-called 'Seleukos excursus' may be found at Primo 2009, 235–49.

[21] Marasco 1982, 125–7 is similarly struck by the romantic and tragic nature of this narrative, and so led to hypothesise that it is derived from one of the 'tragic historians', Duris or Phylarchus.

[22] For discussion see Mehl 1986, 77–82; Grainger 1990, 52–75; Bosworth 2002, 215–17.

[23] Diod. 19.58.5–6.

[24] Diod. 19.60.3–4.

[25] Diod. 19.62.3–6.

[26] Diod. 19.68.3–4.

[27] Diod. 19.75.2.

[28] Diod. 19.80.3.

[29] Cf. Mehl 1986, 316; Kosmin 2014, 80–5 (the latter highly speculative). Alexander's *pothos* features above all in Arrian's writings on him: *An.* 1.3.5, 2.3.1, 3.1.5, 3.3.1, 4.28.2, 5.2.5, 7.1.1, 7.2.2, 7.16.2, *Ind.* 20.1; cf. Ehrenberg 1966.

[30] *AR* 1.11; see also the omens at *AR* 1.33, 3.17, 3.24, 3.30 (cf. *Liber de morte* 90).

[31] Cf. Marasco 1982, 126; Kosmin 2014, 96.

[32] App. *Syr.* 11.44; cf. Plut. *Flam.* 20; Arr. *Byth. FGrH* 156 F 28 = Schol. Tzetzes *Chiliades* 1 line 799.

[33] Hdt. 3.64 (Cambyses at 'Agbatana'); Just. 12.2.3–14 (Alexander I of Epirus at 'Pandosia'); Am Marc. 25.3.9–10 (Julian in 'Phrygia').

[34] Hdt. 6.80; cf. Kosmin 2014, 306 n.10.

[35] Despite the suggestion of Hammond and Griffith 1979, 17 that Seleukos may have been related to the Antiochos of the Orestian royal house referred to by Thucydides 2.80.6; cf. Yardley *et al.* 2009, 267. Seleukos' home town was Europos in Amphaxitis: Arr. *Succ. FGrH* 156 F 1.3; Stephanos of Byzantion *s.v.* Ὀρωπός; *Suda* s.v. Σέλευκος; cf. Heckel 1992, 254.

[36] Mehl 1986, 321.

[37] For suggested restorations, see de Lacey and Einarson 1959 *ad loc.* (p.222 note 1).

[38] For Kleonike see also Plut. *Kim.* 6; Paus. 3.17; and Aristodemos *FGrH* 104 F 1.8; cf. Ogden 2001, 29–32, and 2002.

[39] I.e., substituting διανέμοντα with διανέμοντων.

[40] It is misleading of de Lacey and Einarson 1959 *ad loc.* (p.223 note b) to attempt to elucidate this text with reference either to the proverb-type found repeatedly in the paroemiographers, λαγὼς περὶ κρεῶν, 'A hare [sc. runs] to preserve its meat', applied to those in mortal danger (*CPG* i p.270; cf. also i pp.108, 336–7, ii pp. 37, 121, 496), or to the proverb found in the Coislinian Codex (an important early witness to the Epistles of Paul), λύκος κρέας νέμει, 'a wolf distributes flesh', applied to one that wishes to grab for himself before giving out again (*Proverbia ex codice Coisliniano* 324, at Gaisford 1836, 148).

[41] The immediate context here is not Keraunos' murder of Seleukos but his murders of the children of his half-sister Arsinoe II (Justin 24.2–3).

[42] In rendering *tota acie* in this way I follow Yardley and Develin 1994, though I am not confident that this is what the text contrives to mean, or that it is sound.

[43] Hom. *Il.* 1.5 etc.

[44] App. *Syr.* 62.335–6.

Bibliography

Bosworth, A. B.
    2002   *The Legacy of Alexander: Politics, Warfare and Propaganda under the Successors*, Oxford.

Breebart, A. B.
    1967   'King Seleucus I, Antiochus, and Stratonice', *Mnemosyne* 20, 154–64.

Brodersen, K.
    1985   'Der liebeskranke Königssohn und die seleukidische Herrschaftsauff-assung', *Athenaeum* 63, 459–69.
    1989   *Appians Abriss der Seleukidengeschichte (Syriake 45, 232–70, 369): Text und Kommentar*. Münchener Arbeiten zur alten Geschichte Band 1, Munich.

Capdetrey, L.
    2007   *Le pouvoir séleucide. Territoire, administration, finances d'un royaume hellénistique (312–129 avant J.-C.)*, Rennes.

Chatzis, A.
    1914   *Der Philosoph und Grammatiker Ptolemaios Chennos: Leben, Schriftstellerei und Fragmente*. 1. Teil. *Einleitung und Text*. Studien zur Geschichte und Kultur des Altertums 7.2, Paderborn.

De Lacey, P. H. and Einarson, B. ed. and trans.
    1959   *Plutarch. Moralia*. vii. LCL, Cambridge, Mass.

Ehrenberg, V.
    1966   '*Pothos* in Alexander the Great', in G. T. Griffith (ed.) *Alexander the Great. The Main Problems*, Cambridge, 52–61.

Fraser, P. M.
    1969   'The Career of Erasistratus of Ceos', *Istituto Lombardo-Accademia di Scienze e Lettere, Rendiconti, Classe di Lettere* 103, 518–37.

Gaisford, T.
    1836   *Paroemiographi Graeci*, Oxford.

Goukowsky, P.
    2007   *Appien. Histoire romaine. Tome vi. Livre xi. Le livre syriaque*, Paris.

Grainger, J. D.
    1990   *Seleukos Nikator: Constructing a Hellenistic Kingdom*, London.

Grayson, A. K.
    1975   *Assyrian and Babylonian Chronicles,* Locust Valley, NY.

Hammond, N. G. L. and Griffith, G. T.
    1979   *A History of Macedonia, II: 550–336 BC*, Oxford.

Hartley, B.
    2014   Novel Research: Fiction and Authority in Ptolemy Chennus, diss., Exeter.

Heckel, W.
    1992   *The Marshals of Alexander's Empire*, London.

Heinen, H.
    1972   *Untersuchungen zur hellenistischen Geschichte des 3. Jahrhunderts v. Chr.: zur*

Geschichte der Zeit des Ptolemaios Keraunos und zum Chremonideischen Krieg. Historia Einzelschriften 20, Wiesbaden.

Jacoby, F. *et al.* (eds)
    1923– *Die Fragmente der griechischen Historiker.* Multiple volumes and parts, Berlin and Leiden.

Kosmin, P. J.
    2014 *The Land of the Elephant Kings: Space, Territory and Ideology in the Seleucid Empire,* Cambridge, Mass.

Kuhrt, A., and Sherwin-White, S.
    1991 'Aspects of Seleucid Royal Ideology: the cylinder of Antiochus I from Borsippa', *JHS* 111, 71–86.

Landucci Gattinoni, F.
    1978 'Problemi dinastici e opinion pubblica nel "caso" di Stratonice', in M. Sordi (ed.) *Aspetti dell'opinione pubblica nel mondo antico, Vita e Pensiero,* CISA 5, Milan, 74–84.

Leutsch, E. L. and Schneidewin, F. G.
    1839–51 *Corpus paroemiographorum Graecorum,* 2 vols., Göttingen.

Lightfoot, J. L.
    2003 *Lucian. On the Syrian Goddess,* Oxford.

Marasco, G.
    1982 *Appiano e la storia dei Seleucidi fino all' ascesa al trono di Antioco III,* Florence.

Mastrocinque, A.
    1983 *Manipolazione della storia in età ellenistica: i Seleucidi e Roma,* Rome.

Mehl, A.
    1986 *Seleukos Nikator und sein Reich: Teil 1: Seleukos' Leben und die Entwicklung seiner Machtposition,* Louvain.

Mesk, J.
    1913 'Antiochos und Stratonike', *RhM* 68, 366–94.

Ogden, D.
    1999 *Polygamy, Prostitutes and Death: The Hellenistic Dynasties,* London.
    2001 *Greek and Roman Necromancy,* Princeton.
    2002 'Three evocations of the dead with Pausanias', in S. Hodkinson (ed.) *Beyond the Spartan mirage,* London, 111–33.

Pinault, J. R.
    1992 *Hippocratic Lives and Legends,* Leiden.

Primo, A.
    2009 *La storiografia sui Seleucidi: da Megastene a Eusebio di Cesarea,* Pisa.

Saunders, N. J.
    2006 *Alexander's Tomb,* New York.

Sherwin-White, S. and Kuhrt, A.
    1993 *From Samarkand to Sardis,* London.

Shipley, G.
    2000 *The Greek World after Alexander, 323–30 BC,* London.

Tomberg, K.
    1968 Die *Kaine Historia* des Ptolemaios Chennos, diss., Bonn.

Wheatley, P. V.
    2014   'Seleukos and Chandragupta in Justin XV 4', in H. Hauben and A. Meeus (eds) *The Age of the Successors and the Creation of the Hellenistic Kingdoms (323–76 BC)*, Leuven, 501–16.

Yardley, J.C. and Develin, R. (trans. and ed.)
    1994   *Justin. Epitome of the Philippic History of Pompeius Trogus*, Atlanta.

Yardley, J.C., Wheatley, P. and Heckel, W.
    2009   *Justin. Epitome of the Philippic History of Pompeius Trogus*. ii. *Books 13–15: The Successors to Alexander the Great*, Oxford.

11

THE MEMORY OF ALEXANDER IN PLUTARCH'S *LIVES* OF DEMETRIOS, PYRRHOS AND EUMENES[1]

Sulochana Asirvatham

It has been noted that for Greek writers of the high Roman empire – whose immersion from childhood onwards in the art of declamation formed the basis for their identity as *pepaideumenoi* – [2] 'Greek' history essentially ends with the death of Alexander the Great.[3] As I have argued elsewhere (2008), for a truly Atticist writer like Aelius Aristides Greek history can end with classical Athens, and thus even exclude Alexander,[4] but exceptions to both of these endpoints can be found in Plutarch's Greek *Lives* that are set after Alexander's death in 323 BC. Their subjects include three men who were involved in the Succession: Demetrios Poliorketes ('the Besieger'), Pyrrhos of Epeiros, and Eumenes of Kardia; they also include some later figures: the Spartan kings Agis and Kleomenes, and the Achaean Philopoimen. There is also a *bios* of the Sicyonian Aratos that was written separately from the *Parallel Lives*. By studying these texts together, we can shed additional light on the extent to which Plutarch considers post-classical history to be part of 'Greek' history, beyond the observation that he chose to write relatively few *Lives* that were set in the Hellenistic period.

One very important way in which Plutarch (like other Greek sophists of the empire) is able to incorporate post-classical Greece into 'Greek history' is by emphasising a resurgent panhellenic ideology,[5] which reflects his overall concern with harmony (ὁμόνοια), both within and between states.[6] Plutarch judges Agis and Kleomenes, Philopoimen, and Aratos at least partly in relation to each man's respect for citizen-equality and/or Greek unification against common enemies. Agis and Kleomenes wish to restore the famous Lycurgan system of citizen equality (ἰσότης) in Sparta;[7] Philopoimen is champion of Greek freedom (ἐλευθερία);[8] Aratos is anti-tyrannical[9] and prioritises a collective of states, the Achaean League, over his own state. He also effects the rescue of Acrocorinth from its Macedonian garrison, 'not in the interests of Sikyonians or Achaeans alone, but for the purpose of driving from that stronghold what held all Hellas in a common subjection (κοινήν τινα τῆς Ἑλλάδος ὅλης τυραννίδα) (*Arat.* 16.2)'.

Philopoimen, whom a certain Roman called 'the last of the Greeks, meaning that Greece produced no great man after him, nor worthy of her' (*Phil.* 1.4), finds a rival in his love for Hellas in the Roman Flamininus, who liberated those parts of Greece that were subject to Philip V and the Macedonians with a single proclamation (*Phil.* 15.1).[10] The fact that Plutarch can see Macedon in these last two examples as, in no uncertain words, the enemy of Greece in the *bios* of a Hellenistic Greek raises the question of to what degree Plutarch conceives of Macedonian hegemony – from the rise of Philip II to the defeat of Perseus – as Greek history, for he also tends to idealise Alexander in quasi-panhellenic terms, especially in his two laudatory display-speeches *De Alexandri Fortuna aut Virtute*,[11] in which the king appears as a philosopher-of-action who seeks to unite the world as one ethically and culturally 'Greek' entity, but also in the *Life of Alexander*, which also emphasises his Greek education and philosophical outlook (at least in the earlier part of his life, before his behaviour takes a tragic turn).[12]

I shall argue here that, just as Agis, Kleomenes, Aratos, and Philopoimen are judged in relation to their panhellenism, the protagonists of the *Demetrius*, *Pyrrhus* and *Eumenes* and their allies or rivals are to an important degree judged in relation to this idealised Alexander. These men – a Macedonian, an Epeirote, and a Kardian Greek – are of course all 'Greeks' within the dualistic scheme of the *Parallel Lives*. It is unclear to what degree these men were chosen by Plutarch for their 'ethnic' origins *per se*. Plutarch stresses neither Demetrios' Macedonian origins nor the Antigonid claims to kinship with Alexander,[13] but instead focuses on parallel situations that highlight differences in these men's leadership skills. Pyrrhos' geneaology is, on the other hand, crucial, as it connects him to Alexander genealogically through Neoptolemos and makes him a perfect foil to Alexander's image of a new 'Achilles' in the *Life of Alexander* (a motif that has been well studied by J. Mossman (1992)).[14] His struggles for power in both Epeiros and Macedonia, however, give him the aura of displacement, as was the case for Olympias in the *Alexander*, who went into voluntary exile back to Epeiros after Philip married Kleopatra.[15] Plutarch says that the Greek Eumenes gained the hatred of enemy and ally alike because he, a stranger and alien, used Macedonian power against him.[16] The only overarching 'ethnic' message here, if there is one, is that it is important to keep the Macedonian soldiers loyal, a message that, as I shall argue below, is conveyed to the reader by references to their memory of Alexander's excellent leadership. Beyond that, Demetrios, Pyrrhos and Eumenes are bound together politically as part of a world in which panhellenism – with the exception of Demetrios' brief tenure as head of the Corinthian League – has lost its relevance, in terms of both the unity of city-states and Alexander's

'Hellenic' rule of the world. It is replaced by a sense of statelessness that is caused by the Successors' overenthusiasm for war, blinding personal ambition, and lack of personal loyalty. To this degree, these figures are bound together by a certain (but hardly uniform) level of negative treatment by Plutarch. Notable in this connection is Plutarch's seemingly frequent (if often unspoken) use in these three *Lives* of the anti-Macedonian historian Duris of Samos,[17] as a source to supplement[18] Hieronymos of Kardia who had reason to be well-disposed towards at least Eumenes and Demetrios,[19] and who was also Diodoros' main source for his books on the Diadochs (18–20). We also know that Plutarch read Cornelius Nepos,[20] who is himself considered to have used Hieronymos as a source.[21] Plutarch was presumably influenced by Nepos in some way,[22] but the latter's view of Eumenes (the subject of his only Successor biography) is much more positive than Plutarch's,[23] and Eumenes was evidently esteemed by Alexander himself.[24] Even more interesting perhaps are indications of a change in programme on Plutarch's part from his original intention for the *Lives*, which was to encourage the reader to model his character after the virtues of historical men using history as a 'mirror' (*Aem.* 1.1–4). In an apparent challenge to Plato, who famously worried that witnessing an image of immoral behaviour could have a corrupting influence on the observer,[25] Plutarch proposes at the outset of his *Demet.-Ant.* that men with great natures but bad characters are worth writing about because they provide the reader with examples of moral behaviour to avoid (*Demet.* 1.1–8). Plutarch may have also tacitly applied this principle to Pyrrhos,[26] although he is careful to provide him with a heroic lineage, and Pyrrhos is generally a more positive figure than the *Demetrios*,[27] as his more positive connection to Alexander shows. There are perhaps other motivations involved with *Eumenes*: based on the relative superficiality of the *Eumenes'* treatment of its subject and the pains Plutarch took to create parallels to the figure of Sertorius, A. B. Bosworth has argued that Eumenes was chosen by Plutarch primarily to act as a negative foil to the Roman, about whom he wished to write positively.[28] But it cannot be a coincidence, especially considering Alexander's recurrence in these texts, that none of the Successors (as opposed to the Hellenistic figures from the Greek mainland described above) are men to be emulated. This is especially interesting to consider in the light of Geiger's argument that Plutarch likely composed the five pairs with Hellenistic Greek subjects after he had already found success with his classical heroes.[29]

G. Harrison (1995, 93) has suggested that, just as the *Pericles-Fabius Maximus* anchors the classical lives,[30] the *Alexander-Caesar* anchors the post-classical lives: 'this pair is the centripetal hub from which all of the other later *Lives* radiate and to which parts of the *Moralia* spin in elliptical orbit.'[31] While Harrison is interested in the various forms that *synkrisis* takes amongst these *bioi*, the present article focuses instead on Alexander as a single historical figure – not just any historical figure, but the one most mentioned in the *Moralia* and a very frequent presence in the *Lives*[32] – and the forms his image takes in *bioi* that are set in the years after his death. Only in the *Eumenes* does Alexander appear as a living entity (and there only briefly), but he also has an important role in that *bios* and in the *Demetrius* and *Pyrrhus* as 'historical memory'. I mean memory both figuratively and literally: beyond a number of examples of intertextuality between Plutarch's Alexander-texts and the Successor *Lives* and mentions of various Successors' attitudes towards the deceased Alexander, there are two other, sometimes overlapping, scene-types that are present in all three texts. First are scenes in which a Successor is visited by Alexander in a dream. Beyond the *Demetrius, Pyrrhus* and *Eumenes*, dream-Alexander appears only one other time in a *bios*, to Darius in the *Alexander*, but whereas in the Successor *bioi* Alexander-dreams always convey a direct message to their recipients (even when Plutarch indicates that the dream is invented, as in one instance in the *Eumenes*), in the *Alexander* Darius is forced to interpret a symbolic scene in which Alexander appears, which he does wrongly.[33] The second scene-type is one in which the judgment of a Successor is focalised through the Macedonian soldiery, who measure a potential leader's worth by their recollection of Alexander's leadership. As we shall see, this is all but one case positive. The memory of Philip also emerges in the *Demetrius* when the protagonist is seen to act alongside his father Antigonos Monophthalmos. The bulk of comparisons and contrasts we see, however, deal with Alexander alone, and Philip is generally not given a share of his father's glory in Plutarch (following the pattern found elsewhere in Roman Greek literature).[34] Plutarch often sees Demetrios, Pyrrhos and Eumenes through an abstract philosophical lens, but the strongly ideological presence of Alexander, as well as the Macedonian soldiery, as foils to these men suggest that they are also being judged historically as well. The question Plutarch seems to ask is: how historically significant or insignificant were the Successors, not just as rulers *per se* but as compared to Alexander? The first three sections of this paper draw together evidence of Alexander's presence in the *Lives* of Demetrios and Pyrrhos and Eumenes. The bulk is devoted to the *Demetrius*, since Alexander's appearance there has been somewhat less explored than in the *Pyrrhus; Eumenes* appears last for its relative briefness. A concluding section considers the possible relevance of Plutarch's treatment of Alexander, his Successors, and the Macedonians, to the author's self-presentation as a

'Greek' authority on imperial – that is to say, Roman – rule. Plutarch is, after all, like all his fellow sophists a man of the present as well as the past.

The *Life* of Demetrius

I. A preliminary note on the *Demetrius* and the language of Hellenic virtue

As has been often discussed in relation to Plutarch and other sophists of his era, to idealise a figure is to see him or her as a cultural and ethical Hellene (ethnicity may or may not play a role for particular writers), whose opposite is stated or implied 'barbarism'. These oppositional terms cannot be stabilised as they are subjective categorisations, nor should we expect that someone who is acting as a 'Hellene' in one circumstance will be doing so later. This is especially true of Plutarch's *Lives*, in which, frequently, a statesman of initial promise is shown to experience a tragic 'reversal of fortune'. Nevertheless, Plutarch's oppositional habit allows us to compare the relative moral quality of historical figures. Plutarch makes clear that Demetrios begins life with Hellenic potential – which helps us make a preliminary if not direct comparison with Alexander and others who are endowed with such traits, most obviously Antony, his Roman counterpart in the *Lives*. The *Demetrius* begins with the observation that both Demetrios and Antony are proof of Plato's saying that 'great natures exhibit great vices also, as well as great virtues' (καὶ κακίας μεγάλας, ὥσπερ ἀρετάς, αἱ μεγάλαι φύσεις ἐκφέρουσι: 1.7; the sentiment is repeated for Demetrios specifically in *Demetr.* 20.2).[35] In his early years (ἐν ἀρχῇ), we witness Demetrios' great nature, which is coded in terms Plutarch normally associates with Hellenic virtue: the young man was 'naturally humane and fond of his companions' (καὶ φιλάνθρωπον φύσει καὶ φιλέταιρον: 4.1)[36] and naturally inclined 'towards kindness and justice' (πρὸς ἐπιείκειαν καὶ δικαιοσύνην: 4.4). Later, in 17.1, Plutarch uses φιλανθρωπία alongside εὐγνωμοσύνη, 'kindness of heart', when referring to how Demetrios treated Ptolemy in defeat. Plutarch uses the words φιλάνθρωπος/φιλανθρωπία consistently of Alexander or of his actions. They occur four times in the *Life of Alexander* (21.2, 29.4, 44.3, 71.5), and nine times in *De Alex.* (1.8, 1.11 twice, 2.1, 2.4 twice, 2.6 twice, 2.12); φιλέταιρον is a less common adjective Plutarch uses indirectly about Alexander in *Alex.* 48.1, where we hear that Philotas was second only to Alexander in his love of his friends; and Darius refers to Alexander's treatment of his womenfolk as ἐπιείκεια (*Alex.* 43.2).

II. Barbarian wealth and Greek freedom, *redux*

More telling bases for comparison between Alexander and Demetrios can be found in moments in which Demetrios' actions seem to echo those of

Alexander. Particularly useful in this regard is H. Beck's concept of the 'foil figure' – that is, a personage who appears in a *Life* in which he is not the subject, and who illuminates characteristics of the subject by contrast (2002, esp. 468–469 for the definition of *Folienfiguren*). Beck's foil, however, is by definition negative: to give just one set of examples, Marius, the subject of a 'negative life' whose counterpart is Pyrrhos, acts as negative foil to Sulla in the *Sulla*; in the *Lucullus*, Marius and Sulla are both negative foils to the protagonist (2002, 469–470). Alexander is an interesting case because, in almost all of the passages in which he appears in the *Demetrius, Pyrrhus*, and *Eumenes*, he is a positive figure against which the Successor in question can either be compared or contrasted. In an important sense, then, Alexander's Successors become negative foils – within their very own *bioi* – to Alexander. He is the figure who cannot be surpassed (nor, as we shall see in the dream-passages, escaped) even beyond his death.

Take each man's use of Persian money to gain support from the Greeks. Plutarch tells us in *Demetrius* 8.1 that, after Demetrios and his father Antigonos rescued Halicarnassos from Ptolemy and released Athens from the tyranny of Demetrios of Phaleron (307 BC), Poliorketes used barbarian wealth 'to win glory and honour' from the Greeks:

> The glory won by this noble deed inspired father and son with an admirable eagerness to give freedom to all of Greece (ἐλευθεροῦν τὴν Ἑλλάδα πᾶσαν), which had been reduced to subjection by Kassandros and Ptolemy. No war more noble and just (καλλίω καὶ δικαιότερον) than this was waged by any one of the kings; for the vast wealth they together had amassed by subduing the barbarians (τοὺς βαρβάρους ταπεινοῦντες) they now lavishly spent (ἀνήλισκον) on the Greeks, to win glory and honour (ὑπὲρ εὐδοξίας καὶ τιμῆς). (*Demetr.* 8.1)[37]

This passage resonates with a longer one found in the *Life of Alexander*, whose theme is also that of a Macedonian ruler wishing for honour among the Greeks:

> The battle having had this issue, the empire of the Persians was thought to be utterly dissolved, and Alexander, proclaimed king of Asia, made magnificent sacrifices to the gods and rewarded (ἐδωρεῖτο) his friends with wealth, estates, and provinces. And being desirous of honour among the Greeks (φιλοτιμούμενος δὲ πρὸς τοὺς Ἕλληνας), he wrote them that all their tyrannies were abolished and they now lived under their own laws (ἔγραψε τὰς τυραννίδας πάσας καταλυθῆναι καὶ πολιτεύειν αὐτονόμους); moreover, he wrote the Plataians specifically that he would rebuild their city, because their ancestors had furnished their territory to the Greeks for the struggle on behalf of their freedom (ἰδίᾳ δὲ Πλαταιεῦσι τὴν πόλιν ἀνοικοδομεῖν, ὅτι τὴν χώραν οἱ πατέρες αὐτῶν ἐναγωνίσασθαι τοῖς Ἕλλησιν ὑπὲρ τῆς ἐλευθερίας παρέσχον). He sent also to the people of Kroton in Italy a portion of the spoils (μέρος τῶν λαφύρων), honouring the zeal and valour of their athlete Phaÿllos, who, in the

Median wars, when the rest of the Greeks in Italy refused to help their brother Greeks, fitted out a ship at his own cost and sailed with it to Salamis, that he might have some share in the peril there. So considerate was Alexander toward every form of valour, and such a friend and guardian of noble deeds (οὕτω τις εὐμενὴς ἦν πρὸς ἅπασαν ἀρετὴν καὶ καλῶν ἔργων φύλαξ καὶ οἰκεῖος). (*Alex.* 34.1–2)[38]

It cannot be an accident that the language of 'freeing the Greeks', an entrenched motif in classical thought that carried over into the empire,[39] appears in both *Lives* of Alexander and Demetrios: the latter would soon revive the Corinthian League in memory of and in competition with Alexander (see below). Differences in the use of the cliché in these two passages show Alexander to be the more noble character of the two: since wealth is a traditional Greek signifier of Persian (or, in general, 'barbarian') decadence,[40] an ethical person would be expected to use it carefully and for a worthy cause. Alexander is the model for the proper use of barbarian wealth. Plutarch tells us that when Alexander became King of Asia, he made impressive sacrifices and brought wealth to his friends; his actions towards the Greeks, however, were not primarily focused on money, but on a restoration of their politics. Alexander abolished tyrannies and rebuilt the city of the Plataians precisely as a reward for their role in preserving the panhellenic ideal (they provided the fighting ground on which Greek freedom from the barbarian was won). Plutarch here briefly associates the Greeks with money, but this is only in the context of the panhellenic ideal: the citizens of Kroton in Italy alone received spoils (a portion, μέρος, of them) as an honour to the athlete Phaÿllos, who fitted out his own ship to aid the cause of Greek freedom. Finally, we should note that nowhere in the *Alexander* passage is wealth explicitly connected to Persia or the barbarians, although this is naturally the source; Alexander becomes King of Asia and spends money whose origin should be obvious to the audience but remains unmentioned.

The *Demetrius* passage, by contrast, seems to reflect the mixture of 'great nature' and 'great vices' with which that this *bios* began. Demetrios and his father are waging a war 'more noble and just' (καλλίω καὶ δικαιότερον) than any of the other Diadochs who are presently fighting one another – itself a rather limited compliment – but the connection Plutarch makes between Demetrios, barbarian wealth, and the Greeks is unflattering. Alexander and Demetrios both desire honor from the Greeks, but Demetrios alone uses money to accomplish this: the verb ἀναλίσκειν, which means 'to spend', has metaphorical connotations of waste (in *Aem.* 30.4, Plutarch uses it to refer to 'wasting time with words', in reference to an injurious speech), as well as an extended meaning 'to kill' (e.g. in Thuc. 8.65).[41] The negative association of the Greeks themselves (specifically the Athenians) with money becomes explicit in *Life of Demetrius* 10–12. After Demetrios restores the government of the Athenians, who fourteen years ago had lost their democracy (δημοκρατίαν) – to what was 'nominally an oligarchy but really a monarchy' (λόγῳ μὲν ὀλιγαρχικῆς, ἔργῳ δὲ μοναρχικῆς: *Demetr.* 10.2) under Demetrios of Phaleron – they flatter Demetrios Poliorketes and Antigonos excessively. The corrupting influence of the Athenians, which plays out in a combination of political and religious honours, has made Demetrios 'offensive and oppressive' (ἐπαχθῆ καὶ βαρὺν: *Demetr.* 10.2).[42] We learn that the Athenians, for example, are the first to call Antigonos and Demetrios 'kings', an honour which the Macedonian kings have not themselves asked for, and which had been previously reserved for the descendants of Philip and Alexander (*Demetr.* 10.3). The Athenians are also alone in calling Antigonos and Demetrios Savior-gods; they have the kings' images woven into the sacred robe (τῷ πέπλῳ: *Demetr.* 10.4) of the Panathenaic procession alongside those of the traditional gods;[43] they consecrate an altar on the spot where Demetrios had landed at Athens; and they also create two new tribes called Demetrias and Antigonis, which require an increase in senators. Plutarch devotes *Demetr.* 11–12 to a particularly bad character named Stratokles, who among other things changes the names of the month Mounychion to Demetrion, the last day of the month Demetrias, and the City Dionysia to Demetria (*Demetr.* 12.3).[44] In contrast to an Athenocentric writer like Aelius Aristides, Plutarch does not show unmitigated admiration of Athens throughout his corpus;[45] it is not, therefore, necessarily surprising that he takes the Athenians to task for their behaviour towards the king. In this particular context the author may have been influenced (or his inclinations aided) by Duris, who was apparently bitter towards the Athenians for their treatment of Samos during the Samian Revolt of 441/0 and for their transformation of Samos into a cleruchy from 365/4 until 324 (which probably resulted in the exile of his family).[46] The most important aspect of this story is Demetrios' susceptibility to flattery, considered throughout Greco-Roman antiquity to be a pitfall of power.[47] Plutarch's reference to Alexander and Philip here as the only ones whose descendants deserve the honour of being called 'kings' subtly reminds the reader that Demetrios and Antigonos are not, in fact, Alexander and Philip.

The hitherto implied contrast between Demetrios with Alexander and, to a lesser degree, Philip becomes explicit in *Demetrius* 25.3, when Demetrios is elected to the post of *hēgemōn* of the Corinthian League:

> At the Isthmus of Corinth, where a general assembly was held and throngs of people came together, he was proclaimed commander-in-chief of the

Greeks, as Philip and Alexander had been proclaimed before him; and to these he considered himself in no slight measure superior, lifted up as he was by the good fortune and power which he then enjoyed (τῇ τύχῃ τῇ παρούσῃ καὶ τῇ δυνάμει τῶν πραγμάτων ἐπαιρόμενος). And certainly King Alexander never refused to bestow the royal title upon other kings, nor did he proclaim himself King of Kings, although many kings received their position and title from him; whereas Demetrios used to rail and mock at those who gave the title of King to any one except his father and himself.

An omniscient Plutarch remarks that Demetrios, buoyed by 'fortune and power', felt superior to Philip and Alexander; he also contrasts Alexander's generosity in letting others be called 'king' with Demetrios' wish to limit the title to himself and his father.

The positive appearances of Philip here and in the previous passage are interesting considering Plutarch's marginalisation of him elsewhere (noted above), most conspicuously in his Alexander-texts.[48] The parallel contexts – Athenian honours offered to father-son pairs; the establishment/re-establishment of the Corinthian League – make sense of Philip's presence here alongside his son. But there may be another subtle point to be understood from Plutarch's choice to alternately highlight and suppress the father-son pair analogy. Alexander is continually shown in the *Alexander* in competition with Philip: note, for example, his lament to his friends in *Alex.* 5.4 that his father will anticipate him in every possible achievement, and leave him with nothing to achieve.[49] In the *Demetrius*, Plutarch says that Demetrios was 'exceedingly fond of his father...from genuine affection rather than out of deference to his power' (φιλοπάτωρ διαφερόντως... δι'εὔνοιαν ἀληθινὴν μᾶλλον ἢ θεραπείαν τῆς δυνάμεως: *Demetr.* 3.1); he also calls Antigonos the 'greatest and the oldest of Alexander's Successors' (τὸν μέγιστον τῶν Ἀλεξάνδρου διαδόχων καὶ πρεσβύτατον: *Demetr.* 3.3) and the *synkresis* notes that Demetrios got his power and fame from his father, 'since Antigonos became the strongest of Alexander's Successors, and before Demetrios came of age had attacked and mastered the greater part of Asia.' (*Comp. Demetr. Ant.* 1) Above, in *Demetr.* 25.3, the contrast involved in the conferral of honors on kings is between Alexander, on the one hand, and Demetrios and his father on the other (the fact that the reference to Alexander historically relates to his own rule after Philip's death is part of the point: Demetrios' luck only lasted as long as his father was alive). Perhaps part of Demetrios' failure as a would-be Alexander is that he not only failed to outdo his father, but failed even to wish to outdo him, instead showing a certain overreliance on him. Antigonos is later blamed precisely for leaving the kingdom to his son (*Demetr.* 28.2), in contrast to Philip, who Plutarch suggests in the *Alexander* is at his best when supporting Alexander's ambitions.[50]

III. Alexander-dreaming

Right before the battle of Ipsos in 301, Alexander appears to Demetrios in a dream (*Demetr.* 29.1). This is presented as one of two bad omens (σημεῖα μοχθηρὰ) that quashed the spirits of his men (the second omen: Antigonos takes a bad fall). In the dream, Demetrios rejects Alexander's offer of help towards victory; as a result, dream-Alexander threatens to support Demetrios' enemy Antiochos instead of him:

> Demetrios dreamed that Alexander, in brilliant array of armor, asked him what watchword they were going to give for the battle; and when he replied, 'Zeus and Victory', Alexander said: 'Then I will go away and join your adversaries; they surely will receive me'.

The subject of dreams and dreaming in classical antiquity is of great interest to contemporary scholarship, which has produced a number of recent monographs dedicated to the subject.[51] Dreams are notoriously difficult to categorise, but for our purposes it is sufficient to note that ancient writers and, presumably their audiences, did believe in the prophetic value of at least some dreams.[52] Plutarch records more dreams than any other imperial writer (around fifty), and the narrator of his Plato/Xenophon-inspired *Septem Sapientium Convivium* implies that dreams are 'the oldest kind of divination' (τὸ πρεσβύτατον ἡμῖν μαντεῖον: 159a). While Plutarch does reject the truth-value of some dreams, it is not because he classifies them in general, negatively, as 'superstition'.[53] On the other hand, as F. Brenk has pointed out, Plutarch also had no problem inventing dreams, which provided him with yet another means of characterising his heroes.[54] This is important for our study because we will see parallel dreams in the *Lives* of Demetrios, Pyrrhos and Eumenes that are evidently Plutarchan inventions, but that we are meant to take as true. Inasmuch as these dreams are invented and have Alexander in common, they must be considered relevant to Plutarch's overall sense of the contrast between Alexander's reign and the period that comes after it.

IV. The warrior perspective on a tragic king

The Macedonian soldiery also plays a role in enforcing comparisons and contrasts between Alexander and his Successors. This emerges in a particularly complex way in *Demetr.* 41–42, which deals with Demetrios' regal comportment. After Kassandros' death in 294, Demetrios returns to Macedon and kills Kassandros' son Alexander V in order to take over the Macedonian throne. According to Plutarch, the Macedonians at first openly welcome Demetrios out of hatred of Antipatros, and of Kassandros specifically for the crimes he had committed against the posterity of Alexander (ἃ Κάσσανδρος εἰς Ἀλέξανδρον τεθνηκότα παρηνόμησεν: *Demetr.* 37.2).

But when Pyrrhos comes into the picture as a rival – as always, Plutarch's foil mechanism is in place – the Macedonians' memory of Alexander led them to simultaneously admire Pyrrhos for his personal role on the battlefield, and to scorn Demetrios for enjoying the trappings of kingly luxury.

> For Pyrrhos, who was not so much hated for what he had done as he was admired for making most of his conquests in person, acquired from this battle a great and splendid name among the Macedonians, and many of them were moved to say that in him alone of all the kings could they see an image of the great Alexander's daring; whereas the others, and particularly Demetrios, merely assumed Alexander's majesty and pomp, like actors on a stage (ἐπὶ σκηνῆς). And there was in truth (ὡς ἀληθῶς) much of the theatrical (τραγῳδία μεγάλη) about Demetrios, who not only had an extravagant array of cloakings and head-gear – double-mitred broad-brimmed hats and purple robes shot with gold, but also equipped his feet with gold-embroidered shoes of the richest purple felt. And there was one cloak (ἦν δέ τις χλανὶς) which took a long time to weave for him, a magnificent work, on which was represented the world and the heavenly bodies (εἴκασμα τοῦ κόσμου καὶ τῶν κατ' οὐρανὸν φαινομένων); this was left behind half-finished when the reversal of his fortunes (ἐν τῇ μεταβολῇ τῶν πραγμάτων) came, and no succeeding king of Macedonia ventured to use it, although not a few of them were given to pomp and luxury (*Demetr.* 41.3–5).

The Macedonian perspective only appears briefly, but Plutarch clearly aligns himself with it: he agrees with the soldiers' assessment of Demetrios and 'others' as 'theatrical' ('in truth': ὡς ἀληθῶς), then proceeds to embellish on the motif. This alignment between the Macedonian and Plutarch's authorial perspective is significant because Plutarch characterises the king as 'theatrical' throughout the *Demetrius*. The first instance occurs literally in a theater. In *Demetr.* 34.3, right after Plutarch has told us in a disturbing anecdote about an Athenian father and son who were reduced by hunger to fighting over a mouse that fell from their ceiling (*Demetr.* 34.2), Demetrios enters Athens in triumph, having attacked the city at a moment of vulnerability and starved the Athenians out: 'Such, then, was the plight of the city when Demetrios made his entry and ordered all the people to assemble in the theater. He fenced the stage-buildings around with armed men, and encompassed the stage (τὴν σκηνὴν) itself with his body-guards, while he himself, like the tragic actors (ὥσπερ οἱ τραγῳδοί), came down into view through one of the upper side-entrances.' Note the use of the σκηνὴν here for stage-building; the double-meaning of the word (stage/tent) will later emerge clearly when Demetrios ultimately capitulates to Pyrrhos: 'he went to his tent (ἐπὶ σκήνῃ) and, as if he had been an actor and not a king (ὥσπερ οὐ βασιλεὺς, ἀλλ' ὑποκριτής), put on a dark cloak in place of his stage-cloak, and stole away unnoticed.' (44.6)[55] (The larger context of this passage will be discussed below.) The theatricality continues after his death: Demetrios' funeral ceremonies had something tragic and theatrical' (53.1: ἔσχε...τραγικήν τινα καὶ θεατρικὴν διάθεσιν).[56]

The heavily recurrent motif in this text of Demetrios' theatricality has not, of course, gone unnoticed by scholars. Plutarch's initial inspiration may have come from Duris, whose style elsewhere Plutarch calls 'tragic' (*Per.* 28.1),[57] but the interest in tragedy can also be seen as part of Plutarch's literary arsenal. T. Duff, for example, notes that tragic language is used of both Demetrios and his Roman counterpart Antony, and that by inviting the reader to see these men in tragic terms he is specifically responding to Plato's dismissal of tragedy as morally corrupting.[58] But, as Duff also points out, the tragedy motif is found in many other places in Plutarch's corpus, not least of all in the *Alexander* and in the *Pyrrhus*, on whose epic or tragic elements J. Mossman has written significantly (see below); in the latter, the hero who was Alexander-esque in *Demetr.* 41.3–5 himself becomes a tragic anti-type to Alexander. But there is also a moment in *De Alex.* 1.43 in which Alexander is praised precisely for being non-tragic or theatrical: we are told that he 'rejected the unusual and theatrical varieties of barbarian adornment' (τὰ γὰρ ἔξαλλα καὶ τραγικὰ τοῦ βαρβαρικοῦ κόσμου παραιτησάμενος), and only wore these things when conducting business with non-Macedonians, as a matter of diplomacy: 'As a philosopher what he wore was a matter of indifference, but as sovereign of both nations and benevolent king he strove to acquire the goodwill of the conquered by showing respect for their apparel, so that they might continue constant in loving the Macedonians as rulers, and might not feel hate toward them as enemies.'[59] If we cross-read *Demetr.* 43.3–5 with Plutarch's disclaimer in *De Alex.* that Alexander dressed like a Persian for reasons of foreign diplomacy, Demetrios' court-ceremonial appears as an act of self-aggrandisement without higher purpose.[60]

The cloak is a particularly tantalising image that underlines Demetrios' arrogance in implicit contrast with Alexander. Its original source must be Duris, whom Athenaios cites as his source for a list of rulers who adopted Persian costume (*BNJ* 76 F 14 = Ath. 12.50).[61] The list includes Pausanias of Sparta, Dionysios tyrant of Sicily, and Alexander; it culminates with Demetrios, who 'exceeded them all' (πάντας ὑπερέβαλεν). Duris sandwiches the mention of the military cloaks (χλαμύδες), shiny brown-grey and embroidered with the universe covered in gold stars and with the twelve signs of the zodiac (τὸ δὲ πᾶν [ὁ πόλος] ἐνύφαντο χρυσοῦς ἀστέρας ἔχον καὶ τὰ δώδεκα ζῴδια. μίτρα δὲ χρυσόπαστος ἦν), between references to the purple and gold boots, on the one hand, and to the gold μίτρα and purple fringed καυσία on the other. Plutarch also mentions extravagant robes within his general description of the king's finery, but ends his passage by describing a single magnificent robe that involved considerable labor. This last appears to be Plutarch's addition to Duris' description. The tragic aspect is present: we learn that the robe remained unfinished because of Demetrios' 'reversal of fortune', something that – given the context of Macedonian judgment on kings who are not Alexander – is intricately tied into the question of his (and by extension Alexander's) Macedonian succession: a cloak left incomplete due to a king's downfall is so cursed that even equally pretentious Successors dare not use it.[62]

There may be another more specific intertextual contrast here with *De Alex.* Duris tells us that Demetrios' military robes depicted stars and the zodiac. Angelos Chaniotis (2011, 161–171) makes the case for the historicity of the imagery, and suggests (following P. Thonemann's observations about the timing of Demetrios' entry into the Athenian theater) that it may have been connected with Demetrios' propagandistic self-association with the seasons as 'Master of Time' (2005, 66–82). Support for this is found in the ithyphallic hymn that was dedicated to Demetrios at Athens, which likens Demetrios, with his solemn appearance, to the sun standing in the middle of his friends who are like stars (the source again is Duris via Athenaios: *BNJ* 76 F 13 = Ath. 6.63: σεμνόν τι φαίνεθ᾽, οἱ φίλοι πάντες κύκλῳ, ἐν μέσοισι δ᾽ αὐτός, ὅμοιον ὥσπερ οἱ φίλοι μὲν ἀστέρες, ἥλιος δ᾽ ἐκεῖνος).[63] But Plutarch's cosmic imagery is different: his Demetrian robe has embroidered on it not the sun and the zodiac *per se* but the entire universe. This seems closer to something we see in *De Alex.* 1.6, where we learn that Alexander had desired that everyone, everywhere, consider the entire οἰκουμένη their homeland, his camp their acropolis and garrison, and consider only the good to be 'Greek' and only the wicked to be 'barbarian' (πατρίδα μὲν τὴν οἰκουμένην προσέταξεν ἡγεῖσθαι πάντας, ἀκρόπολιν δὲ καὶ φρουρὰν στρατόπεδον, συγγενεῖς δὲ τοὺς ἀγαθούς, ἀλλοφύλους δὲ τοὺς πονηρούς).[64] In the *Demetrius*, by contrast, we see a man arrogant enough to have commissioned for himself a cloak which represents not only the οἰκουμένη that Alexander had conquered, but the entire κόσμος as well as the οὐρανός, and which significantly lies half-finished after his defeat, serving as a warning to others not to overreach their power.[65]

As noted above, *Demetr.* 41 starts from the perspective of the Macedonians (who prefer Pyrrhos because of his similarity to Alexander) but then shifts to Plutarch's perspective, which is again, at that moment, the same as that of the Macedonians. The Macedonian perspective also appears in *Demetr.* 42, aligned with that of some of the Greek city-states and of Philip. The subject of the passage is Demetrios' lack of accessibility to his subjects, which includes here the Athenians, the Spartans, and the

Macedonians, who were angered and insulted by his treatment of them. The Macedonians in particular are reminded of Philip by contrast: 'This was a great vexation to the Macedonians, who thought themselves insulted, not ruled, and they called to mind, or listened to those who called to mind, how reasonable Philip used to be in such matters, and how accessible.' (*Demetr.* 42.3: καὶ τοῦτο δὴ δεινῶς ἠνίασε τοὺς Μακεδόνας ὑβρίζεσθαι δοκοῦντες, οὐ βασιλεύεσθαι, καὶ Φιλίππου μνημονεύοντας, ἢ τῶν μνημονευόντςν ἀκούοντας, ὡς μέτριος ἦν περὶ ταῦτα καὶ κοινός). The Macedonian perspective is evoked once again during the joint war of Seleukos, Ptolemy and Lysimachos (who also enlisted Pyrrhos) against Demetrios, who Plutarch tells us had the greatest force since Alexander (*Demetr.* 44.1). Here Demetrios becomes aware of the Macedonian perspective, but he underestimates the implicitly Alexander-like qualities of Pyrrhos and thus mistakenly assumes that the soldiers have a preference for Lysimachos. His mistake means, again, that he has to leave the stage as if he were an actor and not a king (see above):

> Demetrios...decided to put as much distance as possible between himself and Lysimachos, and to turn his arms against Pyrrhos; for Lysimachos, as he thought, was a fellow-countryman and congenial to many [of the Macedonians] because of Alexander, while Pyrrhos was a new-comer and a foreigner (ἔπηλυν δὲ καὶ ξένον ἄνδρα), and would not be preferred by them before himself. In these calculations, however, he was greatly deceived. For he drew close and pitched his camp by that of Pyrrhos; but his soldiers had always admired that leader's brilliant exploits in arms, and for a very long time they had been accustomed to think that the man who was strongest in arms was also the most kingly; besides this, they now learned that Pyrrhos treated his prisoners of war with mildness (πρᾴως), and since they were seeking to be rid of Demetrios whether it took them to Pyrrhos or to someone else, they kept deserting him, at first secretly and in small companies. Then the whole camp was in open revolt and disorder, and at last some of the soldiers ventured to go to Demetrios, bidding him to go away and save himself; for the Macedonians, they said, were tired of waging war in support of his luxurious way of living (τῆς ἐκείνου τρυφῆς). Demetrios thought that this was moderate language compared with the harshness of the rest; so he went to his tent, and, as if he had been an actor and not a king, put on a dark cloak in place of his stage-cloak, and stole away unnoticed. Most of the soldiers at once fell to pillaging and tearing down his tent (ἐπὶ σκήνη), and fought with one another for the spoils; but Pyrrhos came up, mastered the camp without a blow, and took possession of it (*Demetr.* 44.4–7).

Alexander here arises as part of Demetrios' memory: Demetrios is aware of the importance of Alexander to the Macedonian soldiery, although he is wrong about the extent of their ethnic loyalty. The Macedonians prefer Pyrrhos to Lysimachos, Plutarch tells us, not only because they always consider the most militarily accomplished man to be the best king, but also because they had heard that Pyrrhos treated his prisoners mildly, which appears in Plutarch as an attribute of Alexander and, as we saw earlier, was once a trait of Demetrios. Once again, Demetrios is characterised as an antitype to Alexander when the Macedonians rebel against his luxurious way of living.

Once Pyrrhos is established as an Alexander-figure, the Macedonian perspective is abandoned in favour of that of Alexander-Pyrrhos, who takes over the camp calmly while the Macedonians revert to a money-hungry mob; a similar contrast was highlighted in *Alex.* 21.11–13 where the Macedonians take to looting Darius' tent while Alexander looks on impassively. Plutarch's treatment of the Macedonians as foils here is typical of the way Plutarch presents soldiers in general,[66] but their use elsewhere as positive foils to the Successors is a testament to the controlling power of Alexander's own positive image as a leader of soldiers, and its importance to the reader's evaluation of both him and his Successors.

The *Life* of Pyrrhus

The epic and tragic aspects of the *Pyrrhus* have been well noted. In a 1988 article, J. Mossman studied the 'chiaroscuro effect' of epic and tragic imagery in Plutarch's *Alexander*; she followed up in 1992 with a study of how the *Pyrrhus* shows a similar 'association of epic, and especially Achillean, characteristics with the positive side of the subject's character, and the tragic patterning and references with his negative aspect'.[67] In his tragic aspects Pyrrhos appears as an inferior doublet of the epic Alexander, whom he had imitated, but he is also glorified by his and Alexander's common ancestral connection to Achilles via Neoptolemos. Plutarch tell us in *Alex.* 2.1 that Alexander is descended from Neoptolemos on Olympias' side; in *Pyrrh.* 1.2–3 we also learn that Pyrrhos is descended from Neoptolemos, who happens to have had the surname Pyrrhos, and who took the land of Epeiros from the Molossians. Mossman (1992, 93) notes that instead of making Andromache's son Neoptolemos' heir as Euripides did in his *Andromache*, Plutarch draws Pyrrhos' ancestry back to Neoptolemos' wife Lanassa, the great-granddaughter of Heracles, who was Alexander's heroic ancestor on his father's side. Beyond these statements of lineage, the invocation of Achilles throughout both the *Alexander* and the *Pyrrhus* is a commentary on each man's character as a leader and a warrior, but only for Pyrrhos is the emulation of Achilles (as well as his emulation of Alexander) connected to πλεονεξία: Plutarch tells us that, like Achilles, Pyrrhos could not stand being idle (*Pyrr.* 13.1). Furthermore, as D. Braund points out, unlike Homer's Achilles Pyrrhos wished for glory above all for himself rather than his people[68] – an indication of the kind of Successor statelessness I referred to in the first section of his chapter.[69] This sense of statelessness is enhanced by the fact that Pyrrhos' story demonstrates the earliest historical confrontation between the Greek world and Rome.[70] (Indeed, of the two parts into which his story naturally falls – the first covering his birth through his rule of Epeiros and Macedonia, Chapters 1–12, and the second covering his conflict with Rome and his death, Chapters 13–34 – the latter is considerably longer). As Braund (1997, 115–116) points out, Pyrrhos' kinship with Alexander inevitably called to mind the old question of whether or not the latter would have defeated the Romans had he met them on the battlefield. The question is answered definitively in the negative by Livy 9.17–19, but Plutarch suggests, at least obliquely, a different answer when he attributes Alexander's conquests to virtue, but Rome's to fortune, respectively, in his speeches *De Alex.* and *De Fortuna Romanorum*. By contrast, Plutarch's answer for Pyrrhos' prospects of defeating the Romans must obviously be 'No'. It is not necessary to review here all of the evidence Mossman and Braund use to argue for Pyrrhos as an Achilles or Alexander figure; the present section aims to supplement their work with some further connections between Pyrrhos and Alexander in the earlier Diadochoi scenes that simultaneously link the *Pyrrhus* to the *Alexander*, and link both to the *Demetrius* and the *Eumenes*.

The connection between Alexander and Pyrrhos becomes explicit at the moment when the Macedonians encounter Pyrrhos for the first time (*Pyrrh.* 7.4–8.1). On their way to attack one another, Demetrios and Pyrrhos fail to meet; Demetrios goes on to plunder Epeiros while Pyrrhos encounters Demetrios' man Pantauchos and kills him, Plutarch implies, as a self-styled new Achilles.[71] We then witness the Macedonians admiring Pyrrhos as someone closer to a true Alexander than to the false ones, who would only imitate the trappings of regality but not Alexander's 'arms and action':

> [The conflict between Demetrios and Pyrrhos] did not fill the Macedonians with wrath and hate towards Pyrrhos for their losses; rather it led those who beheld his exploits and engaged him in the battle to esteem him highly and admire his bravery and talk much about him. For they likened his aspect and his swiftness and all his motions to those of the great Alexander, and thought they saw in him shadows and imitations of that leader's impetuosity and might in conflicts. The other kings, they said, represented Alexander with their purple robes, their body-guards, the inclination of their necks, and their louder tones in conversation; but Pyrrhos, and Pyrrhos alone, in arms and action (τοῖς ὅπλοις καὶ ταῖς χερσὶν) (*Pyrrh.* 8.1).

As was the case in the Demetrios, the Macedonian perspective is reinforced by Plutarch's own verification of the qualities he has described (this time, through Pyrrhos' own writings: 'Of his knowledge and ability in the field of military tactics and leadership one may get proofs from the writings on these subjects which he left' (*Pyrrh.* 8.2)). After the Macedonian troops switch their allegiance from Demetrios to Pyrrhos, they praise Pyrrhos not only as a great warrior, but as a philanthropic king (*Pyrrh.* 11.4):

> After [Demetrios] had pitched his camp over against Pyrrhos, many Beroians [i.e. of Macedonia] came there with loud praises of Pyrrhos; they said he was invincible in arms and a brilliant hero (ὡς ἄμαχον μὲν τοῖς ὅπλοις καὶ λαμπρὸν ἄνδρα), and treated his captives with mildness and humanity (πρᾴως δὲ καὶ φιλανθρώπως).

The combination of military and moral virtues witnessed here is the same as those that were attributed to Demetrios in his *bios* and to Alexander in *De Alex.*, which characterised the latter as a philanthropic 'philosopher-in-arms'.[72]

The Macedonians will eventually abandon Pyrrhos, but first we learn that Alexander has appeared to Pyrrhos in a dream (*Pyrrh.* 11.2–3). While Demetrios had rejected dream-Alexander's offer to help, Pyrrhos tacitly accepts it, to his benefit:

> Pyrrhos dreamed that he was called by Alexander the Great, and that when he answered the call he found the king lying on a couch, and met with kindly speech and friendly treatment from him, and received a promise of his ready aid and help. 'And how, O King,' Pyrrhos ventured to ask, 'when you are sick, can you give me aid and help?' 'My name itself will give it', said the king, and mounting a Nisaean horse he led the way. This vision gave Pyrrhos great assurance.

As with Demetrios' Alexander dream, there is no direct source for Pyrrhos' Alexander-dream: this fact – coupled with its parallel chronological placement to Demetrios' Alexander-dream at the Battle of Issos – makes it obvious that it is Plutarch's invention. As such it serves to align Pyrrhos with Alexander and, with Alexander's support, to distinguish Pyrrhos' leadership qualities from those of Demetrios.

But Plutarch also shows that the Macedonians' memory of Alexander could be used to harm Pyrrhos. After Pyrrhos lost the Macedonians to Lysimachos, the latter 'corrupted (διέφθειρε) the leading Macedonians, upbraiding them for choosing as lord and master a man who was a foreigner (ξένον ἄνδρα), whose ancestors had always been subject to Macedonia, and were thrusting the friends and familiars of Alexander out of the country'. (*Pyrrh.* 12.6) (Here there is an exploitation of the kind of Macedonian fickleness that, as we shall see, is also present in the *Eumenes*.) Even more intriguing is the passage introducing that section:

> For how men to whose rapacity (πλεονεξίας) neither sea nor mountain nor uninhabitable desert sets a limit, men to whose inordinate desires the boundaries which separate Europe and Asia put no stop, can remain content with what they have and do one another no wrong when they are in close touch, it is impossible to say. (*Pyrrh.* 12.3)

Mossman (1992, 97) suggests that Plutarch writes about πλεονεξία here in terms 'that apply rather more accurately to Alexander than to Pyrrhos and Lysimachos' and asks a rhetorical question: 'Is Plutarch reminding us that all this intrigue and ambition is as much a part of Alexander's legacy as the ability to conquer kingdoms with the magic of his name?' I agree that there is a hidden reference to Alexander here, but I am not sure it is meant as a criticism: rather, if we compare this passage to those descriptions found in *De Alex.* of Alexander's aim for world-unification, what emerges is the idea that the Successors are *not* Alexander, not only because they have no philosophical basis for wanting power, but because they presume to make a local event such as the division of Macedonia into a world-scale one.

The *Life* of Eumenes

We turn finally now to the *Eumenes*, which is set in the earliest days of the Succession. As noted above, Plutarch's portrait of Eumenes appears quite negative as compared to those of, say, Diodoros and Cornelius Nepos, whose main source was the laudatory work of Eumenes' countryman Hieronymos of Kardia; Eumenes was likely chosen by Plutarch for the purpose of providing a negative counterpart to his positive Sertorius.[73] The *Eumenes* is also quite superficial and very short and, unusually for a Greek life, comes second and not first in the pair with its Roman counterpart, the *Sertorius*. Even in what is perhaps to be considered a 'throw-away' *Life*, Alexander and Philip (who first brought Eumenes into the fold) have important roles in helping the reader evaluate Eumenes, and connect his *bios* to the *Demetrius* and *Pyrrhus*. The *Eumenes* begins with Philip's perspective on Eumenes as a boy on their first encounter (*Eum.* 1.1). Plutarch rejects the story that is more flattering to Eumenes (he was a poor boy but well-trained intellectually and physically; Philip, on a visit to a *pankration* in Kardia, was so impressed with Eumenes' wrestling that he took him into his following)[74] in favour of the less flattering one (Eumenes advanced because of Philip's guest-friendship with his father).[75] The story of Eumenes' relationship with Alexander before the latter's death is one of conflict (*Eum.* 2.1–5; by *Eum.* 3 Alexander is dead), and establishes the ongoing characterisation in the *bios* of Eumenes as clever and manipulative. We learn that Alexander was suspicious of Eumenes for hoarding money; as a result he orders the Macedonians to set fire to Eumenes' tent, an act which reveals more than a thousand talents of melted gold and silver. (We are told Alexander immediately regrets the action [*Eum.* 2.3], which reflects the commonplace of Alexander's capacity for remorse that is expressed numerous times in the *Alexander*, e.g. at the burning of Persepolis [*Alex.* 38.4] and his murder of Kleitos [*Alex.* 51.6–52.1]). But 'because he was wily and persuasive' (*Eum.* 2.5: πανοῦργος ὢν καὶ πιθανός), Eumenes could also intentionally subvert Alexander's expectations. Aware of Alexander's suspicions of his jealousy towards Hephaestion, when the latter dies (to Alexander's boundless grief, Plutarch tells us in *Alex.* 72.3) Eumenes argues that honors be given the deceased, and he spends lavishly on Hephaistion's tomb (neither Diodoros nor Nepos discusses Eumenes' attitude towards Hephaestion).

Eumenes also goes on to manipulate the Macedonians, whose fickleness emerges here as nowhere else among the *Lives* of the Successors. At first he succeeds: in a dispute between his companions and the Macedonian soldiers that ensues right after Alexander's death (*Eum.* 3.1), Eumenes tacitly agrees with his companions, but appears to hold himself above the fray 'in what he says' (τῷ λόγῳ). This makes him sensible but not quite possessing Alexander's ability to create solidarity between himself and his men (see, e.g., *Alex*: 24.8 where Plutarch tells us that Alexander is 'ever accustomed to cheer the Macedonians in their perplexities by sharing their toils'). But ultimately Eumenes fails to control them. After the battle with Neoptolemos, which results in the death of Krateros – whom, as we shall discuss in more detail below, the Macedonians are seen to admire greatly – the Macedonians are ready to put him to death (*Eum.* 8.2); but when he demonstrates his generosity towards them, they again come over to his side (*Eum.* 8.5–6). Later, Eumenes struggles to prevent them from taking more loot than they can carry (*Eum.* 9.3–4) and has to deal with the envy of the leaders of the Silver Shields (*Eum.* 13.2), who are also guilty of corrupting the rank and file with flattery and lavish expenditure (*Eum.* 13.5).

Again the motif of the Alexander-dream appears. In the *Eumenes* there are in fact two dreams, which Plutarch uses as vehicles to demonstrate another aspect of Eumenes' approach to dealing with the Macedonians that dooms him: his dishonesty. The first Alexander-dream portends Eumenes' victory against Krateros and Neoptolemos; it is a genuine dream, but it has a false purpose, as Eumenes uses it to manipulate the Macedonians into a war with Krateros without disclosing the identity of their opponent (he also cleverly decides to use alternative non-Macedonian troops to meet the enemy at first, lest the Macedonians desert him for Krateros).

He dreamed that he saw two Alexanders ready to give each other battle, each at the head of a phalanx; then Athena came to help the one, and Demeter the other, and after a fierce struggle the one who had Athena for a helper was beaten, and Demeter, culling ears of grain, wove them into a wreath for the victor. At once, Eumenes conjectured that the vision was in his favour... But though he often felt an impulse to speak out and tell his principal officers who it was against whom their struggle was to be...nevertheless he abided by his first resolution. (*Eum.* 6.5–6.7)

The second dream is a lie that Eumenes concocts to gain the allegiance of the Silver Shields (*Eum.* 13.3–4):

[Eumenes] brought superstition to bear. He said, namely, that Alexander had appeared to him in a dream, had shown him a tent arrayed in royal fashion with a throne standing in it, and had then said that if they held their councils and transacted their business there, he himself would be present and would assist them in every plan and enterprise which they undertook in his name... So they erected a royal tent, and a throne in it which they dedicated to Alexander; there they met for deliberation on matters of highest importance.

Interestingly, while Eumenes' Alexander-tent dream is attested elsewhere,[76] the former dream that portends Alexander's victory – like the portent dreams found in both *Demetrius* and *Pyrrhus* – is found only in Plutarch. It is conceivable that Plutarch was inspired by Eumenes' attested Alexander-tent dream to invent these three pre-battle Alexander-portent-dreams. But there is an even better historical possibility: Seleukos' Alexander-portent-dream before the battle of Ipsos – the very same setting in which a dream-Alexander appeared to Demetrios and Pyrrhos. (Seleukos appears in the *Demetrius* but is not given an Alexander-dream.) Seleukos' dream is attested in Diodoros, and couched, incidentally, in language that inevitably calls to mind Alexander's egalitarian attitude towards his men.[77]

When Seleukos saw that [his men] were terror-stricken, he encouraged them, saying that men who had campaigned with Alexander and had been advanced by him because of their prowess ought not to rely solely on armed force and wealth when confronting difficult situations, but upon experience and skill, the means whereby Alexander himself had accomplished his great and universally admired deeds. He added that they ought also to believe the oracles of the gods which had foretold that the end of his campaign would be worthy of his purpose; for, when he had consulted the oracle in Branchidai, the god had greeted him as King Seleukos, and Alexander standing beside him in a dream had given him a clear sign of the future leadership that was destined to fall to him in the course of time. Moreover, he pointed out that everything that is good and admired among men is gained through toil and danger. But he also sought the favor of his fellow soldiers and put himself on equal footing with them all in such a way that each man respected him and willingly accepted the risk of the daring venture (Diod. 19.90.3–5).

R. Hadley has argued that the story originated during the battle of Ipsos and was part of the Seleukid mythology promoted by Hieronymos of Kardia.[78] We can assume that Plutarch knew the Seleukos story from his Hellenistic sources; the logical conclusion, then, is that he simply applied the Seleukos *logos* to the three figures he was more interested in as a means of enforcing comparisons and contrasts between those Successors and Alexander. This is important because it suggests the very loose way in which Plutarch wishes to address *imitatio Alexandri* among the Successors – the focus is both on their general failure to be good leaders, and on their specific failure to match Alexander.

In the end, Plutarch's Eumenes proves himself to be even less of an Alexander-figure than either Demetrios or Pyrrhos, but his biography does contain a true Alexander – one who is at least in one way even better than the original. That is Krateros. Plutarch mentions Krateros' Alexander-qualities on the battlefield after his first clash with Eumenes, saying that 'Krateros did not disgrace Alexander, but slew many foes' (*Eum.* 7.3: οὐ Κρατερὸς τὸν Ἀλεξανδρον, ἀλλὰ πολλοὺς μὲν καταβαλὼν). This is enforced by the Macedonian perspective, which is relayed by Neoptolemos to Krateros and Antipatros when initially seeking their help against Eumenes, and validated by Plutarch (*Eum.* 6.1–2):

> [Neoptolemos urged Krateros and Antipatros] to come to his aid, both of them if possible, but at any rate Krateros; for the Macedonians longed for him exceedingly, and if they should only see his cap and hear his voice, they would come rushing at him, arms and all. And indeed the name of Krateros was really great among them, and after Alexander's death most of them had longed for him as their commander. They remembered that he had many times incurred the strong displeasure of Alexander himself on their behalf, by opposing his gradually increasing desire to adopt Persian customs, and by defending the manners of their country, which, thanks to the spread of luxury and pomp, were already being treated with contempt.

Plutarch here allows Krateros to demonstrate superiority to Alexander in one of the few areas in which Plutarch criticises the latter elsewhere: that is, his (putative)[79] attempt to impose Persian customs on the court. S. Wallace (2017) argues that Plutarch's portrait of Krateros is in fact ahistorical: according to the Ps.-Demetrios of Phaleron treatise *On Style* (289), Krateros did wear eastern dress and comported himself with kingly arrogance, and a fragment from Arrian's *On the Successors of Alexander* (*FGrH* 156 F 177a–b = *Suda* K2335), suggests that the Macedonians (at least after

Alexander's death) admired Krateros because of his splendid apparel, which was almost like Alexander's. It seems then, that Krateros' historical popularity with the soldiers is being used specifically in a way that allows Plutarch to critique Alexander's orientalism. In this respect, his function is much like that the *Alexander*'s Kallisthenes, a Greek historian who is uniquely characterised by Plutarch as a 'philosopher' and, as I have argued elsewhere, becomes a sort of mouthpiece for the dissatisfied Macedonians when Alexander tries to force *proskynēsis* on them.[80] The historical Alexander does not simply exist to be idealised; he also illustrates the potential moral pitfalls of absolute rule, as is amply illustrated by his extended fall in the *Life of Alexander*. Nevertheless, his presence in the Successors as an imperial role model shows that he is still the only imperialist who is capable of being idealised as a true 'Hellene'. Especially given the concomitant lack of parallel Roman role models in his corpus, this has implications for Plutarch's understanding of the true extent of Greek influence over Rome.

Conclusion: Hellenising *Imitatio-Alexandri* in the Empire

On the one hand, the evaluation of Hellenistic kings against Alexander (and sometimes Philip) speaks to 'limits': post-classical Greek history is 'that which can be construed as 'panhellenic'. But the image of a panhellenic Alexander is new to Plutarch's era: it obviously does not belong to the Golden Age of the independent city-states of Demosthenes or even the Philip-loving Isocrates so beloved by Greek imperial sophists, nor is it a feature of extant Hellenistic portraits of Alexander. (By contrast, there is no difficulty for Plutarch in glorifying the attempts of Agis or Kleomenes to recapture the glory days of Lycurgus.) So, at the same time that a panhellenic Alexander can be seen as a limiting 'high-point' in Greek history (the 'greatest individual Greek', as Bowie sweepingly refers to him),[81] his existence also extends the chronological scope of the classical past beyond what is, at least from a purist and Atticist perspective like that of Aelius Aristides, its natural endpoint: the end of Greek freedom under Macedonian hegemony.

But for Plutarch, Alexander is not just an example – when he is at his best – of the best kind of imperial ruler; when we compare him to other imperialists whom Plutarch treats, he is the only one worthy of emulation. What this panhellenic Alexander offers to Plutarch is the opportunity for 'Greek' history to include world-empire, and as would-be Alexanders who ultimately fail, the Successors play a secondary role to Alexander in helping distinguish good from bad imperial rule.[82] This is of course of the greatest relevance to Plutarch's own experience as a self-identified 'Greek' intellectual attempting to navigate the political waters of the Roman empire. As Schepens neatly puts it: 'The mere conception of a corpus of parallel lives, organised into pairs of Greeks and Romans, amounts to a political statement'. While it seems obvious that Plutarch would have had historical *imitatio Alexandri* of Hellenistic kings on his mind as he wove Alexander's image into the *bioi* of Demetrios, Pyrrhos and Eumenes,[83] the fact that he completely ignores the *imitatio* of some of Alexander's most famous Hellenistic imitators (like Ptolemy and Seleukos, or later figures like Philip V) suggests the generalised nature of this critique. Inasmuch as it is general, it logically gets its relevance from present circumstances.[84]

E. Koulakiotis (2006, 150) has suggested that Alexander's importance to imperial Greeks lies in his position at the intersection between Greek cultural Hellenocentrism and the philhellenism and *imitatio Alexandri* of the Roman emperors; it cannot be a coincidence that Plutarch's Hellenised Alexander arises during the reign of Trajan, a philhellene who was a famous imitator of Alexander[85] and also helped foster the kind of literary activity in which Plutarch was engaged.[86] It is important to note, then, that as much as Plutarch treats the Successors' *imitatio Alexandri* rather generally, he says much less about Roman *imitatio*, dealing with it only in the *Pompey*.[87] Even there Plutarch raises the comparison between Alexander and the Republican general only immediately to invalidate it.[88] He questions the similarities in their appearances, and notes how Pompey's apparent enjoyment of the nickname 'Alexander' resulted in mockery. He even complains of those who would 'force the parallel' between their ages and how far each man's fortune had led him by the time of death:

> At the outset, too, he had a countenance which helped him in no small degree to win the favour of the people, and which pleaded for him before he spoke. For even his boyish loveliness had a gentle dignity about it, and in the prime and flower of his youthful beauty there was at once manifest the majesty and kingliness of his nature. His hair was inclined to lift itself slightly from his forehead, and this, with a graceful contour of face about the eyes, produced a resemblance, more talked about than actually apparent, to the portrait statues of King Alexander. Wherefore, since many also applied the name to him in his earlier years, Pompey did not decline it, so that presently some called him Alexander in derision (*Pomp.* 2.1–2).

> His age at this time, as those insist who compare him in all points to Alexander and force the parallel, was less than thirty-four years, though in fact he was nearly forty. How happy would it have been for him if he had ended his life at this point, up to which he enjoyed the good fortune of Alexander! For succeeding time brought him only success that made him odious, and failure that was irreparable (*Pomp.* 46.1).

Pompey's reputation as another Alexander appears here as misguided and superficial – like those of the nameless kings in *Pyrrh.* 8.1 who, as we saw above, 'represented Alexander with their purple robes, their body-guards, the inclination of their necks, and their louder tones in conversation'. But the reputations of at least some of Alexander's Successors could be validated by Alexander after his death through dreams and through his soldiers' memories. By characterising 'good' conquest in Hellenic terms, confining it to Alexander, and allowing some of his better qualities to leak into characterisations of his Successors – but not to any Roman imitators – Plutarch tacitly denies the Romans their own self-aggrandisements as new Alexanders.[89] This has further implications because no Roman imperial figure in Plutarch's corpus has the same combination Alexander can be said to have of Greek education and imperialism – what I have elsewhere referred to as Alexander's *humanitas* in the *De Alex.*[90] – those qualities that could be historically associated with Trajan, whom Plutarch does not mention, or Marcus Aurelius. Caesar and Pompey have the οἰκουμένη,[91] but they do not have Hellenism; Aemilius Paullus has Hellenism, but not the οἰκουμένη.

A final note on the soldiers. Pompey seems to have a very different relationship with his men than the Successors (even Eumenes) do with the Macedonians: in *Pompey* 3.3, the young protagonist, having almost been killed in a murder plot, cries and throws himself on the ground at the mercy of his soldiers, who retreat out of shame. A full study on the role of the Macedonian soldiery in Plutarch and other ancient texts has yet to be accomplished,[92] but inasmuch as Plutarch uses their viewpoint to admire Hellenic qualities in Alexander and Alexander-like qualities in Pyrrhos and Krateros, the Macedonians equip these quasi-Hellenic leaders with the brute military force that they need to appear as idealised precursors to the Roman emperor. The Macedonians are in fact the best tool for subverting the dichotomy between Greek and Roman, because Roman strong-men who imitated Alexander also admired the Macedonians. Nepos in *Eum.* 3.4 had equated the reputations of the Macedonian and Roman militaries (Stem 2012, 151 n. 43); Cassius Dio, whose history of Rome comments on the *imitatio Alexandri* by men ranging from Perseus (whose admiration of Alexander was ignored by Plutarch) to Trajan to Caracalla (Antoninus), is even more vivid. We end here with the Caracalla passage, which demonstrates the emperor's excessive love for Alexander – whom he believes was reincarnated as Augustus – and by extension, the Macedonian phalanx, which he has recreated in obsessive detail (Book 78.7–9). Cassius Dio's final commentary on Caracalla's admiration of Alexander is reminiscent of Plutarch's criticism of Demetrios' *ouranos*-cloak in the *Demetrius* and of the Successors' overweening desire for conquest in the *Pyrrhus*, although Dio's language is considerably stronger:

> Now this great admirer of Alexander, Antoninus, was fond of spending money upon the soldiers, great numbers of whom he kept in attendance upon him, alleging one excuse after another and one war after another; but he made it his business to strip, despoil, and grind down all the rest of mankind (τοὺς δὲ λοιποὺς πάντας ἀνθρώπους), and the senators by no means least (Dio 78.9).

So far from Alexander desiring that all mankind from everywhere (τὰ πανταχόθεν...πάντας) think of the entire οἰκουμένη as their homeland, as he did in Plutarch (*De Alex.* 1.6), Caracalla fixed to destroy all the rest of humanity (τοὺς δὲ λοιποὺς πάντας ἀνθρώπους), using the legacy of Alexander in the worst way a world ruler possibly could.

Notes

[1] This paper has benefited immensely from the excellent set of comments I received on an early draft I posted for feedback on the website Academia.edu in November 2015. I thank all who so generously took the time to read and respond to the paper: Paul Cournarie, Christian Djurslev, Tolga Ersoy, Federico Muccioli, Jonas Scherr, Yannis Stoyas, Kathleen Toohey, Shane Wallace, and Alexei Zadorojnyi. Any infelicities or errors remaining are, needless to say, my own.

[2] See e.g. Swain 1996, 91–6. T. Habinek (2005, 61) is concise and eloquent on the transformative effect of rhetorical training (in both the Greek and Roman context) on the student's mind, as well as in terms of his acculturation, often from a non-Greco-Roman culture, into a shared elite culture.

[3] Bowie 1974, 171.

[4] Asirvatham 2008.

[5] This is not a Plutarchan anachronism; this language was used throughout the Hellenistic period by both Greeks and Romans (see Dmitriev 2011). But whereas its employment appears in Diodoros and Polybios as 'reportage' (Asirvatham 2008, 104–5), in Plutarch the line between the author's panhellenic sentiment and that of his protagonists is often blurred.

[6] Duff 1999, 89–90.

[7] *Agis* 5.1, 9.3; *Cleom.* 18.2.

[8] *Phil.* 11.2; in *Comp. Phil./Flam.* 3.3 he is described as most generous in his love of freedom.

[9] 'A vehement and glowing hatred of tyrants' (τὸ σφοδρὸν καὶ διάπυρον μῖσος ἐπὶ τοὺς τυράννους) grew within him (*Arat.* 3.1); he is described as πικρῶς μισοτύραννος in *Arat.* 10.1.

[10] The proclamation was made at the Isthmian games: *Flam.* 10. Muccioli (2012, 225–6) notes the absence of *bioi* of Philip V and Perseus in Plutarch's programme (but instead, a *Flamininus*, *Aemilius Paullus*, and a lost *Scipio*, perhaps Africanus), despite the fact that Polybius had written about them, and Plutarch was also aware

of a seemingly positive source on Perseus called Poseidonios (not identifiable with others we know of: see Poseidonios, *On Perseus of Macedon* = *BNJ* 169 with commentary by Dowden).

[11] On the speeches see, e.g. Hoffmann 1907, 93–96; Wardman 1955; Asirvatham 2005 and Koulakiotis 2006, 162–8. For the purposes of this paper I will refer to these two speeches together as a single work, as the second was purportedly delivered on the day after the first.

[12] On Alexander's Hellenism in the *Life of Alexander* see e.g. Whitmarsh 2002. Evidently the only salient 'genealogical' aspect of Alexander's character is his descent from heroes (Herakles on his father's side, via Karanos, and Achilles on Olympias' side via Neoptolemos: *Alex.* 2.1); Plutarch nowhere mentions the Argead ruling family's claim to Argive orgins, which he must have known from Herodotos (5.22).

[13] Eckstein 2009, 251 and 262 n. 18.

[14] Ameling (1988) argues for the historicity of Alexander's emulation of Achilles; Heckel (2015), however, sees little reliable evidence for this, especially as compared to Alexander's emulation of Herakles.

[15] Olympias' Epeirote origins are the subtext of Attalos' insult to Alexander during a toast at the wedding of his niece Kleopatra to Philip that finally Philip would have a legitimate (i.e. fully Macedonian) heir to the kingdom (*Alex.* 9.4–5).

[16] Against the ancient commonplace (less common today) that Eumenes was a victim of 'ethnic' hatred on the part of the Macedonians, see in particular Anson 2015, 214–62.

[17] As F. Pownall (2013) has concluded from careful study of his fragments in Athenaios; see Sweet 1951 for Duris as a source for the *Demetrius*; Kebric 1977, 59 n. 31, for the *Pyrrhus*; and Geiger 1995, 180–1, for the *Eumenes* (Plutarch names Duris as a source in *Eum.* 1.1 as well as in a number of other *bioi*).

[18] As is the general consensus (Roisman 2012, 11).

[19] On Hieronymos in general see Jacoby's *RE* and *FGrH* (1913; 1929–1930) articles; Brown 1947, and Hornblower 1981. Hieronymos' work is known only from fragments, but his *testimonia* show that he had a personal relationship with Eumenes, who was his compatriot. Hornblower (1981, 6) and Billows (1990, 390–91) have suggested that Hieronymos was Eumenes' nephew but, as Anson (2015, 11–12, n. 20) notes, the suggestion is based on a single reference in Arrian (*Ind.* 18.7) and is hardly secure. Diodoros tells us that, after Eumenes' death, Antigonos held Hieronymos in honor (19.44.3 = *FGrH* 154 T 5); another reference indicates that Antigonos entrusted Hieronymos with taking over the supply of bitumen that the Nabataeans were accustomed to sell to the Egyptians (resulting in his defeat: 19.100.1–3 = *FGrH* 154 T 6). For Hieronymos' pro-Eumenes bias, see Roisman 2012, 9–30. We also learn from Plutarch (*Demet.* 39.2) that Demetrios made Hieronymos the governer and harmost of Boiotian cities.

[20] *Marc.* 30.4; *Comp. Pel.-Marc.* 1.6; *Luc.* 43.1; *TiGr.* 21.2; see Stadter 2015, 130–48, on Plutarch's Latin reading including Nepos.

[21] Roisman 2012, 11 (see notes 7 and 8 for bibliography).

[22] There are, however, significant differences between the works. Nepos compared non-Romans as a group with Romans rather than constructing a series

of non-Roman/Roman pairs (Geiger 1981, 96), and Plutarch's biographies were longer and more elaborate than Nepos' (Geiger 1988, 106; Stem 2012, 16–17, who notes that 'Nepos' *On Foreign Generals* should be regarded as comparable to an abridgement of all of Plutarch's Greek *Lives* into a single book.' (17)). J. Geiger (1985, 105–6; 117–20) argues that Plutarch's choice of subjects was influenced by Nepos, but Moles (1989, 233) points out (here following Russell 1973, 106–8), that Plutarch's Latin was weak by his own admission (in his *Demosthenes* (2.2–3), which was the first of his fifth pair of *Lives*). It seems unlikely, then, that Nepos could have been Plutarch's starting point for planning the *Lives*.

[23] One only need notice the distinction between Nepos' *Eumenes*, who shows supreme control over the Macedonians soldiers (who like all soldiers are prone to corruptibility (Nep. *Eum.* 8.1–3)) and whose virtue the Macedonian soldiers recognised as exceeding his (Nep. *Eum.* 1.3), and the hated Eumenes of Plutarch, who gains Macedonian loyalty only by trickery (see below).

[24] Geiger 1995, 173.

[25] Duff 2004.

[26] Duff 1999, 101.

[27] Schepens (2000a) argues strongly, in particular against Mossman, for the general positivity of Pyrrhos' portrait.

[28] Bosworth 1992.

[29] J. Geiger (1981, 90–95. He bases his conclusion not only on the change of program implied by the *Demetrius*, but also on the fact that many of these *bioi* contain rare justifications for why Plutarch chose their subjects, and the fact that neither the Greek subjects in these pairs, nor their Roman counterparts, have significant presences in the *Moralia*.

[30] As he takes Stadter 1989, xxix–xxx, to suggest (1995, 92 n. 7); see also Stadter 2014, 286–302.

[31] His examples are *Dem.-Ant.* and *Ages.-Pomp.*, which provide 'a riposte and a frame of reference to Alexander and to Caesar.' For cross-readings of *Alexander-Caesar* and *Pyrrhus-Marius*, see Mossman 1992 and Buszard 2008; for a reading of the *Agesilaus-Pompey* that includes cross-references to Agamemnon alongside Alexander, see Nevin 2014.

[32] Alexander appears at least once (and, often, much more than once) in each of the following works of Plutarch: *Aem., Ages., Alex., Ant., Arist., Caes., Cam., Cleom., Comp. Ages. Pomp., Comp. Demetr. Ant., Comp. Nic. Crass., Dem., Demetr., Eum., Flam., Galb., Pel., Per., Phil., Phoc., Pomp., Pyrrh., Thes., De Lib., Adulator, Quis Suos, De Amic., De Fortuna, Cons. Ap., De Tuenda, De Super., Regum Apoph., Inst., Mulier., Para., De Fort. Rom., De Alex., De Iside, De Pyth., De Virt. Mor., De Cohib., De Tranq., De Frat., De Vitioso, De Invidia, De Se Ipsum, De Sera, De Exilio, Quaes. Conv., Amatorius, Ad Princ., An Seni, Praecepta, De Unius, Vit. Dec., De Herod., De Soll., De Stoic., Non Posse, Adv. Col.*

[33] Darius dreams that the Macedonian phalanx was fire, and that Alexander was waiting on him as a royal courtier. See Harrisson 2014 for the (admittedly her own, but useful) distinction between 'message' and 'symbolic' dream-reports.

[34] As I have previously discussed (Asirvatham 2010a) for Plutarch, Dio

Chrysostom and Arrian, Lucian, who likes to surprise his audience, presents the rare instance of Philip righteously mocking Alexander (in *Dialogues of the Dead* 12: even having met his father after death, Philip points out, Alexander cannot admit that he is mortal!)

[35] We do not know to which Platonic text Plutarch is referring. See Duff 2004 on the Platonic tragic argument of the *Demetrius'* preface.

[36] This is true of φιλανθρωπία in particular: 'These three concepts-philanthropia, civilization, Hellenism-seem almost inseparable for Plutarch.' (Martin 1961, 167) The word occurs often in Polybius as well, who interestingly uses it of Philip but not of Alexander.

[37] Translations are modified from the Loeb Classical Library translations of B. Perrin (Plutarch's *Lives*); F. Babbitt (Plutarch's *Moralia*); R. Geer (Diodoros); and E. Cary (Cassius Dio).

[38] Elsewhere Alexander chides his men for falling prey to the seductions of wealth (*Alex.* 40–1.3). Towards the end of his life, Alexander himself will spend extravagantly in order to please his Macedonians (by paying their debts) and join them to the Persian nobility. It is possible that Plutarch considers Alexander's use of money as a sign of barbarism, but Alexander's orientalism tends to be manifested in the *Life* more in religious and cultural contexts (Asirvatham 2001) and in physiological/hereditary/geographical contexts (Whitmarsh 2002, 188–90) than in monetary contexts *per se*. Indeed, Plutarch seems to make a specific effort to pin money-lust onto his men. Take, for example, the scene in which Alexander and his men first encounter Darius' tent. Alexander 'finds' the soldiers carrying off Darius' loot; it is they who 'choose' for Alexander the tent of Darius, which was overflowing with riches (*Alex.* 20.11). I see an ironic contrast here between the soldiers' response and Alexander's understated response to it: 'This, as it would seem, is to be a king'. Note, too, that among the pre-justifications Plutarch offers for Alexander's suspicions of Philotas, the latter is said to have an abundance of wealth that is inappropriate for a private man (*Alex.* 48.2).

[39] See especially Dmitriev 2011. A similar moment is recorded in detail (along with the text of an edict) by Diodoros for Polyperchon who, upon gaining the regency of Macedonians calls a council to 'free the Greeks' from Antipatros' oligarchies and restore their democracies (*Diod.* 18.55.2–57.1). An almost unrecognisably brief version of this occurs in *Phoc.* 32.1, where we are simply told of Polyperchon's accession and his purported desire to restore the democracy of Athens (not Greece) – which Plutarch calls a plot against Phokion, who was an Athenian known as 'the Good' (Nepos *Phoc.* 1.1; Plut. *Phoc.* 10.4 – not without irony) whose eventual death at the hands of his own countrymen, Plutarch tells us, reminded the Greeks all over again of Socrates, as 'they felt that the sin and misfortune of Athens were alike in both cases' (*Phoc.* 38.23). The *Phocion* is interesting for our purposes because, while it takes place during the Succession, its nostalgia is for the last days of the democracy, not for Alexander's glorious empire, as I argue for *Demetrius, Pyrrhus* and *Eumemes*.

[40] The *locus classicus* is Aesch. *Persae* (see, e.g. Hall 1989, 126–9) but the motif persists throughout antiquity in literature from tragedy (see, e.g., Saïd 2002, 64–7 on Euripides) to Herodotos to Plutarch and Athenaios. For a discussion of

'Persian decadence' in Greek writers from Classical to Roman Greek writers, see Briant 2002.

[41] In a later scene, wishing to join his father against Egypt but not wanting to abandon the 'more noble and glorious' (καλλίω καὶ λαμπρότερον) war to liberate the Greeks, tries unsuccessfully to bribe Ptolemy's governor to release Sikyon and Corinth (*Demetr.* 15.1–2).

[42] Later, when Demetrios helps the Athenians ('who imagined', Plutarch will note with some sarcasm, 'that because they were rid of their garrison they therefore had their freedom': *Demetr.* 24.5) against siege by Kassandros, they showed themselves to be 'new and fresh in devising flatteries' (πρόσφατοι καὶ καινοὶ ταῖς κολακείαις φανῆναι: *Demetr.* 23.2), specifically ones that encouraged Demetrios' sexual excess: they gave him the rear chamber of the Parthenon on the Akropolis, which he filled with the abuse of both free-born youths and Athenian native women (ὕβριν εἰς παῖδας ἐλευθέρους καὶ γυναῖκας ἀστὰς) and where he lived with a few courtesans (*Demetr.* 24.1); he also used Athenian money to buy soap for these women (*Demetr.* 27.1), including Lamia who according to Plutarch sexually overpowered Demetrios when she was his prisoner: *Demetr.* 16.3–4. (On the symbolic value of courtesans for Hellenistic kings as Aphrodites incarnate, see Müller 2009.) Earlier, Plutarch pointed to Demetrios' indifferent treatment of his many wives, to whose company he apparently preferred that of courtesans; one of these neglected wives was Phila, daughter of Antipatros and wife of Krateros, a man who had been particularly esteemed by the Macedonians (*Demetr.* 14.1–3). The last item finds correspondence in *Eum.* 6.1–2, where Krateros is named as a hero to the Macedonians (for resisting Alexander at his worst, in fact; see on that *bios* below), but taken together, all these details concerning Demetrios' sexual behaviour provide an impression of general contrast with Alexander, whose sexual restraint is emphasised by Plutarch, most notably after his capture of Darius' womenfolk on the Great King's death (*Alex.* 21.3). This includes Darius' daughter Stateira, whom Alexander marries at the mass wedding at Susa (*Alex.* 70.2), but the Greco-Roman tradition is less interested in her as a wife than as a reflection both of Alexander's piety towards women as well as of his combination of respect towards or dominance over Darius (for discussion, see Ogden 2011, 133–8).

[43] On Demetrios's effect on traditional cult at Athens, see Kuhn 2006.

[44] In *De Alex.* 2.5, Plutarch makes a succinct contrast, touching on ruler cult, between the self-controlled Alexander and his Successors Demetrios and Lysimachos (as well as the Macedonians Kleitos and Klearchos, and the Syracusan Dionysius the Younger), whom he accuses of styling themselves as Poseidons, Zeuses and Apollos.

[45] See Podlecki 1988.

[46] Samian Revolt: *BNJ* 76 F 65–67; family exile: T 4 and F 13. See Pownall 2009.

[47] For a survey of Greco-Roman attitudes towards flattery, see Konstan 1996.

[48] See Asirvatham 2010a and note 34 above.

[49] See Asirvatham 2010a, 201–2 for more examples.

[50] E.g. when he cries for joy at Alexander's taming of Boukephalas, saying that Macedonia is not big enough for his son (*Alex.* 6.5). Antigonos' support of

Demetrios, by contrast, is less innocent: he excused his son's extreme sexuality and drinking because his son was so good at war, and able to compartmentalise war and pleasure (*Demetr.* 19.3–8).

[51] Most recently Weber 2000; Näf 2004; Harris 2009; Harrisson 2013.

[52] See esp. Pelling 1997.

[53] See e.g. Näf 2004, 104.

[54] Brenk 1975, 347. The tendency to invent dreams may be due to the chronological distance between writers and their subject matter, coupled with the fact that these are literary texts: 'it is precisely the force of the literary tradition that makes these stories plausible when told about the distant past, but less plausible when told about the present.' (Harrisson 2013, 77, following Harris 2009, 133–4)

[55] Demetrios appears three times in robes – and once 'on' a robe. At the height of his power he appeared in his outlandish royal robes (*Demetr.* 41.3–5; see above); here in *Demetr.* 44.6, with his royal ambitions destroyed, he dons a robe as disguise as he leaves camp. Early in the *bios* we see him escaping his enemies in a shabby cloak once they discover him vulnerable on his way to a secret tryst with Polyperchon's daughter-in-law Kratesipolis (*Demetr.* 9.3–4) – δρόμῳ φεύγων ἐξέφυγεν – which altogether anticipates his future troubles as he attempts to establish his rule as an inferior version of Alexander; it hardly needs mentioning that there are no passages in the *Alexander* in which Alexander is said to be in flight. (If P. Wheatley (2004) is correct in placing the (presumably historical) tryst chronologically later, its placement by Plutarch here can be read as a foreshadowing of his later womanising, as his shoddy cloak is a foreshadowing of his fall from power.) We also see Demetrios and his father in *ekphrasis* as figures embroidered into the robe the Athenians used to flatter him in *Demetr.* 10.4 (see above).

[56] Tatum 1996 suggests that Plutarch's tendency to use physical description mostly of regal figures is part of an overall critique of traditional royal ideology, and points to the fact that Plutarch's description of Demetrios' appearance is the most elaborate of any figure in the *Lives* (1996, 141–3). To this extent, perhaps Plutarch is making Demetrios responsible for trends that were in fact begun by Alexander. For the 'poetics of clothing' in the *Demetrius*, see Mossman 2015.

[57] Scholars have called Duris 'tragic history' based on analogy with Phylarchus whom Polybius criticised for being more like a tragic poet than a historian (2.56) as well as supposed association with the Peripatetics; the latter association has been denied by Walbank (1960) and Dalby (1991); see Pownall 2013, 43–44.

[58] Duff 2004. Note, e.g., *Demetr.* 53.10, which makes the transition between *Demetr.* and *Ant.* with the words: 'And now that the Macedonian 'play' (δρᾶμα) has been performed, let us introduce the Roman', and Plutarch's description in *Comp. Demetr. Ant.* 6.2 of Antony as having 'made his exit' (ἑαυτὸν ἐξήγαγεν).

[59] Koulakiotis (2006) argues that the idealising *De Alex.* is not necessarily a work of youth, contrary to what has often been supposed based on its highly rhetorical character (e.g. Brown 1967, 359; Jones 1966, 70), noting its political-philosophical sophistication. (173). Despite its generic differences from the *Alexander*, I consider its treatment of Alexander as part of Plutarch's entire complex of ideas surrounding the king, be they idealising or admonitory, based in history or generalising.

If P. Thonemann (2005) is correct in thinking that theatrical Demetrios is not simply a literary conceit but has a historical basis in Demetrios' own self-fashioning, we may well wonder whether the 'theatrical varieties of barbarian adornment' in *De Alex.* 1.43 is a tacit displacement on the part of Plutarch of a well-known historical characteristic of Demetrios onto the barbarians. In that case, just as Demetrios is a negative 'theatrical' foil to Alexander, via the memory of the Macedonians, in the *Demetrius*, the barbarians are negative 'theatrical' foils to Alexander's superior character in *De Alex.*

[60] The only explicitly 'theatrical' moment in the *Alexander* happens to be positive: Plutarch describes the moment when Alexander, deciding to trust his doctor Philip, who Parmenion had warned Alexander was planning to kill him, as θαυμαστὴν and θεατρικὴν (*Alex.* 19.7), but Alexander does have tragic moments that allow him to be compared, at least on a scale, with Demetrios. It is instructive, for example, to notice each man's relationship with Dionysus. An early passage in the *Demetrius* links Demetrios' eventual tragic downfall to Alexander's in the *Alexander* through Dionysus, whom we are told Demetrios held as a model because he was great at both war and pleasure (*Dem.* 2.3; Pownall 2013, 44–6) suggests that a Dionysian connection is behind the description of a decadent and androgynous Demetrios in Athen. 12.542b–e and that it originates with Duris. As the god of tragedy, Dionysus has of course an internal relevance to the stage-references we see throughout the *Demetrius*, but Dionysus is also a somewhat problematic figure for Alexander. Before his son's birth, Philip sees Olympias sleeping with a snake stretched out next to her and takes the creature to be the incarnation of Zeus Ammon (*Alex.* 2.4; on the complexities of Alexander's serpent-sire tradition see Ogden 2011, 14–56). Plutarch implies, however, a Dionysian origin for the scene: Olympias was a Bacchant who followed the more 'extravagant and superstitious' (the latter a classic negative buzzword for Plutarch) ceremonies of the Edonian and Thracian women, and even among these women she indulged in a particulary barbaric (βαρβαρικώτερον) sort of dancing that included snake-handling (2.7). As I have argued elsewhere (Asirvatham 2001), Plutarch is careful in the *Alexander* to disassociate the king from any 'true' belief that he was Zeus' son by interpreting any sign that he promoted rumours concerning his own divine sonship as an attempt to impress barbarians. This tendency to approve a 'stateman's manipulation of the common people's irrational fears in order to achieve a greater end' happens elsewhere in Plutarch's corpus (Duff 1999, 131; see n. 3 for references). Olympias' barbaric worship of Dionysus does not directly affect Alexander's image – his *bios* will not be a narrative reflection, as it is in the case of *Demetrius*, of Dionysian extremes, – but we learn in *Alex.* 13.4 that, as a result of his destruction of Thebes (i.e., Dionysus' birthplace), Alexander was accustomed to blaming Dionysus for his murder of Kleitos 'in his cups' as well as for his men's refusal to persist into India. This is a clear Euripidean foreshadowing of Alexander's own tragic downfall: Kleitos quotes Euripides' *Andromache* just before his death by Alexander's sword at the banquet at Maracanda (*Alex.* 52.4), and Alexander quotes the *Bacchae* when goading Kallisthenes to denounce the Macedonians (*Alex.* 53.5), and prefigures his demise for refusing to perform obeisance – which itself had tragic connotations for a classically-read author like

Plutarch, in Clytemnestra's implied bowing to Agamemnon in Aesch. *Ag.* 918–22) – to the king (*Alex.* 54.3). (Both incidents are less subtly pointed to by Arrian as part of his so-called 'great digression' on Alexander's orientalism (*Anab.* 4.7.4–14.4), a 'sustained moral commentary, which stands outside the chronological sequence of the Sogdian campaigns' in which the mutilation of Darius' murderer Bessos serves to introduce 'the larger theme of the king's lack of moral balance'. (Bosworth 1995, 45)). All told, however, the tragic motif is nowhere as prominent in *Lives* than in the *Demetrius*, *Antony*, and *Pyrrhus*, and it is this degree of difference that distinguishes Alexander as heroic in contrast to his Successors.

[61] Duris = *BNJ* 76 F 14 with commentary by Pownall (2009).

[62] It is hard not to see a reference to Jason here, especially given Plutarch's use of the tragic motif of reversal of fortune to describe Demetrios' robe (ἐν τῇ μεταβολῇ τῶν πραγμάτων). Jason's royal robe appears as a cursed robe in Euripides' *Medea*, which the Khalchian sorceress – having experienced her own reversal of fortune in her abandonment by Jason – poisons in order to kill her husband's new wife and her father-in-law; it appears again, but very differently, in Apollonius of Rhodes' *Argonautica*: embroidered with seven famous mythological scenes and possessing an ancient pedigree, it serves to validate the importance of Jason's quest for the Golden Fleece (see Bulloch 2006). In my reading, Plutarch here combines historical detail (Demetrios' cloak; his Successors' reaction to the cloak) with literary/mythical allusion in the service of a larger, implicit contrast between Demetrios and Alexander.

[63] On the idea of the king as the sun in Hellenistic and Roman thought, see Bergmann 1998. The hymn also gives Demetrios the parentage of Poseidon and Athena (patron deities of Athens), on whose symbolic importance for the Macedonian king's self-presentation see Holton 2014.

[64] We see something similar in Diodoros' description of Alexander's last plans (Diod. 18.4.4), which includes, among other things, *synoecism* on a grand scale: that is, a desire 'to establish cities and to transplant populations from Asia to Europe and in the opposite direction from Europe to Asia, in order to bring the largest continents to common unity and to friendly kinship by means of intermarriages and family ties' (πόλεων συνοικισμοὺς καὶ σωμάτων μεταγωγὰς ἐκ τῆς Ἀσίας εἰς τὴν Εὐρώπην καὶ κατὰ τοὐναντίον ἐκ τῆς Εὐρώπης εἰς τὴν Ἀσίαν, ὅπως τὰς μεγίστας ἠπείρους ταῖς ἐπιγαμίαις καὶ ταῖς οἰκειώσεσιν εἰς κοινὴν ὁμόνοιαν καὶ συγγενικὴν φιλίαν καταστήσῃ). As I have argued elsewhere (2005), however, Plutarch here explicity imagines this as a 'civilising' act – that is, Hellenisation – of the entire world, a variation on classical panhellenic rhetoric that is not a feature of extant Hellenistic historiography.

Furthermore, while Alexander is indeed frequently used as a chronological marker in the *Bibliotheke*, Diodoros also emphasises the limits of his conquests (Sacks 1990, 179). The historian's greatest heroes are Caesar with whose Celtic conquest he ends the work, rather than bringing it to Caesar's assassination or his own present day (Laqueur 1958, 287–8) – and at the end of a text whose focus was on the progress of humankind through necessity and periodic benefactions of great men (Sacks 1990, 55–82). Second in importance to Diodoros was his countryman Gelon (Sacks 1990, 122–5).

[65] Antigonos also shows an exaggerated sense of self in *Demetr.* 8.2: 'He said that the goodwill of a people was a noble gangway which no waves could shake, and that Athens, the beacon-tower of the whole world, would speedily flash the glory of their deeds to all mankind.' (Similarly, Plut. *Regum* 29: 'When he sent Demetrios his son, with many ships and forces, to make the Greeks a free people, he said that his repute, kindled in Greece as on a lofty height, would spread like beacon-fires through out the inhabited world (εἰς τὴν οἰκουμένην).' Incidentally, we learn here too that Antigonos realises his possibilities for Alexander-level glory are slim: 'Antigonos was persistent in his demands for money, and when somebody said, 'But Alexander was not like this,' he replied, ' Very naturally; for he reaped Asia, and I am picking up the straws.')

[66] See, e.g., de Blois 2008 on Galba and Otho.

[67] Mossman 1992, 90; for Euripidean overtones in the *Pyrrhus*, see also Braund 1997.

[68] Braund 1997, 118–19.

[69] Schepens (2000a, 430–431 n. 48) provides ample evidence that Pyrrhos' emulation of Achilles was in fact historical, and thus had probably little or nothing to do with Alexander; he also points out that the overt references to Achilles far outnumber references to Alexander and Heracles. The task of the present article is not to propose that the entire *Pyrrhus*, or the *Demetrius* or the *Eumenes* for that matter, are somehow really 'about' Alexander: Plutarch is far too complex for that. It is, rather, to suggest that a comparison between Alexander's treatment as an imperialist vs. three other plausibly 'Greek' imperialists, especially given the similar ways in which he appears in all three texts, constitute a way of articulating positive and negative aspects of imperial rule in ways that ultimately privilege Alexander – an observation made more interesting, as we shall discuss in the conclusion, by the absence of such an 'Alexander figure' among his Roman subjects.

[70] With – as Schepens 2008b suggests – the early Roman Republic idealised against Pyrrhos in this *Life*. Schepens (2000a, 416) also notes the difficulty of Plutarch's rhetorical task given the various settings in which Pyrrhos' story takes place: 'The writing of this biography confronted him with different historical backgrounds – Epirus, the Hellenistic World, Rome, Sicily, Sparta and the Peloponnese – constituting as many settings against which he had to elaborate a coherent view of his hero's tumultuous life.'

[71] On the Homeric touches here, see Mossman 1992, 95.

[72] See Asirvatham 2005.

[73] Bosworth 1992.

[74] Plutarch attributes this story to Duris, who Anson (2015, 35 n. 1) thinks is probably the source for such 'rags-to-riches' stories about the Successors.

[75] Nepos, by contrast, says that Eumenes became intimate friends with Philip when he was very young because he was 'conspicuous even in his youth for his high character' (18.1.4–5: *fulgebat...iam adulescentulo indoles virtutes*).

[76] E.g. D. S. 18.60.4–61.3 and Polyaenus 4.8.2, with a probable origin in Duris.

[77] This attitude is represented as well by Appian (*Syr.* 10.61).

[78] Hadley 1969; on Seleukos' use in general of Alexander imagery to promote his own reign, see Erickson 2012.

[79] Bowden 2013 questions the historicity of Alexander's attempt to impose *proskynēsis* on his court.

[80] Asirvatham 2001, 117–23.

[81] Bowie 1974, 170.

[82] These 'failures' are, needless to say, hardly to be taken at face-value: for example, Plutarch's assignation of seventy city-foundations to Alexander in *De. Alex.* 1.5 ignores the Diadoch's city-foundations (Muccioli, 2012, 196), in addition to being a complete exaggeration (Fraser 1996, 201). For an interpretation of Plutarch's use of Demetrios and Pyrrhos (and their failures to become Alexanders) as a cautionary example for Trajan, see Caterine 2017.

[83] The appropriation of Alexander's royal style by the Successors goes far beyond the figures treated by Plutarch: see Wallace 2017. Also on Hellenistic *imitatio*: e.g Bohm 1989; Stewart 1993; Meeus 2009.

[84] See Muccioli 2012, 193–194.

[85] E.g. Cassius Dio 68.29.1–30.1; *Hist. Aug.*, *Hadrian* 4.9.

[86] Plutarch says little on the emperors in general on the *Lives* and *Moralia* (see Ash 2008), but direct reference should not be expected: compare both Pliny's *Panegyricus* (see Stadter 2002) and Dio Chrysostom, who dedicated his four 'kingship orations' (1–4) to Trajan and uses Alexander as a stand-in for the emperor rather than addressing him directly (see e.g. Moles 1990 and Koulakiotis 2006, 154–8). On Plutarch's relationship to Trajan, see the collection of essays by Stadter and Van der Stockt (2002). On Plutarch, Alexander and Trajan, see also Koulakiotis 2006, 159; the connection between the *De Alex.* and Trajan was made by Eicke in 1909 (53). As for chronology: Jones (1966, 100–6) shows that, despite Eusebius' attestation of Plutarch's death sometime in the reign of Hadrian, nothing in Plutarch's texts proves that he was still writing after Trajan, which supports the idea that there is a connection between Trajan's reign and the practice of writing about Alexander. If we accept the 'topical' nature of Plutarch's interest in Alexander, then his Hellenic Alexander becomes a complex act of self-reflection, in which the boundary between physical and philosophical 'conquest' of the οἰκουμένη, between Roman political domination and Greek cultural domination becomes completely blurred.

[87] As Swain notices (1990, 126 and n. 1). On Roman *imitatio*, see Bruhl 1930; Heuss 1954; Weippert 1972; Wirth 1976; Kühnen 2008; and Spencer 2009.

[88] The image of Pompey as a failed Alexander is discussed in detail by Nevin (2014, 59–65).

[89] Mossman 2005 demonstrates the complex ways in which the *Pyrrhus* problematises the distinction between Greek/colonised and Roman/coloniser.

[90] Asirvatham 2005.

[91] Caesar: *Caes.* 23.2 (he carried Roman rule beyond the limits of the world); Pompey: *Pomp.* 25.2 (the Roman world, over which Plutarch tells us Gabinius gave him 'irresponsible power over all men'; δύναμιν ἐπὶ πάντας ἀνθρώπους ἀνυπεύθυνον) and 38.2 (speaking to Pompey's desire to recover Syria and expand to the ocean); *Cat. Mi.* 45.2 (Cato points out that he got more riches without war than Pompey had having stirred up the world); *De fort. Rom.* 11 (where the description of Pompey's triumphs ends with a comment on his overthrow by

fate); there is needless to say no equivalent note concerning Alexander's failure to maintain his world-empire in Plutarch's corpus.

For a critique of Roman imperial self-aggrandisement put in a Roman's mouth, see Plut. *Ti. Gr.* 9.5, where the Republican hero Tiberius Gracchus laments the 'homelessness' of Roman imperialists, who are 'self-styled masters of the earth' but have 'not a single clod of earth that is their own.'

[92] In the *Alexander*, Plutarch at times characterises the Macedonians/ Macedonia/ Macedonian-ness in quasi-barbaric terms in obvious contrast to Alexander (Asirvatham 2001, 109–15); Muccioli (2012, 134; 179) refers to Alexander's 'demacedonisation' in Plutarch's Alexander texts; the opposite seems to be the case in the *Demetrius, Pyrrhus* and *Eumenes*, in which a close association between Alexander and the Macedonians is contrasted with the inability of these new leaders to impress Alexander's old soldiers. (Interesting to note in this connection: when Plutarch has Alexander shout Μακεδονιστί – 'in Macedonian' – (*Alex.* 51.4), it is a sign of his descent into barbarism, but when the Macedonians use their native tongue in the *Eumenes* it is a (very temporary but positive) sign of their loyalty to Eumenes (*Eum.* 14.5)). For a brief survey on the image of the Macedonians in Roman Greek literature, see Asirvatham 2010b 107–11; see also Roisman (2012), although the latter's project is concerned less with the ideological uses of the Macedonian image *per se* than with recovering the real-life experiences of soldiers, typically ignored by elite ancient sources and modern scholars alike. Mossman (2005, 513) notices the way in which the Macedonians can be seen negatively in the *Pyrrhus* as befits their traditional ambiguity.

Bibliography

Ameling, W.
  1988   'Alexander und Achilleus. Eine Bestandsaufnahme,' in W. Will and J. Heinrichs (eds) *Zu Alexander der Große : Festschrift G. Wirth, vol. II*, Amsterdam, 657–92.

Anson, E.
  2015   *Eumenes of Cardia – A Greek among Macedonians. Ancient Mediterranean and Medieval Texts and Contexts; Studies in Philo of Alexandria, 3.* 2nd edition, Leiden.

Ash, R.
  2008   'Standing in the Shadows: Plutarch and the Emperors in the *Lives* and *Moralia*', in A. Nikolaidis (ed.) *The Unity of Plutarch's Work*, Berlin, 557–75.

Asirvatham, S. R.
  2001   'Olympias' Snake and Callisthenes' Stand: Religion and Politics in Plutarch's *Life of Alexander*', in S. R. Asirvatham, C. Pache and J. Watrous (eds) *Between Magic and Religion: Interdisciplinary Studies in Ancient Mediterranean Religion and Society*, Lanham, MA, 93–125.

  2005   'Classicism and *Romanitas* in Plutarch's *De Alexandri Fortuna aut Virtute*', *AJP* 126, 107–25.

  2008   'No Patriotic Fervor for Pella: Aelius Aristides and the Presentation of the Macedonians in the Second Sophistic', *Mnemosyne* 61, 207–27.

2010a 'His Son's Father? Philip II in the Second Sophistic', Oxford, 193–204 and notes 294–9.

2010b 'Perspectives on the Macedonians from Greece, Rome, and Beyond', in J. Roisman and I. Worthington, *A Companion to Ancient Macedonia*, New York, 99–124.

Beck, H.
2002 'Interne synkrisis bei Plutarch', *Hermes* 130, 467–89.

Bergmann, M.
1998 *Die Strahlen der Herrscher. Theomorphes Herrscherbild und politische Symbolik im Hellenismus und in der römischen Kaiserzeit*, Mainz.

Billows, R.
1990 *Antigonos the One-Eyed and the Creation of the Hellenistic State*, Berkeley.

Bohm, C.
1989 *Imitatio Alexandri im Hellenismus: Untersuchungen zum politischen Nachwirken Alexanders des Großen in hoch- und späthellenistischen Monarchien*, München.

Bosworth, A. B.
1992 'History and Artifice in *Eumenes*', in P. A. Stadter (ed.) *Plutarch and the Historical Tradition*, London, 56–89.

1995 *A Historical Commentary on Arrian's History of Alexander,* vol. II, Oxford.

Bowden, H.
2013 'On Kissing and Making Up: Court Protocol and Historiography in Alexander the Great's 'Experiment with *Proskynesis*', *BICS* 56, 55–77.

Bowie, E.
1974 'The Greeks and their Past in the Second Sophistic', in M. I. Finley (ed.) *Studies in Ancient Society*, London, 166–209 (slightly revised from *Past and Present* 46 (1970), 3–41).

Braund D.
1997 'Plutarch's Pyrrhus and Euripides' Phoenician Women: Biography and Tragedy on Pleonectic Parenting', *Histos* 1, 1–11.

2000 'Athenaeus, *On the Kings of Syria*', D. Braund and J. Wilkins (eds) *Athenaeus and his World*, Exeter, 514–22.

Brenk, F.
1975 'The Dreams of Plutarch's Lives', *Latomus* 34, 336–49.

Brown
1947 'Hieronymus of Cardia', *The American Historical Review*, 52.4, 684–96.

Bruhl, A.
1930 'Le souvenir d'Alexandre le Grand et les Romains', *Mélanges d'archéologie et d'histoire Année,* 47.1, 202–21.

Bulloch, A.
2006 'Jason's Cloak', *Hermes* 134, 44–68.

Buszard, B.
2008 'A Combined Reading of Plutarch's "Alexander-Caesar" and "Pyrrhus-Marius"', *TAPA* 138, 185–215.

Caterine, M. M.
2017 'Alexander-Imitators in the Age of Trajan: Plutarch's *Demetrius* and *Pyrrhus*', *CJ* 112.4: 406–430.

Chaniotis, A.

2011 'The Ithyphallic Hymn for Demetrios Poliorcetes and Hellenistic Religious Mentality' in P. Iossif, A. S. Chankowski and C. C. Lorber (eds) *More than Men, Less than Gods: Studies in Royal Cult and Imperial Worship*, Louvain, 157–96.

Dalby, A.

1991 'The Curriculum Vitae of Duris of Samos,' *CQ* 41, 539–541.

de Blois, L.

2008 'Soldiers and Leaders in Plutarch's Galba and Otho', in H. M. Schellenberg, V. Hirschmann and A. Krieckhaus (eds), *A Roman Miscellany: Essays in Honour of Anthony R. Birley on his Seventieth Birthday*, Gdansk, 5–13.

Dowden, K.

2013 'Poseidonios (87).' *Brill's New Jacoby*, Leiden.

Dmitriev, S.

2011 *The Greek Slogan of Freedom and Early Roman Politics in Greece*, Oxford.

Duff, T.

2004 'Plato, Tragedy, the Ideal Reader and Plutarch's "Demetrius and Antony"', *Hermes* 132, 271–91.

1999 *Plutarch's Lives: Exploring Virtue and Vice*, Oxford.

Eckstein, A. M.

2009 'Hellenistic Monarchy in Theory and Practice', in R. K. Balot (ed.) *A Companion to Greek and Roman Political Thought. Blackwell Companions to the Ancient World. Literature and Culture*, Malden, MA, 247–65.

Eicke, L.

1909 Veterum philosophorum qualia fuerint de Alexandro Magno iudicia, diss. Rostock.

Erickson, K.

2012 'Seleucus I, Zeus and Alexander', in L. Mitchell and C. Melville (eds) *Every Inch a King: Comparative Studies on Kings and Kingship in the Ancient and Medieval Worlds*, Leiden, 109–27.

Fraser, P.

1996 *Cities of Alexander the Great*, Oxford.

Geiger, J.

1981 'Plutarch's Parallel Lives: The Choice of Heroes', *Hermes* 109, 85–104.

1985 *Cornelius Nepos and Ancient Political Biography*, Stuttgart.

1988 'Nepos and Plutarch: From Latin to Greek Political Biography', *ICS* 13, 245–56.

1995 'Plutarch on Hellenistic Politics: the case of Eumenes of Cardia', in I. Gallo and B. Scardigli (eds) *Teoria e prassi politica nelle opere di Plutarco*, Naples, 173–85.

Habinek, T.

2005 *Ancient Rhetoric and Oratory*, Malden MA.

Hadley, R.

1969 'Hieronymus of Cardia and Early Seleucid Mythology', *Historia* 18, 142–52.

Hall, E.

1989 *Inventing the Barbarian: Greek Self-Definition through Tragedy*, Oxford.

Harris, W. V.
   2009   *Dreams and Experience in Classical Antiquity*, Cambridge MA.
Harrison, G. W. M.
   1995   'The Semiotics of Plutarch's Συγκρίσεις: The Hellenistic Lives of
          Demetrius-Antony and Agesilaus-Pompey,' *RBPhil* 73, 91–104.
Harrisson, J.
   2013   *Dreams and Dreaming in the Roman Empire: Cultural Memory and Imagination*,
          London; New York.
Heckel, W.
   2015   'Alexander, Achilles, and Heracles: Between Myth and History', in
          P. Wheatley and E. Baynham (eds) *East and West in the World Empire of
          Alexander. Essays in Honour of Brian Bosworth*, 21–33, Oxford.
Heuss, A.
   1954   'Alexander der Große und die politische Ideologie des Altertums',
          Antike und Abendland 4, 65–104.
Hoffmann, W.
   1907   *Das literarische porträt Alexanders des Grossen im griechischen und römischen
          Altertum*, Leipzig.
Holton, J. R.
   2014   'Demetrios Poliorketes, Son of Poseidon and Aphrodite. Cosmic and
          Memorial Significance in the Athenian Ithyphallic Hymn', *Mnemosyne*
          67, 370–390.
Hornblower, J.
   1981   *Hieronymus of Cardia*, Oxford.
Jacoby, F.
   1913   'Hieronymos von Kardia (10)', *RE* 8, 1540–60.
   1929–1930 'Hieronymos von Kardia', *FGrH* 154.
Jones, C. P.
   1966   'Towards a Chronology of Plutarch's Works', *JRS* 56, 61–74.
Kebric, R. B.
   1977   *In the Shadow of Macedon: Duris of Samos*, Wiesbaden.
Konstan, D.
   1996   'Friendship, Frankness and Flattery', in J. T. Fitzgerald (ed.) *Friendship,
          Flattery, and Frankness of Speech: Studies on Friendship in the New Testament
          World*, Leiden, 7–19.
Koulakiotis, E.
   2006   *Genese und Metamorphosen des Alexandermythos im Spiegel der griechischen nicht-
          historiographischen Überlieferung bis zum 3. Jh. n. Ch*, Konstanz.
Kuhn, A.
   2006   'Ritual Change during the Reign of Demetrius Poliorcetes,' in
          E. Stavrianopoulou (ed.) *Ritual and Communication in the Graeco-Roman
          World*, Liege, 265–281.
Kühnen, A.
   2008   *Die imitatio Alexandri in der römischen Politik (1. Jh. v. Chr. bis 3. Jh. n. Chr.)*,
          Münster.

Laqueur, R.
   1958   *Diodorea, Hermes* 86, 257–90.
Martin, H.
   1961   'The Concept of *Philanthropia* in Plutarch's *Lives*', *AJP* 82, 164–75.
Meeus, A.
   2009   Alexander's Image in the Age of the Successors', in W. Heckel and
          L. Tritle (eds) *Alexander the Great: A New History*, Malden, MA, 235–50.
Moles, J.
   1989   Review of J. Geiger, *Nepos and Biography, The Classical Review* 39, 229–33.
   1990   'The Kingship Orations of Dio Chrysostom', *PLLS* 6, 297–375.
Mossman, J. M.
   1988   'Tragedy and Epic in Plutarch's Alexander', *JHS* 108, 83–93.
   1992   'Plutarch, Pyrrhus and Alexander', in P. A. Stadter (ed.), *Plutarch and the
          Historical Tradition*, London, 90–198.
   2005   'Taxis ou barbaros: Greek and Roman in Plutarch's *Pyrrhus*', *CQ* 55,
          498–517.
   2015   'Dressed for success? Clothing in Plutarch's Demetrius', in R. Ash,
          J. Mossman and F. B. Titchener (eds), *Fame and Infamy*, Oxford, 149–60.
Muccioli, F.
   2102   *La storia attraverso gli esempi. Protagonisti e interpretazioni del mondogreco in
          Plutarco*, Milan.
Müller, S.
   2009   'In Favour of Aphrodite: Sulla, Demetrios Poliorketes, and the Symbolic
          Value of the Hetaira', *AHB* 23, 38–49.
Näf, B.
   2004   *Traum und Traumdeutung im Altertum*, Darmstadt.
Nevin, S.
   2014   'Negative Comparison in Plutarch's *Agesilaus-Pompey*', *GRBS* 54, 45–68.
Ogden, D.
   2011   *Alexander the Great: Myth, Genesis and Sexuality*, Exeter.
Pelling, C.
   1997   'Tragical Dreamer: Some Dreams in the Roman Historians', *Greece and
          Rome*[2] 44, 197–213.
Podlecki, A.
   1988   'Plutarch and Athens', *Illinois Classical Studies* 13, 231–43.
Pownall, F.
   2009– 'Duris (76).' *Brill's New Jacoby*, Leiden.
   2013   'Duris of Samos and the Diadochi', in V. A. Troncoso and E. Anson
          (eds) *After Alexander: the Time of the Diadochi (323–281* BC*)*, Oxford/
          Oakville, CT, 43–56.
Roisman, J.
   2012   *Alexander's Veterans and the Early Wars of the Successors*, Austin.
Russell, D. A.
   1973   *Plutarch*, London.
Sacks, K.
   1990   *Diodorus Siculus and the First Century*, Princeton.

Saïd, S.
 2002 'Greeks and Barbarians in Euripides' Tragedies: The End of Differences?', in T. Harrison (ed.), *Greeks and Barbarians,* New York, 62–100.
Schepens, G.
 2000a 'Rhetoric in Plutarch's *Life of Pyrrhus*', in L. Van der Stockt (ed.) *Rhetorical Theory and Praxis in Plutarch*, 413–41.
 2000b 'Plutarch's View of Ancient Rome: Some Remarks on the *Life of Pyrrhus*', in L. Mooren (ed.) *Politics, Administration and Society in the Hellenistic and Roman World,* Leuven, 349–64.
Spencer, D.
 2009 'Roman Alexanders: Epistemology and Identity', in W. Heckel and L. Tritle (eds) *Alexander the Great: A New History*, Malden, MA, 251–74.
Stadter, P.
 1989 *A Commentary on Plutarch's* Pericles, Chapel Hill.
 2002 'Platonic and Trajanic Ideology', in P. Stadter and L. Van der Stockt (eds) *Sage and Emperor: Plutarch, Greek Intellectuals and Roman Power in the Time of Trajan (98–117 AD)*, Leuven, 227–41.
 2015 *Plutarch and His Roman Readers*, Oxford.
Stadter, P. and Van der Stockt, L. (eds)
 2002 *Sage and Emperor: Plutarch, Greek Intellectuals and Roman Power in the Time of Trajan (98–117 AD)*, Leuven.
Stem, R.
 2012 *The Political Biographies of Cornelius Nepos*, Ann Arbor.
Stewart, A.
 1993 *Faces of Power: Alexander's Image and Hellenistic Politics*, Berkeley.
Swain, S.
 1990 'Hellenic Culture and the Roman Heroes of Plutarch', *JHS* 110, 126–45.
 1996 *Hellenism and Empire: Language, Classicism and Power in the Greek World, AD 50–250*, Oxford.
Sweet, W.
 1951 'Sources of Plutarch's *Demetrius*', *The Classical Weekly* 44, 177–81.
Tatum, J.
 1996 'The Regal Image in Plutarch's *Lives*', *JHS* 116, 135–51.
Thonemann, P.
 2005 'The Tragic King: Demetrios Poliorketes and the City of Athens', in O. Hekster and R. Fowler (eds) *Imaginary Kings: The Royal Image in the Near East, Greece and Rome,* Stuttgart, 63–86.
Walbank, F. W.
 1960 'History and Tragedy', *Historia* 9, 216–34.
Wallace, S.
 2017 'Court, Kingship, and Royal Style in the Early Hellenistic Period', in A. Erskine L. Llewellyn-Jones, and S. Wallace (eds) *The Hellenistic Court*, Swansea, 1–30.
Wardman, A. E.
 1955 'Plutarch and Alexander', *CQ* 5, 96–107.

Weber, G.
  2000   *Kaiser, Träume und Visionen in Prinzipat und Spätantike*, Stuttgart.
Weippert, O.
  1972   *Alexander-imitatio und römische Politik in republikanischer Zeit*, Augsburg.
Wheatley, P.
  2004   'Poliorcetes and Cratesipolis: A Note on Plutarch, *Demetr.* 9.5–7, *Antichthon* 38, 1–9.
Whitmarsh, T.
  2002   'Alexander's Hellenism and Plutarch's textualism', *CQ* 52, 174–92.
Wirth, G.
  1976   'Alexander und Rom', in E. Badian (ed.) *Alexander le Grand: image et réalité*, 181–221.

INDEX